1990

1990

Russians Remember
A Turning Point

Edited by Irina Prokhorova

Abridged and translated from the Russian by Arch Tait

With a Foreword by Bridget Kendall

MACLEHOSE PRESS
QUERCUS · LONDON

First published in the Russian language by
New Literary Observer in two volumes:
"1990: opyt izucheniia nedavnei istorii" ("1990: an attempt to study recent history"), vol. 1, *Novoe Literaturnoe Obozrenie*, No. 83 (1/2007); "1990: opyt izucheniia nedavnei istorii" ("1990: an attempt to study recent history"), vol. 2, *Novoe Literaturnoe Obozrenie*, No. 84 (2/2007)

First published in Great Britain in 2013 by

MacLehose Press
an imprint of Quercus
55 Baker Street
7th Floor, South Block
London W1U 8EW

The publication was effected under the auspices of the
Mikhail Prokhorov Foundation TRANSCRIPT Programme
to Support Translations of Russian Literature

 transcript

Contents

List of Illustrations

For Illustration Source Notes see p. 503

List of Contributors

Marietta Omarovna Chudakova – Literary critic, historian, Doctor of Philological Sciences, columnist, writer, memoirist, editor-in-chief of the *Tynyanov Collections*, public figure

Boris Vladimirovich Dubin – Translator, sociologist, director of the Levada Centre's Department of Socio-political Research in Moscow

Tamara Natanovna Eydelman – History teacher at Grammar School No. 1567 (Moscow), chairwoman of the History Teachers' Association, Distinguished Teacher of Russia

Vadim Eduardovich Goncharov – Associate Professor of social and political science at Bonch-Bruevich State University of Telecommunications, St Petersburg

Hasan Chingizovich Guseynov – Professor in the Philological Faculty of Lomonosov Moscow State University, author of books on Classical culture and the philosophy of language

Sergey Gennadievich Karnaukhov – Research fellow at the Centre for Independent Social Research, Irkutsk, postgraduate student in the History Faculty of the European University, St Petersburg

Mark Sergeyevich Kharitonov – Prose writer, essayist, translator, winner of the Russian Booker Prize (1992)

Sergey Vladimirovich Khramov – Inspector-general of the Union of Trade Unions of Russia

Olesya Igorevna Kirchik – Research fellow at the Higher School of Economics, St Petersburg, Nizhny Novgorod and Perm

Svetlana Sergeyevna Koroleva – Sociologist, researcher at the Levada Centre, Moscow

Nikolai Aleksandrovich Mitrokhin – Historian, fellow at the Research Centre for East European Studies, University of Bremen

Pavel Vladimirovich Pavlov – Reporter and producer at the South Urals state broadcasting company, postgraduate student in the Department of the Theory of Mass Communications of Chelyabinsk State University

Vladimir Vladimirovich Pozner – First President of the Russian Television Academy (1994–2008), presenter and producer of the talk show *The Times* (*Vremena*) (2000–2008), presenter of *Pozner* on Russia's national Channel 1 (2012)

Irina Dmitrievna Prokhorova – Founder and editor-in-chief of the New Literary Observer publishing house

Pavel Vasilievich Romanov – Professor of socio-economic systems and social policy at the Higher School of Economics, St Petersburg, Nizhny Novgorod and Perm, director of the Centre of Social Policy and Gender Research, Saratov, editor of the *Journal of Social Policy Research* (Zhurnal issledovanii sotsial'noi politiki)

Eduard Amvrosievich Shevardnadze – Former President of Georgia

Sergey Anatoliyevich Turkin – Political scientist, senior analyst of the Lukoil Inform Analysis Centre, Moscow, head of political projects at the Centre for Economic and Political Research and Development, Moscow

Yelena Rostislavovna Yarskaya-Smirnova – Professor, head of the Department of Social Anthropology and Social Work at Saratov State Technical University (1997–2006), lecturer at the Moscow Higher School of Social and Economic Science (2004–7), co-editor of the *Journal of Social Policy Research* (Zhurnal issledovanii sotsial'noi politiki)

Vitaliy Pavlovich Yelizarov – Associate Professor of the theory and history of the state and law at the State University of Economics and Finance, St Petersburg

Aleksey Vladimirovich Yurchak – Associate Professor of socio-cultural anthropology, University of California, Berkeley

FOREWORD

Bridget Kendall

B.B.C. Moscow Correspondent 1989–1993

There is little doubt that the disintegration of Soviet Communism in the second half of the 1980s and early '90s was one of the most important episodes of the late twentieth century. But even for those of us who had a ringside seat, how much do we remember?

I arrived in Moscow as B.B.C. Correspondent in the summer of 1989 and was instantly plunged into a reporting job that left little time to eat and sleep. Scrambling to keeping up with the frenzy of political developments was exhilarating and exhausting.

There was no shortage of interest in what I was witnessing: the world's attention was on the Soviet Union. I recall a comment from one of my London news editors at the time: "If one of our four world headlines does not reflect some aspect of what is happening in the Soviet Union right now, we must be missing something." Every fresh law and decree, every rally and every pronouncement by a senior politician was of interest to the news desk.

But it was not only the developments in Moscow which drew interest. By early 1990 a mood of insurrection was beginning to emerge in many of the republics. The Baltic states led the way, and the ever-unruly Caucasus. It was not long before Ukraine began to wake up too.

I remember an unsanctioned rally held in Western Ukraine in support of the Uniate Church, which was still illegal. News reached Moscow reporting that the police had set dogs on the crowds. Two weeks later I travelled to the region myself, to attend another rally.

This time there were no dogs and no police either. The crowd was huge. One incident remains clear in my mind: a local party official pushed his way forward, saying he wanted to give the B.B.C. an interview. Sinking to his knees, he spoke in Ukrainian into my microphone, appealing to the crowd for their forgiveness; he had betrayed them by working for the Communist Party. It was a mesmerising moment.

But even as I felt I was living through revolutionary times, I was also wary of where these changes might be heading.

My arrival in Moscow coincided with several of my colleagues in the British media being expelled in a tit for tat espionage scandal. It was a reminder that the Cold War was not yet over. For all the dizzying pace of change, many Soviet rules and attitudes were still in place. The authorities regarded us Western journalists as objects of suspicion. Bureaucratic hurdles ensnared us. Yes, there was plenty of talk of openness, but our movements were still restricted.

I first recognised that conditions had changed less than the rhetoric suggested when one Sunday I set off to drive out of the city and into the countryside for some fresh air. I did not get beyond the first police check-point on the ring road before I was turned back. A new directive was in force, requiring all foreigners to stay inside the Moscow perimeter unless they had express permission to travel.

More seriously, in January 1990 we were blocked from flying to Azerbaijan to cover the riots and subsequent emergency crackdown in Baku, which left more than a hundred dead. The department of the Soviet Ministry of Foreign Affairs which oversaw foreign journalists declared it would only issue visa support once we had bought air tickets. But the state airline Aeroflot would not issue tickets unless we first had visas.

It was a typical Soviet "catch-22", and also an effective means of censorship. As this volume reveals, that appalling massacre in Baku dismayed many in Moscow and contributed to a feeling that Mikhail Gorbachev's commitment to reform might be wavering.

But the incident made far less impact abroad (unlike the crackdown in Vilnius a year later). This was the era before mobile phones. There was no internet, no Twitter or Facebook. If a journalist was not present at an event to report on it themselves, the chances were that no-one else would hear about it. The official Soviet media was still heavily controlled and gave away little. With no foreign journalists in Baku, there were no compelling television pictures or eyewitness reports sent abroad, so the outside world took little note of it.

★

As the year 1990 progressed, mounting economic chaos and intensified political battles meant old rules began to break down. It became easier to travel and easier, too, to gain access to those at the top of the political hierarchy.

For decades the governance of the Soviet Union through the Communist Party had been conducted in secret. The nearest you could get to the main Central Committee building next to the Kremlin was the other side of a public square. Even the pavement nearby was cordoned off by police. What went on when the ruling Politburo gathered inside the Kremlin was even more of a mystery.

But in 1990 the process of government was no longer inaccessible to all but the party elite. A journalist's pass would get you into the press gallery of the Soviet parliament (or Supreme Soviet), which held its sessions in a red velvet furnished hall inside the Kremlin complex. It also gave you access to M.P.s (or Deputies) as they hung about in the foyer during breaks. And as most government ministers and many prominent reformers were also members of parliament, and as Mikhail Gorbachev (as chairman) regularly ran the sessions and frequently used them to release political bombshells, it was the swiftest and most effective way of finding out about political developments.

I spent a lot of my time there, listening to the fractious debates or seeking reactions from politicians during the breaks. It was extraordinary to be able to go up to the Interior Minister to ask for a quote; access was significantly easier than it would have been in London. Much of my focus was therefore on politics, rather than on the broader social changes. But it was incredibly illuminating, both in an anecdotal way, and for tracking major political changes.

I remember I spent one morning in late 1990 watching K.G.B. chief Vladimir Kryuchkov as he perched on his seat near the Praesidium. While monitoring the parliamentary debate, he silently worked his way through a mountain of documents, scrutinising each one carefully before adding his signature and placing it on another pile. Who knows what he was authorising? But his cold-blooded and methodical precision stuck in my mind – it was so out of step with the passionate speeches from the floor, and spoke so eloquently of his disdain for the whole parliamentary process. Only later did it transpire that he was one of the main instigators of the hard-line conspiracy in 1991 who tried to overturn reforms. Watching him in parliament had been a valuable forewarning.

Perhaps the most significant parliamentary moment of 1990, however, came in May, at the convening of the first Russian parliament. This was also held in a Kremlin hall, a long, awkward, echoing chamber in which it was difficult to see or hear speakers if you were standing at the back.

Most telling was the presence of Mikhail Gorbachev, a lonely figure seated on his own on a balcony halfway along the hall. You might have thought that the Soviet President would have better things to do than to watch parliamentary proceedings. But day after day he sat there in silence, following the vote to decide who would win the election to head the new Russian parliament.

In the end Boris Yeltsin scraped through, winning by only four votes. It was an early sign that Mr Gorbachev had recognised from the outset that this would be a crucial moment, the emergence of a rival who was to pose a mounting threat to his own continued power as Soviet leader.

*

The increasingly embittered political battle at the top was only one strand of the story of 1990. What is especially valuable about this anthology of timelines and essays is that it seeks to paint a broader picture and make sense of some of the trends which marked this year as a moment of transition.

Month by month, each chapter provides a catalogue of selected events. Diary excerpts and reminiscences add colour and context. Essays explore different ways in which 1990 was pivotal.

Some contributors focus on politics. One describes how the waning legitimacy of the Communist Party was echoed in mounting criticism of

Lenin and Leninism. Another looks at the sidelining of political parties once the Soviet Communist Party had relinquished its leading role, as a power struggle ensued between rival presidents. Another essay explores the re-emergence of the Russian Orthodox Church as a political and social force. A further essay explains the dwindling influence of Russian miners and other blue-collar workers, whose strikes and rallies began to lose support in 1990, irrelevant in a country engulfed in full-scale economic chaos.

Other essays reflect the mood of the time. There is the mismatch between endless discussions of grand economic plans and the frightening pace of economic collapse, which saw ration cards become a way of life for most people, as food output dropped and the heavily centralised system of the Soviet planned economy fell apart. There is the curious explosion of interest in faith healers from a bewildered, anxious public, which had lost its faith in "scientific materialism" and now clung to miracles to provide certainty and meaning. Reminiscences from teachers from around the country reinforce this sense of uncertainty, some grimly hanging on to old orthodoxies, others groping for new ways of teaching that would reflect the giddy times they were living through.

And perhaps the most poignant of all are the thoughts of members of the liberal intelligentsia, revealing their growing disillusionment with Mikhail Gorbachev's ability to keep pace with the demands for change, their alarm at the stirrings of an ugly anti-Semitism and racism, and their mixed feelings about the flood of Russian intellectual talent being lost to emigration. We can see an anguished recognition that scholarship and literature were losing their central position in Russian life, and that Russian writers, once the revered prophets of society, risked becoming peripheral.

*

It is true that at first glance 1990 might seem an odd year to profile; some might question if it really was a turning point.

For those who look back on the perestroika era from abroad, some pinpoint 1985 as the key moment: the year in which Mikhail Gorbachev came to power and launched his reforms from the top down. Others identify

1991 as most significant – the year of the abortive coup by Kremlin hard-liners, which precipitated the U.S.S.R.'s final implosion. And inside Russia not everyone even remembers the proper sequence of events. As Irina Prokhorova notes in her Introduction, recollections can be blurred or tinged with confusion.

Travelling through villages and former collective farms in the northern region of Vologda a few years ago, I was puzzled to hear locals talking dismissively of perestroika as a catastrophic event which took place at the end of 1991. "But what about the earlier years of perestroika reform from 1985 onwards?" I asked them, "What about 'glasnost', or openness, the lifting of censorship? What about the laws that sanctioned private enterprise? What about the political battles that ended seventy years of the Communist Party's monopoly on power and rocked the Kremlin's authority? And yes, the food shortages and ration cards."

They remembered the ration cards, but the empty shelves which so horrified Muscovites in 1990 were for the people of Vologda just an extension of the chronic shortages which provincial Russian towns and villages had endured for decades.

As for the other changes in Soviet society in the perestroika era, these were dismissed as simply the latest meaningless party slogans. "We didn't pay much attention," the Vologda villagers told me. "Our kolkhoz director would tell us perestroika and glasnost were important, but why would we believe him? We watched the rallies and speeches on television, but it was nothing to do with our lives."

One essay in this volume analyses the role played by local television, and concludes that although media organisations in the provinces could have galvanised Russia's grass roots by unearthing local stories people really cared about, in fact they lagged behind the national media. As the essay argues, and as I found in Vologda, in the provinces "many people felt detached from what they watched". The sometimes scarcely credible events unfolding in Moscow were for them little more than empty political theatre.

What they did not realise at the time was that they too were about to be affected. When at the end of 1991 the Soviet Union ceased to exist and a

Russian reformist government embarked on shock therapy, lifting price controls overnight to speed up the transition to a market economy, everyone was suddenly confronted with a new, frightening reality: rampant inflation, plummeting industrial output, the alarming prospect of job losses and the shock of finding that relatives in Ukraine and Belarus now lived in another country. That, for the villagers of Vologda, was why 1991 was the year of perestroika.

So 1990 is often a forgotten year, a year of progression rather than endings or beginnings. But it is the process of what ordinary people went through which is so fascinating: their private thoughts on this "revolution without shots", which in six short years transformed the world in which they lived.

This book goes some way to telling their story.

Bridget Kendall
January 2013

1990

INTRODUCTION

Irina Prokhorova

This book began its life as a two-volume special issue of Moscow's *New Literary Observer*, in which the journal's editors set out to study a single year in Russian history: 1990. Why did we choose this unspectacular year for scrutiny rather than, for example, 1989, a year crucial for the whole of Europe as the Berlin Wall came down? Or at least 1991, when the Soviet Union collapsed, and with it the Communist hold over many other lands?

The project arose not only out of an academic interest in recent history, but also as a result of profound personal experiences. I was privileged to be a witness and active participant in the historic events of the late 1980s. I spent three unforgettable days on the barricades defending the Russian government's White House during the August 1991 coup attempt, and came away from that experience a free, no longer Soviet, person. In all the years which have passed since then, I have never ceased to wonder that the great and terrible Evil Empire could fall apart overnight, and to wonder also why no-one foresaw that it was going to happen. What explains the fact that the militaristic Soviet Union collapsed peacefully and almost bloodlessly, while Yugoslavia, which, compared to the U.S.S.R., seemed a much better adjusted country, became mired in a bloody civil war?

A religious person might see this as a miracle, the working of divine Providence, but the intellectual, the researcher, needs more rational explanations. The obvious conclusion is that we have precious little understanding of how a "closed society" is structured and functions, of what concealed transformations may be taking place beneath that deceptive mantle of totalitarian "stability", or of which, sometimes quirky, paths it may choose to follow in order to move towards democratic changes. The recent wave of Arab revolutions, which so astonished the world, only confirms my idea.

This close study of 1990, the last year of the Soviet Union's existence, is one attempt to answer these questions. My initial hypothesis was that this year, which had slipped Russian society's cultural memory and been overshadowed by the more dramatic years of 1989 and 1991, was in fact a turning point in the modern history of Russia, and that the events which occurred during it had determined the country's future development. In order to test that hypothesis, we compiled a comprehensive chronicle of 1990, which reads like a thriller. Around it we set articles analysing aspects of life in Russia at the time: the transformation of the economy, of politics and daily life, of the artistic and scholarly communities, of public consciousness and institutional structures. We interviewed major players of the period, we tracked down diaries and memoirs of eyewitnesses.

Our "total" description of 1990 bore out my initial belief that this brief period was truly revolutionary, with a critical mass of changes in every sphere of life making the collapse of the Soviet empire irreversible. A whole new way of life, all the achievements and shortcomings of the two decades that followed, stemmed from 1990. For us, however, the most important discovery concerned the character of late-Soviet society. In flat contradiction of a widespread belief that the peoples of Russia had shown themselves disastrously unready to display constructive initiative, our researches revealed that, at this critical moment in history, the country succeeded in averting catastrophic developments. This resulted from the efforts of diverse social groups, the courage and creative endeavour of individuals, and the general spirit of the times which demanded change. After taking a close look at the dire experience of its existence under totalitarianism, our people found the strength of mind to build a new social system.

It has to be said that, as we worked on the project, we encountered a whole raft of problems, both social and professional. We had naively supposed that historians would find this an attractive and rewarding prospect, recent history having an abundance of the kind of sources they can only dream of when studying more distant periods. Alas, we soon found that some major social, economic and cultural processes of the late 1980s had simply not been registered by Soviet and foreign media or commentators, and, if they had, then often tendentiously. A further blow was the chaos that engulfed the Russian nation's memory banks as the Soviet empire disintegrated, funding dwindled, and ideological assumptions were undermined. Most depositories lack, or have only very incomplete holdings of, the non-official press from the latter years of perestroika. In 1990–91, television and radio stations repeatedly recorded over earlier tapes "in order to save money", we were told, but perhaps also because diehards were taking revenge by imposing a kind of retrospective censorship. Many broadcasts are simply not preserved where you would expect to find them.

As regards the testimony of those actively involved in the events of the time, we encountered blanket social amnesia. There was a marked reluctance to revisit "the follies of youth". The remorseful tone in which brave, idealistic actions, creative initiatives and political commitment to the cause of democracy were recalled, and a stubborn repudiation of the undeniable achievements of the 1990s, were unexpected. A similar block had frustrated historians and journalists in the perestroika period when interviewing war veterans and former prison-camp inmates. Instead of receiving searing, authentic accounts of lived experience, interviewers were fobbed off with platitudes and the weary clichés of Soviet propaganda. We came to see that no less sophisticated methods of reconstruction were called for when researching recent history than when researching the history of the distant past.

While respecting the cultural historian's traditional tools, we felt a need to seek new approaches to studying the recent Soviet past. The difficulty of describing 1990 stems from the short-lived, unstable coexistence at every social and symbolic level of the old and the new, from elites to the economy, from public to institutional consciousness, in discourse and in art. Analysing this situation called for a sound grounding in the peculiarities of Soviet discourse and an ability to read between the lines. This was something all Soviet citizens were brilliantly able to do, in both the Brezhnev "Era of Stagnation" and the perestroika period. Russian society has gradually lost this ability, which was essential to survival in the freewheeling 1990s. It has yet to be generally recognised that it remains an essential tool for anyone researching the Soviet era.

This deficiency made it easier to manipulate public opinion in the 2000s, inducing a wave of witless nostalgia but also leading researchers in the humanities, especially younger ones, to idealise the "grand style" of the Stalinist past and the Soviet era generally. The result has been that academics, instead of creating an alternative history of Russia, essentially repeat the mental processes behind the official Soviet version, concealing this

3

lamentable fact behind an intricate screen of fashionable terminology. The lack of new approaches for analysing Soviet civilisation makes it difficult to characterise 1990, a year on which many look back as merely a time when the continuity of Russian history was disrupted and society degraded.

Today's cultural elite like to reproach the late 1980s as a time when "professionalism" was lost, across the board. The latter years of perestroika were indeed an era of idealistic, almost militant, amateurism: in the economy, with its home-grown cooperatives, independent farmers and joint ventures; in politics, with the carnivalesque proliferation of political parties; in culture, obsessed with eroticism and denigration of both past and present; in literary language, "desecrated" by mockery, anglicisms and prison slang; and in the new mass media, with their programmes tossed out seemingly without any awareness of international best practice.[1]

If we take a different perspective and link the anarchic birth of the new media with the Russian tradition of the singer-songwriter, the ways of the artistic underground, and the tradition of comedy skits, where "sincerity", artlessness, self-irony and depiction of run-of-the-mill life were potent aesthetic weapons against the totalitarian factory of lies, we can see that there was more to the society and culture of this period than meets the eye. Its apparent amateurism was no mere dilettantism but a hard-hitting alternative to the castrated "professionalism" of the Soviet epoch.[2]

Another problem we encountered was a shortage of researchers who were comfortable working with different media. To this day, scholars in the humanities can be divided into the respectable readers of paper archives and more frivolous listeners to and watchers of audio-visual materials. In order to understand this transitional period, however, we needed analysts able to compare the presentation of events across different media. If we

---

1 On the vagaries of the new media, see articles below by Pavel Pavlov and Vladimir Pozner.
2 Many people fondly remember the Moscow Ventilation Factory advertisements screened in 1990 ("Time for you to sign a contract/With the Ventilation Factory./If you think you can't afford/a system that is really nice/We'll refurbish one that's old/For a reasonable price./If you fancy keeping cool/We're the lads will show you how./Moscow Ventilation Factory./Lift the phone and call us now!"). These are now included in textbooks as examples of effective advertising in which a self-aware jingle successfully advertises the work of a "serious" industrial enterprise.

had restricted ourselves to traditional periodicals and personal diaries of 1990, we would have concluded that the dominant mood was one of foreboding, bewilderment and disillusionment. Giving due emphasis to the new radio, and in particular television, stations we found a quite different, positive, dynamic perception of reality.

Thanks to the recent appearance of satellite T.V. channels like Nostalgia, Retro T.V., Times Far and Near, and the thoroughgoing "retromania" of present-day television, we had a unique opportunity to view large numbers of programmes from the latter half of the 1980s. In next to no time, the presentation and design of programmes changed, along with the body language and appearance of presenters. The lifeless blue backdrop of the Time (Vremya) news programme gradually retreated under the onslaught of colourful special effects. The hairstyles and clothing of newsreaders lost their severity until, after 1988, "professional" readers were replaced by presenters whose diction was barely comprehensible and whose facial expressions were entirely unexpected in the context of ideological programmes. The camera would pan over the auditorium during concerts and discussions, infallibly registering the physical transformation of the audience, the disappearance of tell-tale signs of "Sovietness" in their deportment – relaxation of the facial muscles, a wider repertoire of individual gestures, an open, friendly look, unconstrained movement. These visual clues provide irrefutable evidence that the humanising and liberation of Soviet society were very real, that the overall thrust of this period was constructive rather than destructive.

Finally, and most crucially, we confronted the predicament of the researcher. When studying the present, how do you combine the traditional requirement of scholarly objectivity, the historian's impartial gaze, with the observer's personal experience of events, their emotional and intellectual baggage, indeed their political convictions? Being experienced in surviving a totalitarian society with its "professionally" perfected system for discrediting and devaluing everything possessing value and meaning, shall we not restore to the guild of historians their ancient, long-forgotten privilege of travelling in the wake of the army as impartial and enlightened chroniclers, preserving our shared past, however diverse and individual, and thereby giving meaning to the present?

LATE 1989: A TIMELINE

9 November

The Council of Ministers of the German Democratic Republic decides that it will allow "all who wish to" to leave the G.D.R. temporarily or permanently without restriction. (In the summer of 1989, a large number of its citizens had escaped to the Federal Republic of Germany.) On the night of 9 December, residents of East and West Germany began jointly to demolish the Berlin Wall.

15–19 November

At the U.S.S.R. Student Forum held at the Palace of Youth in Moscow, Mikhail Gorbachev, asked about the introduction of private property rights in the Soviet Union, replies, "I stand by the *Communist Manifesto*. That does not stop me from making proposals to reform the structure of industry and property relations. I do not believe the working class supports those who are calling for our society to choose the path of capitalism" (*Komsomol'skaia pravda*, 17 November). The students also meet Andrey Sakharov, who says, "I believe now is a critical moment in our history. It is vitally important to get some fundamental laws passed at the Congress [of People's Deputies of the U.S.S.R.], or at least to discuss them. We are not sure the Congress will do this. The first priority is a law on land and a law on property. It is essential to discuss the Communist Party's monopoly on power in order to have a political guarantee that perestroika will go forward irreversibly. If economic change is not introduced in 1990, everyone will lose confidence in perestroika. I do not think it is too late yet for a peaceful transition to a new set of mutual relationships" (*Komsomol'skaia pravda*, 16 December).

17 November

In Prague, the Velvet Revolution grows out of an anti-Communist student demonstration joined by townspeople. The demonstrators' main demands are for free elections; the resignation of Miloš Jakeš, the General Secretary of the Communist Party of Czechoslovakia; and abolition of the Party's monopoly on political power. The demonstrations continue for several weeks, and, although periodically dispersed by the police, the crowds grow more numerous, finally causing the downfall of the regime.

19 November

The Supreme Soviet of the Georgian Soviet Socialist Republic passes an amendment to the Georgian constitution giving it the right to veto U.S.S.R. laws and declaring its own natural resources the property of Georgia. It reaffirms Georgia's right to freely secede from the U.S.S.R. (*L'Année internationale* [Paris, 1992], p. 268).

22 November

Boris Gidaspov, First Secretary of the Leningrad provincial Party committee and Leningrad municipal soviet, organises a mass rally in Leningrad against perestroika (*Ogonek*, 50 [1989], p. 26). A report shown on national television produces strong reactions throughout the U.S.S.R. "I was in Moscow at the time and saw just a fragment of the 22 November meeting on television. The ferocity and atmosphere of mob hatred horrified me" (Anatoliy Sobchak, *Khozhdenie vo vlast'* [Leningrad, 1991]; http://fragments. spb.ru/sobchak_1.html).

29 November

Death of Natan Eydelman (b. 1930), the outstanding historian, author and political commentator.
    The parliament of Czechoslovakia deletes the article in the country's constitution relating to the Communist Party's monopoly on power.

7

1 *December*

A meeting takes place between Gorbachev and Pope John Paul II, during which both sides express their wish to establish diplomatic relations between the Vatican and the U.S.S.R. (which duly occurred). From Gorbachev's speech at the Vatican: "I have to say, Your Holiness, that I was astonished by the way the people responded to our proposals and reflections. We are not so arrogant as to suppose we bear some exalted redemptive mission. One cannot claim to possess absolute truth, or try to impose it on others. Some people are claiming that Europe should be renewed solely on the basis of Western values, and that everything that differs from those should be excised. It is wrong to treat peoples, their history, traditions and identity like that. The U.S.S.R. used to be accused of exporting revolution. Now, however, attempts are being made to export other values. That is not the right path. In this, as in other issues, the supreme authority for us is the people. Everything depends on what choice it will make" (Mikhail Gorbachev, *Gody trudnykh reshenii* [Moscow, 1993], pp. 166–72).

2–3 *December*

Gorbachev and George Bush meet on the *Maxim Gorky*, off the coast of Malta.

9 *December*

At a meeting of the Interregional Group of Deputies, formed in the summer of 1989 and the most democratic group in the U.S.S.R. Supreme Soviet, members call for abolition of the Communist Party's monopoly on power and the introduction of a multi-party system.

A plenum of the Communist Party of the Soviet Union (C.P.S.U.) Central Committee considers issues arising at the forthcoming Second Congress of People's Deputies of the U.S.S.R., the formation of a Russian Bureau of the Central Committee etc. It reaffirms the desirability of retaining a one-party system.

12 December

The Congress of People's Deputies rejects a draft resolution on the introduction of a multi-party system by 1,138 votes to 939.

12–24 December

The Second Congress of People's Deputies of the U.S.S.R. During the Congress, many workers' groups hold a token two-hour strike on the initiative of Andrey Sakharov in favour of abolition of Article 6 of the U.S.S.R. Constitution (which enshrined in law the "leading role of the Communist Party").

14 December

Sakharov (b. 1921) dies suddenly in Moscow. He had been a physicist, political activist, one of the leaders of the dissident movement in the U.S.S.R. and, in 1980, won the Nobel Peace Prize. On 27 November, Sakharov had given Gorbachev, who was Chairman of the Constitutional Commission, a draft "Constitution of the Union of Soviet Republics of Europe and Asia", a voluntary association of sovereign republics (*Novoe vremia*, 52 [1989]). In his final days Sakharov was still making amendments to the draft.

Presidential elections in Chile end the dictatorship of General Augusto Pinochet Ugarte, who had come to power in a military coup in September 1973.

20 December

The Democratic Workers' Movement is established, based on the strike committee of the Vorgashorsk coal mine. It had only forty or so members but was very active in the 1989–90 election campaign. All the candidates it supported were elected people's deputies (http://www.nasledie.ru/oborg/ 2_16/t2/14.htm).

U.S. troops invaded Panama to overthrow the dictatorial regime of Manuel Noriega. The U.S. government had earlier accused Noriega of personal involvement in the drugs trade and suppression of democratic freedoms (Ivan Konovalov, "'Pravoe delo' Pentagona", *Voenno-promyshlennyi kur'er*, 22 [2005]; http://vpk-news.ru/articles/471).

In Romania, massive popular uprisings topple the dictatorial regime of Nicolae Ceauşescu. Power passes to the Council of the National Salvation Front.

24 December

The Congress of People's Deputies approves a directive "Concerning the political and legal assessment of the Soviet–German non-aggression pact of 1939" (i.e., the Molotov–Ribbentrop Pact). The congress acknowledges the existence of secret protocols to the pact regarding "spheres of influence" in Europe which, even in 1989, the Soviet leadership had been denying. It condemns and declares them null and void from the moment of signing. The Congress also condemns the invasion of Afghanistan in December 1979 on political and moral grounds (*Pravda*, 26 December).

25 December

In Romania, former dictator Ceauşescu and his wife Elena are executed by firing squad.

Gorbachev sends a message to the Chairman of the Council of the National Salvation Front of Romania, Ion Iliescu, which reads, "Understanding the complexity and importance of the challenges facing the National Salvation Front, I wish to assure you that our friends, the people of Romania, will enjoy the support of the people and leaders of the Soviet Union on their path of renewal" (*Pravda*, 27 December).

The Federal Assembly of Czechoslovakia elects as president Václav Havel, leader of the dissident movement, human rights activist and playwright.

The Polish Sejm amends the republic's constitution to abolish the Communist Party's monopoly on power, introduce a multi-party system and protect private property. The name of the country is changed to the

Republic of Poland (*Mezhdunarodnyi ezhegodnik. Politika i ekonomika: 1990* [Moscow, 1990], p. 411).

31 December

How Is Perestroika Doing?

(from surveys conducted by the U.S.S.R. Centre for the Study of Public Opinion)

	1988	1989
What was the past year like for you?		
More difficult than last year	42.5	55.6
Easier than last year	11.4	13.6
The same as last year	46.1	30.8
What was it like for our society?		
More difficult than last year	79.6	83.4
Easier than last year	7.1	4.3
The same as last year	13.3	12.3
How did the availability of food change in the past year?		
For the better	15.6	6.0
For the worse	46.3	78.4
No change	33.7	13.9
Don't know	4.4	1.7
How did the availability of manufactured goods change in the past year?		
For the better	8.2	3.1
For the worse	58.8	83.3
No change	27.5	9.5
Don't know	5.5	4.1
How did relations between people of different nationalities change in the past year?		
For the better	19.5	7.0
For the worse	37.6	71.5
No change	26.5	10.9
Don't know	16.4	10.6
How has the personal security of citizens changed in the last year?		
For the better		4.5

	1988	1989
For the worse		58.4
No change		21.0
Don't know		16.1

How has the influence of ordinary people on state affairs changed in the past year?

Increased		25.5
Decreased		7.7
No change		41.0
Don't know		25.8

What, in your opinion, are the reasons for our present difficulties?

Low vocational and professional qualifications	26.4	24.1
Technological backwardness	42.0	42.9
Corruption, drunkenness, profiteering, thieving	56.8	58.5
The legacy of Stalinism	12.7	13.8
Too much power in the hands of bureaucrats	41.4	39.1
Loss of faith in the ideals of socialism	15.6	18.3
Destruction of national traditions	10.7	15.3
People are work-shy	28.0	27.3
Incompetence of bosses	18.7	17.9
Failure of morality	13.3	15.9
Hidden enemies	5.9	8.8
Errors by the country's political leaders	23.7	31.2
Degeneration of the population	3.2	5.5
Politics of envy, suppression of people with initiative	22.7	19.5
Loss of religious faith	7.4	10.3
Policies of imperialist countries	1.9	2.1
Lack of concern for problems of federalism and autonomy of peoples		12.7
Mafia and organised crime		35.9
One-party system		20.2
Don't know	5.4	6.4

	1988	1989
Who is mainly benefiting from the changes taking place in the country?		
People who work conscientiously	30.0	19.5
Windbags	7.4	14.1
Peasants	6.9	4.9
Executives	8.3	18.3
Owners and workers of cooperatives	39.6	41.8
Skilled workers	9.1	7.5
Sole traders	13.6	16.9
The working class	7.1	5.7
Other private traders	10.8	22.9
People who have moved to full-cost accounting	15.2	10.1
Intellectuals	3.6	2.0
Scam artists, swindlers	20.7	38.7
Don't know	15.8	11.7
Who, then, in your opinion, is losing out?		
Bureaucrats	23.2	11.3
Low-income families	30.4	46.0
Lonely people, old people	25.4	36.8
Ordinary hard-working people	15.7	23.6
Layabouts, drunkards	23.0	10.8
Honest white-collar workers	10.3	22.5
Former bosses who have been demoted	9.4	5.3
People with no education or training	12.9	9.7
Employees made redundant	16.1	15.0
Don't know	15.8	11.6

(Est' mnenie! Itogi sotsiologicheskogo oprosa [Moscow, 1990]).

"IF LENIN WERE ALIVE TODAY, HE WOULD KNOW WHAT TO DO"

Aleksey Yurchak

Throughout the history of the U.S.S.R., Lenin was the main legitimising symbol, the "master-signifier", of Soviet ideology, external to the ideological discourse.[3] In other words, the postulate that Lenin's ideas were correct and incontrovertible was the premise underlying all ideological statements, and hence could not be called into question by them. As a result, all reforms and changes in the Soviet system were carried out under the pretext that they were combating perversion of Lenin's ideas in order to revert to what he really meant.

This was also the task which perestroika initially set itself. In 1990, however, the Communist Party press changed the way in which the the task was formulated. If in the past the speeches of Party leaders had explained that distortion of Lenin's ideas had occurred during particular periods (under Stalin or Brezhnev), the suggestion now was that Lenin's ideas had been distorted throughout the whole of Soviet history. This cast doubt on the authenticity of any of Lenin's statements to be found in Soviet sources. That apparently minor shift in 1990 created a paradox within Party discourse. On the one hand, it was declaring that the main task of the perestroika reforms was to return to the ideas of the real Lenin, while on the other it was asserting that the real Lenin was unknown.

A typical early 1990 article in *Kommunist*, the Central Committee's official theoretical journal, begins in familiar vein: the main task of perestroika is to "rid socialism of Stalin's perversions, to restore to it the ideals of Marx

---

3. See Alexei Yurchak, *Everything Was Forever, until It Was No More: The Last Soviet Generation* (Princeton, 2006), pp. 73–4.

and Lenin, its heart and soul, which Stalin had cut out . . ."[4] Later, however, the article formulates the task of perestroika somewhat differently: "to proceed by way of experimentation rather than dogma, enriching the ideals of socialism with new, hitherto unknown meaning".[5] Returning to the ideals of Marx and Lenin was going to be a leap in the dark. The emergence of this contradiction in Party discourse in 1990 was one of the most significant events of that eventful year. It greatly hastened the undermining of the principle that legitimised Soviet ideology, and accelerated the irreversible collapse of the Communist Party and the Soviet system as a whole.

This process began and ended in 1990.

I

Admitting that Lenin's words and ideas had been distorted throughout Soviet history created the necessity to establish the Leader's authentic, undistorted identity. The first step was to understand how and why his words had been distorted. Party writers, debating the issue in the spring of 1990, noted that this had been done by all manner of commentators, paraphrasers and editors. Some had done it as a result of misunderstanding, some with the best of intentions and some maliciously. Other people's reports of what Lenin said had occasionally been treated as tantamount to what he actually said. *Kommunist* observed that, "Sundry views, opinions and statements by the authors of reminiscences" of Lenin were still being treated as "fundamental propositions by Lenin himself."[6] For example, the journal continued, although in a well-known publication on the Party's cultural policy, Clara Zetkin was only reporting a conversation she had had with Lenin, her paraphrase was treated "as if the words were written by Lenin himself". Moreover, ". . . for many years we have been using a far from perfect translation", even of the paraphrase. In this instance, Lenin's words and ideas were doubly distorted, having been inaccurately reported

4. Vladimir Sogrin, "Levaia, pravaia gde storona?", *Kommunist*, 3 (February 1990), pp. 33–4.
5. *Ibid*. p. 36.
6. V. Polevoi, "Khudozhnik i vlast'", *Kommunist*, 2 (January 1990), pp. 66–75.

and then inaccurately translated. If these strictures apply to the account of one of Lenin's closest "comrades-in-arms", what must be the situation where people wrote down and edited what Lenin said for reasons of political expediency during a particular historical period? "Is it not time we found out?" *Kommunist* asked. That is, was it not time to check the authenticity of everything Lenin is reported to have said, in order finally to identify his real voice? The journal proposed not merely to improve the accuracy of particular statements but to carry out a complete "inventory of texts, records and interpretations" of what the Leader said.[7]

It soon became apparent, however, that merely compiling an inventory would not solve the problem. Lenin's words were distorted, not only by inaccurate paraphrasing and interpretation but also because he had been canonised by Soviet history, and everything he said along with him. Living speech had been transfigured into a set of quotations. Lenin's discourse had been frozen and rendered unable to develop in tandem with the advance of history. This, *Kommunist* observed, was the source of the greatest distortion of Lenin's words.

Gorbachev began an official speech marking the 120th anniversary of Lenin's birth in April 1990 by saying, "Lenin remains with us as a leading thinker of the twentieth century." He immediately added, "We need to reinterpret Lenin, his theoretical and political legacy, shaking off distortions and the canonisation of the conclusions he came to. It is time to put a stop to a mindless attitude towards the name and image of Lenin which treats him as a figure in an icon."[8] Since the canonical doctrine established on the basis of Lenin's ideas is Leninism, a movement away from that and a return to a more authentic Lenin was tantamount, blasphemous as it might sound, to a rejection of Leninism. In an attempt to fudge this considerable issue, Gorbachev went on to explain that *Leninism* was a term coined by the Mensheviks as a means of ridiculing the Leader's ideas.[9]

7. *Ibid.*, p. 69. 8. "Slovo o Lenine prezidenta SSSR, General'nogo sektretaria TsK KPSS M.S. Gorbacheva", *Pravda*, 21 April 1990, p. 1.
9. *Ibid.* Nina Tumarkin gives a different account of the origin of the term. She claims that it

The real Lenin, unlike the canonical image, *Kommunist* explained, often changed his mind and corrected errors in the light of changing historical circumstances. What he had to say was not static but had evolved. Building on this idea, Aleksandr Yakovlev, a Party theoretician, member of the Politburo and the 'foreman of the perestroika building site', wrote in *Kommunist* that spring that the real Lenin was to be found, not in particular political positions but in the ability to change one's position in accordance with the situation. "Something which I personally greatly admire in Lenin's personality," Yakovlev explained, "is his ability to revise his position when that was what life itself called for."[10] Two other writers in *Kommunist* developed this by noting that, in the light of the practical experience of building socialism, Lenin was constantly correcting not only his own errors but those in the theoretical works of Marx and Engels.[11]

These assertions in the spring of 1990 led naturally to the conclusion that, since Lenin's practical experience of building socialism had been limited to a few years, he could not have corrected every error and adapted every policy. Consequently, *Kommunist* argued, those views in his works and those of the Marxist classics which he was unable to correct were continuing to mislead us. This was because ". . . until the epistemological mechanism of error is revealed and understood, thought is unable to argue with and correct itself".[12] In other words, Party theorists had to learn to correct and augment Lenin's texts in the spirit of Lenin himself. They had to correct and add to them as Lenin would have done if he had still been alive. The old formula of Party ideology claimed "Lenin is more alive than the living". It celebrated a canonical, changeless and hence, paradoxically, dead Lenin. The new ideological formula introduced in 1990 can be

was first publicly used on 3 January, 1923 by Vladimir Sorokin, head of the Agitation and Propaganda Department of the Moscow Party Committee, when he spoke of the need to study Leninism as a unique component of Marxism. See Nina Tumarkin, *Lenin Lives! The Lenin Cult in Soviet Russia* (Cambridge, MA , 1997, p. 120).

10. Aleksandr Yakovlev, "Sotsializm: mechty i real'nosti", *Kommunist*, 4 (March 1990), p. 21.

11. I. Pantin and E. Plimak, "Idei K. Marksa na perelome chelovecheskoi tsivilizatsii", *Kommunist*, 4 (March 1990), pp. 28–45, esp. p. 36. 12. *Ibid*.

summarised in a catchphrase which became current in the latter years of perestroika: "If Lenin were alive today, he would know what to do". The task facing the Party's ideologues was becoming increasingly fanciful. They needed to recreate a living Lenin, able to reflect on today's problems in today's language. If the Party's publications and pronouncements in 1990 did not call directly for the physical resurrection of Lenin, that is transparently what they desired.

An example of this wishful thinking is a propaganda poster titled "Let Lenin speak!" and issued in 1990 by the Central Committee's Plakat publishing imprint (figure 1).[13] The centre of the poster is taken up by a massive red podium with microphones and the Soviet crest, which represents the canonical quoting of Lenin in official party speeches. Lenin himself is depicted in a deliberately non-monumental way. A small, hunched figure in black and white, he crouches to one side in the lower part of the poster, beneath the podium, intently jotting down his thoughts about the current situation in a notebook. We cannot see his thoughts, and to know what they are we have to let Lenin speak, to allow him to come to the podium and hear him "live" in the present day.

Another example is the new look of Kommunist itself, which was unveiled in April 1990.[14] For decades, the cover had had a conservative, bureaucratic look, like the cover of most other Soviet Party and academic publications. The title had been printed in a clunky Soviet font on a blue-grey background (figure 2). In April 1990, the magazine had a sudden facelift (figure 3). In a letter to its readers the editors explained, "This issue of Kommunist, dedicated to the 120th anniversary of the birth of V. I. Lenin, has been redesigned by Vladimir Panteleyev. The title on the cover is a magnified facsimile of Vladimir Ilyich's handwriting. Our intention is to indicate our attitude to the legacy of the founder of the Soviet state and the legacy of Marxism generally,

13. The artist was V. Chumakov.
14. The change in the cover design of Kommunist was also analysed by Thomas Wolfe in a paper presented at the annual conference of the American Anthropological Association in Washington, DC, in 1993.

on which the journal today bases its theoretical and political work."[15] The title thus becomes part of an authentic Lenin manuscript and of his revived, topical, dynamically developing discourse.[16]

Right: Fig. 2 *Kommunist*'s "bureaucratic" look.

Above: Fig. 1 "Let Lenin speak!"

Fig. 3 *Kommunist* in Lenin's hand-writing

15. *Kommunist*, 5 (1990), p. 128. Subsequent issues in 1990 and 1991 followed the new style.
16. This changeover from the old, frozen discourse to a new, rapidly developing one is reflected in every aspect of the design. The title is placed diagonally; the colour saturation of the background diminishes from top to bottom; the canonical symbols of the Order of Lenin and the slogan "Workers of all countries, unite!" are removed; and the date is written in a modern, casual format as "5'90" instead of "No. 5, 1990". See figs 2, 3.

II

In talking of the need to let Lenin speak, both the Party poster and the new cover of *Kommunist* were thinking subjunctively: "If Lenin could speak . . ." But how was that to be achieved in practice? How could Lenin's voice be replicated so that he was not just repeating the old, familiar quotations but making new, up-to-date pronouncements which would still really be coming from Lenin? How could you not just go back to the thoughts of a long-dead Leader, but instead formulate new ideas from Lenin for the present day? Throughout 1990, the Party's theoreticians ransacked their brains for a solution to this less-than-obvious problem. The Central Committee theorist Georgiy Shakhnazarov proposed to solve it by injecting into the familiar discourse of Lenin the ideas and utterances of other thinkers about socialism, thinkers to whom Lenin had turned, and to whom he would doubtless have had recourse again, had he been living in the 1990s. Shakhnazarov instanced Plato, Aristotle, Locke, Rousseau, Kant and Hegel, offering a solution not so much discursive as organic, even agronomic, grafting the sayings of other thinkers on to the familiar texts of Lenin. The outcome of this hybridisation would be the appearance of entirely new statements by Lenin, different from what he had already said and yet genuinely by him. It would not be so different from a tree which, having received a graft, produces entirely new fruit which nevertheless belongs to it. According to Shakhnazarov, this modelling of Lenin's thought would be tantamount to "a revolution in our theoretical consciousness". "No-one," he averred, "would approve of such a revolution" more than Lenin – if he had been alive at the time.[17]

The search for the real Lenin was gradually moving in a biological direction, which doubtless explains the growing interest in his pedigree, health, psychology and physical features, and the details of his death. These were unquestionably authentic aspects of his existence, free from outside interference and the myth-making of the past, and hence available

17. Georgiy Shakhnazarov, *Kommunist*, 4 (March 1990), p. 56.

for endowment with new and topical meaning.

An increasing number of articles and broadcasts in 1990 related the details of Lenin's last days, hours and even moments, when he was ill and helpless, dying but not yet dead, suspended for an instant between life and death. In this intermediate state he was no longer a political player or the Leader but a "bare" human being. There is increasing interest in that part of Lenin's nature which Giorgio Agamben terms the "bare" or "naked" life of an individual, the physiological component of a human being that remains when the citizen's political life has been reduced to nothing.[18]

Unlike political life, bare life is outside history and politics, free from political distortion. Hence it seemed that here it should at last be possible to find the true, undistorted Lenin.

Of all his political pronouncements, Lenin's last, made literally when he was at death's door, suddenly appeared to be the most authentic, most expressive of his real, biological identity. Gorbachev said in April 1990 that it was by turning to "Lenin's last works" that he drew "confidence that [we] have embarked on a correct, if difficult, path".[19] Ogonyok magazine published Lenin's last texts under the general heading of "Lenin's political testament", including in it "eight short letters and articles dating from late 1922 and early 1923".[20]

18. Giorgio Agamben has proposed, developing the thesis of Hannah Arendt in The Human Condition (Chicago, 1958), that any modern individual has a "political life", or bios, and a "bare life", or zoe. The first component involves the political and legal existence of the individual in relation to the "sovereign" (the monarch or state), while the second is their elementary biological existence. The life of an individual whom the sovereign political power recognises as a citizen includes both components, with all their accompanying rights and restrictions. If, however, the individual loses their political component, they lose not only such legal rights as those conferred by citizenship but, in the eyes of the sovereign power, their claim to be regarded as a valid human being. This can lead to their physical annihilation with impunity on the part of the executioner, as has occurred regularly in modern history. See Giorgio Agamben, Homo Sacer: Sovereign Power and Bare Life (Stanford, 1998).
19. "Slovo o Lenine prezidenta SSSR, General'nogo sektretaria TsK KPSS M.S. Gorbacheva", p. 2.
20. Including a letter of 4 January, 1923 in which Lenin warns the Central Committee about serious faults in Stalin's personality and proposes that he be removed from the post of General Secretary. See Nikolai Gul'binskii, "K 120-letiiu so dnia rozhdeniia Vladimira Il'icha Lenina", Ogonek, 17 (1990), p. 3.

This increase of interest in the Leader's bare life took a variety of forms. For decades before 1990, Lenin was principally commemorated on the anniversary of his birth, 22 April. The anniversary of his death, 21 January, was observed, but more modestly, and had less symbolic impact.[21] Pravda's coverage of the topic was printed not on the front page but on the inside of the newspaper. The emphasis was less on Lenin's death than on his role as Leader of the world revolution. Many Soviet citizens did not know the significance of the date, which was certainly not the case with 22 April. In 1990, however, the priority was again suddenly changed: for the first time since the mid-1950s, Lenin's death was commemorated as extensively as his birth, with Pravda devoting its entire front page to the anniversary under the heading "Remembering that January".[22]

This reflected increased interest not so much in the diagnosis of Lenin's final illness, or in the political situation surrounding his death, as in the details of the physiological process of his dying and the undistorted, "organic" nature of the man, his bare life suddenly revealed. Publishing little-known eyewitness accounts, the front page of Pravda described his death in unfamiliar, straightforwardly physical terms. The emphasis in a passage from Nikolai Bukharin's memoirs was on the Leader's physical features. "Never again shall we see that great brow, the magnificent head which radiated revolutionary energy in every direction, those lively, piercing, attentive eyes, the firm, powerful hands, his whole sturdy, powerful figure . . ." These accounts seem sometimes not to be describing death but an existence between life and death. In an excerpt from the memoirs of Vladimir Bonch-Bruevich, we read: "The right hand is clenched, the grey stain of a small bruise on the right ear relentlessly holds our attention.

21. This had not always been the case. In the years immediately following Lenin's death, the anniversary of it was observed far more expansively than that of his birth. However, just over a year before his historic criticism of Stalin's "personality cult", Khrushchev reversed the emphasis. On 11 January, 1955, the Central Committee adopted a resolution moving the annual celebration of Lenin's life from 21 January to 22 April. See Nina Tumarkin, Lenin Lives!, p. 257.
22. John Gooding, "Lenin in Soviet Politics, 1985–91", Soviet Studies, 44/3 (1992), p. 409.

Look, his eyes seem to be opening. His cheek is trembling slightly . . ."[23]

Interest in these physical details became part of the process of decanonisation of Lenin which Gorbachev had called for. The other side of this process, however, was that the Leader ceased to be sacrosanct. Deprived of his political aura, he also lost his status as the infallible superman you just knew was always right. There was still little overt criticism of Lenin in the media in 1990, but increasingly he was discussed in terms which presented him as neither good nor bad, merely human.

In one of the 1990 issues of *Ogonyok*, the magazine's editor Vitaliy Korotich describes a recent visit to the Lenin Mausoleum, writing that, in place of his usual sense of religious awe, he was surprised to register the complete banality of the ritual surroundings and the body in the coffin. On this occasion, Red Square was closed to the public, and Korotich entered the mausoleum without the usual stream of visitors: "For the first time I was face to face with Lenin in the semi-darkness of his public tomb, dimly lit and melancholy, as are all resting places of the dead."[24] For Korotich, Lenin no longer appeared as the Leader "alive for all eternity" but as a man whose fate was to have been stranded between life and death. In this condition, he was deprived of his political status and its associated grandeur and reduced to his bare life, a life not only banal but tragic, because it has not been allowed to proceed to its natural end: "A short man in his best suit was lying in a bulletproof coffin in the middle of a chamber, one hand clenched and the other with its fingers outstretched. 'Poor Lenin,' I thought. 'A man not allowed to rest in peace. In every age, one of the most terrible humiliations was not to have your body consigned to the grave. How [had] he deserved such a fate?'"[25]

In the eyes of most Soviet citizens, the totem of Lenin was still, at the end of 1990, revered and unassailable. Desacralising the Leader was, nevertheless, gradually rendering him more vulnerable to overt criticism. In

23. "Pamiat' o tom ianvare", *Pravda*, 21 January 1990, p. 1.
24. Introduction by Vitaliy Korotich to "Rasstavanie s bogom" [discussion between Oleg Moroz and Vladimir Soloukhin], *Ogonek*, 51 (1990), p. 26. 25. *Ibid*.

December 1990, Oleg Moroz wrote in *Ogonyok* that "for our readers today, the idea of debunking Lenin is almost as shocking as debunking Christ would be to Christians, a thoroughly dubious enterprise in every respect. People have become accustomed to believing that Lenin is God, and have no wish to have that belief questioned."[26] "It is time to tell the truth about this person," Moroz's fellow contributor Vladimir Soloukhin added.[27] The "truth" that most of Lenin's critics wanted to reveal, however, was to be found not so much by analysing his views on particular historical events as by revealing secrets and mysteries about his ancestry and physiology. Calls to tear away his mask and expose his true colours took the form of demands to reveal his human nature. A. A. Matyshev suggested abandoning the "false" name of Lenin and using his real surname, Ulyanov. The time had come, he wrote, to reveal people's "real names and surnames". That would make it "easier to say goodbye to myths".[28]

III

This interest in real names points to a wish to dig deeper into the real Lenin's ancestry and ethnic origins, and indeed his "hidden roots" were discussed more and more freely. In April 1990, the newspaper *Arguments and Facts* published a pioneering interview with his niece on the subject of the Ulyanov family's antecedents. Rumours were already circulating in the press about Lenin's un-Russian pedigree, and his elderly niece went out of her way to emphasise that the family "through the line of Ilya Nikolayevich [Lenin's father] were Russian people. Vladimir Ilyich and his sisters always wrote in official forms that they were Russian and that their native language was Russian. I can't tell you anything definite about the line through Mariya Aleksandrovna. She was Russian too, although there has

---

26. *Ibid.*, p. 27.   27. *Ibid.*, p. 30.
28. A. A Matyshev's manuscript "Diktator" had been offered to the magazine *Neva*. Quoted by Vitaliy Startsev in "Politik i chelovek", *Neva*, 3 (1991), pp. 148–59. Matyshev's article was written in early 1990 when there was a controversy on this subject.

been talk of a Swedish branch. There is no documentary evidence of that, though."[29]

In October 1990, *Man of Letters* (*Literator*), a Leningrad newspaper, published previously unknown facts uncovered in secret archives of the Central Committee's Institute of Marxism-Leninism. At the request of its readers, *Word*, a magazine with a much larger circulation, reprinted the information,[30] and it was subsequently also reported in *Book Survey*, a literary newspaper.[31] The article focused particularly on the continuing investigation into Lenin's Swedish roots, which had been mentioned only as unsubstantiated rumour. Although there was now more information, the newspaper reported, the full facts were not yet known: "Carl Reinhald Östedt, a glove-maker in Uppsala, and Grigory Ulyanin, a serf, are the earliest forebears to whom researchers have traced the family tree (albeit without dates for their births and deaths)."[32]

The stream of articles and broadcasts about Lenin's antecedents increased. Most are a cross between the investigation in a detective novel

29. "I vnov' o Lenine. Ol'ga Dmitrievna Ul'ianova, plemiannitsa V. I. Ul'ianova (Lenina), otvechaet na voprosy korrespondenta 'AiF'", *Argumenty i Fakty*, 16 (1990), p. 1. This was the first serious effort to establish Lenin's genealogy since the 1930s. Marietta Shaginian made an early attempt in her 1938 novel *Bilet po istorii* (The History Exam), part of a trilogy about the Ulyanov family. Shaginian mentions Lenin's Kalmyk grandmother but characterises his Jewish grandfather, Aleksandr Blank, as a "Little Russian" (i.e., Ukrainian). She was roundly condemned for the novel. On 5 August, 1936, the Politburo of the C.P.S.U. (the Bolsheviks) adopted a resolution "On Marietta Shaginian's novel *The History Exam*, Part 1: 'The Ulyanov Family'". Shaginian and Lenin's wife, Nadezhda Krupskaya (who had given her an interview and material), were accused of having turned the "generally accepted manner of compiling works about Lenin into a private family affair and presented themselves as having a monopoly on interpreting the public and private life and work of Lenin and his family, something to which the Central Committee has never given anybody any rights whatsoever". See Academician Aleksandr Iakovlev, ed., *Vlast' i khudozhestvennaia intelligentsiia: Dokumenty TsK RKP(b)-VKP(b), VChK-OGPU-NKVD o kul'turnoi politike, 1917–1953 gg.* (Moscow, 1999). See also Efim Melamed, "'Otrekis' ot iudeiskoi very' (Novonaidennye dokumenty o evreiskikh predkakh Lenina)", *Vestnik*, 21 (332), 15 October, 2003.
30. *Slovo*, 2 (1990).
31. A. Kochergina, "Pochta: massovyi vopros", *Knizhnoe obozrenie*, 22 (1991).
32. Mikhail Shtein, "Genealogiia roda Ul'ianovykh (ili kakie tainy khraniat do sikh por seify Instituta Marksizma-leninizma pri TsK KPSS", *Literator*, 38 (October 1990).

and a scientific enquiry into secrets of nature which were expected to show the entire course of Soviet history in a new light. The apotheosis of the genre is Stanislav Govorukhin's documentary *The Russia We Lost*. He began shooting at the Mosfilm studios in 1990 when interest in this issue was at its height.[33] The film contrasts the pre-revolutionary Russian empire with contemporary Soviet Russia, partly through a comparison of two opposing families: that of Tsar Nicholas II and the Ulyanovs. Govorukhin acts as the film's main narrator, walking through archives, viewing newsreel footage and quoting from previously classified documents. He stresses that both families had complex, non-Russian antecedents. The roots of the tsarist royal family were West European: "All the tsars of Russia, from Catherine the First onwards, had German blood in their veins. Nicholas II also had Danish blood. His mother, Mariya Fyodorovna, was a Danish princess. Here he is with his cousin, King George V of England [shows photo]. His wife, Aleksandra Fyodorovna of Hesse-Darmstadt, was a German princess brought up at the English court."[34] Despite their origins, Govorukhin continued, members of the royal family were genuinely Russian in their culture and religion. The tsar's wife voluntarily converted to Russian Orthodoxy, refused to have her children taught German, and even employed simple Russian nannies who told them Russian fairy tales and taught them to speak like ordinary Russians.

Govorukhin then comes to Lenin's family. Sitting in the Leningrad History Archive, he comments,

> For many decades Lenin's ethnic background has been shrouded in mystery. And understandably so, because there is plenty in it to knock the feet from under any true-believing Communist. On the paternal side we find his father, Ilya Nikolayevich [shows photo]; Lenin's grandmother, Anna Smirnova, was a Kalmyk; his grandfather, Nikolai Ulyanin, was a Chuvash. The maternal line is even

33. The film was completed in 1991 and shown on Central Television in early 1992.
34. My transcription from a video recording of the film – A. Yu.

more problematical. This is his mother, Mariya Aleksandrovna [shows photo]; Lenin's grandmother, Anna Groschopf, was German with an admixture of Swedish blood. Pay attention, now, anti-Semites: Lenin's grandad, Aleksandr Blank, was a Jew. Here we have a register of Department of Medicine staff. We know Lenin's grandfather, Aleksandr Blank, was trained as a medic and graduated from the Academy of Medicine. Pages 520–23 are missing, and it took us six months to find them.[35]

Govorukhin was only able to track down the missing pages the following year, in 1991, when, after the failed August putsch, the Communist Party archives were declassified. Sitting in a room at the archive, he continues his story:

Here we found documents removed from the History Archive in St Petersburg. What terrible secret did the Party need to conceal from its members? There is a document explaining why the Blanks, who were Jewish, converted to Christianity. It reads, "Information regarding Dmitriy and Aleksandr Blank, Jewish children who accepted the sacrament of baptism, pupils of the Imperial Academy of Surgery and Medicine. The aforementioned Blanks are descended from burgers of Starokonstantinovo and are children of the Jew Moshka Blank.

"That's all there is to it," Govorukhin remarks pensively, before concluding, "The brothers Abel and Israel Blank took the Christian names of Dmitriy and Aleksandr. They were forced [Govorukhin emphasises the word] to convert to Russian Orthodoxy because higher education institutions did not admit Jews."[36]

The film offers a simple conclusion. Despite the complex antecedents of the two families, members of the royal family can be considered

35. Ibid.   36. Ibid.

genuinely Russian and with a good European pedigree. Those who were not born into Orthodoxy voluntarily adopted it. The ethnic origins of Lenin's family are less straightforward and contain "problematical" facts. While some of Lenin's ancestors were said to be Russian, they were in fact Kalmyks, Chuvashes and Germans "with an admixture of Swedish blood". Lenin's Jewish ancestors, moreover, did not convert to Orthodoxy and take Russian names willingly but only for tactical reasons.

This sub-genre of investigative journalism in which Lenin was unmasked and his true nature revealed, and the influence this had on how Russian history was explained, became very familiar to readers and viewers in 1990–91.

IV

The whiff of nationalism and anti-Semitism some of these reports gave off generated a counter-discourse of parody and satire. The most substantial, but not the only, "counter-investigation" is a hoax brilliantly perpetrated by Sergey Kuryokhin in a popular programme broadcast on the Fifth (Leningrad) T.V. channel, which at the time was carried nationwide.[37] It was conceived by Kuryokhin in late 1990 in response to the mounting interest in the mysteries surrounding Lenin's identity.[38]

At the beginning of the programme, the compère, Sergey Sholokhov, introduced Kuryokhin as "the well-known politician and movie actor" who had recently returned from Mexico, where he had been studying

---

37. Another, less spectacular, example is a short note by Tatyana Tolstoy in a spring 1990 issue of *Ogonyok*. In response to the growing enthusiasm for investigating the hidden Jewish roots of personalities in Russian history, from literary figures to revolutionaries, and to a very noticeable surge of anti-Semitism in Russian society, Tolstoy wrote, "Pushkin was a Jew. His real name was Pushkind. His signature is frequently reproduced in facsimile, so anyone can see this with their own eyes. There it is in black and white, 'Pushkind'. In addition, his brother's name was Leo, his great-grandfather was Abram, and to cap it all his grandmother was called Sarah. Which words don't you understand? And the stuff he wrote!" (Tat'iana Tolstaya, "Ne mogu molchat'", *Ogonek*, 14 [1990], p. 31).

38. Broadcast in the spring of 1991 (author's interview with Kuryokhin, 1995).

the influence of hallucinogenic drugs on social revolution. Kuryokhin explained that this was to be the first in a series of programmes offering a "completely new approach to familiar events of Russian and world history, and to some familiar facts".[39] He then proceeded to employ his favourite technique, starting with an entirely serious talk and gradually reducing it to total absurdity, remaining earnest and po-faced all the while. As practised by Kuryokhin, this provoked a mixture of puzzlement, fascination, a desire to believe and complete uncertainty as to whether or not he was serious.[40] This was the style in which he delivered to camera a lengthy academic lecture about Lenin's secret nature and its influence on the Bolshevik Revolution. He began: "My talk today concerns the most important secret of the October Revolution of 1917. Not everything in the revolution was quite as straightforward as it might seem."[41] Kuryokhin explained that Lenin, like his fellow revolutionaries, liked going out into the woods to gather mushrooms for the table. Many Russian fungi, the *mukhomor*, or fly agaric, in particular, alter consciousness no less than the famous Mexican hallucinogenic peyote cactus, *Lophophora Williamsii*.[42] After consuming these mushrooms over a period of many years, "a human being's personality is subtly displaced by the personality" of the mushroom; the fungus "very gradually takes over his being. To put it another way, the individual is little by little turned into a mushroom". Kuryokhin then went on to make what was to become his most famous pronouncement: "I have incontrovertible evidence that, from start to finish, the October Revolution was the work of people who for years had been using the fungi

39. My transcription from a video recording of the film – A. Yu.
40. For analysis of this style and the skit genre generally, see Aleksei Iurchak, "Nochnye tantsy s angelom istorii", in A. Etkind, ed., *Kult'tural'nye issledovaniia* (St Petersburg, 2006); Alexei Yurchak, "Gagarin and the Rave Kids: Transforming Power, Identity, and Aesthetics in Post-Soviet Night Life", in Adele Barker, ed., *Consuming Russia: Popular Culture, Sex, and Society Since Gorbachev* (Durham, N.C., 1999); Alexei Yurchak, "Dead Irony", in *Everything Was Forever, until It Was No More: The Last Soviet Generation.* 41. Ibid.
42. Kuryokhin had read about this cactus in the 1980s in a *samizdat* translation of Carlos Castaneda's *The Teachings of Don Juan*. It was used for its hallucinogenic properties by Mexican Indians (author's interview with Kuryokhin, 1995).

referred to. The mushrooms being used by these individuals drove their personalities out of them and they themselves became fungi. Quite simply, not to mince words, Lenin was a fungus."[43] Citing philosophical treatises and running a pointer over various diagrams, Kuryokhin adduced an immense weight of evidence to show that, unquestionably, Lenin's personality was transformed from that of a human being into that of a mushroom. Throughout the broadcast, this highly original discovery was presented elegantly and with Kuryokhin's trademark solemnity and persuasiveness.

Many viewers phoned the studio in a panic to ask for clarification. Not only less educated viewers but reputable intellectuals, most of whom had never heard of Kuryokhin, fell for the hoax. Among them was the satirical actor Konstantin Raikin, which suggests that what was operating was not mere naivety on the part of the audience but an acceptance by this time that it was natural to be investigating the mysteries of Lenin's personality and physiology, and that these had influenced not just his own destiny but Russian history itself.[44] Raikin recalls that he was fooled

> as an ordinary Soviet citizen accustomed to take on trust anything presented in a serious tone of voice. Kuryokhin's acting was brilliant. I fell for it completely. We all like to think no-one can make a fool of us and that we will spot when we are having our leg pulled, but this was about Lenin. It was still very daring at that time. Kuryokhin is one of the people who made me feel a new era in our national life was beginning. When I saw what was possible, and that it could be done so cleverly, and that you could have a big laugh at something we had believed was unshakeable and beyond the reach of humour, and at the whole lot of us into the bargain, it

43. My transcription from a video recording of the film – A. Yu.
44. For more about the popular fascination with parapsychology, biorhythms, horoscopes, Gumilyov's theories of ethnogenesis and the biosphere, televised "psycho-therapeutic sessions" with Anatoliy Kashpirovsky and much else besides, see the essay below by Pavel Romanov and Elena Yarskaya-Smirnova.

was amazing. It was a wonderful feeling, a breath of freedom.[45]

Kuryokhin's skit was a kind of summing up of 1990, a year in which the image of Lenin in Party and public discourse was transformed. From a canonical Leader above criticism, he morphed into an unknown entity whose very nature concealed mysteries and secrets which had influenced the course of history.

In conclusion, let us return to our initial thesis. Throughout Soviet history, "Lenin" the ideologeme occupied a special, outside position in relation to the Soviet ideological construct. From this external point it legitimised that ideology. During 1990, however, Lenin's privileged position in the structure of ideological discourse was lost. At the outset, the notion was articulated in the press that Lenin's words and ideas had been distorted throughout Soviet history. This questioning of the authenticity of his pronouncements published in Soviet primary sources led to a contradiction in the structure of the ideological discourse. On the one hand, it was being claimed that the main aim of perestroika was to return to the real Lenin, while on the other hand it was being said that the real Lenin was unknown.

The main result of the changes in how Lenin was perceived was to accelerate a structural crisis in Soviet ideology that was already underway. The ideology ceased to be able to appeal to Lenin as a source of absolute, exter-

45. Discussion between Konstantin Raikin and Sergey Sholokhov on the programme *Tikhii Dom Remembers Kuryokhin*, July 1996 (my transcription of a video recording – A.Yu.). Vitaliy Komar and Aleksandr Melamid, the founders of Sots art, had treated Lenin's image satirically as early as the 1970s. During the years of perestroika, there was a dramatic increase in the number of such "unofficial" artworks (for example, by Aleksandr Kosolapov). Kuryokhin's skit did, however, differ from these and other forms of irony in 1990–91. His barbs were directed not so much at Lenin as at the public enthusiasm for investigations into Lenin's "real" nature and its secret influence on Soviet history. Unlike Sots art, Kuryokhin's irony was directed not at Soviet ideology but at its critics (although he was not championing the ideology). His focus was not just on the topic but on the culture and ideology behind it. Kuryokhin's skit was performed on national television in front of millions of viewers. The important thing is that, by early 1991, a broadcast of this kind had become possible.

nal, unquestionable truth. It began rapidly to lose legitimacy in the eyes of society and became just one of several, more or less equal truths which could be publicly called into question. Accompanying this was a questioning of the legitimacy of the Communist Party of the Soviet Union itself. Its right, as the vessel of Soviet ideology, to lead and guide was also losing its absolute and indisputable status. Among the events of the latter years of perestroika, it was perhaps the loss of Lenin's legitimising function during 1990 which most facilitated the rapid collapse of the entire system.

Lenin's loss of status was dramatically illustrated by the renaming of Leningrad. Although early in 1990 several members of the new, democratically elected Leningrad City Soviet tried to raise the question of returning to Leningrad its historical name of St Petersburg, most of the deputies, including the city's first mayor, Anatoliy Sobchak, voted against even putting the issue on the agenda. At the end of 1990, however, it was raised again, and in May 1991 the Soviet voted in favour of holding a referendum within the city. In June of that year, a majority voted in favour of restoring the original name.[46]

In March 1990 the Third Congress of People's Deputies of the U.S.S.R. voted to delete Article 6 of the Constitution (on the leading and guiding role of the C.P.S.U.). In June a conservative section of the Party attempted to re-assert the legitimacy of Soviet ideology and the guiding role of the Communist Party by forming the Communist Party of the R.S.F.S.R. In July the C.P.S.U. held its twenty-eighth (and final) Congress. A group of democratically minded participants failed to convert the C.P.S.U. into a parliamentary-type democratic party, and a number, including Boris Yeltsin, Anatoliy Sobchak and Gavriil Popov, announced that they were resigning from the Party. In fact, throughout Russia there was a sharp increase in the exodus from the Party. In 1989, 140,000 members resigned. In 1990, particularly in the second half of the year, the numbers

46. Of eligible residents, 64.7 per cent voted in the referendum, 54.9 per cent in favour of renaming the city.

increased vastly, reaching a total of 2.7 million.[47]

In the autumn of 1991, the U.S.S.R. Supreme Soviet adopted two decrees: one renaming Leningrad as St Petersburg, and another banning the Communist Party. Although the immediate cause was a failed attempt by conservative forces in the Party leadership to organise a putsch, the very possibility of formulating them was due to the lost legitimacy within state ideology of the authority of Lenin and the Party. These decrees gave legislative form to a transfer of legitimacy which had already largely occurred the previous year. In 1990.

47. SSSR v tsifrakh v 1990 godu: Kratkii statisticheskii sbornik (Moscow, 1991), pp. 104, 105. The exodus was particularly marked after the Twenty-Eighth Congress: between the summers of 1990 and 1991, some four million members left the Party. See Sergei Konstantinov, "S"ezd obrechennykh", Nezavisimaya gazeta, 12 July, 2000; http://www.ng.ru/ style/2000-07-12/16_siezd.html

JANUARY

1 January

In 1989, the Central Committee of the C.P.S.U. deregulated subscriptions to newspapers, magazines and journals, allowing all titles to compete on an equal footing. Subscriptions increased to the newspapers *Komsomolskaya pravda* (by 3.6 million) and *Labour* (by 160,000), and to *Arguments and Facts*, and to the magazines *Health*, *Peasant Woman*, *The Worker*, *Ogonyok* (*The Spark*) and *Novy mir* (*New World*). Subscriptions fell to the newspapers *Pravda*, *Izvestiya*, *Rural Life* and *Soviet Russia*, and to the magazine *Friendship of the Peoples*. Sales of *Arguments and Facts* rose to an unprecedented 32,959,458 copies (*Argumenty i Fakty*, 1 [1990], p. 3; *Izvestiia TsK KPSS*, 12 [1989]).

2 January

The bells of St Basil's Cathedral on Red Square ring out for the first time since Stalin banned them (services there had ceased in 1929).

    Izvestiya publishes Mikhail Gorbachev's New Year address to the American people and George Bush's New Year address to the Soviet people (*Izvestiia*, 2, p. 1).

3 January

Late at night on 2 January, the national Soviet radio station Youth broadcasts U2's New Year concert, which had gone out live to the rest of Europe on New Year's Eve. Organisational assistance is provided by Greenpeace.

4 January

The U.S.S.R. Ministry of Health criticises the televising of "psychotherapeutic" seances conducted by Anatoliy Kashpirovsky and Allan Chumak (*Izvestiia*, 5, p. 6).

6 January

The Red Guard Scientific Equipment Production Association in Leningrad commences production of laboratory facilities for the rapid diagnosis of A.I.D.S. (*Izvestiia*, 7, p. 6).

7 January

On the night of 6 January, the Christmas service at the Patriarchal Cathedral of the Epiphany, Moscow is broadcast for the first time on national television (*Moskovskie novosti*, 2, p. 2).

A hammer is wrenched from the hand of the blacksmith's statue in the square by Elektrozavodskaya metro station during a fracas between cooperatives trading legally and protection racketeers. Witnesses are asked to phone the police (*Moskovskii komsomolets*, 5, p. 1).

"Discussion of the black market economy is warped by the fact that the problem is being exploited by those opposed to reform [. . .] They use the undeniable fact of a revival of the underground economy to discredit the very idea of a free market, and to let off the hook the real culprit for this state of affairs, our bureaucratic administrative system" (Tat'iana Koriagina, "Podarki tenevoi ekonomike", *Moskovskie novosti*, 1, p. 10).

8 January

In Moscow, *Kommersant*, a business newspaper, begins publication. Its masthead reads, "Published since 1909. Not published 1917–1990 owing to circumstances beyond our control."

Sergey Kuznetsov, described by the press as "the last Soviet political prisoner", is released from detention. He had been arrested in Sverdlovsk for writing a leaflet entitled "Stop Repression by the Interior Ministry and the K.G.B.", which had been distributed in September 1988 by the Democratic Union, an unregistered political party.

An article about the persecuted film-maker Andrey Tarkovsky is published in *Izvestiya*. His later films had finally been released in the U.S.S.R. in 1989

(N. Izmailova, "Vozvrashchenie Tarkovskogo", *Izvestiia*, 9, p. 3).

9 January

The Israeli Habima Theatre gives guest performances at the Taganka Theatre. Founded in Bialystok in 1909 and later based in Moscow, the theatre had gone on a European tour in 1926 and had not returned to the U.S.S.R. This was the first tour of the U.S.S.R. by an Israeli theatre (*Izvestiia*, 11, p. 6).

10 January

Shortages in Leningrad. A meeting of the city and provincial Soviets agrees on the need to temporarily introduce a system under which the sale of certain goods will be regulated on the basis of "special I.D. business cards" (*Izvestiia*, 11, p. 1).

Fighting breaks out between the armed forces of Armenia and Azerbaijan, with the use of heavy artillery, over the disputed territory of Nagorno-Karabakh.

11 January

Gorbachev goes to Vilnius for a week to resolve a conflict between two rival Communist parties of Lithuania. At a meeting with workers in Šiauliai, he says, "We must renew our society. We are not talking about minor repairs or cosmetic measures. A revolutionary overhaul is needed everywhere. We need to renew every aspect of life, all the institutions of the state and society. We need to change the very foundations, beginning with reform of ownership of property and economic relations" (*Pravda*, 14 January, p. 1). He is unable to reconcile the two Communist parties.

In an unprecedented move, the Public Prosecutor quashes charges against Rano Abdullayeva (*Izvestiia*, 13, p. 7). Abdullayeva , the Secretary of the Central Committee of the Communist Party of Uzbekistan, had been arrested in 1986 by investigators Telman Gdlyan and Nikolai Ivanov. She had been accused of corruption and held in custody for two years. Criminal proceedings on corruption charges against the higher echelons of Party and state officialdom in Uzbekistan and the U.S.S.R. had been abruptly terminated. After her release, Abdullayeva had launched a counter-attack on Gdlyan and Ivanov. She had been rapidly re-admitted to membership of the Communist Party but, as Gdlyan remarked, ". . . a number of disappointments awaited her when she got home. All the profitable positions in the republican leadership had already been sold" (Tel'man Gdlian and Nikolai Ivanov, *Kremlevskoe delo*, 2nd edn [Moscow, 1996], pp. 116–17).

The first columns of humanitarian aid arrived in Moscow. "Herr Dietrich Bahner (West Germany) sent 82 vehicles loaded with many tons of medical supplies, food and other goods for Soviet orphanages, hospitals and soldiers wounded in the Afghanistan conflict" (*Moskovskii komsomolets*, 9, p. 1).

12 January

Pogroms against Armenians start in Baku after a meeting of Azerbaijani nationalists and the appearance on Azerbaijani television of Nemat Panahliya, one of the leaders of the Popular Front of Azerbaijan. "Panahliya said that Baku was full of homeless refugees while thousands of Armenians were living in comfort, thereby provoking Azerbaijanis to violence against the Armenians" (Thomas de Waal, *Black Garden*; http://news.bbc.co.uk/hi/russian/in_depth/newsid_4664000/4664799.stm). Subsequently, a political scientist, Vagif Guseynov, giving members of the Popular Front as his source, calls Panahliya an agent provocateur (Vagif Guseinov, "Aliev posle Alieva", *Nezavisimaya gazeta*, 19 March 2004). As a result of civil unrest, control of a number of cities passes into the hands of the Popular Front of Azerbaijan for several days.

A recital of works composed by Sofiya Gubaidulina takes place in the Great Hall of the Moscow Conservatoire as part of the Russian Winter Arts Festival. One of the main figures of the musical avant-garde, Gubaidulina's work is celebrated throughout the world but had previously been all but unknown in the U.S.S.R.

A first press conference is held by the heads of State Television and

37

Radio. The decision to block the 29 December 1989 edition of the current affairs programme *Viewpoint* is discussed (*Moskovskii komsomolets*, 10, p. 1; 11, p. 3).

13 January

Chairman of the Committee of the Supreme Soviet of the U.S.S.R. for Construction and Architecture, People's Deputy of the U.S.S.R. Boris Yeltsin tells the editor of *Moscow News* that the Communist Party should give up its monopoly of power, but "cannot do so in such a rush that the economy, finances, and Union collapse" (*Moskovskie novosti*, 2, p. 2).

U.S.S.R. People's Deputy and journalist Anatoliy Yezhelev, a member of the working group to prepare a draft law on freedom of the press, reports that, in compliance with the Vienna Accords of 1990, public access will be given to duplicating technology and that "it will even be possible to buy Xerox photocopiers" (*Moskovskie novosti*, 2, p. 2).

15 January

The Supreme Soviet of the U.S.S.R. declares a state of emergency in the Nagorno-Karabakh Autonomous Region. More riots in Baku, aimed at expelling all Armenians from Azerbaijan, leave 148 people dead and 503 injured. Thousands of houses and apartments are looted and most remaining Armenians flee the country. The P.F.A. and its "Defence Committee" take control of Baku.

The Bulgarian parliament abolishes the Communist Party's monopoly on power (*Nezavisimaya gazeta*, 14 January 1995).

16 January

Gorbachev signs a decree of the Presidium of the U.S.S.R. Supreme Soviet restoring the Soviet citizenship of cellist Mstislav Rostropovich and opera singer Galina Vishnevskaya, cancelling a 1978 decree which had deprived them of their state honours.

Train station, Stepanakert,
Nagorno-Karabakh.
Kalachevsky Brigade of
interior troops training,
Spring 1990

18 January

The State Committee for Technical and Material Supplies makes proposals to the government for developing wholesale trade in the means of production. It urges the use of market regulators such as prices and tax incentives, and recommends that suppliers should be encouraged to act as distribution agents (*Izvestiia*, 19, p. 1).

There is uproar at an open meeting of the April writers' association held at the Central Writers' Club. The meeting is disrupted by thugs from the Pamyat' (Memory) society, led by Konstantin Smirnov-Ostashvili, one of the society's leaders. Anti-Semitic slogans are shouted, and the assembled writers are insulted and assaulted. Smirnov-Ostashvili is arrested in the summer for inciting ethnic hatred, and is sentenced on 12 October to two years' imprisonment. He dies in prison in mysterious circumstances, having apparently hanged himself, in 1991.

April, which supports perestroika, adopts a declaration against racism. "Extremists in Pamyat' and the organisations which support them appear to be fomenting riots in the hope that this will lead to an imperial military dictatorship. One of today's most dangerous forms of organised crime is racism, which makes a cynical pretence of campaigning for the people's interests. In fact, it is merely a tool used to manipulate the people in order to advance the careers of a narrow reactionary group" (*Ogonek*, 6, p. 18).

The Moscow City Executive Committee sets up a commission to discover where victims of Stalin's purges are buried and approves the charter of the Moscow Association of Victims of Baseless Persecution (*Moskovskie novosti*, 3, p. 2).

The first meeting of the management committee of the *Ogonyok* Anti-A.I.D.S. Foundation takes decisions on the use of foreign currency and medical equipment donated to the foundation.

19 January

The Presidium of the U.S.S.R. Supreme Soviet declares a state of emergency in Baku. During the night of 20 January, troops and armoured vehicles enter the city. Officially, over 130 people are killed and 700 wounded in armed clashes with the army. At least 21 soldiers die, some possibly as the result of friendly fire. At 7.30 p.m. the national television electricity supply station in Baku is blown up by "unidentified persons", thus halting broadcasts. According to eyewitnesses, soldiers shoot at people who are fleeing, and execute the wounded (Thomas de Waal, *op. cit.*).

20–21 January

The Democratic Russia "electoral association" is founded in Moscow to coordinate the election campaign of candidates for the Congress of People's Deputies of the R.S.F.S.R. Over 170 attend the founding conference, and by 20 February the association has more than five thousand candidates. The board of the Moscow branch includes Yeltsin and Sergey Stankevich. Nikolai Travkin states, "We will seek to gain genuine sovereignty for Russia, with primacy of republican legislation over U.S.S.R. legislation in fundamental areas of economic and cultural life" (*Argumenty i Fakty*, 8, p. 8). The association's founding declaration announces, "The overall political direction of this broad alliance will be based on the policies of the Inter-regional Group of Deputies, the humane ideas of our great contemporary, Andrey Sakharov, his draft decree on government power and his draft new Soviet Constitution" (*Ogonek*, 6, p. 17).

The U.S.S.R. Conference of Communist Party Clubs, an unofficial association of Communists supporting democratic transformation of the Party, is held in Moscow and attended by 455 delegates from 102 cities. On 20 January the conference establishes the Democratic Platform of the C.P.S.U.. Its executive committee includes Boris Yeltsin, Telman Gdlyan, Gavriil Popov, Nikolai Travkin, Yuriy Afanasiev, and Igor Chubais.

21 January

Investigators Gdlyan and Nikolai Ivanov are expelled from the Communist Party at a general meeting of Party members of the Public Prosecutor's Office of the U.S.S.R., "for gross violations of the law and the Party constitution". In response, there are protest strikes in Zelenograd, part of Gdlyan's parliamentary constituency.

American chicken drumsticks appear in Moscow shops, part of a major programme to ensure adequate food supplies for Muscovites (*Moskovskie novosti*, 3. p. 2).

Production line, Istra-Senezh Broiler Association, Moscow Province, November 1990

41

Workers, Istra-
Senezh Broiler
Association,
Moscow Province,
November 1990

22 January

In Lvov, a General Council of the Uniate Ukrainian Greek-Catholic Church
declares invalid the decision of the Lvov Council of 1946 (which repealed
the 1596 Union of Brest and reunified the Uniate Church with the Russian
Orthodox Church). Registration of parishes of the previously banned
Uniate Greek-Catholic Church begins after Gorbachev's meeting with
Pope John Paul II. In protest, Ukrainian Orthodox priests announce the
creation of a Ukrainian Autocephalous Orthodox Church. It declares that
church buildings still belong to it and a struggle begins between the two
denominations. See essay below by Nikolai Mitrokhin.

23 January

Fifty-three aircraft airlift ten thousand refugees from Azerbaijan to
Moscow (*Izvestiia*, 26, p. 6).

The Inter-Sector Commercial Bank for the Development of Wholesale
Trade carries out its first transactions (*Izvestiia*, 24, p. 1).

27 January

An open letter is published in *Ogonyok* (20–27 January), signed by prominent People's Deputies of the U.S.S.R., on the situation in the Nagorno-Karabakh Autonomous Region. It comments that "evidently some people in this country are displeased by the prospect of a difficult but peaceful compromise resulting from M. S. Gorbachev's visit to Lithuania."

In Moscow, an Extraordinary Congress of Moscow Cooperatives discusses the Moscow City Soviet's "Temporary Provision on the Operation of Cooperatives in Moscow". This is said to violate the U.S.S.R. Law "On Cooperatives in the U.S.S.R.". Academician Vladimir Tikhonov remarks that the fivefold growth of the cooperative movement in the previous year, which contrasted with decline and cutbacks in the public sector, as well as a flight of labour to cooperatives, is undermining the economic monopoly of state-owned enterprises and with it the monopoly of political power. The congress passes a vote of no confidence in the administrative apparatus of the City Soviet and demands its resignation (*Argumenty i Fakty*, 5. pp. 1, 6).

28 January

At the beginning of 1990, the population of the U.S.S.R. was 288.8 million, an increase on the preceding year of 2.1 million. The birth rate fell from 18.8 to 17.6 births per thousand of the population, and average life expectancy was 69.5 years, approximately the same as in 1988 (*Izvestiia*, 29, p. 1.).

The founding congress takes place in Tallinn, Estonia of the Social-Democratic Association. Its Declaration notes, "Five years of perestroika have made it clear that the U.S.S.R. is in an economic, political and moral crisis. The hyper-ideological model has reached an impasse. For the interests of the workers it substitutes the 'interests of the state', behind which the bureaucracy clings to power. Economic laws continue to be violated and the inclination is still to resolve matters by administrative measures. The domination of the bureaucratic class leads to lawlessness and arbitrariness, driving the country towards disaster" (*Moskovskie novosti*, 4, p. 7)

30 January

An illustrated calendar of the Russian royal family goes on sale; it is

Poster of the Tsar, displayed in Pushkino (formerly Tsarskoye Selo) in May 1990.

available in the subway between Revolution Square and Sverdlov Square metro stations (*Moskovskii komsomolets*, 24, p. 1).

31 January

The first McDonald's fast-food restaurant opens in Moscow, attracting over four hundred television, radio and newspaper reporters. "The menu is truly amazing: a Hamburger (a cutlet re-formed from chopped beef); a Cheeseburger (the same, but with a slice of cheese). Yum-yum! And the price? In Russian roubles! A Big Mac is 3 roubles 75 kopecks. A meal comes in at just over 5 roubles" (*Moskovskii komsomolets*, 26, p. 1). McDonald's gives a free meal on its first day to seven hundred orphans (*Izvestiia*, 27, p. 7). The restaurant advertises in popular magazines.

The [nationalist] journal *Our Contemporary* gives its readers an opportunity to meet members of the editorial board and writers in the Tchaikovsky Concert Hall. The entrance is closely guarded, and no journalists are admitted (*Moskovskie novosti*, 6).

Also in January

In Moscow, the founding meeting was held of the Committee for the Protection of Free Speech and Journalists' Rights. Its aim is "to protect people from disinformation, and journalists from threats and lawlessness".

The Gorky Moscow Art Theatre was renamed the Chekhov Moscow Art Theatre. The theatre had split in 1987, one of the companies now retaining the name of the Gorky Moscow Art Theatre. Shortly after its renaming, Gorbachev and his family attended the performance of a play based on Lyudmila Petrushevskaya's *The Moscow Choir* (*Moskovskie novosti*, 2, p. 2).

The journals *Star*, *Our Contemporary* and *Neva* published Aleksandr Solzhenitsyn's epic *The Red Wheel* (1969–88). During the year, seven editions of *The Gulag Archipelago* were published, along with some twenty other works by Solzhenitsyn. In 1990, he was awarded the U.S.S.R. State Prize for *The Gulag Archipelago* (*Noveishaia istoriia otechestvennogo kino: 1986–2000*).

The Moscow office of the Sputnik youth travel bureau offered a new service, tourist trips abroad (payable in convertible currency) (*Moskovskii komsomolets*, 16, p. 3).

MY DIARY FOR JANUARY 1990

Mark Kharitonov

More than forty years ago, I started using a slightly adapted form of short-hand for everyday purposes. Its main advantage was speed, but in the Soviet period the technique also provided necessary privacy. My diaries contained notes about the events of the day, literary and other reflections, impressions of people I met and conversations, observations of the life around me and working notes. I found rereading them years later unexpectedly interesting and decided to decipher some of the entries for 1975–99. The result was a book, *A Transcript of the End of the Century*, published in 2002 by New Literary Observer.

Looking once again at my account of 1990, I found that most of the entries on current political events had been left undeciphered. Over the years, I recorded these less, because as freedom of speech became more of a reality it seemed less essential. In future, I reasoned, if need be, people would be able simply to read about what had happened in back issues of newspapers. I find, however, that the Timeline given above doesn't overlap very much with what I noted down. The following entries are less a commentary on the Timeline than a supplement to it:

2.1.90. Dmitriy Rachkov phoned from Tambov. "Have you heard the competing views of what the Year of the White Horse signifies? It's either a reference to White Horse Whisky or to the Pale Horse of the Apocalypse." [Rachkov was a professor at Tambov Institute of Culture, a literary scholar, writer and memoirist. Most of the people commented on here are long-standing friends.][48]

48. Notes in square brackets are Mark Kharitonov's comments, written in 2006.

I can't listen to the radio [by which I meant, of course, Western radio broadcasts. My batteries had run out and there was nowhere to buy replacements].

People say that when the "Tbilisi incident" was being discussed, not only the Georgian delegates walked out but also Shevardnadze and Yakovlev, who are members of the Politburo. Viewpoint (Vzglyad) is said to have been blocked for trying to show the incident. It's the talk of Moscow.

3.1.90. Karabchievsky phoned. In spite of the flu quarantine regulations, he managed to visit Batkin in hospital. He is immersed in politics, writing an Afterword to the Sakharov Constitution.[49] Batkin said that without Sakharov, everything at the Interregional Group of Deputies and Moscow Tribune is going to pot. He cares less and less for Gorbachev. "Perhaps it's time he was replaced." "Who with?" "See how depleted the nation is," Karabchievsky said. "There really is no other leader of similar substance." I protested: "Perhaps we just don't know who they are. There is no way of finding out, no way for them to make their mark." [Nobody was yet taking Yeltsin seriously. He wasn't being "hyped". How remarkably this chimes with our current situation, where there seems to be no serious alternative to the current president. You really can't think of anyone. It is still a misfortune for Russia.] "According to the Talmud," Karabchievsky said, "the world must contain no fewer than thirty-six righteous men. If one of them is lost, he must be replaced by another, but if no-one can be found the world will end. God will destroy it. There will be no point in its continued existence."

Yelena Makarova rang, in ecstasies over Israel. "It's my country, my people, our children, our army." She is wondering whether to emigrate. She feels there's no point in staying here. Well, why not emigrate? Who says you have to live your whole life in the same country? [Yuriy Karabchievsky

49. A "Constitution of the Union of Soviet Republics of Europe and Asia" was drafted by Andrey Sakharov in 1989. See http://www.yabloko.ru/Themes/History/ sakharov_const.html. The Afterword mentioned is published in Leonid Batkin, "O konstitutsionnom proekte Andreia Sakharova", Konstitutsionnye idei Andreia Sakharova: sbornik (Moscow, 1990).

was a writer, poet and essayist; Leonid Batkin is a cultural historian, essayist and public figure; Yelena Makarova is a prolific author with a special interest in the Theresienstadt concentration camp. She now lives in Israel, having emigrated in 1990.]

4.1.90. There are rumours that Gorbachev is ill, supposedly with heart disease. Without my radio I am deaf. The newspapers are full of pessimistic speculation about our future, but what cause is there for optimism? [The rumours of Gorbachev's illness were evidently false, but, as we know, rumours can influence public opinion and events no less than genuine facts, and they can be started deliberately.]

7.1.90. A gathering to mark the fortieth day since Natan Eydelman died was held at the Herzen Museum. Stanislav Rassadin,[50] Voldemar Smilga,[51] Aleksandr Svobodin,[52] Fazil Iskander, Bulat Okudzhava, Aleksandr Gorodnitsky and others spoke. Yuliy Kim sang his "Letter to the R.S.F.S.R. Writers' Union" to an appreciative audience.[53] Yuliya [Madora-Eydelman, Eydelman's widow] spoke movingly about her last conversations with him. These past few months he had a presentiment, and now she could recall many allusions to the imminence of death. For all his outward gaiety, there was an abiding sadness in his heart, such as we all have, I suppose. In Gorodnitsky's poem his death was seen as a harbinger of disaster.

Someone recalled a conversation with Eydelman. "You know, it's like in

---

50. Stanislav Rassadin (b. 1935), literary critic, political essayist, author of literary parodies.
51. Voldemar Smilga, Doctor of Physics and Mathematics, theoretical physicist, author of popular science books and scientific papers, friend of Eydelman.
52. Aleksandr Svobodin (1922–1999), dramatist, author of *Narodnovol'tsy* (1967), screenwriter, theatre critic.
53. "Letter to the R.S.F.S.R. Writers' Union" (subtitled "On the occasion of the Sixth Plenum of the Secretariat of the Writers' Union, which considered the issue of who should be considered Russian, and who should be classified as only a Russian-language writer"). Popular in 1989–91, the song ridicules the Writers' Union's anti-Semitic sentiments. In the spring of 1990, Kim would preface the song by remarking, "Sung to the tune of Yuz Aleshkovskii's 'Comrade Stalin, You're a Doughty Scholar', a tune I don't know but remember as plaintive and alternative" (Transcript of a tape recording of April 1990). The last stanza runs, "To you I say, defenders brave of Russia,/Your leaders' antecedents too look grim,/Your Mikhalkov was pals with Leon Kassil/And Bondarev's Gran's name was Karaim."

an American saloon bar," Natan said. "When a shoot-out starts, half the people get down on the floor while the other half get on with the shooting. I don't want to lie on the floor." I thought of the pianist sometimes present on such occasions, who carries on playing beneath a sign reading, "Please don't shoot the pianist – he's the only one we've got".

Fazil, prompted by Yuliy's song, said, "That crowd reckon I'm worse than a Jew." "How so?" "That's what they say in the Writers' Union: 'Fazil Iskander is even worse than a Jew'." "Where they're coming from, perhaps they've got a point," someone remarked.

Walking to the metro (from Sivtsev Vrazhek to Park of Culture station), I talked to Vladimir Lukin about the "pessimistic hysteria" and how things may develop. He believes something unforeseen could happen at any moment. The best we can hope for is that in May Gorbachev succeeds in getting the Party Congress to do as he wants; the Central Committee changes; we get a new Supreme Soviet (without the Congress of Soviets) and a strong presidency. Gorbachev firmly suppresses any attempts to overstep the line he lays down, with a certain amount of bloodshed if need be, in order to forestall much more bloodshed later, much as the "blood-thirsty dog" Gustav Noske did in Germany in 1919,[54] thereby contributing to the creation of the Weimar Republic. National unity has to be preserved by all means necessary, otherwise who knows how the Russians will react? Civil war, bloodshed etc. If economic reforms can be pushed through, in fifteen or twenty years we will have the makings of a normal society. Only the preconditions, mind. It can't come any sooner than that. Such is the real state of the country, the situation in society, and the people's psychological level. And that was his most optimistic forecast. [55]

54. Gustav Noske (1868–1946). In early 1919, as Social-Democratic Minister of Defence, he used units of the so-called *Freikorps* (paramilitary volunteer forces) to suppress demonstrations by German Communists and Left Social Democrats who planned to proclaim Soviet rule in Germany. The ringleaders, Karl Liebknecht, Rosa Luxembourg and several others, were killed. Noske declared, "Someone has to become a bloodthirsty dog, and I'm not afraid of assuming that responsibility."
55. Vladimir Lukin, politician and diplomat, presently Human Rights Ombudsman of the Russian Federation.

There is a story in the press and on T.V. about a man who ran away to hide in 1947 after threats from a secret policeman against whom he had dared to speak out. He has been living in the forests ever since, built a hut there, hunting for food. Someone must have been helping him, but so far he has not revealed where he has been hiding. He didn't trust anybody, and has come out now because he believes he no longer needs to be afraid. Only in Russia! He fought in the war, and, although he has been able to follow the news, his mentality and understanding of reality are frozen at the age of twenty-five. He is sixty-seven now and, interestingly enough, was never ill in the forest.

8.1.90. In the morning, Yelena Makarova phoned and talked for a long time about her experiences in Israel. Jews born in Israel don't like talking about the catastrophe which befell European Jews. They despise the sheep-like submissiveness with which some six million people went to their deaths. Friedl Dicker-Brandeis (a Czech artist who perished in Auschwitz) had an invitation in 1938 to emigrate to Palestine but chose not to leave, claiming everything was fine. Even on her way to Theresienstadt, robbed and humiliated, she noted in her diary that things were not as bad as she had expected. Living in her world of lofty spirituality, she paid no attention to Theresienstadt and taught her children to behave the same way.[56] Many of the six million could have escaped if they had acted in time, but they didn't notice history. They clung to Europe, their routines and spiritual values which were not contingent on where you lived.

The parallels are obvious. I just asked Yelena why she was more interested in Friedl than in Israel's pilots. Did she see greatness of spirit only in tragedy? God forbid, of course, but there could be something the Jews of Israel don't know about. Then again, perhaps we should thank God for that. Dubious speculation.

56. Yelena Makarova later wrote a play and a documentary novel, *Friedl*, about the fate of Friedl Dicker-Brandeis (1898–1944). An abridged version was published in *Druzhba narodov*, 9 (2000); http://magazines.russ.ru/druzhba/2000/9/makar.html. Makraova has organised several exhibitions of the work of Friedl and her students.

Thinking the way Yelena does now is to think in terms of national confrontation, the inevitability of anti-Semitism and pogroms. To be realistic, that is the way it looks, but you don't want to give in, to think yourself into this system of coordinates, because then Israel will have no choice but to confront the Arabs, fight, kill, commit atrocities. Is it really not possible to imagine a world where you can feel you are a normal human being among other people, a representative of one particular culture among other cultures, in fact of a single world culture? Our dreadful experience, our dreadful lives tell you that such aspirations are too starry-eyed. But in that case, you will have to repudiate not just your country and your culture but the beliefs, the values you have built up over a lifetime. Only if life becomes absolutely impossible, only if you fear for your children.

Yelena has been sent the internal review of her book from the Soviet Writer publishing house. One of their reasons for rejecting it is that "almost 90 per cent of the characters are Jewish". She wants to make a big fuss, not to try to get it accepted; she is no longer very interested in that, I don't think that psychologically she is still living in Russia. The incident has confirmed to her how remote she feels from life here and she would just like to give them a good smack in the face.

9.1.90. The December issue of Novy mir has a publication of amazing letters by Vladimir Vernadsky.[57] In 1923–4 he was preoccupied by the same issues as we are now: Russia's dire present and dire future, the miracle which enables scholarly thought to endure and young, new talent to appear; whether to emigrate, and the problems that would entail; religion and the Church. These were the people who truly sustained Russia's spirit through all those years, not the ones everybody saw standing on mausoleums. Perhaps I'll find the time and energy to write "A Reader's Notes . . ." [In the days that followed, I did make notes for an essay which later became "Between Hopelessness and Hope". Here is an abridged version of the beginning:]

57. B. S. Sokolov, ed., "'Ia veriu v silu svobodnoi mysli ...': Pis'ma V.I. Vernadskogo I.I. Petrunkevichu", Novyi mir, 12 (1989), pp. 204–21.

Russian history has an extraordinary feature which I shall call its persistence. The pre-revolutionary poetry of Sasha Cherny could be used in a quiz: "When was this written?" ("Freedom calls . . . to perestroika all the land is striving" – 1905). Today when you read some of the documents of bygone years, you have a weird feeling, as if the familiar things which people are saying, thinking or feeling today have been displaced in time, as if historical conflicts are either being endlessly repeated or are suspended in time with the same problems and issues unresolved to this day:

"All this is unstable, but we are accustomed now to instability. The future is obscure to me, but I think that it will be harsh. A dark nationalistic mood is growing, a peevish sense of humiliation and false pride which is fraught with disaster."

Look at the date. That was written on 10 March 1923. Vernadsky's letters, only recently published, don't just seem topical as we read them today; they seem unexpectedly, from all that distance, to illuminate our present state of mind. Our deliberations, for example, on whether or not to emigrate. "If I were much younger, I would emigrate," Vernadsky writes on 24 April, 1924. "My sense of loyalty to humanity is much stronger than to any one nation, but it would be difficult now, indeed impossible. It always takes years to get established. I have no illusions. Living in Russia is extremely hard, and you aren't properly rewarded for your work. Perhaps I will leave soon."

You find echoes in almost every line, but now they seem to me to matter not just in themselves. For all their consonance with our own attitudes and assessments, their distance in the past enables us to affirm them. Our own future is, as always, obscure and unknowable, but for us Vernadsky's future is already in the past. Let us listen very carefully once more to his thoughts and forecasts:

"The more I ponder what is going on, the more I am persuaded that the situation in Russia is dismaying. I do not rule out the possibility that this crisis may continue for another ten or fifteen years, and I wonder whether Russia will not then collapse.

"If this state of affairs lasts several more years, Russia will not recover from the consequences for generations."

This was written in 1923–4. Since then, considerably more than ten or fifteen years have passed, and perhaps what is most surprising is that the same concerns and forecasts are being repeated seemingly unaltered: they have not been proved wrong, they have not been withdrawn, but seem merely to have been extended in time. Contrary to notions of what is conceivable, the tragedy, the collapse, the catastrophe are permanent, seeming to leave no hope for even the immediate future, but also without reaching any culmination. Each new decade manages to muddle through; from somewhere new strength is found, new people appear.

For some reason, I suddenly thought about Solzhenitsyn. Even a year or six months ago, I could picture him returning in triumph, although with uncertain consequences. The situation has changed quickly and dramatically. Now his arrival would be an embarrassment, the rejoicing too late. The truth he had to tell us no longer tops the agenda, as he himself is probably aware. Will he return at all? It is becoming less important than it once was, and it looks as if he's afraid of making no significant impact. Although it might now be a really courageous act, because of the lack of certainty.

12.1.90. Worked in the library on the monthly report. Read Sinyavsky's article in the *Frankfurter Allgemeine* about anti-Semitism in the Soviet Union, along with his thinking that it is currently the most interesting country in the world. What is unfolding here can be viewed as a work of fiction in which it is impossible to predict how the plot will develop. It must be comfortable to feel you're a member of the audience, sitting there in Paris, but he talked like an aesthete even in the prison camp. [For around twenty years I was a freelance reviewer and wrote a monthly digest of the German,

Austrian and Swiss press for *Foreign Literature* magazine. This gave me unfettered access to German-language newspapers and magazines, at first in the closed depositories of the Library of Foreign Literature, and later on open access.]

15.1.90. In the morning I drafted the essay on Vernadsky's letters. [Here is the end of the essay. There really are surprising parallels, not only with 1990 but even with the present day:]

"Nevertheless, the most important power, which will eventually overcome everything else, is thought and intellectual creativity, science, philosophy, religion and art. That shows no sign of drying up in Russia today," Vernadsky wrote on 20 April 1924. "Logic never succeeds in encompassing the diversity of life, and, despite all our calculations, many things are happening which, it seems to us, ought not to be possible under the present circumstances. I have a pessimistic view of the immediate future for Russia – and these strivings and achievements don't strike me as long-lasting, – but they exist and have been achieved at immense cost by hard work and force of will. Perhaps this is the main hope for rebirth. I am sure everything depends on the individual rather than the collective, a country's elite and not its *demos*. In large measure its revival is governed by laws unknown to us which determine the appearance of major personalities. If new powers really are coming to replace the old, and to my great surprise the facts seem to be pointing in that direction, Russia may revive sooner than I think. Only, of course, if the same process is manifest in the various fields of culture and not only in science. I don't really believe in miracles, and think it will all come to pass rather gradually" (21 August, 1924).

From the vantage point of the years which have passed since then, we can see how things actually turned out. Cultural and spiritual life, science, literature and art continue to progress against all expectations and probability, and against the logic Vernadsky mentions. The Earth has no shortage of talent. It is amazing mentally to list the names, old and new, in different areas of intellectual endeavour through the decades. In Russia in the 1920s, '30s, '40s and '50s, there were people of whom any culture could have been proud. It is largely the same as the list of those who were shot, deported, exiled or vilified – and yet in every period, from one decade to the next, people were there to be persecuted, and what people they were! The wonder is where they all kept coming from, in music, biology, literature and physics. How did they survive, propagate, how did they re-appear in a climate so inimical to normal life? After all the wars and waves of terror, physical and spiritual, when teachers were destroyed along with whole schools, movements, areas of science and cultural life, when they were hacked down and pulled out by the roots? Russia is truly a great country with a great culture. How many others could have held out against so much for so long?

Vernadsky in the 1920s saw only the beginning of this process, but from one year to the next he repeats the refrain. "Logically, I can see no favourable outcome, but I am mindful that my logic cannot encompass everything, and perhaps something I have overlooked will radically alter the result. I have to admit that my first appalled impressions are weakening, not worsening, the more closely I examine life. I was more afraid than I am now of biological degeneration. The race seems really quite healthy and very talented. Perhaps it will survive" (14 June 1927).

It is particularly affecting to read these lines at the present time when we have such an acute sense of crisis. Do they hold a promise for us us too? On the one hand, we know that Vernadsky's worst fears were realised, and with a vengeance. Russia was to endure the terror of the 1930s and a terrible war, but it did survive! Paradoxically, Vernadsky's glimmer of hope, in defiance of logic, was not wholly unjustified. Even now it has not been totally extinguished, although the arguments in favour and against have changed. On the one hand, thank God, the cultural elite are no longer physically exterminated as in Vernadsky's times, although they emigrate.

On the other, may not the growth medium have been fatally damaged which is essential if major cultural phenomena are to develop? They do not spring from nowhere, without the necessary environment and soil, without schools and teachers. It is all very well for someone in my profession. All you need is paper and a pencil, the universe and the life around you. You need great books and a head on your shoulders, but the rest is up to you. Complaining about material difficulties or the problems of getting into print are no excuse. You are not the first to face that. To be a dancer, however, is simply impossible without a school; a musician needs not only teachers of sufficient quality but decent instruments; anyone conducting experiments or a software engineer needs up-to-date equipment and computers. Is there perhaps a tipping point beyond which the ability of culture, intellectual creativity, and spiritual experience to replicate itself is in jeopardy?

Our hopes have been and are maintained not least by the unremitting and selfless work of people like Vernadsky, who did in fact remain in Russia, people who preserve and revive traditions, create schools and educate young researchers. There are not so many of them now, and there seem to be fewer with every passing year, but so far they are still managing to accumulate and maintain the energy essential for Russia to continue.

In times such as ours, the mood of despondency and despair not only feeds on reality but itself influences reality, and therefore gives real cause for concern. This makes it all the more important for us to listen to the voice of people like Vernadsky. Looking back, we see more clearly that we have faced emergencies in the past, but we have also known hope, and that we need more than ever. It is worth reminding ourselves. We may just win through. [This essay was first published in 1991 in the émigré journal *Russia and the World* (*Strana i mir*) and then in the *Independent*, and was included in the book *Mode of Existence* ('*Sposob sushchestvovaniia*') (Moscow, 1998).]

18.1.90. In the evening, a T.V. programme about Russian émigrés in Germany. Interviews with Lyubarsky, Kopelev, Zinoviev at Radio Liberty, made at the very time I was there – that is, two or three months ago.[58] Permission to broadcast it has only now been granted.

19.1.90. It is painful even to write about the unrest in Azerbaijan.

21.1.90. In the evening, Yevgeniy Popov's Gala at the Central Writers' Club. Yursky, Chuprinin, Prigov and Kublanovsky spoke. Popov read his "Tales of the Communists". Quite funny.[59] Heard from Karabchievsky that there had been a brawl at April's evening at the C.W.C. on the 18th. The club was invaded by bruisers from Pamyat', with megaphones. They yelled, "Push off to Israel. This is our patch!" and started a punch-up. Anatoliy Kurchatkin had his glasses smashed and Tanya Bek was beaten up. The worst of it is that, when they reported it to the police, they openly scoffed at them and refused to note down their injuries. They said, "That's not our job. Go and see a doctor." People from Pamyat' were openly parading about in the police office and sneering, "Make sure you write that all down!" Karabchievsky thinks it was a demonstration by fascist organisations controlled by the regime, or at all events by the Moscow K.G.B. The only reason there haven't been pogroms is because they haven't yet been given the order. "After this incident," Yuriy said, "I believe something I haven't said before: it's time for Jews to leave. Not just because of the physical threat, although that is serious enough, but because of the humiliation. I felt I had been spat on." What could they have done? The writers looked on helplessly. Of course, there will be articles written, but nobody pays the slightest attention to those now.

Garry Kasparov spoke on the radio [about the Soviet army's occupation of Baku]. He has evacuated several hundred refugees by plane from Baku. He said Gorbachev is completely discredited. Karabchievsky said he's paying the price for his failure to deal firmly with the Sumgait race riots in

58. Kronid Lyubarsky (1934–1996), astronomer, human rights activist, political essayist; in 1977–93 lived in exile in Germany; in 1984–91 edited the magazine *Strana i mir*. Lev Kopelev (1912–1997), literary critic, cultural historian, human rights activist, public figure, memoirist; emigrated to West Germany in 1980.

59. Yevgeniy Popov (b. 1946). His stories were published in *Znamia*, 3 (1991) and in E. Popov, *Restoran "Berezki". Poema i rasskazy o kommunistakh* (Moscow, 1991).

1988, for refusing to face up to what was going on and punish the perpetrators. There is bound to be an outburst of anti-Russian sentiment in Azerbaijan, which can only make things worse. Poor Russia!

I went to see Kublanovsky.[60] He will stay in Moscow until February. He said he was very shocked at first, but has got over it a bit now. He had been travelling in the Kaluga region and had the impression everything was falling apart, total breakdown. While we were speaking, though, he was brought some skimpy photocopies for an autograph and inscribed them. He doesn't get much of that in Munich.

22.1.90. In the morning Karabchievsky phoned. "I was appalled by Yevgeniy Popov's talk yesterday," he said. "Popov seemed to be saying both sides should sacrifice their principles and be nice to everyone. Chuprinin put it well when he asked which principles he personally was willing to sacrifice. If he, a real Russky, a Siberian, had stood up and said they were fascist bastards, it would really have counted for something. Trying to butter everyone up and smooth everything over and stay on good terms with everyone – Belov, Rasputin – is the politics of Munich. I realised they won't stand up for us any more than they did in Germany. I saw it at the Central Writers' Club: they stood by helplessly, perplexed. Only a few intervened, like Nataliya Ivanova, mostly women. It will be just the same if things get nastier."

He had heard a Radio Moscow programme today. The reporter stated unambiguously that the events in Azerbaijan had not just erupted of their own accord. They were directed by identifiable forces, and those were forces of the U.S.S.R. Gorbachev really seems to be turning into a mere figurehead. There was talk about him retiring at the last plenary session [of the Central Committee]. He managed to fight them off and thought he had won, but in fact they had won. The Second Congress [of People's Deputies of the U.S.S.R.] showed him following their line, and he may push it further just in order to survive.

60. Yury Kublanovsky is a poet. In early 1990, he was still only considering the possibility of returning from emigration. He talked to me about it in the autumn of 1989 when I was in Germany, and returned to Russia in 1990.

One can only indirectly get a sense of what is going on in Armenia and Azerbaijan, sifting through the torrents of official lies. My radio still isn't working, but the impression I have is that everything is more serious, more terrible and irreparable than we thought. You hear hints that someone at the top is directing it, but nothing is being said openly, which means that nothing will be put right. All non-Azerbaijanis are being driven out of Baku. Rumour has it that representatives of the Popular Front [of Azerbaijan] in Moscow are compiling lists of Armenians. Outbreaks of violence can be expected anywhere at any time.

23.1.90. In the morning Lyuba Berger phoned. She came back recently from a three-month trip to Europe. One of her impressions from working in an acoustic music centre is that we are at a completely different stage of civilisation. They are developing computer acoustics, computer musicology. Entirely new possibilities are opening up there for musicians, composers and researchers in just the same way that the development of instrumental music and modern orchestras was contingent on discoveries in physics, in particular the discovery of harmonics. "It makes you sad for the life you haven't lived," she told someone, and they replied with a smile, "We heard people say those very words in Moscow."[61] I told her we can't allow ourselves to think like that until the very end, even if there is an element of truth in it.

I'm trying to decide whether the fact that there are certain highly talented individuals in various fields (our situation) is not yet sufficient grounds to talk of the existence of culture. It depends on what you mean by culture. Maybe it's something like a mycelium, which is essential if individual mushrooms are to sprout and swell, since without it there is nowhere for them to come from. Or can you compare it to a well-tended plantation where something remarkable can be born, and, even if it isn't, the culture is still there? Or can a wonderful plant just blow in on the wind and grow on waste ground? Serious research is being written up now about

61. Lyubov Berger is a musicologist. Her aesthetic ideas are expounded in her *Epistemologiia iskusstva* (Moscow, 1997).

the culture of the Stalin and, more generally, the totalitarian era, which dispassionately analyses its stylistic features (monumentalism), mythology and so on, as one might the culture of the Egyptian pharaohs, without judgements as to morality or good taste.[62] Highly educated people living in that period, however, suffocated for lack of air and felt culture was decaying and being destroyed.

[A recurring theme of my diary entries is, of course, work. In January 1990, I was translating Kafka's letters and wrote a cycle of stories called *Voices*. The stories, although in a different way from the diary entries, were inevitably imbued with the atmosphere, attitudes and everyday reality of the time.] "It was a time memorable for a general falling of standards, indeed for progressive dissolution and chaos: puddles of urine in telephone kiosks, queues for synthetic diamonds, road surfaces permanently broken up." [These lines are from my short story "Music". I had observed the queue for artificial ("Japanese") diamonds a short time before in the Leningradsky Arcade. There were long queues for literally everything. You could say it was the archetype of life at that time. Mikhail Epstein found a more accurate label – the 'kenotype'.[63] A joke of the time has a bus driver announcing, "This stop, the wine store. Next stop, start of the queue." Queues could be formed without anyone knowing what they were for. People would join first and then ask, "What's come in?" If nobody knew, they would wait until someone did. People were registered in the queue, given a number and checked at roll calls. My story, "The Queue", which I wrote that January, was based on this absurd routine. The heroine, an elderly lady, spends days and months in a queue without knowing what she's queueing for. It becomes her way of life, more natural and meaningful than sitting at home alone. She is horrified to hear a rumour

62. Shortly before this, when I was in Cologne, Boris Groys talked to me about his ideas on the stylistic unity of cultures in the middle of the last century. See Boris Groys, *The Total Art of Stalinism* (Princeton, 1992).

63. For a definition, see Mikhail N. Epstein, "Teoreticheskie fantazii", *Iskusstvo kino*, 7 (1988). See also his essay "Ochered'" (The Queue), written in the late 1980s, in *Vse esse*, 1 (Ekaterinburg, 2005), pp. 79–85.

that the queue isn't leading anywhere but goes round in a circle:]

> Why do they torment us so with new worries every day? One day everybody's talking about fire victims from another district who are being served out of turn, or even foreigners who've turned up. Haven't we had enough suffering in our lives? What more do they want from us? Why are they still checking up on us? We're not looking for anything special. Everything can stay just as it is as long as it doesn't get any worse. We don't need much: radishes from the vegetable garden, enough bread, a little salt. We don't mind waiting as long as need be . . . Even if we don't get to that door, never get through it . . . nobody knows how many days we have left to us. Let it last and last and never end. While we're here, among other people, we're not afraid of anything and there's everything to look forward to. We'll sleep here, sweep the street for nothing . . .

[I did not know that at about the same time a novel of the same name and with a similar theme had been written by Vladimir Sorokin. Many years later, director Lev Dodin's students conflated excerpts from both tales and also from "Music" in their graduation production, *Claustrophobia*. It found a place in the repertoire of Dodin's theatre.[64]]

I worked on the story. *Literaturnaya gazeta* and *Ogonyok* arrived. Depressing reading. We were born and have lived our lives at the hands of political thugs who stop at nothing. The same type are in power to this day. That makes it difficult to take much pride in personal achievements, creative, scholarly or otherwise. We have failed to pass on a decent life in a decent country to our children. We can explain why we couldn't, but it is hard to excuse ourselves. All my life I have had this humiliating sense of

64. *Claustrophobia* was staged by Lev Dodin in 1994. It combined excerpts from works by Mark Kharitonov, Venedikt Yerofeyev, Vladimir Sorokin and Lyudmila Ulitskaya. "Ochered'" and "Muzyka" were first published in *Znamia* and *Druzhba narodov* respectively, and later included in *Golosa*; see Kharitonov, *Izbrannaia proza*, 2 vols, vol. 2 (Moscow, 1994).

powerlessness. Of course, I could have performed some dramatic act of civil protest, but, knowing myself, I am certain that I would have been broken and perished, like Ilya Gabai[65] and many others, and would never have become a writer.

In the morning, worked on the story, then went to get money from *Izvestiya*. On Pushkin Square it is as lively as Hyde Park by the windows of *Moscow News*. A great variety of newspapers are on sale, including those from the Baltic States. People are debating. In their window is a display of materials relating to Yeltsin, Gdlyan and Ivanov (they've assembled an entire dossier), appeals, proclamations, cartoons. One was put up while I was there by a woman who opened the *Moscow News* stand with a triangular key. In a chair labelled "Party Boss" sits a fat official with guard dogs labelled "K.G.B." and "Interior Ministry" chained to it. Stooped in front of them, slaves are toiling, goaded on by overseers from the Partocracy. One has straightened his back and is raising a placard which reads, "We are not slaves". There are barbed attacks on the K.G.B., satirical poems and an ordinary girl standing there selling a slim typewritten volume of her own poetry. There is a sense that people are not going to let the Party bosses have a free hand.

Nevertheless, anxiety is in the air. My mother, whom I went over to see in the evening, feels this more acutely than I do. She is afraid to go out of the house, to go to the shop. She is afraid of anti-Semitic attacks or just thuggish behaviour.

Yesterday, several of the features in the T.V. show *Viewpoint* were devoted to the question of who is really in charge of the country. The wife of someone who works at the Council of Ministers knocks down a child and manages to avoid ending up in court; the Public Prosecutor steps in to protect the thugs who attacked people in the Central Writers' Club;

65. Ilya Gabai (1935–1973), poet, literature teacher, teacher of the deaf and dumb, human rights activist; participated in the *samizdat* publication *Khronika tekushchikh sobytii*; actively assisted the Crimean Tatars' movement to return to their homeland; repeatedly arrested; committed suicide after intolerable psychological pressure was applied by the investigating authorities. See "Uchast'" in Mark Kharitonov, *Sposob sushchestvovaniia* (Moscow, 1998).

generals get awarded lavish houses in the country; Communist Party staff get outrageous wage increases etc.

I translated Kafka. Phoned Grigoriy Pomerants.[66] He was at a meeting of Moscow Tribune, where they were discussing racial issues. On Azerbaijan they agreed that, no matter how disgusting martial law may be, race riots are worse, and they might start up again. Moscow's problems are more tractable. Averintsev repeated that we need to call a spade a spade, call fascism fascism, and not try to talk people round in the hope of re-educating them. Criminal charges should be brought. They set up a special group to initiate legal action, get in touch with the Prosecutor's Office etc. It is difficult to tell whether that will help. Pamyat' held a protest at Ostankino with openly anti-Semitic slogans. In a night-time broadcast, which I didn't watch, someone has already shrilly demanded that the government should take action to head off a pogrom scheduled for 5 May. Forces within the regime are openly trying to provoke a pogrom in order to provide a pretext for a military coup. According to Grigoriy, a mysterious shoot-out near the Azerbaijani Legation in Moscow was clearly instigated by the K.G.B. Some of those detained were immediately transferred to the K.G.B.'s Lefortovo Prison. Troops moved into Azerbaijan only when Russians started getting attacked. Armenians got no protection. These people, Grisha says, only want to hold on to their dachas. Sooner or later the mobs will come for them, but they just want to put that day off. All this, and hostility on the part of the common people, are even more obvious than race hatred, although there are forces very actively trying to channel it into that. [I had attended several meetings of Moscow Tribune, having been introduced by Pomerants and Leonid Batkin, and witnessed furious arguments between Armenians and Azerbaijanis. An Armenian had only to talk about what was happening in Azerbaijan for an Azerbaijani to come to the podium and protest it was all propaganda, hearsay, and nothing of the sort was going on. "You name names, but these are Uzbek, not Azeri,

66. Grigoriy Pomerants is a cultural historian, philosopher and essayist.

names" etc. You could see the whites of both their eyes. They were seeing nothing and had no wish to listen. Not for the first time I experienced a sense of helplessness. Ashamed as I am to admit it, it only confirmed my suspicion that I have little aptitude for political activism.]

I talked about the same topic to Lyubov Berger, who came to visit us in the evening. Jews from Baku whom she knew had come to see her. They are shocked and just want to emigrate without delay. (Refugees from Baku are said to be getting visas for Israel without having to go through the formalities.) They were asking, "Do you really not understand that you will have the same thing here?" More than likely. Everybody is preoccupied now with the same issue. I would like to stick it out. At all events, I'll be one of the last to leave, always assuming I don't leave it too late.

29.1.90. I went looking for a birthday present for Galya, a cup to replace one that got broken, and was shocked by the catastrophic emptiness of the shops. I haven't been into a tableware shop for a long time. Empty shelves, empty rooms, no sales assistants, nothing but crystal or glass ashtrays and nesting matryoshka dolls. One shop was still selling expensive table settings, for which there was a long queue. Instead, I bought batteries for my radio and clock, and today for the first time was able to listen to Western radio. Nothing particularly new. It confirmed the sense of impending disaster, and there is probably little point in pinning our hopes on some extraordinary act by Gorbachev, on the popular indignation against the leaders of the state (they showed a protest rally in Volgograd) or the bosses' sense of self-preservation. All these people are interested in is hanging on to their privileged rations at all costs. They will succeed in the short term, and alas, they are incapable of looking beyond that, even into their own future.

Last thing at night, I reread the diaries of Thomas Mann for 1933, with a very peculiar feeling. The start of his exile. A broken life. The depression of someone who has been ejected from his own house, from his native land. Is that what I am going to face? I am reading with new eyes the memoirs of Nadezhda Mandelstam: why did these people not leave when they still had the opportunity? Why did Pasternak not stay in the West, or the others?

I phoned Karabchievsky. He was in Gorky at the Sakharov Readings. Said there are a lot of fine intelligent people there, but the people in charge are dreadful. Literally nothing in the shops and it looks like there's a famine, but at home people somehow get by. A mood of panic. It is not only Jews who are desperate to leave immediately but Russians are also asking Jews to arrange an invitation for them so they can get out. Someone Yuriy knows, a war veteran, a captain, lives on the fifteenth floor. He says that if they start breaking the door down, he'll throw himself out the window. Yuriy's wife is insisting on leaving, threatening him with divorce, but he is still hesitating, wondering whether he should just let her go with their son and stay himself. [We know now, alas, how tragically that disagreement played out. His wife remained in Israel and Karabchievsky committed suicide in Moscow in 1992. I wrote about this in my essay "Three Jews" in *Mode of Existence*.[67]]

31.1.90. Today Gorbachev, officially, on T.V., denied rumours that he is planning to resign as General Secretary of the Communist Party.

---

67. Kharitonov, *Sposob sushchestvovaniia*.

FEBRUARY

1 February

From 1 February, residents of Leningrad city and province require a photo-ID "business card" in order to buy meat, meat products, butter and cheese, citrus fruit and tobacco, furniture, refrigerators, radios, bicycles, motorbikes, household appliances, electrical goods, knitwear and hosiery, children's goods and leather footwear (*Moskovskii komsomolets*, 24 [30 January], p. 1).

Moscow "business card", 1990

Left: Zelenograd food-ration coupons from 1990

1–28 February

During February, the liberal economists Grigoriy Yavlinsky, Mikhail Zadornov and Aleksey Mikhailov work at the State Commission on Economic Reform of the U.S.S.R. Council of Ministers on the 400 Days programme, intended to greatly expedite transition to a market economy (*Mirovaia ekonomika i mezhdunarodnye otnosheniia*, 11 [1990], p. 112).

2 February

"2 February, 1990 is the fiftieth anniversary of the death, or rather execution by shooting, of the celebrated theatre director Vsevolod Meyerhold. For the first time we will be commemorating this tragic date publicly" (Valeriy Fokin, Director of the Yermolova Theatre, Moscow) (*Moskovskie novosti*, 5, p. 13).

4 February

Between 150,000 and 200,000 people attend a rally in Manège Square, Moscow, demanding abolition of Article 6 of the Soviet Constitution and protesting against anti-Semitism. The rally is in response to the tumult caused by ultra-nationalists at the Central Writers' Club in January (*Moskovskii komsomolets*, 30, pp. 1–2).

People's Deputy Sergey Averintsev is elected President of the Bible Society of the Soviet Union. "Christians of various denominations – Orthodox, Catholics, Protestants – may become members. Their main task will be publication of the Bible and translating it into the languages of the peoples of the U.S.S.R. The new society plans also to engage in research and charitable work" (*Moskovskie novosti*, 5, p. 2).

Moscow's Muslims are allowed to register a second community and establish an Islamic religious and cultural centre. Ravil Gainutdin, *Imam Khatib* of the Moscow mosque, comments, "Moscow City Soviet has promised to help us with transferring to this second community a building on Zemlyachka Street. It is the oldest mosque in Moscow and, according to legend, was given as a token of appreciation from the city authorities of the role played by Tatar regiments in repelling the French invasion in 1812" (*Moskovskie novosti*, 5, p. 2).

5–7 February

The Plenum of the Central Committee of the C.P.S.U. voluntarily relinquishes the Party's monopoly on power and recommends establishing the post of President of the U.S.S.R. Eduard Shevardnadze says at the plenum,

Renewal of the Party requires a fundamental change in its relations with governmental and economic bodies, abandoning the practice of giving them orders and usurping their functions. The Party can exist and fulfil its leading role as society is renewed only as a democratically accepted force. This means that its status should not be imposed by the constitution. Within the Party, power should lie with Party members rather than with the administrative apparatus . . . We remain committed to the choice made in October 1917 and to the socialist ideal, but are moving away from interpreting this dogmatically. We repudiate sacrificing the real interests of the people to schematic ideology" (*Moskovskie novosti*, 6, p. 1; *Argumenty i Fakty*, 6, p. 1).

6 February

The Politizdat publishing house issues an anthology entitled *V. I. Lenin on Glasnost* (*Izvestiia*, 37, p. 3).

8 February

The Palace of Culture at the Likhachov Automobile Factory hosts *Love Street*, an exhibition of hippy art.

9 February

An evening to mark the centenary of the birth of Boris Pasternak is held at the Bolshoy Theatre. It is attended by many members of the Party elite, including Vladimir Kryuchkov, Yegor Ligachov, Anatoliy Lukianov, Yevgeniy Primakov and Aleksandr Yakovlev (*Izvestiia*, 42, p. 2). UNESCO declares 1990 the Year of Pasternak. In the spring of 1990, *Rilke – Pasternak – Tsvetaeva: Letters of 1926* (Moscow, 1990) will appear after numerous agonising previous attempts to publish the correspondence between these great poets (information from Konstantin Azadovsky).

10 February

In Moscow, negotiations are conducted between Mikhail Gorbachev and Chancellor Helmut Kohl of Germany on the issue of German reunification. "Gorbachev stated, and the Chancellor agreed, that there is no dispute between the U.S.S.R., the Federal Republic of Germany and the German Democratic Republic that the question of reunification of the German nation must be decided by the Germans themselves. It is for them to make their choice, and to decide what form of government, what timeframe, at which speed and under which conditions they may wish to effect reunification. Gorbachev refers in this connection to his recent conversation with the Chairman of the G.D.R. Council of Ministers, Hans Modrow (Pravda, 11 February).

11 February

Independent experts estimate the number of refugees in the country as at least half a million (Moskovskie novosti, 6, p. 1).

"The food shop at No. 206, Moskovsky Prospekt in Leningrad has an abundance of fruit and vegetables, including apples, citrus fruits, cleanly washed carrots, fresh green spring onions and cabbage (without rotten leaves). The reason? The Moskovsky district fruit and vegetable distribution centre has set up a wholesale and retail association which itself purchases produce in different parts of the country" (Moskovskie novosti, 6).

12 February

The Soviet government issues a statement in connection with developments in Europe, reaffirming its previously stated position: by 1995–6, withdrawal of all foreign troops from the territory of Eastern Europe, and by 2000, dismantling of all military bases on foreign territory. "The Soviet Union is already negotiating with Czechoslovakia and Hungary to withdraw its troops from those countries. If the government of the Republic of Poland expresses such a desire, the U.S.S.R. will discuss the question of Soviet troops in that country with its representatives. As regards the Western Group of Forces located in the G.D.R., the Soviet Union is already unilaterally reducing its troops there" (Izvestiia, 44, p. 1).

14 February

In Moscow, the founding conference of the Association of Independent Cinema opens with some pomp. It includes fifty-six non-state-owned film and video studios and associations, as well as the Cinematographers' Union of the U.S.S.R. This marks the beginning of an unprecedented flowering of film-making, which has gone down in history as "Cooperative Cinema" (Noveishaia istoriia otechestvennogo kino, 5 [St Petersburg, 2004]).

15 February

Founding of the Union group, which includes such influential People's Deputies of the U.S.S.R. Supreme Soviet as Viktor Alksnis, Yegor Ligachov and Veniamin Yarin. Its stated purpose is to defend the territorial integrity of the Soviet Union by countering separatism in the Baltic republics, the Caucasus and other regions of the country.

21 February

Moscow hosts the Forty-Fourth International Congress of Evangelical Baptist-Christians (Izvestiia, 53, p. 6). In the U.S.S.R., Baptists, although registered as an officially recognised religious community, have been persecuted. In 1981, all but one of the independent members of the Council of Churches of Evangelical Baptist-Christians , a group which had refused state registration, were arrested.

23 February

"The Motherland or Death!" Nina Andreyeva chants at the Wings of the Soviets indoor sports arena. A counter-revolutionary tendency is, she states, now predominant in perestroika. The acceleration of socialist progress which Gorbachev had so loudly proclaimed to the whole world is proving a social disaster. Instead of humane socialism, we are seeing the ugly snouts of mafiosi turning a fast buck and intent on seizing power.

Around fifteen hundred people pay 3 roubles each to attend "Russia, My Motherland", an evening of music and literature organised by the Soviet Russia publishing house. Of the promised celebrities, only Vladimir Soloukhin turns up. Men wearing the uniform of the tsarist army unfurl banners of St George.

Andreyeva is welcomed with a standing ovation, flowers are thrown, and two dozen cameras capture the historic moment. "Long live the indissoluble unity of the army and the people!" is how she concludes her speech. "Long live the unity of the patriotic and socialist forces!" (*Moskovskie novosti*, 9, p. 2). A teacher at the Leningrad Institute of Technology, Nina Andreyeva came to prominence after her letter, "I cannot sacrifice my principles", was published in *Soviet Russia* on 13 March 1988 (on the recommendation of Yegor Ligachov). It called for a scaling down of democratic reforms.

24 February

Elections to the Supreme Soviet of the Lithuanian S.S.R. Sajūdis, a movement campaigning for the independence of Lithuania, is the clear winner.

25 February

A rally is held on Zubovskaya Square, Moscow in support of democratic reform and the Democratic Russia candidates. Similar meetings are held in Volgograd, Sverdlovsk, Novosibirsk and Stavropol [as well as in Leningrad, Tomsk, Tbilisi and Kharkov]. The February rallies play a crucial role in the success of democrats in elections to the Supreme Soviet and regional government institutions (*Moskovskii komsomolets*, 47, p. 2).

26 February

President-elect Václav Havel flies to Moscow from Czechoslovakia for two days. An agreement on the withdrawal of Soviet troops from Czechoslovakia is signed.

A rally, winter 1990

28 February

A gala celebration of the centenary of the birth of Vaslav Nijinsky is held at the Bolshoy Theatre. The anniversary is celebrated by all the U.S.S.R.'s major music theatres.

The first echelon of troops withdrawn from Czechoslovakia arrives back at the Soviet border town of Chop (*Izvestiia*, 60, p. 1). Complete withdrawal of Soviet troops from Czechoslovakia is to be completed by 1 July 1991 (*Argumenty i Fakty*, 9, p. 8).

Also in February

A list of all locations of missile bases in the U.S.S.R. and of missile support facilities in the U.S. was published for the first time in the *Foreign Ministry Bulletin* (*Vestnik MID SSSR*), 2 [1990]). The list was reprinted in *Argumenty i Fakty*, 12, p. 7.

Marina Tsvetayeva's "Letter to an Amazon", an openly lesbian lyrical essay, was published for the first time in the U.S.S.R. in the February issue of *Star* (*Zvezda*). The original had been written in French, and the magazine published Konstantin Azadovsky's 1970s translation, made from a photo-copy. The publication opened up a discussion of homoerotic themes in the works of Russian writers of the early twentieth century, and in Russian literature generally.

THE YEAR OF UTOPIAS REALISED:

SCHOOLS, TEACHERS AND EDUCATIONAL REFORMERS IN 1990

Tamara Eydelman

I

What happened in Russian education in 1990? There is no simple answer to this question, because different, sometimes even polarised, trends made themselves felt. Innovators could be over the top while traditionalists were determined not to retreat a single step. Teachers were being deluged with more information than they could take in, as were students and parents. Some were exultant, others appalled. Headteachers and administrators were unsure what was now allowed and what wasn't. It was a good time if you knew what you wanted.

The changes had a drastic effect on school life, but everywhere was different. We posted an invitation on the Innovative Teachers website (http://www.it-n.ru) for readers to share their memories of 1990, and responses came from teachers in Moscow, small towns and remote villages. Some remembered a year of wonderful experimentation and breathless innovation, others a period of penury and despair. But no-one said it was a time of business as usual when nothing changed. The schools were fizzing with vitality.

Everyone remembered 1988, when the perplexed authorities cancelled the history exams throughout the U.S.S.R. because nobody knew what to teach or what questions to set.[68] An admirable government instruction had

68. One Western researcher reports that the 1988/9 school year began without new textbooks or an approved syllabus. See Robert W. Davies, *Soviet History in the Yeltsin Era* (New York, 1997). See also Anton Sveshnikov, "Bor'ba vokrug shkol'nykh uchebnikov

been issued specifying that students were not to lose marks for expressing their own opinions. The Innovative Teachers' Union had been founded;[69] teachers' associations began springing up one after another; 1990 saw the founding of the U.S.S.R. Association of History Teachers. In many places, the most noticeable innovations in school life were in the activities of the Pioneers and Young Communist League (*Komsomol*). In the past, many of the livelier schools had made good use of these movements – the only option at the time – to do considerably more than conduct pointless meetings. Now those schools saw perestroika as an opportunity to breathe new life into old forms.

Gulnur Nasibullina, History Teacher, Alpastovo Village, Tatarstan

Today I looked out my old notes at school and was interested to reread them. I was Deputy Head in charge of pupil development at the time, and some records have survived. You can see that everybody had their hands full and there was a great deal of variety. On the one hand, democracy was the buzzword of the day, turning up repeatedly in plans and projects. On the other hand, the Pioneers and Young Communist League had deep-rooted traditions. Pioneer meetings had changed since, say, 1986, and were now more like character-training mediated through games. Political-indoctrination lectures were still important, and were discussed and assessed at staff meetings. 1990 was the 120th anniversary of Lenin's birth, and he was much in evidence in themed lessons and events. I remember the school putting on a big concert for the village on the anniversary. Reviews and sketches were all the rage. I remember two reviews called "The Capital Show" and "Get With It, Guys". [Items on the programme of the concert.] Our own national Pioneer organisation was being

istorii v postsovetskoi Rossii: osnovnye tendentsii i rezul'taty", *Neprikosnovennyi zapas*, 36 (2004), pp. 70–77.
69. Its founding congress was held in Krasnodar on 11–14 May, 1989. The Innovative Teachers' Union initially combined aspects of a campaigning movement and a trade union. It consisted of several regional associations and spawned local organisations in cities which had never known anything of the kind before. The idea of a "Teacher of the Year" award was mooted at its founding congress, and implemented from 1990.

set up in Tatarstan, the "Union of Pioneers, Heirs of Tatarstan". I still have my notes on a visit to one of their meetings. It was informal but topical, and the children found it interesting. That was the kind of year 1990 was. The winds of change affected us all but had not yet swept away the things that were good in Soviet society, and gave us faith that everything was being renewed. That was the mood in the classroom too. Now, unlike in the 1980s, teachers were allowed to have their own opinions and express them.

Oksana Cherkasova, Deputy Head for Pupil Development, Barnaul, Altai

In 1990 I was a troop leader in the dying days of the Pioneer movement, when ideology had been reduced to a minimum. The meetings were more like sports competitions, but we still did jobs for the frail and elderly and collected waste paper. In 1990 our district had its first revivalist Communard Gathering, a great school of activism. That summer, under the direction of the city's Young Communist League committee, I and other troop leaders took a group of fifty "difficult" children off to the Altai Mountains. Back then everything was still free of charge. That same summer we travelled with the city Y.C.L. staff to a remote part of our region for a Communard Gathering. We camped in the woods and felt perfectly safe. Those are my memories of 1990.

Yuriy Alekseyev, Teacher of History and Computer Science, Pskov Province

In the summer of 1990, I was working as an activities organiser at a summer camp where Byelorussian children from Gomel province were spending an extended holiday recuperating. The Chernobyl disaster had taken place just over four years previously. They were brought to our province to "aerate" their bodies and get rid of radioactive isotopes.

It was interesting and it was fun. We roamed through the pine forests, swam in the forest lakes, and in the evenings the children taught me Byelorussian. I remember two comical but scary incidents. Once, when we were not far from the main buildings, we were caught in a warm summer downpour. It was nothing out of the ordinary, but the girls suddenly shrieked and rushed back inside. I didn't know what was going on, but the boys explained that they were afraid of losing their crowning glory because the rain might contain fall-out. It was a reflex with them.

Another day, when we were out hiking through the woods and swamps, we came upon a meadow full of blueberries. It took a long time for me to persuade them, by example, to treat themselves to the fruits of the forest. They said berries and mushrooms were full of radiation. Afterwards, though, their tongues and teeth were blue for days.

I had to give them a kind of reverse course in health and safety.

It wasn't like that everywhere. Good schools had always taken advantage of any opportunities which presented themselves. Bad or lifeless schools and colleges got into a worse and worse mess, which they blamed, of course, on the growing national chaos.

Nadezhda Malova, Music Teacher, Kostroma Province

In the 1989/90 school year, having graduated, I came to teach music at my old Chernopenskaya Secondary School. The first year was difficult and very hard work. There was little in the way of audio-visual aids or teaching materials. I had to write all the song lyrics on huge sheets of drawing paper, and the gramophones were constantly breaking down. The children did not take me very seriously as a teacher, but it was interesting to be starting a new phase in my life. The salary was 170 roubles, which seemed to be enough for every-thing. It's difficult now to believe that was all so long ago and yet so recent.

Irina Ivanova, Moscow

I taught computer science on the Soviet B.K. personal computers. Membrane keyboard, cathode ray monitor. I also taught physics. You couldn't buy equip-ment or ask the school office for anything. I wasn't conscious of any change for the better. All I can remember is very minor key, I'm afraid.

Aleksandr Morozov, History Teacher, Editorial Staff of History Teaching in Schools, Moscow

I wouldn't bother writing in about any other year than 1990, but that was the year I graduated and began teaching at a school in Shcherbinka, Moscow province. The headmistress greeted me as if I were her long-lost son and said she would make sure I had everything a young professional needed. I would only have to teach one year, the five ninth-year sets (or perhaps then it was the eighth, I don't remember). I was suitably grateful, and only later found there was a sting in the tail. The "A" set were the top kids, the elite, and in the four other sets were all the rest, mostly children of shop-floor workers in the nearby lift factory. Some of them were already working hard to qualify for a career in prison. I remember a whole gang turned up to a lesson. I had to punch one in the face and they turned nasty. I was called to see the headmistress immediately after the lesson. She said, "Take care. They're thugs." That was the back-up. I had plenty of problems with the girls too. Some were very eager to get after-hours lessons. As soon as I got home from school, I would crash out and sleep for three hours. I've never known anything like it since. I don't remember any Y.C.L. or Pioneer groups. I think they had already evaporated. In fact, I don't remember any social activities at the school.

That is one way things developed. The old institutions crumbled and nothing came in their place. Everything could be very different, however. In some schools there was a great deal of political activity, with no guarantee that the Young Communist League and Communist Party organisations would side with the teachers. Sometimes the teachers too were tired of playing the old games.

Irina Ivanova, Computer Science Teacher, Moscow

In 1990, I resigned from the Y.C.L. because it was becoming intolerable to be responsible for the teachers' Y.C.L. organisation. I was constantly getting it in the neck from the Party organisation because our pupils did so badly in the

*"Leninist tests" of their political knowledge, and because "bad" (i.e., demo-
cratic) influences were affecting pupils in the Y.C.L. Now it's just a pain to
remember all that inane drivel.*

Leonid Katsva, author of Russian history Textbooks, History Teacher at No. 1543 Grammar School, Moscow

*In the autumn of 1990, I had been working for ten years as a history teacher
at No. 43 School (as it then was). In September 1990, I resigned from the
Communist Party, which I had joined in 1985.*

In 1990 people were beginning to leave the Communist Party, not in droves
like after the August 1991 coup attempt, but in considerable numbers.
Among those handing in their Party cards were not only prominent politicians but also teachers. Schools were considered ideological institutions,
and it would have been particularly difficult not to be a Party member if you
were teaching history. I remember how hard our Party administrator tried
in 1989–90 to get me to join. I just laughed nervously and said I had two
children and simply didn't have time for Party work. If the conversation had
taken place a few years earlier, I would probably have been barred from
teaching children in the more senior grades. In 1990, all that happened was
that the deputy headteachers took me aside one by one to tell me how much
they admired my civic courage, but that I must realise I was destroying my
career prospects. That was as far as it went. No-one in my school had actually left the Party yet, but the meetings for Party members, both public and
private, were very fiery.

II

It is difficult today to remember the shortages teachers faced, from a lack of useable history books to chalk, which somebody had somehow to get hold of from somewhere and distribute in rationed quantities. On the other hand, there was tremendous scope in those years for experimentation. Looking back today, Irina Ivanova may recall with horror having to teach computer science on the old B.K., but this was a time when the vast majority of pupils and teachers had never seen a computer. Computer science had been introduced into the curriculum, but nobody knew how to teach it. Our pupils went to a "Computer Science Centre" where the teachers did little more than draw a few diagrams and explain on their fingers what a com-puter was. In our school, at least, the appearance of the first B.K.s occasioned much joy and was regarded as a great triumph. This was the seed from which all later computer classes grew.

Of course, schools need good equipment, but the amazing advances in those hungry, penniless years show how much teachers can do without chalk, books or computers, just as long as they have freedom.

Mikhail Goldenberg, History Teacher, Petrozavodsk

The school received its first Russian computers. They were called Agate and looked exactly like a Youth television set. You inserted a cartridge in the drive and could then play a game of chess. We were receiving humanitarian aid from abroad. In the Maths Department, sausage sent from Germany was cut up using a metre ruler. There was a sense that the end of an era was imminent, but I imagined the future as a daunting mountain range.

Irina Ukolova, History Teacher, Moscow

In 1990, there was a spectral organisation called Rainbow (Raduga), a "construction and educational unpaid labour detachment" which sponsored an orphanage for deaf-and-blind children in Zagorsk. My friends from Rainbow and the Computer Club, which Garry Kasparov sponsored, kitted out our computer room with computers and printers and taught classes there. Our political backer was Tanya Nikitina, famed singer of the children's song "The Rubber Hedgehog with a Hole in His Side".[70] Our supporters were hoping with her help to secure a building near the school for a children's centre. (Having battled for a year, they failed, and of course it is now occupied by a bank.) Meanwhile, Rainbow arranged for teachers of architecture, music and English to come out and give classes on a voluntary basis to our after-school society.

Lyudmila Kozhurina, Journalist on September the First Teachers' Newspaper

In the autumn of 1989, I moved from Moscow to a village in Vladimir province. This was arranged by the Institute for In-Service Teacher Training.[71] A new school was being opened in the village with a young head-master, bright people were being brought in to create a rural "lyceum", and they were looking for a good literature teacher. There was a national mood of renaissance. New life was burgeoning everywhere except, it seemed to me, in my old school, where it was "no change". I accepted, the state farm sent a car, gave me a two-bedroom apartment with mod cons, and we all got stuck in: a visiting historian, a doctor of philosophy, a visiting physics teacher, a mathematician and me. Needless to say, we didn't manage to create our lyceum in the country, but the school ran well and we were all very happy. Was it the unfamiliar location, the people, the situations you never encountered in city schools or the heady anticipation of great achievements? I don't know, but I've never enjoyed life more than I did then. From every direction we were getting the green light. We did all sorts of incredible things and somehow it all added up! Where else would I have found myself digging up ground which spilled out museum exhibits, or headed off with the children to the provincial archives in the hope

70. Tatyana Nikitina in 1990 was head of the Cultural Department of the October District Soviet Executive Committee in Moscow, and in 1992–4 Deputy Minister of Culture of the Russian Federation.
71. The Moscow City Institute for In-Service Teacher Training, now the Moscow Institute of Open Education.

of discovering where exactly Ivan the Terrible hid his library, or tacking up a horse for a day's riding? Of all our endless political discussions, one stands out. We were wondering what was needed if Russia was to be even more successfully transformed. People suggested all sorts of things: political will, a love of hard work, education . . . I remember I said, "Confidence." People laughed. "Well, that's different." I often go back there to be reminded of those great days. There's nothing that special about the village, or the school, or the people, but when we meet up it's all, "Oh, do you remember . . . ?" People's eyes light up, as if they haven't known anything better either.

Gulnur Nasibullina, Tatarstan

As at any other time, there were difficulties, but when we meet up with ex-pupils who finished their schooling in 1989 and 1990, we find they have only good memories. We were young then, we wanted action and change, and we had the opportunities.

Aleksandr Drakhler, Director of the Internet Association of Methodologists, History Teacher, Moscow

In 1990, while I was in my fifth year of college, I went to work at a lyceum specialising in medicine and philosophy. They gave me the fifth and sixth grades to teach. Nobody seemed much bothered what I was teaching them or how. It was all based on trust. The odd thing is that I can hardly remember what I did teach. Later, towards winter, I was asked to teach the tenth grade because the main teacher was ill, and afterwards the kids went to see the head to ask if I could carry on teaching them. That I do remember, and also later failing one pupil. Nobody pulled me up for it! That was actually allowed!

I remember too the relief we all felt when we found we were allowed to put "fail" in the school-leaving certificate. It was nothing to do with malign teachers blighting the future of hapless children. We saw it as one further step towards telling the truth. We were no longer being compelled to award unjustified scrape passes to truants and layabouts but could give them the marks they had earned. They left school with those certificates, and some of them still managed to get into college. That dispensation only lasted a couple of years before registering failure on certificates was again prohibited.

It was a time when some fantastic, unimaginable perspectives opened up. In early 1990 our school was suddenly invited to organise an exchange with a school in Rome. One dark February evening, we met a group of Italians who had travelled to Moscow. I don't know who was more stunned, them or us. For the reception we put cloths on the school tables and set out the best food we could find: open sandwiches with smoked sausage and fruit juice in cut-glass tumblers. For ten days our teachers, pupils and parents went out of their way to entertain our guests and look after them properly. Then it was our turn to go to Rome. Apart from one of the girls, it was the first time in our lives any of us had been abroad. We didn't have a lira between us. "Foreign currency" still suggested black market dealings and imprisonment, but we were making our trip at the perfect moment. Train tickets to Rome were still at a price everyone could afford, and people were just beginning to be allowed out of the U.S.S.R. We travelled for three days and two nights and spent most of that time just staring out of the window. I remember everyone cheering when we crossed the border at Chop in Ukraine. One of the kids said the air smelled different abroad, but none of us were expecting the rapturous reception we received when we arrived. Even an ice cream vendor said, "Gorbachev is my friend" and reduced his prices. In the morning, the families we were living with took us to school. While we were all assembling, the kids ran into a food shop just to gaze at the displays and came out shrieking with delight. During the ten blissful days we spent in Italy, Hungary had its velvet revolution. The border guard on the way back had a new crest on his cap. I wanted to congratulate him and reached out my hand, but he recoiled. He must have thought I wanted to pull it off.

Irina Ukolova, Moscow

Back in October 1990, I took twenty-five children in the eighth to eleventh grades to Denmark for almost a month. It came about through some sort of unofficial Red Cross arrangement. The children's names were included in five adult passports. The Soviet embassy in Germany had no idea a lot of Moscow schoolchildren had already been in Copenhagen for a couple of weeks, during which time the German Democratic Republic was reunited with the Federal Republic of Germany. We couldn't get back home because we didn't have transit visas for reunified Germany, which hadn't existed on our way out and was now only issuing visas in Moscow, only we couldn't get to Moscow without a German transit visa.

In the summer of 1990, we flew with children in the ninth grade to archaeological excavations in Bashkiria, also without any official documents or authorisations. The freedom was real and total. The state authorities were as bewildered as anyone else, and generally just wearily rubber-stamped each and every grassroots initiative.

III

Another feature of teaching in 1990 was that everyone was looking for totally new approaches. We were literally groping around in the dark. Few of us had a clear idea of what we wanted, but very many headteachers, deputy heads and teachers at the coalface certainly wanted change. In some places, that proceeded in the traditional Russian manner of razing everything to the ground first, confident in the belief that whatever came afterwards was bound to be better. In quite a few schools, teachers or administrators stopped teaching subjects which, for whatever reason, they disliked. In one place they abolished geography, in another, chemistry. At that moment, they could get away with it, but it was also a time when serious thinking was going on about developing new educational models.

The renewal of education proceeded in two directions. On the one hand, it was essential to revise the content of lessons, certainly in the humanities, and particularly in history and literature. The school history syllabus was excruciatingly behind the times, as most people recognised.

Teachers, especially those of the older generation, found themselves in a distressing predicament. For years they had been feeding their students an ideologically biased view of history, particularly in respect of the Soviet period. Many genuinely believed what they were teaching, while others had forced themselves to believe it, since how else could they live with themselves, facing the children every day and teaching them things they didn't believe? Now the whole country, including teachers and pupils alike, was being deluged with information which often flatly contradicted what was written in the textbooks. For some, the change was welcome. They could bring in facts which previously had to be kept secret, without fearing that parents would complain to the Party's district committee and that they would get a flea in their ear from the headteacher. Others were horrified, some even refusing to teach senior pupils, which had always been considered more prestigious.

Oksana Cherkasova, Barnaul, Altai Region

In 1990, when a new head was appointed, she decided to adopt the "Aesthetic Upbringing" model for our school and new syllabuses were devised accordingly. That same year, she decided in October or November to stream the children in grade six by ability. There was a long drawn-out pupil rebellion, with home-made posters demanding a return to the old system. It didn't happen.

Mikhail Goldenberg, History Teacher, Petrozavodsk, Karelia

1990 was a watershed year for me, both in the purely formal sense that I had been teaching for fifteen years, exactly half my teaching career, and in a more personal sense: the U.S.S.R. was sunk in profound lethargy. There was an imperative to rethink the history syllabus. In the cinemas they were screening Govorukhin's merciless This Is No Way to Live!, and teachers were thinking, "This Is No Way to Teach!"

I subscribed to nine or ten literary journals. Their circulation numbers were *astronomical. I had two mailboxes and a box at the post office besides, which was also full to overflowing. There was a song I couldn't get out of my head, "We're Going to Live a New Way Now". It seemed certain that everything was going to change, and for the better. The Party organisation at school just fell to pieces. I used texts in my lessons which I had just been able to read for the first time myself: "Cursed Days", Ivan Bunin's diary covering the first half of 1918; Vladimir Korolenko's "Letters to Lunacharsky"; Fyodor Raskolnikov's 1939 "Open Letter to Stalin"; Martemian Ryutin's 1932 "Appeal to All Members of the C.P.S.U. (b)", and other shocking documents which made the case against totalitarianism. The problem of ethnic-conflict "hot spots" was freely discussed at the political indoctrination sessions, which were still being held. I clearly remember us discussing the violent events in Baku in January 1990. We weren't too interested in teaching methodology, and the textbooks were left over from the Stone Age, so we concentrated more on what to teach rather than how to do it. Many history teachers on the in-service courses were clearly perplexed: "How are we supposed to present Lenin now?" Others decided they were going to stick to their guns: "I have not the slightest intention of re-thinking anything!"*

Aleksandr Morozov, Moscow

Teaching history was difficult. In the first place, I didn't know how to teach anything, and in the second place, the textbooks were out of date and no new ones were yet available. It's curious that, even though I soon fled from that school and enrolled on a graduate course, the experience gave me an interest in teaching which I have never lost. I have taught in schools almost uninterruptedly ever since.

By 1990, the old Soviet history textbooks seemed simply ridiculous. In search of alternative sources, teachers rushed to the literary journals, newspapers and television broadcasts. In 1990, *History Teaching in Schools* was packed with articles on twentieth-century history. Documents were published illuminating 1917, the 1920s and 1930s, the Second World War; there were biographies of leaders of the anti-Bolshevik White movement; an article about Pavel Milyukov, the Constitutional Democrat Foreign Minister of the 1917 Provisional Government; and, under the heading of "Assignments on the Topic of World War II", the text of the Molotov–Ribbentrop Pact was published and the existence of its secret protocols acknowledged.[72] There was an article on the history of the human rights movement in the U.S.S.R.[73] and another on how to teach human rights in the classroom, including, in an appendix, the 1948 Declaration of Human Rights, which had been banned until recently.[74] Another sign of the times was role-playing for lessons on citizenship, with "The Political Rally" as one example.[75]

The new textbooks on twentieth-century history were still only being prepared, but already the journal was publishing excerpts. Teachers could not wait: they had a class to teach every day. In an article titled "Educating with the Truth of History", next to the standard quotations from Marx and Engels we find the words of Nikolai Berdyaev, a philosopher deported from Soviet Russia in 1922. The same article quotes a telegram from Lenin calling for brutal suppression of all uprisings and containing the words "ruthless extermination is essential". The author described the Solovki prison camp as the firstborn of the Gulag, blessed by Lenin.[76]

72. Elena Gevurkova and Anatolii Koloskov, "Zadaniia k teme 'Vtoraia mirovaia voina'", *Prepodavanie istorii v shkole*, 3 (1990), pp. 88–99; 4 (1990), pp. 100–109.
73. M. M. Meier, "Ocherk istorii pravozashchitnogo dvizheniia v SSSR", *Prepodavanie istorii v shkole*, 5 (1990).
74. *Prepodavanie istorii v shkole*, 4 (1990), pp. 124–30.
75. *Ibid.*
76. V. V. Pomogaev, "Vospityvat' pravdoi istorii", *Prepodavanie istorii v shkole*, 1 (1990), pp. 47–59.

IV

At this time, significant changes were being made to the very structure of the subjects taught at school. The unbearably ideological courses in social science and on the foundations of the Soviet state and law, reeking of mothballs, were replaced by a new course on "Man and Society". It cannot be said to have been a complete success, and indeed controversy about how to teach what is today called Social Studies continues to rage, but the most important change had begun: Marxist ideology was being squeezed out of the syllabus. In vocational colleges the traditional courses on "The Basis of Economic Knowledge" and "Political Economy" were replaced by "Fundamentals of Modern Economics and Industrial Administration". Schools were offered an unprecedented choice between "Fundamentals of Law", "Aesthetics", "Ethics", "History and Theory of Religion and Atheism" and "History of Science and Technology". We may smile wryly and say that all these things were being taught by the same old teachers, and that in many cases this was a freshened-up version of the same old social science. Maybe so, but for many teachers it was a breath of fresh air and an opportunity to talk to their pupils about completely new things in completely new ways.

History Teaching in Schools in 1990 held several round tables on topics of concern. At one, painful attempts were made to correlate the history of the U.S.S.R. with world history, and to elaborate principles for combining the history of Russia in the syllabus with that of the other republics.[77] The Soviet Union was falling apart and everybody wanted to study their own, national history. Somehow, a way needed to be found to accommodate that demand. Additionally, the fall of the Iron Curtain called into question the appropriateness of keeping the course on Soviet history entirely separate from that of the rest of the world. There was great enthusiasm for a course integrating Russian and world history, which unfortunately has been put on the back burner in recent times.

77. "Istoricheskaia nauka i shkol'noe istoricheskoe obrazovanie. 'Kruglyi stol' v redaktsii zhurnala 'Prepodavanie istorii v shkole' 28 marta 1990 goda", *Prepodavanie istorii v shkole*, 4 (1990), pp. 7–30.

Another round table considered the hot topic of whether to teach the history of religions in schools.[78] Actually, the question had already been answered because, in the 1990/91 academic year, schools introduced an elective course on "The History of Religions of the World". Topics which had recently been strictly banned suddenly surfaced. When Father Aleksandr Men gave a talk at my school in October 1988, it came as a tremendous shock to everyone, teachers, pupils and parents, irrespective of whether or not they were believers. Just the fact of a priest coming into a school seemed completely incredible.

Today, I would be unambiguously against the representative of any faith coming into a school, even one as reasonable, sensitive and intelligent as Father Aleksandr, but at that moment it was another gust of freedom! *Izvestiya* reported his visit and some of our pupils were interviewed by Italian journalists. Our headmaster Yevgeniy Topaler immediately found himself being invited to all meetings on matters of religion. He was a celebrity: the first headmaster to invite a priest to talk at his school! At one of those meetings, he found himself next to Metropolitan Yuvenaliy and promptly asked him for some copies of the Bible for our teachers. Two of the more muscular young teachers were sent to the Patriarchate to collect them. Ironically, one was the Party administrator and the other a member of the school's Party committee. The Bibles were brought back and handed round. Some of the old Communists were bristling with indignation, not because the school was being poisoned by "the opium of the people" but because books nobody could get hold of had been distributed without consulting the Party organisation as to who should get them.

Olga Strelova, Historian, Methodologist, Khabarovsk, Russian Far East

In 1989 I flew to a Eureka seminar. The topic was "What should school

78. "'Kruglyi stol' 'Nuzhno li prepodavanie istorii religii v shkole?'", *Prepodavanie istorii v shkole*, 5 (1990), pp. 9–21; 6, pp. 8–14.

textbooks be like?" The participants were selected by The Teacher's Newspaper on the basis of a questionnaire. One of the questions had been, "What should school textbooks be like?" and I answered, "Interesting."

We will return to Eureka below, but for the moment let us consider that remembered vignette. Teachers were willing to come together from every corner of the U.S.S.R. to discuss the problems of school textbooks. They had probably been unhappy with them before, but there had been no choice, and anyway nobody had ever asked their opinion. Now there was a choice, and they could speak out, not just in their kitchen at home but at a meeting with colleagues.

Olga Strelova was a well-known teacher-training specialist and in response to that survey question could have written at length about the principles on which she would have liked to have seen textbooks based. It is worth asking ourselves how many interesting textbooks we have seen in our lives as teachers, and in the lives of our schoolchildren.

Leonid Katsva, Teacher, No. 1543 Grammar School, Moscow

In 1990, I realised that I just could not work with Soviet-style textbooks any longer. Considerably more to the point, I was getting a sense that, if I wrote a book myself, there might even be a possibility of getting it published. I set to work. If I remember, it was in late 1990 that I was introduced to Aleksandr Shevyryov, who headed up the history laboratory at a research centre which later became the Moscow Institute for the Development of Educational Systems (M.I.R.O.S.). He was looking for someone to write a textbook on the history of Ancient Rus.

In 1988, under the direction of Eduard Dneprov, a remarkable ad hoc research team called "School Basics" was set up. Its interest was not in cosmetic tinkering but in devising a new comprehensive vision of teaching in Russia. I am sure that all the members of that team must today look back fondly at those tumultuous years. I was one of the originators of the history-teaching concept it produced, and the ideas we discussed then have provided the foundation for all my subsequent teaching. In the cramped rooms where the subject groups met, debate was exceptionally intense. It has to be admitted that many of our ideas in 1988–9 were fairly cuckoo, but we were buoyed up by an unshakeable faith in future success which it is hard even to imagine today.

Aleksandr Abramov, Corresponding Member of the Russian Academy of Sciences

By the beginning of 1990, we had already been working for several years with the School Basics research team on conceptualising and devising syllabuses for all subjects. In November 1990, at the Moscow Institute of In-Service Teacher Training, a research department under my direction was created from the Schools Basics curriculum laboratory. The idea arose at that point of creating a set of new textbooks and overhauling the entire curriculum. The suggestion was put forward that we might make use of market mechanisms. The need was not only to write but also to publish and sell textbooks.

Aleksandr Shevyryov, Associate Professor, Moscow State University, Head of School Basics History Syllabus Group, Moscow

At our first group meeting we decided to develop an ideal concept of history teaching, abstaining from self-censorship and ignoring the political constraints prevailing at the time. We decided first to create an ideal project and then to subject it to self-censorship. In other words, we would write two drafts: one "for the desk drawer", of interest, probably, only to future historians, and another, more realistic, for Basics. Change came about so rapidly in the country, however, that in December 1988 our "unrealistic" ideas were approved by School Basics.

Today, we smile at our idealism when we reread our vision of "Problems of History Teaching in Secondary Schools and Ways to Improve It", published in 1989 by School Basics. We excoriated the untoward politicisation of teaching, the fact that in history the main emphasis was on studying socio-economic processes and the class struggle. We condemned existing textbooks for their dismissiveness towards small nationalities and derided the very idea of having just one official history textbook. We described the main aim of future educational reform as "Developing the pupil's personality on the basis of knowledge of the past and the ability to make up his own mind about the most important achievements of world culture; socialisation of someone who is embarking on living their life; facilitating his self-determination as an individual and understanding his place in society". We went on to say that what should be taught in school was "not so much passive memorisation of facts and assessments of them as the ability to evaluate for oneself the mass of historical data, to find causal connections between historical events, to distinguish what was of primary importance in the historical process from what was of secondary importance". We stated that man should be placed at the centre of historical understanding by paying more attention to individuals in history, and to the personality of the pupils.

Much in our language at that time now strikes me as naive and comical, but I still stand by most of the School Basics ideas. The other subject groups seem to have been moving in much the same direction. At all events, the general concept of how education should develop which School Basics created professed the same values. In his recent book Education and Politics, Eduard Dneprov, the director of School Basics, writes, "The bonding, the interpenetration of the premises, the goals and objectives, the underlying principles of the reform of education in Russia, is in effect its ideology and its ethical foundation. At its core are two fundamental concepts, two keywords: democracy and humanity."[79]

These were the years during which Eduard Dneprov formulated for himself the principles which, in 1990, saw him elected Minister of Education of the R.S.F.S.R., far ahead of the other contenders. He then brought into the ministry many of the School Basics team. Those principles were: democratisation, pluralism, respect for popular wisdom, frankness, regional

79. Eduard Dneprov, *Obrazovanie i politika. Noveishaia politicheskaia istoriia rossiiskogo obrazovaniia*, vol. 1 (Moscow, 2006), p. 97.

devolution, humanisation, inculcation of the humanities, differentiation, development of character and continuity of education. Today, many of these words stick in our throats and we find it difficult to take them seriously; but if we reflect on them, they are based on admirable ideals. Just formulating these principles helped the educational reform in 1990 make a great advance. It moved from formulating general principles, concepts and syllabuses to introducing specific changes.

By 1990, School Basics, initially so lively, had outlived its usefulness. The concepts and syllabuses had been written and it was time to move on. The next step was establishing a research centre at the Institute of In-Service Teacher Training, to try to put into practice the ideas School Basics had generated. As far as history is concerned, the most original and lively textbooks were conceived at School Basics, discussed at the Research Centre in 1990 and, from 1992, began to be published by the newly established Moscow Institute for Development of Education Systems (M.I.R.O.S.). In 1990, work had already begun on what was to become a quite outstanding anthology of Russian history. The texts presented did not cover every topic in the syllabus, but drew teachers' attention to matters which had been neglected.[80] There were not only primary source materials but also excerpts from historical research, many of which had not previously been available to teachers. Volume I contained an excerpt from *A History of Russian Culture* by Milyukov! Rather pointedly, the first segment to be published in *History Teaching in Schools* in 1991 was on Ivan the Terrible. It included very varied, sometimes outspoken, comments by historians about the Tsar's personal militia, the *oprichnina*, and provided both an excellent basis for in-depth historical study and a starting point for discussion of the present day.[81]

The anthology included texts describing people's everyday life and

80. I. V. Babich *et al.*, eds, *Khrestomatiia po istorii Rossii*, vol. 1, *Mezhdunarodnye otnosheniia* (1994); vol. 2 (I) (Moscow, 1995); vol. 2 (II) (Moscow, 1997).
81. "Rossiia v tsarstvovanie Ivana Groznogo (fragmenty khrestomatii)", *Prepodavanie istorii v shkole*, 4 (1991), pp. 33–55; 5, pp. 19–36; 6, pp. 16–19.

particular significant individuals. It enabled teachers to put right precisely the shortcomings of school education which School Basics had been aiming to rectify. It was very noticeable that neither the Research Centre, nor later M.I.R.O.S., rushed to plug the gaps in twentieth-century history about which so much was being written and said. Changing the content of teaching began with the earliest times. The first textbook to be worked on was Aleksey Vigasin's *History of the Ancient World*. It was followed by Nataliya Trukhina's totally brilliant books on the history of ancient Greece and Rome, Mikhail Boytsov and Rustam Shukurov's *History of the Middle Ages*, and a textbook on Russian history by Leonid Katsva and Andrey Yurganov. These books varied widely in their methodology, language and scope, but all of them possessed in full measure that rarest of qualities: they were interesting.

V

An important corollary soon became apparent. You couldn't modernise the content of education without changing the teaching methods. The traditional system of education, whether Russian or Soviet, had been based on memorisation of great quantities of facts and their subsequent more or less accurate regurgitation. This was true of almost all subjects, with the obvious exception of mathematics, which explains why, in the Soviet era, schools specialising in physics and mathematics were so often breeding grounds for independently minded people. Moscow's No. 2 School of Physics and Mathematics was legendary in this respect. In most school subjects, whether history, geography or biology, the pupils' main requirement was to recite a paragraph from the textbook. Even foreign languages, which it would seem impossible to learn without active participation and repeated communication, were mostly studied by memorising "topics". In later, freer times, one lady about to travel to the United Kingdom remarked wistfully, "I can tell you all about Gagarin's biography in English, but I'm unlikely to be able to make myself understood in a shop." New techniques were desperately needed, and everybody was looking for them. Teachers sought them in the same place as everybody else in that era: in the principle of personal freedom.

Gulnur Nasibullina, Tatarstan

It was in the spring of 1990 that I and our physics teacher gave a joint sample lesson at republican level on "The Laws of Dialectics" in sociology. Delivering it was pure creative delight and I still remember it vividly. It was a great success. I would love to try repeating it, but times have changed.

It gradually became clear that updating content was not enough. The gaps in Soviet history were filled in quite rapidly, and it was then no longer enough simply to tell children about the high price paid for collectivising agriculture, or what it was like in a prison camp under Stalin. New teaching techniques were needed, and the quest began for developmental teaching methods.

Nikolai Idatchikov, History Teacher, Krasnoyarsk

There were a lot of new ideas around. They were published one after the other, but not put into practice. Independence! Initiative! The Local Education Department had some money in the budget for training assignments, so I went to Poltava to study how to use Viktor Shatalov's "reference summaries". I took part in a business game to develop a concept of education for Byelorussia under the direction of Pyotr Shchedrovitsky. In our district there was a lot of seeking of new ways of teaching. In particular, a group of Krasnoyarsk academics had a project called "Noogen", looking at the best ways of working with students.

Innovative teachers were one of the bright features of that stormy era. Most of them had been discovered and championed back in 1986 by Simon

Soloveychik, a tireless idealist and educational reformer.[82] The innovators included many interesting teachers, some people who were simply nuts, and a few out-and-out opportunists. What is really interesting here, however, is less the quality of their teaching than how eagerly people read about them, how attentively they were listened to and how they were imitated. When else could teachers have been invited to the main studio at Ostankino Television Centre to perform before a packed house, and for the programmes then to have been broadcast to the whole of the U.S.S.R.? Yevgeniy Ilyin, literature teacher; Viktor Shatalov, mathematician; Sofiya Lysenkova, primary school teacher, held the country spellbound, only to retreat back into the shadows without trace later on. Each of them was seen as proof that the entire system of teaching was going to be overhauled. Everything they said or wrote seemed like a revelation.

The "Noogen" Nikolai Idatchikov mentions was also born of the quest for new ways to teach. Its founders have this to say on their website:

> In 1988–9 a regional summer school brought together academic staff from the Siberian Branch of the U.S.S.R. Academy of Sciences and teachers and students from the University of Krasnoyarsk. The intention was to invent a new, non-traditional approach to practical teaching. The underlying principle was to be the personal development of both teachers and students, who would jointly attempt to solve problems which not only had not yet been solved by modern science but had not even been identified as problems. These problems, specially created and formulated through the use of insight, were called "noogens". The approach to working

82. Simon Soloveychik (1930–1996) was an educator, journalist, writer and educational theorist. In 1960, he started a column in *Komsomolskaya Pravda* entitled "Crimson Sails" which published articles on social morality. In the mid-1980s, working on *The Teachers' Newspaper*, Soloveychik set about popularising a new, scientifically based, practical teaching movement (and himself largely provided the theoretical basis in his books and articles). It was a pedagogics of cooperation, in which education was viewed not as something visited on a child but as a dialogue between teacher and pupil. In 1992, Soloveychik founded and edited the newspaper *Pervoye sentyabrya* (September the First).

on them was derived from the techniques of organisational and mental activity-related games originated by the Moscow Methodological Circle. The core activity was intense, team-based intercommunication to induce the conceptualisation of problems and push participants into thinking. Concentrating experts from different fields (physicists, biologists, philologists, mathematicians) in one place made it possible to overcome the restrictive boundaries of academic subjects and comprehend the categories of science and scientific thinking, thereby opening up new directions and areas of activity [www.noogen.ru].

Today these words strike us as slightly mad, although the academics in Krasnoyarsk were clearly moving in a perfectly understandable and indeed predictable direction. They wanted primarily to encourage their students to think, and were combining that preoccupation with interdisciplinary research. Solving noogenic problems cannot constitute an education, but it does stimulate thinking and invites students to take a fresh look at the world. Is that not what was happening to everybody as the 1980s made way for the 1990s?

Here are some examples of noogens:

– Imagine a world in which objects are not clearly distinguishable from each other. Describe how it would be possible to perform an action in that world.

– Establish and prove whether I manage time or time manages me.

– Imagine a world in which everything is inside out.

The year 1990 saw the opening of the first Waldorf school in Moscow. It was called "Family Harmony"[83] and, along with Rudolf Steiner's anthroposophy, which had been very popular in the early years of the twentieth

83. Experiments with elements of Waldorfian theory had begun earlier, and particularly from 1988 at Moscow's No. 734 Secondary School under A. V. Khutorskoy. See the chronological table in A. V. Khutorskoi, *Pedagogicheskaia innovatika: metodologiia, teoriia, praktika* (Moscow, 2005). A selection of articles on Waldorfian educational theory was published in *Sem'ia i shkola*, 12 (1990).

century, took on a new lease of life. The school took the view that the first priority was to develop a child's soul, its personality, which the Waldorfians believed traditional schooling choked with superfluous knowledge, hindering the forming of the person. Growth must be achieved through the common, joyous efforts of children, their teachers and parents. This year also saw the resurrection of Maria Montessori's pedagogical ideas, which enjoyed respect all over the rest of the world and had been applied in Russia up until the 1920s. The first new Montessori kindergarten now opened in Moscow. The children were not compelled to do anything, and the aim was to create conditions for them to develop freely and harmoniously.

Both the Waldorf and Montessori schools are open to criticism on many grounds. The main complaint is that they are so focused on personal development that they keep children in hothouse conditions and fail to provide the basic knowledge needed for living in the real world. Be that as it may, what is of interest here is the very fact of theories which had been so thoroughly suppressed coming back into play, winning a substantial number of supporters and, significantly, continuing to exist to the present day.

Less "alternative", but for Soviet traditionalists still rather startling, innovation was offered by the Eureka project. This was a pedagogic society dating from 1986 which, thanks to the dynamism of its founder, Aleksandr Adamsky, rapidly developed into a movement influential throughout the U.S.S.R., with its own schools, gatherings and summer courses. Today Eureka is a think tank, the Institute of Educational Policy, but in 1990 it was developing retraining programmes for teachers, organising rallies, gatherings and congresses. Eureka acted as a focus for other groups interested in developmental education, or which subscribed to the educational theories of psychologists like Vasiliy Davydov and Daniil Elkonin,[84] or adhered to

84. The Soviet psychologists Vasiliy Davydov (1930–1998) and Daniil Elkonin (1904–1984) in the 1970s worked on "developmental education". In September 1990, Eureka-Development (No. 9 Secondary School), based on the concept, was opened by Aleksandr Adamsky in Tomsk. A private school, Bakalavr, opened in Moscow in 1998, and a number of other schools work on the basis of the concept.

the cultural theories of Vladimir Bibler and Georgiy Shchedrovitsky, or were admirers of Montessori. Eureka is no longer booming the way it was in 1990. Alternative theories of teaching have found their niche and no longer aspire to transform the world. Of course, in 1990 it did seem that education could be revolutionised from top to bottom, and that it was just a matter of agreeing how best to do it.

VI

It gradually came to be accepted that education did not necessarily have to be the same for everyone.

Leonid Katsva, Teacher, No. 1543 Grammar School, Moscow

The school introduced a third specialised subject stream in biology. A stream for maths had been operating for two years already, and a humanities stream for one. From 1990, we extended this streaming from the earlier two or three years to a full four years, from eighth to eleventh grade. The school had almost arrived at its final model, with general education up to seventh grade and subject streams after that.

Irina Ukolova, Moscow

In 1990 we created a humanities stream, devising the syllabus and time-table entirely by ourselves on the basis of common sense and the staff we had available. That was unbelievably radical. We reduced mathematics to an option, which gave us problems the following year when we faced the require-ment of having something to write about it in the children's school-leaving certificates. We hastily improvised an intensive half-year maths class for the eleventh grade. No administrator above the headmaster heard about it or made a fuss. When we spotted the problem in April 1991 I was at the Second Congress of the Innovative Teachers' Union. I asked Vladimir Shadrikov, the Deputy Minister of Education at that time, and he said, "If you don't want to teach it, you don't have to." Nobody knew what you could get away with and what you couldn't.

Yevgeniy Yamburg, Headmaster, Moscow

At this time we began to develop our school by adding Classical subjects and a kindergarten, devising remedial teaching, and going to great lengths to set up medical, psychological and educational support services.

From 1988 there were discussions going on with the Ministry of Education about establishing grammar schools (gimnazii) in Moscow. What is taken as a matter of course today caused astonishment and bafflement back then. For some this was mixed with enthusiasm, for others with horror. It was not so long ago that Boris Yeltsin, as Secretary of the Moscow City Party Committee, had criticised the foreign-language special schools, mainly for being elitist. I remember how the schools were quaking at the prospect of losing their puny, much diluted right of selection, even though the magic words "catchment area" overrode everything else. A child would be assigned to a nearby school, much as a serf used to be registered to his master. Now, suddenly, the idea appeared of establishing schools which would be different from the others, in terms of both their teaching methodology and their selection process. The statute was a year in the drafting, but finally in spring 1989 it happened: three Moscow headteachers, Aleksandr Bubman, Anatoliy Kasparzhak and Yevgeniy Topaler, became the principals of grammar schools.

There was a great desire back then for diversity, as a result of which there was no standard plan for the grammar schools. The three selected had a reputation for high-quality education, but otherwise had little in common. Bubman's No. 1513 Grammar School was created from a successful German-language special school; Kasparzhak's used its existing, established classes; and our own No. 67 School further developed its profession-orientated teaching which had been operating for decades. For all their differences, however, there were certain agreed, common principles: grammar-school education would offer different professional specialisations; it was designed for gifted children; there would be structured choice of courses and supplementary special subjects. There was to be provision for inviting outside speakers, and there would be a wide range of optional subjects.

Much has changed in our school since then, but Latin has invariably been an extremely popular special subject. Today it is taught by a graduate from our first intake as a grammar school.

It seems strange to be writing this today, when all kinds of new courses are being offered from one year to the next and there are plans to introduce professional specialisation in the senior grades throughout Russia. When we held the exams for entrance to the eighth grade of our new grammar school in the spring of 1989, we couldn't fit everyone into the school building and had to overflow into the yard and give instructions over a tannoy. I remember a girl from Krasnodar whose parents had heard about this sensational innovation on television. They wanted their twelve-year-old daughter to rent a room in Moscow for the joy of going to a school that wasn't like all the others. Fortunately, we managed to talk them out of this lunacy, although we were well aware of the reason for their enthusiasm: they didn't mind where she got her education, just as long as it was not the bog-standard Soviet neigh-bourhood school for their catchment area.

In January 1990 we had been teaching our first grammar-school pupils for six months, and we later recognised that they had been the most high-powered cohort in the school's history. Why was that? Was it coincidence, or was it something in the air at the time?

Also in the 1989/90 school year, we admitted first-graders to our grammar school for the first time. In the autumn of 1989 they still had to be enrolled as little Red Octobrists, but our school abolished the Octobrist organisation shortly thereafter, and it was not long before the Pioneer and Young Communist League organisations withered away too. I remember a divided meeting of first-year parents at the end of 1989, when one father welcomed the school's proposal while another shouted that for the past seven years, almost from birth, his child had been looking forward to getting his Octobrist star badge and Pioneer neckerchief. After the general meeting, we all went to the various classrooms and the teacher of 1B, which my daughter had just joined, exclaimed exultantly, "I've been dreaming of this day for years!" She ran to the stand with the little Red Octobrist rules, tore them down, and immediately replaced them with a list of the Ten Commandments. It was amusing, but that too was a sign of the times.

Yevgeniy Yamburg, Headmaster, Moscow

Much was permitted. The state had more urgent concerns than us. It was marvellous.

MARCH

2 March

The so-called "Letter of the 74", a manifesto of nationalistic and patriotic writers, is published in *Literary Russia*. The signatories include almost the entire leadership of the Writers' Union; editors of several literary magazines, including Anatoliy Ivanov, Sergey Vikulov, Stanislav Kunyaev, Mikhail Lobanov and Aleksandr Prokhanov; the ideologues of anti-Semitism, Igor Shafarevich and Vadim Kozhinov; and the writers Valentin Rasputin, Yegor Isayev, Pyotr Proskurin, and Leonid Leonov. The letter is not, however, signed by Viktor Astafiev, to whom the writers frequently refer in their letter. Astafiev had signed an "anti-perestroika" letter condemning *Ogonyok* (*Pravda*, 18 January, 1989), but after 1990 engaged in outspoken disputation with ultra-right politicians and commentators. The Letter of the 74 declares Russia's main enemy to be "Russophobia", and urges the Supreme Soviets of the U.S.S.R. and the R.S.F.S.R. to combat it.

4 March

The first round of balloting is held in elections throughout the U.S.S.R. for local and republican soviets.

"Donetsk. Rallies, calls for strikes and then a hunger strike by members of the miners' Donetsk Strike Committee which continued for three days in the square in front of the Donetsk Provincial Party Committee" (*Izvestiia*, 65, p. 2).

"It is difficult to find vodka and particularly brandy in shops in Moscow. Yuliya Safonova, Deputy Director for food supplies at the Moscow City Trade Association, reports that provincial manufacturers have refused to supply

Labels of low-quality alcoholic beverages which people were obliged to drink in 1990 because of the vodka shortage

the capital with liquor; some for accountancy reasons, while others, like the Tula and Kuibyshev distilleries, say simply, 'We are short ourselves.' Safonova complains, 'We have repeatedly reminded the suppliers of their obligations under the five-year plan, but they do not even respond to requests from the government. Our Armenian and Azerbaijani colleagues inform us that they will not be able to fulfil the first-quarter plan for brandy owing to their local difficulties.' The executive committee of the Moscow City Soviet responded to the liquor shortages by increasing the number of late-night shops selling 35 per cent-proof fortified wines and spirits" (*Moskovskie novosti*, 9, p. 2).

A hunger strike announced on 13 February by thirty-eight members of a sit-in on behalf of large families in the Gagarin-district executive committee building, obliges the K.G.B. and the administrative department of the C.P.S.U. Central Committee to re-allocate a number of flats to the families in blocks built for their own staff (*Moskovskie novosti*, 9, p. 2).

5 *March*

The U.S.S.R. Supreme Soviet instructs the Prosecutor's Office, K.G.B. and Interior Ministry of the U.S.S.R. to investigate crimes committed in Baku on 20 January, taking account of the findings of a parliamentary commission of inquiry of the Azerbaijan Supreme Soviet. (On 20 December, 1990 the Military Prosecutor's Office finds no criminal liability in the actions of military personnel associated with the events, and closes the case.)

The Moscow branch of Memorial holds a rally by the walls of the K.G.B. headquarters in memory of victims of political repression. The event is attended by former prisoners of the Gulag as well as members of the Popular Fronts of Moscow and of Russia and of the U.S.S.R. Anti-Fascist Centre. By agreement with the Moscow City Executive Committee, no more than five hundred people attend. "The protest was symbolic. Its significance related not to its size but to its subject matter and to the fact of its being held in this place on the day Stalin died. Many wondered why it was necessary for the protesters to be almost outnumbered by militia, vigilantes and 'unidentified individuals in civilian clothing'. Patrol cars, a yellow special-operations troop bus with curtained windows . . . The precautions were manifestly disproportionate. This level of security is never seen at rallies of the 'national-patriotic' associations" (*Moskovskie novosti*, 11, p. 2).

12 March

The Third (Extraordinary) Congress of People's Deputies of the U.S.S.R. opens (*Izvestiia*, 71, p. 1).

Speaking on behalf of the Inter-Regional Group of Deputies against the introduction of the post of President of the U.S.S.R., Yuriy Afanasiev insists that the the legal status of the president must be integrated into the coherent, organic text of a new democratic constitution. He lists a number of conditions which, in his opinion, are vital if a presidency is to be established in the Soviet Union. It should be balanced by a robust legislature, a multi-party system and an effective parliamentary opposition (*Izvestiia*, 72, p. 2.).

Soviet troops begin withdrawing from Hungary. An agreement on the terms and timetable for withdrawal is signed on 10 March during a working visit to Moscow by Gyula Horn, the Hungarian Foreign Minister (*Izvestiia*, 71, p. 1).

13 March

At the Congress of People's Deputies of the U.S.S.R., 1,817 deputies vote in favour of introducing the post of President of the U.S.S.R., 133 vote against, and 61 abstain.

15 March

Mikhail Gorbachev is elected President of the U.S.S.R. There are 1,329 votes in favour (59.2 per cent of the total number of deputies at the Congress), with 495 against. "Supporters of electing the president by a national ballot found themselves in a minority, and the people could only watch on television as their fate was decided" (*Argumenty i Fakty*, 11, p. 1). "In conclusion, the Congress was addressed by President Mikhail Gorbachev. The Congress could not disperse, he said, before it had formed a judgement about events in Lithuania. 'We have reached a point beyond which events will follow which we need to stop. We have to help the Lithuanian people to be aware of everything that is happening.'"

16 March

Replying to a question about how he would react to the dismissive attitude of the Congress of People's Deputies of the U.S.S.R. towards the Supreme Soviet of Lithuania, Vytautas Landsbergis says, "It is a decision taken by a foreign country and not binding on us. Nobody has any right to rescind our decisions" (*Izvestiia*, 76, p. 10).

20 March

Statement by the Government of the U.S.S.R.: "Although the Government of the U.S.S.R. is understanding of the issues relating to the political, social, economic and cultural development of the Lithuanian S.S.R. and respects the desire of its people to renew society and strengthen the republic's sovereignty, the government of the U.S.S.R. considers that these objectives can only be attained in strict compliance with the legislation of the U.S.S.R. and taking due account of the mutual interests of the peoples of the Lithuanian S.S.R. and other republics. Chairman of the Council of Ministers of the U.S.S.R. Nikolai Ryzhkov" (*Izvestiia*, 80, p. 1).

Vytautas Landsbergis comments on the Statement by the Government of the U.S.S.R.:

"The Statement by the government of the U.S.S.R. is on the whole fairly positive. It accepts the need for economic relations between Lithuania and the U.S.S.R. to continue in compliance with provisions in the 1990 treaty. This is in line with our proposal to Prime Minister Nikolai Ryzhkov. The concern expressed over the proposed introduction of Lithuanian currency is somewhat surprising, as this has long been recommended by Lithuanian and Estonian economists, and no dire warnings were previously heard from the Council of Ministers of the U.S.S.R. More surprising is the untruth about a supposed hasty transference of state-owned enterprises to private ownership.

"As regards concerns over the security of the nuclear power station, the biggest threat to it is from its own design.

"On the whole, it has to be said that, as people over the age of fifty are very aware, the current situation has a great deal in common with the climate of 1940 when we faced the same pressure, the same threats and the same uncertainty" (*Moskovskie novosti*, 12, p. 5).

21 March

Independence is proclaimed in Namibia, a territory rich in mineral resources which had been occupied for several decades by South Africa. At the independence ceremonies in Windhoek, Eduard Shevardnadze has meetings with the South African fighter for the rights of the indigenous peoples, Nelson Mandela, and, for the first time, with the South African President, F. W. de Klerk (*Pravda*, 21 and 22 March).

23 March

A Presidential Council is formed to advise the president of the U.S.S.R. The following individuals are appointed: Eduard Shevardnadze, Yuriy

Maslyukov, Vladimir Kryuchkov, Dmitriy Yazov, Chingiz Aitmatov, Stanislav Shatalin, Valentin Rasputin, Aleksandr Yakovlev, Veniamin Yarin, Albert Kauls, Yuriy Osipian, Yevgeniy Primakov, Valeriy Boldin, Vadim Bakatin and Grigoriy Revenko (*Izvestiia*, 85, pp. 1–2; 86, p. 1).

The results of the second round of voting for Russian republican and local soviets show that in Moscow Democratic Russia has won a landslide victory. Of sixty-five Moscow constituencies for people's deputies of the R.S.F.S.R., fifty-seven have been won by Democratic Russia candidates. Seven out of nine delegates from Sverdlovsk are supported by the analogous Democratic Choice association. In Leningrad, twenty-five of thirty-one deputies elected support the democratic platform. This is typical of large industrial and scientific cities of the R.S.F.S.R., but many provinces will have less radical leaders at provincial and republican level (*Moskovskie novosti*, 12, p. 4).

"At a meeting of the Russian P.E.N. Centre's Executive Committee, its president, Anatoly Rybakov, read out a decree of the U.S.S.R. Council of Ministers granting the centre the status of an international, non-governmental organisation, with the right to set up its own publishing company, to publish a newspaper and magazine, to own premises and so on. The P.E.N. Centre's first events will take place on 12 and 13 April, when Andrey Bitov and Mikhail Zhvanetsky, Bulat Okudzhava and Yevgeniy Yevtushenko, Vladimir Lakshin and Igor Shklyarevsky will speak" (*Moskovskie novosti*, 12, p. 2).

30 March

The Supreme Soviet of the Estonian S.S.R. adopts a decree "On the National Status of Estonia", which views the operation of the laws of the U.S.S.R. on its territory as a violation of its sovereignty. The Estonian Congress is recognised as a "parallel parliament", and the beginning of a transition to restoration of Estonia's independence is declared.

31 March

Memorial's department for monitoring public opinion asks 2,097 residents of Moscow to assess the Lithuanian situation. One question asks, "Is it acceptable, in your view, to use armed force to resolve the conflict with Lithuania?" Seventy per cent of respondents reply, "No" (*Moskovskie novosti*, 16, p. 11).

Also in March

Soviet Literature published articles representative of a wide spectrum of ideological opinion. The journal's Atlas of Ideologies included neo-socialists (Boris Orlov); Westernisers (Viktor Kurierov), pacifists (Andrey Nuikin); supporters of "defence awareness" (Oleg Baklanov and Aleksandr Prokhanov); adherents of the Russian Idea (Vadim Kozhinov), and of the "Jewish version" (Yevgeniy Satanovsky); and Dmitriy Balashov, author of historical novels with a nationalist slant (*Noveishaia istoriia otechestvennogo kino*, 5 [St Petersburg, 2004]).

The First Channel of National Television broadcast (at midnight) a pioneering non-ideological news programme, prepared by the Television News Service (*Ibid.*).

Ogonyok published an open letter from the chairmen of the boards of three commercial banks (Vladimir Vinogradov, Aleksey Titov and Aleksandr Smolensky) to the Finance Minister of the U.S.S.R., Valentin Pavlov. They expressed bafflement as to why the Finance Ministry should be seeking to tax the net profit of banks at 60 per cent. "No country in the world taxes profits at more than 35–45 per cent, and the tax is payable at the end of the fiscal year rather than quarterly, so the money is constantly in circulation. Is it really the aim of the Finance Ministry, under the pretext of fighting the good fight against the budget deficit, to crudely choke off commercial banks?" (*Ogonyok*, 10, p. 27).

THE IRRATIONAL IN SOCIETY: DIAGNOSES OF 1990

Pavel Romanov and Yelena Yarskaya-Smirnova

"He predicted my future eight years ago. I laughed at the time . . ." So begins a substantial article on palmistry published in the highly popular *Ogonyok* in 1990.[85] Now, Dmitriy Biryukov tells us, there is a two-month waiting list to see that well-known and legally operating fortune-teller. People come to consult him not because their lives are full of joy, or to escape the regime's propaganda, but because they are seeking liberation from the psychological enslavement they have brought upon themselves by "cutting themselves off from the world" and wilfully ignoring readily avail-able information about the significance of the lines on the human palm. These lines, the article claims, can set us free because, if we know the future, we can change it.

How did "alternative" knowledge come to be seen as a way of liberating people from the old ideology? Was it simply that once forbidden fruit has its own particular sweetness? Was the upsurge of interest in the supernat-ural just as socialist planning was coming to an end purely coincidental, or did it answer a need people felt at that moment in history? How and why did such a major shift occur in widely held beliefs? What role did the state and the scientists play in all this, and how does a culture produce new myths? Why did so many people seek answers from alternative science, folk healers and other providers of irrational services? What changes took place in how information was disseminated to the public during the

85. Dmitrii Biriukov, "Znak sud'by", *Ogonek*, 37 (1990), p. 32.

years of perestroika? How were folk healing and alternative medicine viewed? More broadly, how did society at that time differentiate science from non-science? And finally, what cultural processes were taking place alongside the social upheavals of the late 1980s and early 1990s which tended to legitimise the irrational?

"RELAX, SIT BACK, MAKE YOURSELF COMFORTABLE . . .": PERFORMING PAINLESS SURGERY ON PUBLIC OPINION

Public interest in parascience and the paranormal began to grow in the U.S.S.R. beginning in the mid-1980s, with waves of interest in formerly forbidden topics rising and falling. The newspapers, magazines and television programmes of the perestroika era took up first one and then another passing sensation.

What had happened to the famous Soviet rationalism? The drive for modernisation, which had turned Soviet people into individualistic unbelievers, atomised and isolated them from one another, might seem to have been even more pronounced under perestroika, with its ethos of efficiency, accelerating intellectual processes, glasnost (transparency) and its "appeal to humane values". However, the wave of perestroika as it engulfed the cultural industries swept aside every prohibition and restriction imposed by the censorship on rational, industrial Soviet Man. People found themselves in a state of cultural dislocation or rebirth. After "the soporific decades of Soviet scholasticism",[86] a philosophical, cultural and psychological awakening occurred for which the ground had been prepared by samizdat (illegal "self-publication") in all its forms.

Opinion pieces in the press were hugely influential during this period. Subscribers to The Spark (Ogonyok) exceeded five million; by the late 1980s, the circulation of Arguments and Facts had scaled unimaginable heights, taking it into the Guinness Book of Records. In the literary journals, previously

---

86. Mikhail Epstein, "Tret'e filosofskoe probuzhdenie (1960–1980-e)", Kontinent, 122 (2004); http://magazines.russ.ru/continent/2004/122/epsht21.html

banned books were being published, "shelved" films were being rehabilitated and new ones appearing, old canons were collapsing and new ones
being established. As Nadezhda Azhgikhina put it, "A civil war was being
waged in literature between 'Westernisers' and Russian traditionalists, and
everywhere there was a desire for change and renewal."[87] In this situation,
literature, philosophy, religion, and all manner of quasi-religious and
quasi-scientific alternatives were eagerly put forward to explain what was
going on, to "renovate a discredited cultural model and to enable people to
find their place in the new social environment".[88]

It is not so surprising, then, that the above dithyramb to palmistry as an
authentic branch of knowledge should have appeared in a magazine with a
reputation for emotional pro-perestroika exposés and a penchant for
genres outside the traditional boundaries of journalism. Hard-hitting
political investigations, polemics and scholarly articles rubbed shoulders
with feature articles and photographs of everyday life with its "excesses,
failures, and joys, unfeigned astonishment and sympathy for suffering
which no-one was yet openly mentioning".[89] The official press was
publishing horoscopes and recipes for traditional folk remedies.

Horoscopes had been in vogue even after the Communists had come to
power, then in the 1920s, and then again during the "Khrushchev Thaw" of
the 1960s. In the 1970s astrologers formed unofficial societies in Moscow,
Kiev, Kharkov, Leningrad and Vilnius. For a full seventy years, the Soviet
people had had it drummed into them that religion was the opium of the
people. Astrology took over religion's role in explaining the ineffable.[90]

87. Nadezhda Azhgikhina, "Na puti k obreteniiu sily", We/My, Special Issue (2000); http://
www. owl.ru/win/info/we_my/2000_sp/05.htm
88. Oleg Pachenkov, "Ratsional'noe zakoldovyvanie real'nosti: sovremennye rossiiskie
'magi'", in Nevidimye grani sotsial'noi real'nosti, ed. V. Voronkov et al., Tsentr nezavisimykh
sotsiologicheskikh issledovanii, Trudy, 9 (St Petersburg, 2011), pp. 96–109; http://www.
indepsocres. spb.ru/sbornik9/9_patch.htm
89. Nadezhda Azhgikhina, "Epokha 'Ogon'ka': bitva s sistemoi", Zhurnalist (May 2005), p.
65; http://old.journalist-virt.ru/mag.php?s=200505651
90. Herman J. Obermayer, "Russia's Dysfunctional Media Culture", Policy Review Online;
http:// www.hoover.org/publications/policy-review/article/7560

From the late 1980s on, astrologers were to be found in the media, the first regular astrological predictions in the Soviet press being published from 1990 in *Moskovsky komsomolets*. This was evidently one of the factors contributing to a huge increase in the number of its subscribers, from two hundred thousand in 1990 to eight hundred thousand in 1991. Sergey Vronsky, an astrologer, provided the daily predictions. He also wrote articles and in 1990 had a book published by Nauka, the U.S.S.R. Academy of Sciences' press.[91] Before long, horoscopes were a regular feature in *Arguments and Facts*, the government's official newspaper *Rossiyskaya gazeta* and the new provincial media. Some daily newspapers would publish three or four separate astrological predictions in every issue. Innovative television news programmes were very popular. They aired contentious political issues relating to ecology, the economy and culture, and their presenters were very different from the static, monotonous Soviet newsreaders of old. *600 Seconds*, *Viewpoint* and *Before and After Midnight* went out late at night but attracted enormous audiences. Horoscopes made them even more popular.

Telekinesis, clairvoyance, astrology, healing, psychics, magicians . . . The media coverage both created demand and corresponded to the public's existing mood. For some citizens, faith in a bright future with market capitalism co-existed with "apocalyptic forebodings and anticipation of inevitable punishment for the duplicity of their lives, the living a lie which had become habitual", while others had long ceased to pin any hopes on the state and its market revolution and wanted only to "build capitalism in a single apartment and among their immediate friends". The eschatological fears of others saw no future for Russia, and this caused people to "flee from the current situation to just about anywhere – Australia, the U.S., Israel, South Africa – or to decide everything would work out fine in spite of everything and that a Messiah would come and put everything to rights".[92] According to polls conducted by the U.S.S.R. Centre for the Study of Public

91. Sergei Vronskii, *Astrologiia: sueverie ili nauka?* (Moscow, 1990).
92. "Anomal'noe iavlenie", *Vek XX i mir*, 12 (1990); http://old.russ.ru/antolog/vek/1990/12/yavl.htm

Opinion, two-thirds of respondents surveyed in April 1990 did not believe that Gorbachev's perestroika would succeed, but did believe in miracles and the powers of paranormal practitioners like Anatoliy Kashpirovsky, Allan Chumak and Yevgeniya Dzhuna, in witchcraft, the biofield, telekinesis and telepathy.[93]

"DO YOU BELIEVE THE FOLLOWING?" (APRIL 1990)

	Yes	No	Undecided
Illnesses can be treated by hypnosis	62.4	11.4	26.2
Illnesses can be treated by television psychotherapy (e.g., Anatoliy Kashpirovsky)	56.6	16.7	26.7
Illnesses can be treated through the biofield (e.g., Yevgeniya Dzhuna)	51.5	13.1	35.4
Omens	49.8	25.5	24.7
Some people can predict the future or your destiny by the stars, using horoscopes	41.6	23.0	35.4
Some people can transmit thoughts over a distance (telepathy)	42.2	24.8	33.0
Some people can cast spells or hex	35.0	35.6	29.4
UFOs have appeared on Earth	33.9	26.7	39.4
Illnesses can be treated in the way practised by Allan Chumak	29.0	34.0	37.0
Objects can be moved by willpower	23.0	41.3	35.7
It is possible to communicate with the souls of the dead	11.3	64.6	24.1

Anatoliy Kashpirovsky, who first surfaced on Alma-Ata television in 1986 and on national television in 1988–9, became an "icon of the first five years

93. *Ibid.*

of perestroika T.V."[94] Franz Boas once said of a Kwakiutl medicine man that he did nòt become a great shaman because he cured his patients but because they believed in him. This he achieved by cultivating their ignorance, expressed in mythological and magical images.[95] Much like that shaman, Kashpirovsky enjoyed the unqualified trust of his audience. His hypnosis sessions, "painless surgery" and demonstrations of his unique "gifts", broadcast live on the highly popular *Viewpoint* programme, came to be seen as representative of the period and, according to more sober later estimates, "testimony to over-exuberant embracing of the new freedoms".[96]

Kashpirovsky's evening sessions of hypnotherapy had millions of Soviet citizens glued to their screens, their popularity even rivalling that of the Brazilian soap opera *Isaura the Slave Girl*. The streets were deserted. The population took enthusiastically to the notion of restoring its health and obtaining amazing remedies without having to leave the comfort of home, stand in queues or spend money on doctors. People were eager to free themselves of illnesses and ailments by tuning in to the healing silence of a psychic on television and radio, or charging water, medicines, food and ointments with positive energy from the same source. Kashpirovsky and Allan Chumak, Yuriy Longo and Gennadiy Rutsko, Pavel Globa and Yevgeniya Dzhuna were no less popular than pop star Alla Pugachova. They went on tours in the U.S.S.R. and abroad; they published in newspapers and rapidly increased both their own celebrity and the newspapers' circulation figures. They involved themselves in business and government matters, giving consultations to politicians and officials. Professors and members of the Academy of Sciences spoke out on television and in the press in praise of the merits, or decrying the harmfulness, of their sessions. Their public appearances were accompanied by warnings from the Russian

94. Aleksei Isaev, "Videoart i al'ternativnoe televeshchanie. TV-art? (2002)", Tsentr medi-atekhnologii, iskusstva i kommunikatsii;http://www.mediaartlab.ru/db/tekst.html?id=67
95. Quoted in Il'ia Kasavin, "Magiia: ee mnimye otkrytiia i podlinnye tainy", in Il'ia Kasavin, ed., *Zabluzhdaiushchiisia razum? Mnogoobrazie vnenauchnogo znaniia* (Moscow, 1990), p. 69.
96. Dmitrii Bykov, "'Vzgliad' i Nechto", *Iskusstvo Kino*, 3 (1998); kinoart.ru/1998/n3-article22.html

Orthodox Church about the works of evil, or from the Order of Wizards of Russia praising their dedicated professionalism, as well as letters from people who had been healed or whose health had deteriorated.

In 1990, Kashpirovsky's "wellness sessions" were dropped by Soviet television after high-profile denunciation by scientists and journalists in a number of countries, including Russia and Bulgaria.[97] His popularity declined, but he continued to perform in Poland, where, in 1990, he was awarded the Victor Prize for television personality of the year. He is said to have been awarded a commemorative medal in the U.S. in 1995 for work with Second World War veterans. The denunciations did not detract from the magic sessions and, paradoxically, only consolidated the popularity and affection Russians felt for their wizard, allowing him now to present himself as one wrongly persecuted and maligned. A similar career path was followed by Chumak and most of the other paranormal show-business celebrities as well as, later, the investment fraudsters, the Mavrodi brothers. These gentlemen founded the MMM pyramid scheme and steered it through boom to ultimate bust. Crowds of their defrauded admirers demanded outside the courthouse that their heroes should be acquitted.[98]

The authorities eventually banned mass healing events, "either out of concern for the nation's mental health or because they were jealous of

97. In October 1990, Russian viewers were warned by Todor Dichev, a Bulgarian professor, that the methods used by psychics and psychotherapists like Anatoliy Kashpirovsky were damaging to mental health: "This is typical psycho-fascism. In Bulgaria, after Kashpirovsky's televised sessions there was a rise in instances of mass psychosis." See Elena Vysotskaia and Natal'ia Makarova, eds, *Katastrofy v predskazaniiakh i prorochestvakh* (Minsk, 1997), esp. "Predskazateli i proroki. Kashpirovskii, Chumak, Rutsko"; http://tonos.ru/articles/predafer

98. There is a curious similarity between the addictiveness of the wellness sessions and the mass enthusiasm for financial pyramid schemes in the 1990s. We can observe the same contagion and uncritical reception of advertising, as well as the important role of word of mouth in disseminating information about these phenomena and their outcomes. Massive pyramid scams engulfed many post-Soviet countries, in Albania in 1997 causing what was effectively a civil war. See "Albania Crisis Briefing", International Crisis Group; http://reliefweb.int/node/40004

the new celebrities' fame".[99] In 1996 the Russian Ministry of Health issued instructions bringing unconventional therapies under government control, and televising of the psychics' therapeutic sessions ceased.[100] It was too late, however, to halt the advance of parascience, which had become integrated into the spheres of medicine, politics, defence and people's everyday lives. Witchcraft and the doings of psychics became accepted as perfectly normal, and miracles were no longer regarded as anything out of the ordinary.

By the mid-1990s, by some estimates, there were more than fifty thousand "practitioners of alternative medicine" in Moscow, while in Russia as a whole hundreds of thousands of sorcerers, witches and fortune-tellers were in business. They received massive official endorsement in the form of state licences, government positions, and the support of politicians and elected representatives. Dr Nikolai Kasian, a hugely popular chiropractor, was a member and hero of the First Congress of People's Deputies of the U.S.S.R. (May–June 1989). The Academy of Astrology opened its doors in 1990 after receiving state registration as an educational institution.[101] Between 1993 and 1995, Kashpirovsky was a Member of Parliament in the Duma and is said to have harboured aspirations before that of running the country: "I had every possibility of occupying the position that went to Yeltsin. 1990 was drawing to a close and I would have been several times more popular. I had immense resources at my disposal. I could have run for president, and am more than confident that I would have won."[102]

99. Natal'ia Zharkova, "Ekstrasens stuchit dvazhdy! Tuk-tuk!" *Rodnaia gazeta*, 8 February 2006; http://flb.ru/info/36281.html

100. Ministerstvo zdravookhraneniia i meditsinskoi promyshlennosti Rossiiskoi Federatsii, Order No. 245, 13 June, 1996, "Ob uporiadochenii primeneniia metodov psikhologicheskogo i psikhoterapevticheskogo vozdeistviia".

101. State licence 2269/861-H; http://astroacademia.narod.ru/index. htm

102. Serzh Isakov, "Interv'iu s Anatoliem Kashpirovskim. Chast' 2. Paradoksy politiki", Server "Zagranitsa", 3 March, 2001; http://world.lib.ru/s/serzh_i/kashpirowskijchastx2.shtml. Chumak registered a patent in Russia for "producing energy from water-bearing media". See Allan Chumak, "Protsess poznaniia cheloveka edin (nasha anketa)", *Chudesa i prikliucheniia*, 6 (1995); http://bibliotekar.ru/chip/695-19.htm

PSYCHOANALYST, SHAMAN, MESSIAH, MARKET PLAYER OR
(SELF-)MARKETING MANAGER?

In popular health publications, interest in alternative therapies was at its height in the early to mid-1990s, after which it declined.[103] In 1990 there was a clear difference of opinion among those writing for the magazines *Science and Life* and *The Doctor* on how promising the prospects were for developing folk medicine. Many saw it as potentially having a wide range of applications "from the practical organisation of medical assistance to its use in space during orbital flights".[104] The "growing authority of this movement among medics" was noted, and there were calls to "work harder to bring together reflexologists and doctors working in folk medicine with physiologists, biochemists, mathematicians and engineers. Such an alliance would be effective if it received widespread public support".[105]

Not everybody was so enthusiastic. Professor Donat Sarkisov, a member of the U.S.S.R. Academy of Medical Sciences, said unambiguously that the champions of "so-called folk medicine are an evil which must be combated".[106] Sarkisov believed that the propaganda in favour of alternative medicine could have "grave consequences for patients" and laid the blame primarily on the media: "Propaganda in support of the activities of charlatans is immeasurably more widespread nowadays. If in the past they were to be found only in small and relatively infrequent advertisements, their 'work' is now written about comprehensively, systematically and in great detail in the national press, on television and radio."[107] Alongside his article, *The Doctor* published two other articles in favour of folk medicine, which gave advice on how to make use of it.[108]

103. Elena Iarskaia-Smirnova and Ol'ga Grigor'ieva, "'My – chast' prirody'. Sotsial'naia identifikatsiia narodnykh tselitelei", *Zhurnal sotsiologii i sotsial'noi antropologii*, 9/1 (2006), pp. 151–70.
104. L. Uskova and A. Vodianoi, "Vozvrashchenie traditsii", *Vrach*, 7 (1990), p. 27.
105. *Ibid.*   106. Donat Sarkisov, "Meditsinskaia nauka i lzhenauka", *Vrach*, 7 (1990), pp. 58–60.   107. *Ibid.*, p. 59.
108. L. Seilanova, "Vozvrashchenie traditsii", *Vrach*, 7 (1990), p. 27; S. Yakushina, "Kak lechit' travami", *Vrach*, 7 (1990), p. 12.

Opinion in the early 1990s appears to have been predominantly favourable, however. In issue No. 10, an "Appeal to Doctors" from L. Khundanova, a Doctor of Medical Science, was published. It urged doctors "not only to recognise folk medicine but to professionally publicise its successes in the treatment of a number of illnesses".[109] The same issue contained two further articles about new and unconventional methods of treatment.[110] Issue No. 12 introduced a new section on "Folk Medicine", which appeared a further three times in 1991 and became a permanent fixture in 1992.[111] Each subsequent issue included two or three articles on alternative therapies. The "Folk Medicine" section disappeared in 1996, and a permanent section was reintroduced only in 2003 under the more professional medical title of "Phytotherapy" (i.e., Herbal Medicine). These authors evidently believed that folk medicine and conventional medicine were converging as the result of technological progress. As L. Uskova and A. Vodianoi put it:

> Folk medicine is not static. It is constantly incorporating the latest scientific and technological discoveries. Reports on reflective diagnostics, based on acupuncture pressure points, show that a person's condition can be established using modern electronics while taking account of traditional ideas. Work on biological processing of communication has shown a potential for further developing concepts relating to meditation.[112]

Since the 1990s, Health magazine has had a section, under various titles, devoted to the medicinal use of herbs from ancient times to the present. In 1991 it introduced a section titled "The ABC of Homeopathic Remedies" and published a set of remote exercises relating to Dzhuna's "contactless

109. L. Khundanov, "Obrashchenie k vracham", Vrach, 10 (1990), p. 3.
110. V. Arnol'dova, "Terapiia po Gritsenko", Vrach, 10 (1990), pp. 18–19; A. Sitel', "Manual'naia terapiia: pokazaniia i protivopokazaniia", Vrach, 10 (1990), pp. 20–21.
111. Iu. Makarov and I. Esina, "Refleksoterapiia pri gormonal'noi migreni", Vrach, 7 (1990) 12 (1990), pp. 40–43.
112. Uskova and Vodianoi, "Vozvrashchenie traditsii", Vrach, 7 (1990), p. 27.

massage". In 1993 a section titled "Alternative Medicine" contained articles about folk healers. Publications from this time suggest that the professional standing of a folk healer derived less from diplomas or academic degrees than from continuity of knowledge and abilities, evidenced by the practitioner's "lineage". The legitimating insignia used by conventional medicine, which only a few years previously had clearly differentiated "us" from "them" and enabled individuals without the requisite regalia to be barred from professional practice, were now appropriated by folk healers. Conventionally qualified doctors and even graduate scientists began appearing among the alternative practitioners. Academician Donat Sarkisov noted that the ever-increasing army of charlatans was unprecedented in the annals of medicine.[113]

Meanwhile Russian health-care provision was in a dire state. There was little take up of modern methods of diagnosis and treatment in publicly available medical care, professionalism was in short supply, and there was an acute shortage of even essential drugs and equipment. Medical science, the pharmaceutical industry and medical services in general were far below international standards. Patients were dissatisfied with the attitude of medical staff in the heavily bureaucratised clinics and hospitals. As the Soviet era drew to an end, the training and attitudes of medical staff and the social services on offer were simply not fit for adequately supporting people who were ill, afflicted or undergoing severe mental stress.[114]

An article critical of homeopathy in *Science and Life*, commenting on the persistence of belief in miracles among the ignorant and uneducated, quoted Marx to the effect that "ignorance is immensely powerful". The author commented that, if to this were added "the patient's legitimate fear for the only life he has", then that power would become irresistible.[115] The patient himself would become the facilitator in the "shaman–patient–group" relationship. Whether the magical healing process is actually

113. Donat Sarkisov, "Meditsinskaia nauka i lzhenauka", p. 58.
114. A. Vein, "O dvukh formakh vrachevaniia", *Nauka i zhizn'*, 2 (1990), p. 61.
115. A. Uspenskii, "O gomeopatii i allopatii", *Nauka i zhizn'*, 1 (1990), p. 83.

successful, Claude Levi-Strauss had observed, "is relatively less important than how convincing the ritual is to the community".[116]

Unlike the shaman in a traditional community, the faith healer in a consumer society is seen as a preacher, a kind of messiah. The "highly democratic nature of his sessions, which can as well be watched and participated in by a government minister as a peasant, by someone living in the capital or far out in the provinces", results in his "teaching" becoming extremely widespread.[117] This is accentuated during a period of transition, when the loss or painful revision of political ideals induces a mood of uncertainty. Society becomes less stable, and peripheral trends in politics and culture manifest themselves more freely. Views become polarised, and many incline towards mysticism and occultism.[118] The willingness to accept a messiah is accentuated in the first instance if the popular mind is accepting of paternalism because people lack confidence in their own abilities or are worried about their financial situations. They wait passively for outside help. Secondly, it may be deeply rooted, as in Russia, in traditional beliefs about what constitutes a normal relationship between the community, the individual and the state.[119] This can almost be seen as a kind of "cargo cult", the belief that the solution to problems will be air-freighted in from one's ancestors.[120] Some theoreticians believe this attitude is to be found in the consciousness even of fairly well-educated people in modern Western societies.[121]

In Russia, the "healers" of the 1990s gradually lost their democratic aura and became stratified, targeting separate social classes. The industry

116. Quoted in Il'ia Kasavin, "Magiia: ee mnimye otkrytiia i podlinnye tainy", p. 75.
117. A. Vein, "O dvukh formakh vrachevaniia", p. 64.
118. Ibid. p. 61.
119. Natal'ia Tikhonova, "Rossiiane: normativnaia model' vzaimootnoshenii obshchestva, lichnosti i gosudarstva", Obshchestvennye nauki i sovremennost', 6 (2005), p. 43.
120. See, for example, Mircea Eliade, Aspects du mythe (Paris, 1963).
121. Quite a few articles in Sotsio-Logos, a Franco-Russian collection compiled in 1990, consider the "irrationality" of social institutions and the foundations of social rationality. See especially Michel Maffesoli, "Okoldovannost' mira ili bozhestvennoe sotsial'noe", Sotsio-Logos: Sotsiologiia. Antropologiia. Metafizika (Moscow, 1991), pp. 274–83.

was no longer typically an aged neighbour who could tell fortunes, or old Annie the folk healer from the free advertising newspaper. It came to include corporate sorcerers, wizards and exclusive certificated herbalists in salons known and accessible only to the elite.[122] The fad among political and pop-music trendsetters enabled some healers to make a considerable killing as a result of their exotic status.

Demand for folk medicine and the services of healers, sorcerers and miscellaneous medicine men flourished in a time of socio-economic uncertainty and in the unfamiliar conditions of the new free market. With such rapid expansion in the 1990s, accreditation of any sort was in short supply, and professional credentials were no longer a monopoly of the academic community or the state. They were created by the entrepreneur himself, legitimised largely by clever advertising and market demand and, of course, customer satisfaction.

PSEUDOSCIENCE: LEGITIMISING THE IRRATIONAL

By 1990, there had been an enormous increase in the appetite for paranormal phenomena, the occult, sects and discoveries in areas which official science disparaged. What were the broader factors in Russia's social history and contemporary institutions which led to such rapid growth of religiosity and the flourishing of alternative learning in both the natural sciences and the humanities? On offer were unexpected ways to revitalise, heal and spiritually develop clients, to predict their future, resurrect their dead relatives, ensure success in their personal life and the prospering of their businesses.

An important contribution to the growth of alternative sciences in the 1990s had to do with their assuming the appearance of respectable institutions. Discourse about paranormal phenomena mimicked the scholarly papers of educational and academic institutions. There were references to

122. A typical newspaper advertisement of the early 2000s read, "Witch for the Elite. Expensive."

state registration and professional qualifications like diplomas, Bachelor's and Master's degrees, and the subsequent "academic" careers of para-science graduates who gave lectures, conducted classes, engaged in consultancy and worked in the media. Such marginal, quasi-scientific disciplines as palmistry, modern alchemy, kabbalah, astrology, UFOlogy and extra-sensory perception were institutionalised with reference to their ancient traditions, research institutes, monographs and specialised periodical publications, book series and publishers. The press went to great lengths to popularise the work of the parascientists. Unlike most traditional academic writing, here was information which fascinated the general public, its authenticity vouched for, at least partly, by the same mechanisms that lent credibility to evidence from rigorously scientific sources.

Popularising less usual scientific results comes naturally to journalism, both in Russia and elsewhere. The twentieth century saw greatly increased interest in the wonders of science, not least because of the contribution which technological innovation made to raising living standards and which science, more generally, made to the conquest of nature as well as, seemingly, humankind's domination of the planet. Unlike Nazi Germany, the U.S.S.R. banned all public mention of the irrational, but the achievements of Soviet science and technology in physics, nuclear fusion and space exploration led to a relaxation of restrictions on the debating of unexplained natural phenomena. From the 1960s on, such magazines as *Technology to Youth* and *Science and Life* published items about aliens, Unidentified Flying Objects, cutaneous vision, telekinesis, mind-reading, the Loch Ness monster, the Abominable Snowman, the Bermuda Triangle and Reichian bioenergetics.[123] Some of these articles aimed to expose

123. On the Loch Ness monster, see D. Dmitrieva, "Nessi otmechaet svoe stoletie", *Tekhnika – molodezhi*, 8 (1975); on the Abominable Snowman, Maiia Bykova, "Chaar parne, pe miye!", *Tekhnika – molodezhi*, 10 (1990), pp. 58–62; on cutaneous vision, Vladimir Shcherbakov, "Poslednii eksperiment Rozy Kuleshovoi", *Tekhnika – molodezhi*, 8 (1978); on telekinesis, Iurii Kobzarev, "Beseda o telekineze, ili Na poroge 'magicheskoi' fiziki", *Tekhnika – molodezhi*, 2 (1988), pp. 38–41; on Unidentified Flying Objects, Gennadiy Eremin, "Utseleet li drevniaia zagadka?", *Tekhnika – molodezhi*, 9 (1970), p. 57; "Murav'inaia zvezda", *Tekhnika – molodezhi*, 9 (1970), pp. 19–21.

charlatanism, but the authors of others were making strenuous efforts to find evidence in support of these phenomena. For example, Boris Porshnev, a celebrated Soviet historian, took a great interest in press reports about a British expedition to the Himalayas to search for the mysterious yeti, or Abominable Snowman, particularly after sightings of humanoid creatures (a "wild man", a "forest man") were reported in various parts of the Soviet Union. On Porshnev's initiative, the U.S.S.R. Academy of Sciences in 1958 established a scientific commission to investigate the yeti and sent an expedition to search for it in the Pamir Mountains.[124]

In 1965, the Popov Radio Electronics and Communications Society established a laboratory of bioinformation, which in 1975 was incorporated into a special department of bioelectronics. Its first Chairman was the philosopher Aleksandr Spirkin, a corresponding member of the Academy of Sciences, and its laboratory was instructed to investigate physical fields which exist around living organisms and their effect on other organisms. Since unidentified biological fields could not be researched without examining the activities of psychics, the laboratory also studied telepathy and telekinesis. According to some authors, Spirkin's enthusiasm for psychic phenomena contributed to his being barred in 1990 from full membership of the Academy of Sciences.[125]

The publication in science journals and popular magazines of articles about unexplained phenomena, and mention of work being carried out in classified or semi-classified research groups, saw the spread into the public sphere of discussion of matters previously blocked by academic censors who considered it to undermine science itself. The irrational ceased to be a topic only for kitchen conversations and non-political samizdat. It graduated from secret laboratories to mass-circulation popular

124. Zhanna Kofman, "U istokov novoi nauki. K 100-letiiu so dnia rozhdeniia professora B.F. Porshneva", Mediana, 6 (2004). See also Oleg Vite, Tvorcheskoe nasledie B.F. Porshneva i ego sovremennoe znachenie (Moscow, 1998); http://www.2lib.ru/book/win/2261.html
125. Leonid Medvedev, Za granitsei real'nosti (Novosibirsk, 2003). Quoted from Leonid Medvedev, "O fenomene psevdonauki", Sibirskii obozrevatel' (2004–6); http://ssop.kspu.ru/book_medvedev.htm # 0

science writing and ceased to be the object of automatic derision.

Back in the 1970s, in parallel with the emergence of political dissidence, there had been renewed interest in the occult. Unsanctioned groups of adherents of esoteric doctrines were mostly intellectuals protesting against a stifling ideology, state-sponsored atheism and official science. Many of these groups were persecuted, and it was their leaders who, in the perestroika era, took the initiative in institutionalising alternative science. Alternative science is not homogeneous; it takes established scholarly disciplines, from history and philosophy to biology, physics and chemistry, and pushes them into speculative realms. Which theories are dispatched to the category of pseudoscience is not a purely objective and rational matter, but reflects interaction between such parties as the state with its various interest groups, mainstream science institutions, religious communities and professional organisations.

The year 1990 was a milestone in this struggle. Liberalisation of the media undermined the state's monopoly on truth, and afforded greater opportunities in the adjacent spheres of politics and science for openly challenging official viewpoints. Certain alternative sciences were drafted in to support particular political doctrines. Thus the Pamyat' movement, neo-pagans and other ultranationalist groups sought legitimation of their programmes by reference to what they claimed were academically respectable "historical" explanations and to systematised and inventoried facts, evidence, publications and research.

In fact the power base of official science was considerably undermined by liberalisation. Announcements by its spokesmen were devalued, and anything unofficial or on the fringes was in a position to establish itself, gain institutional status, and enjoy public support from the state and society's new activists. Despite their apparent openness, these discourses were disseminated over controlled networks and could be manipulated by the technologies involved in forming public opinion. Some commentators believed there was a deliberate promotion of obscurantism using the mass media.[126] However, this popular but naive suspicion failed to take account of how diverse the factors were which influenced production of discourse in the media. The official science bureaucracies in both the Soviet and post-Soviet periods were fairly flat-footed, and it was not until the second half of the 1990s that the Russian Academy of Sciences got its act together to demarcate science from pseudoscience and combat the latter.[127]

There were many causes underlying the increased interest in the paranormal which began in 1990. These included developments within the crumbling institutes of the Russian Academy of Sciences, other state academies and universities which enabled alternative science and mysticism to emerge triumphantly from the underground. Strange textbooks were written, and Ph.D. dissertations in physics, chemistry and philosophy were devoted to paranormal topics. Issue No. 3 (1992) of the Physics series of *Proceedings of the Universities*, for example, is a special edition devoted to anomalous phenomena.[128] Alternative science in Russia was not outside the body of mainstream science but born within or parallel to it. It deployed the same discursive strategies and, unlike religion, appealed not to faith but to reason. Its explanations were rational, its conclusions based on evidence apparently obtained using the methods of science.

In the 1960s and 1970s a revolution occurred in the Western understanding of scientific epistemology, sociology and the methodology of science. An American sociologist, Robert K. Merton, demonstrated the impact social norms have on the production of scientific knowledge, their contingency on the social behaviour of scientists, their status and the

126. Petr Trevogin, SMI *propagandiruiut mrakobesie*, Radio Petersburg, 29 June, 2000; http://www.humanism.al.ru/ru/debate.phtml?date=2000.06.29
127. In November 1998, a special commission to combat pseudoscience was established with the support of Academician Yuriy Osipov, President of the Russian Academy of Sciences. See Eduard Krugliakov, *Doklad Komissii po bor'be s lzhenaukoi i fal'sifikatsiei nauchnykh issledovanii na prezidiume RAN 16 marta 1999*; http://www.philosophy.nsc.ru/journals/philscience/5_99/10_ KRUG.htm. The commission's findings were addressed not only to the Academy of Sciences but also to the government.
128. For information about the series, see http://www.ntl.tomskinvest.ru/site_content. php?itemID=457

prestige of the organisations for which they work, as well as the political, economic and cultural environment.[129] That scientific research cannot be understood solely in terms of methodology, without reference to its social, cultural and psychological dimensions, had been argued by such theoreticians as Ludwik Fleck,[130] Thomas Kuhn[131] and Paul Feyerabend. Already in the 1930s, Fleck had written that scientific "facts" are products of the social environment, of certain "thought styles" characteristic of a particular scientific collective, and not a flawless reflection of objective reality.[132] His ideas were only appreciated much later, with the publication of papers by Kuhn and Feyerabend. In the late 1970s, Feyerabend formulated the concept of methodological anarchism, or pluralism, stating, "People in the distant past knew very well that attempts at rationalist investigation of the world have limits and yield incomplete knowledge."[133] Feyerabend believed that understanding this provided an opportunity to free the thinking of scientists from dogmas and prejudices which impeded the process of scientific enquiry.

The problem was, however, that differentiating science from pseudo-science and demarcating robust boundaries between different types of intellectual activity[134] were integral parts of the institution of science.[135] These were essential ideological efforts if scientists were to achieve their goal of enhancing their authority and advancing their careers, denying

129. Robert K. Merton, "The Matthew Effect in Science, II: Cumulative Advantage and the Symbolism of Intellectual Property", *ISIS*, 79 (1988), pp. 606–23.

130. Ludwik Fleck et al., *Genesis and Development of a Scientific Fact* (Chicago, 1981).

131. Thomas S. Kuhn, *The Structure of Scientific Revolutions* (Chicago, 1962).

132. Ludwik Fleck, "Zur Krise der 'Wirklichkeit'", *Die Naturwissenschaften*, 17 (1929), pp. 425–30.

133. Paul K. Feyerabend, Introduction to *Wider den Methodenzwang* (German edition of *Against Method*) (Frankfurt, 1980).

134. Thomas F. Gieryn, "Boundary-work and the Demarcation of Science from Non-science: Strains and Interests in Professional Ideologies of Scientists", *American Sociological Review*, 48/6 (1983), pp. 781–95.

135. For a list of 138 works combating pseudoscience, see V. P. Kaznacheev, ed., *Nauka protiv antinauki: Bibliografiia 1986–2004* (Moscow, 1990). A title by Sergey Vronsky has been included by mistake; http://prometeus.nsc.ru/biblio/spravka/antisci.ssi

"pseudoscientists" access to resources and defending the autonomy of research from political interference. The boundaries are drafted and redrawn, shifting during the course of history and becoming ambiguous, the criteria of comparison evolving in the light of circumstances.[136] From time to time, experiments in redrawing or doing away with boundaries lead to public controversy around the ethics of science and the meaning of the word *scientific*. Relevant notable examples were, firstly, a hoax article published by Alan Sokal in 1996 in *Social Text*, a postmodernist journal, and described in his co-authored book, *Fashionable Nonsense: Postmodern Intellectuals' Abuse of Science*.[137] The second instance was the Bogdanov Brothers Affair, which purported to show a similar lack of academic rigour in certain French physics periodicals in 2001–2.[138]

Science is never based solely on rational explanation. It cannot exist without trust and indeed faith in certain facts or evidence. The rationalisation of modern urban life engenders faith in unchallengeable scientific and technological progress, but modern scientific knowledge has an institutional dimension. There are two problems here, the first related to the fact that in the functioning of "normal" science a role is played by populism and sensations based on debatable, not fully verified sources. Individuals

136. The situation is further complicated if official bodies appear not to be respecting the boundaries they are supposed to defend. The website of the psychic Grigoriy Grabovoy is festooned with scanned certificates and diplomas conferred not only by the exotic academies one might expect but also (seemingly) by the National Commission of Attestation of the Ministry of Education and Science of the Russian Federation. His website displays certificates purporting to show that in April 1999 he was awarded the degree of Doctor of Technological Science and, two months later, that of Doctor of Physics and Mathematics. If the certificates are to be believed, the commission appears also to have awarded him the title of Professor of Safety of Highly Complex Objects and Professor of Analytical Equipment and Systems of Structural Analysis. Grabovoy's website can be viewed at http://www.grigori-grabovoi.ru/sertif/index.htm
137. Alan Sokal and Jean Bricmont, *Fashionable Nonsense: Postmodern Intellectuals' Abuse of Science* (New York, 1999).
138. Richard Monastersky, "French TV Stars Rock the World of Theoretical Physics", *Chronicle of Higher Education*, 5 November, 2002; http://chronicle.com/free/2002/11/2002110501n.htm

with official status who occupy key positions in the academic hierarchy become fountainheads of error. Russian examples include the experiments and supposed discoveries of the likes of Olga B. Lepeshinskaya in embryology or Trofim Lysenko in genetics, along with the proponents of torsion fields and alternative hypotheses about the nature of superconductivity. They can spawn whole schools on the periphery of disciplines which the scholarly community at best views askance and at worst considers to be mere pseudoscience and charlatanism. Examples are the "new historical chronology" of Academician Anatoly Fomenko (which postulates a vast mediaeval empire centred on Russia, encompassing almost the whole of Europe and Asia, and dismisses all evidence to the contrary as forgery); bioenergetics; the search for universal mathematical equations which would explain everything in the world; the search for living dinosaurs and primates generally believed to be extinct; and the quest for Shambhala (an undiscovered ancient super-civilisation in the Altai Mountains, Tibet or the Gobi Desert).

The second problem is the relationship between governments and science. The view taken by ruling regimes of the political acceptability of academic disciplines varies from one epoch to another, from one discipline to another. This demonstrates the uncertainty and imprecision attending any attempt to draw a universally valid distinction between official and unofficial science, science and parascience. The most striking Russian examples have been the vagaries in the reputation of cybernetics and genetics, both now regarded as wholly legitimate but, in the mid-twentieth century, declared pseudosciences in the U.S.S.R. Against that, in Hitler's Germany, astrology, kabbalism and searching for the mystical centres of the spiritual energy of Aryans were officially approved of and considered legitimate.[139] The authoritarian Soviet regime encouraged research into

139. Hitler talked about "Nordic National Socialist science which stands opposed to Jewish-liberal science". The former was esotericism, which justified everything the Nazis were doing on earth by reference to celestial events. See Louis Pauwels and Jacques Bergier, The Dawn of Magic (London, 1963).

aspects of cytology, botany and eugenics which today are acknowledged to have been nonsensical.[140]

It is no longer a state secret that in the 1970s research was conducted deep in the recesses of the military-industrial complexes of both the U.S.S.R. and the U.S. into paranormal phenomena.[141] Even today the Ministry of Emergency Situations and the Ministry of Defence of the Russian Federation support research in astrology. The institutional boundaries of science are constantly being redrawn under the influence of an ever-changing configuration of legitimising bodies: the scientific community and its various interest groups; outside bodies such as the regime, the media and publishers; consumers of forecasting and other scientific services; social and religious organisations; businesses; and, last but not least, public opinion.

---

140. See Oleg Shishkin, *Sekretnye eksperimenty* (Moscow, 2003) about the "Russian Franken-stein" (Professor Ilya I. Ivanov), who in the 1920s attempted to cross human beings with apes; Sergey Voronov's rejuvenation projects involving the grafting of apes' testicular tissue on to human testes; and other "secret Kremlin experiments"; http://lib.rus.ec/b/199211. On the context of these experiments and subsequent scientific discussion, see Kirill O. Rossiianov, "Opasnye sviazi: I.I. Ivanov i opyty skreshchivaniia cheloveka s chelovekoobraznymi obez'ianami", *Voprosy istorii estestvoznaniia i tekhniki*, 1 (2006); http://vivovoco.rsl.ru/vv/papers/ecce/ivapitek.htm
141. On the Soviet development of "psychotechnologies" for the economy and for military purposes, see an interview with Yuriy Malinin, a former K.G.B. officer and consultant to the Federal Security Service under Yeltsin, in "Kremlevskikh ekstrasensov otpravili v otstavku", *Komsomol'skaia pravda*, 5 January, 2005; an interview with Boris Ratnikov, princi-pal adviser to the Security Service of the President of Russia and to the head of the Federal Security Service, in Sergei Ptichkin, "Chekisty skanirovali mysli Madlen Olbrait", *Rossii-skaia gazeta*, Weekend Issue, 4254, 22 December, 2006. Inspired by the K.G.B.'s experi-ments on telekinesis, American intelligence agencies in the 1960s allocated $20 million to the Stargate programme, work on which continued until 1980. See "Pseudoscience intelli-gence studies", 2003; http://www.answers.com/topic/pseudoscience-intelligence-stud-ies. On attempts to develop paranormal weapons in the U.S., see W. Adam Mandelbaum, *The Psychic Battlefield: A History of the Military-Occult Complex* (New York, 2000); David A. Morehouse, *Psychic Warrior: Inside the C.I.A.'s Stargate Program: The True Story of a Soldier's Espi-onage and Awakening* (New York, 1996). On developments in the U.S.S.R., see Sheila Ostran-der and Lynn Schroeder, *Psychic Discoveries Behind the Iron Curtain* (Englewood Cliffs, 1970).

SOCIETY, SCIENCE, AND PSEUDOSCIENCE

Commentators on the explosion of public interest in alternative science offer a variety of explanations. Some blame the Soviet education system for failing to provide citizens with intellectual defences against scams and quackery. Soviet Marxism, unlike Marxist movements abroad, did not encourage critical thinking, emphasising legitimation of the institutions and values of the status quo. Others suggest that the collapse of Communist ideology (which Pitirim Sorokin describes as a secular religion) left a spiritual vacuum, anomie and a sense of desolation which was addressed not only by various religious institutions but also by a proliferation of unscientific models of the world.

Both these viewpoints are perfectly sound, but it was the new openness and market orientation of the media which made possible widespread dissemination of ideas that had recently been marginal, semi-clandestine and known only to oppositionally inclined intellectuals. The collapse of the monopolising materialistic, scientistic mentality took place in the context of the fall of the Iron Curtain, and the formerly banned ideas which now flooded in were not only liberal and democratic notions. Boris Dubin observes:

> In Russia during the 1990s the public sphere, controversy, the rudiments of a public language developed in clusters around the semantic deficits and failures of the previous era and of earlier decades of Soviet life. There were different concepts of society ("liberalism", "democracy", "totalitarianism"); issues of national self-determination; the topic of memory, history which had been experienced firsthand and responsibility; the historical relativism (and conditioning) of values, norms and canons; the notion of everyday life as a less value-rich version of culture; a new confrontation of the mass of the population and the elite, and the issue of the place of success and money in a culture; concepts

related to religion and such other belief systems current in today's Russia as magic, occultism and ritualism.[142]

Many aberrations, recognised as such in democratic societies, were newly available and welcomed.[143] By 1990, the intellectual ground in Russia had been prepared for a massive expansion of alternative doctrines. Representatives of organisations and schools of this ilk arrived to check out the situation, and there followed a great influx of new teachings and a revival of forgotten arts. From the late 1980s on, the management of the Moscow Ventilation Factory was in close contact with foreign management consultants who were adepts of the Church of L. Ron Hubbard, the founder of Scientology, which several European countries had classified as a totalitarian sect (although a number of other countries officially recognised it as a religious organisation).[144] Hubbard's books were subsequently published in Russia in enormous editions, and the practice of business consultancy based on his ideas became widely accepted.

Hubbardism, scientology and businesses specialising in astrological prediction, UFOlogy, and extrasensory perception are no less a product of West European rationalism than astronomy, the discovery of genes and

142. Boris Dubin, "Mezhdu kanonom i aktual'nost'iu, skandalom i modoi: literatura i izdatel'skoe delo v Rossii v izmenivshemsia sotsial'nom prostranstve", *Neprikosnovennyi zapas*, 4 (30) (2003); http://magazines.russ.ru/nz/2003/4/dubin.html
143. Sergei Filatov and Dmitrii Furman, "Religiia i politika v massovom soznanii", *Sotsiologicheskie issledovaniia*, 7 (1992), pp. 3–12. The authors note a sharp increase in 1990–91 in the number of people identifying themselves as believers, a move towards Russian Orthodoxy and its political derivative of "reactionary romantic authoritarianism". They suggest that this can largely be ascribed to the state of ethical uncertainty during the early democratic reforms and the insubstantiality of Russian democracy, which easily degenerated into anarchy. This motivated people to embrace clearly defined and/or authoritarian meta-narratives.
144. "Saientologiia – 'vedushchaia religiia' ili 'destruktivnaia sekta'?", *Regnum.ru News Agency*, 1 June, 2005; http://www.regnum.ru/news/463516.html; Richard Behar, "The Thriving Cult of Greed and Power", *Time Magazine*, 6 May, 1991, p. 50; "France Urged to Ban Scientology", B.B.C. News, 8 February, 2000; http://news.bbc.co.uk/1/hi/world/europe/635986.stm. An empirical study of the effects of Scientology on the transformation of management of enterprises is Veronika Kabalina *et al.*, "Capitalism and Scientology", in Simon Clarke, ed., *The Russian Enterprise in Transition* (Cheltenham, 1996), pp. 125–247.

THE IRRATIONAL IN SOCIETY: DIAGNOSES OF 1990

nuclear power. Opinion poll data suggest that in the U.S. and Europe belief in pseudoscience grew strongly during the 1990s and at the beginning of the third millennium, before declining somewhat between 2001 and 2005. This parallels similar measures of public opinion in Russia. Data from surveys and focus groups confirm that faith in astrology and irrational explanatory models does not correlate directly with marginalisation and lack of education of respondents, but is distributed over very varied social groups in towns, cities and villages.[145] Grigoriy Kertman believes that adherence to popular astrology is a symptom of modernisation, a rationalist strategy to identify optimal behaviour in a high-risk, unpredictable environment.[146]

Coming back to 1990, we see that Soviet citizens' sense of uncertainty was aggravated by the lack of consensus about which knowledge was scientific and which unscientific. The discord among the experts left people bewildered, and the policy of popular science magazines made things worse. Their editors wanted, on the one hand, to hold their readers' interest and attention, while on the other they wanted to be seen as responsible and respectable channels for scientific information. We can see the results in a 1990 issue of *Science and Life*, where the reader is first told that homeopathy is pseudoscience,[147] only to find the following article presenting empirical evidence in support of the view that homeopathy is scientifically legitimate, complete with references to facts and clinical trials.[148] One of the most heated discussions of 1990 was over the scientific credentials of astrology. Of 101 publications between 1960 and 1992 which debated the scientific status of astrology, the highest number (37 items) appeared in 1990.[149]

A curious response from Soviet philosophers to the popular interest in unexplained phenomena was a collection of essays brought out by the

145. Liudmila Vorontsova *et al.*, "Religiia v sovremennom massovom soznanii", *Sotsiologicheskie issledovaniia*, 11 (1995), pp. 81–91.

146. Grigorii Kertman, "Astrologiia v massakh – mezhdu prikolom i kul'tom", *Sotsiologicheskie nabliudeniia (2002–2004)* (Moscow, 2005).

147. A. Uspenskii, "O gomeopatii i allopatii", *Nauka i zhizn'*, 1 (1990), pp. 80–83.

148. A. Vozianov *et al.*, "Perspektivy gomeopatii nachinaiut proiasniat'sia", in *Ibid.*, pp. 84–6.

149. *Astrologiia: Sueverie ili nauka? (Otechestvennaia literatura 1960–1992 gg.)*, Comp. I.G. Yudina; http://www.prometeus.nsc.ru/biblio/cards/astro.ssi

official Politizdat publishing house under the title *Is Reason Losing Its Way?* [150] In 1990, the most authoritative and "advanced" Soviet philosophers addressed the problem of irrational knowledge and, to some extent, legitimised it as something which "paradoxically meets real social needs".[151] These philosophical articles, read in the context of ideas fashionable at that time, evince a desire to find a way of incorporating the popular fascination with inexplicable phenomena into the system of rational thought, to join together discrepant ways of explaining the world.

STATE TECHNOLOGIES, MASS-MEDIA TECHNOLOGIES

Theodor Adorno in 1953, analysing the content of the astrology column of the *Los Angeles Times*, drew attention to the pseudo-rational nature of certain worldwide phenomena. "It would be a mistake," he argued,

> to call these mass phenomena entirely "irrational", to regard them as completely disconnected from individual and collective ego aims [self-preservation and the striving for personal happiness]. In fact most of them are based on an exaggeration and distortion of such ego aims rather than on their neglect. They function as though rationality of the self-maintaining body politic had grown malignant and therewith threatened to destroy the organism. This malignancy, however, can be demonstrated only after the autopsy . . . Irrationality is not necessarily a force operating outside the range of rationality: it may result from the processes of rational self-preservation "run amuck".[152]

Adorno considered this pattern of interacting rational and irrational forces in modern mass culture, pointing out the subtle and manipulative nature of

150. *Zabluzhdaiushchiisia razum? Mnogoobrazie vnenauchnogo znaniia* (Moscow, 1990).
151. Il'ia Kasavin, "Magiia: ee mnimye otkrytiia i podlinnye tainy", pp. 70, 60.
152. Theodor Adorno, *The Stars Come Down to Earth and Other Essays on the Irrational in Culture*, ed. Stephen Crook (London, 1994), p. 34.

such beliefs and thought patterns and comparing them with Nazi propaganda. He concluded that the astrologer's column supported proto-fascist dependence and social conformism, and that the same principles operated in mainstream products of the "culture industry".

We recall that, even in the 1980s, Soviet society was showing increasing interest in tradition, as evidenced by the activities of movements for the "revival of traditional culture" and a "return to our roots". These were very varied in their politics and popularity. As *Science and Life* wrote in 1990, "[M]any people were having second thoughts and, before reaching for powders and tablets, sought alternative, more straightforwardly physiological remedies aimed not at prosthesis but at restoring physical function. This was an important shift in our contemporaries' psychology."[153] This change in the popular mood coincided with a fashionable interest in mysticism, folk healing[154] and Russian folklore (partly in the youth subculture)[155] which had become evident some time before. It was informed by an intuitive urge to search for new cultural niches and stimulated by the freer flowing of information. The government was selective in which of its publicly proclaimed ideological principles it adhered to, and from the 1960s connived in spreading a Soviet patriotism which appealed directly to irrational beliefs and a sense of roots and Russian soil and which was a version of officially banned Russian nationalism.[156]

153. Petr Gaponiuk and Bella Luk'ianova, "Vechnye retsepty. Iz naslediia vostochnoi i zapadnoi meditsiny", *Nauka i zhizn'*, 6 (1990), p. 26.
154. Vladimir Makanin's novel *The Forerunner* (*Predtecha*) caused a sensation in 1983. It focused less on the controversial issue of folk healing than on the difficulties caused by possessing a "gift". The psychic, Yakushkin, is an ambivalent character. Makanin wrote later, "I had a presentiment, long before Kashpirovsky and his ilk came along. I remember when I first heard about this topic having a strange idea that when those at the top start lying and deceiving, life is so wonderfully arranged that the grassroots protest by giving birth to weird forms of anti-order. Its destructive power may cause those at the top to lie even more." Interview with Andrey Maksimov on the TV show *Night Flight* (*Nochnoi polet*).
155. Tat'iana Shchepanskaia, *Simvolika molodezhnoi subkul'tury. Opyt etnograficheskogo issledovaniia sistemy. 1986–1989 gg.* (St Petersburg, 1993).
156. See Nikolai Mitrokhin, *Russkaia partiia: dvizhenie russkikh natsionalistov v SSSR. 1953–1985 gody* (Moscow, 2003).

The return to Russia's roots after years of Bolshevik "forward looking", suppression and denial of tradition and religion often entailed a return to nationalism. This was fed by the writings of a school of village prose writers, the *derevenshchiki*. It became institutionalised in the 1980s in various conservative-leaning heritage preservation societies and, in the 1990s, in fully fledged political parties and official organisations. These were permitted to indulge not merely in anti-American rhetoric but in the preaching of openly racist "blood and land" ideology.[157] The discourse of a return to historical roots and spiritual values of a particular people was in opposition to the dusty supranational Soviet traditions which were supposedly "identical in content but national in form". However, the same rhetorical clichés can be used by both sides in polemics, and even much later supporters of "genuine science and common sense", opposing the "well-organised predictions of false prophets" and the "promotion of obscurantism", write in the idiom of conspiracy theory about machinations of the secret services and the inculcation of irrationalism as a "deliberate policy of intellectual genocide of the Russian people".[158]

Be that as it may, the media industry is interested primarily in what sells, what people want to read, and what creates a buzz, raises circulation figures and generates profits. This leads to accusations against the media and unregulated book publishing of "systematically duping a significant section of our people".[159] The main characteristics of the new media were not only openness, a critical attitude and democratic credentials. The previous loyalty to principles dictated from above was replaced, as is typical of mass culture, by dependence on the consumer, entertainment value, standardisation, commercialised mass production, a focus on mass distribution and open or covert propaganda in favour of the current conventional way of life. This led to a passive, uncritical attitude and development of a

157. Aleksandr Ianov, *Posle El'tsina. "Veimarskaia" Rossiia* (Moscow, 1995).
158. Trevogin, *SMI propagandiruiut mrakobesie*; http://www.humanism.al.ru/ru/debate.phtml?date=2000.06.29
159. Eduard Krugliakov, *Doklad Komissii po bor'be s lzhenaukoi i fal'sifikatsiei nauchnykh issledovanii na prezidiume RAN 16 marta 1999*.

personality type highly susceptible to manipulation.[160]

This is a culture industry which aims to delineate the boundaries of loyalty as against activism, reconciling the needs and opportunities of the average member of the modern middle class. "In astrology, for example," Roland Barthes tells us, "ill luck is always followed by equal good luck; they are always predicted in a prudently compensatory perspective; a final equilibrium immobilises values, life, destiny, etc: one no longer needs to choose but only to endorse."[161]

In 1990, as Russia moved towards becoming a free market society, the irrational did broaden people's intellectual horizons after decades of dogmatic dialectical materialism. It was one way to free them from closed thinking. As capitalist relations developed and increased social inequality, the irrational became part of an ideological environment, reflecting social and cultural changes. Astrological predictions in glossy magazines had a different look and served a different purpose from horoscopes in free newspapers handed out in the metro. A system has developed out of oppositional trends of the past, out of the deeply personal spiritual questing of intense individuals, out of once clandestine movements, which is now an integral part of market institutions, politics, the regime, and sometimes even of education and science. It is a system which exploits the passivity and uncritical thinking this type of knowledge encourages, and nowadays it works to entrench the status quo rather than to challenge it.

The year 1990 was a milestone in the transformation of Soviet rationality. One era came to an end and another began. Alongside the scientistic Soviet model which had taken root over decades, a broad spectrum of sometimes

160. See Ol'ga Aksiutina, "DIY pank-kul'tura kak fenomen molodezhnoi kontrkul'tury v postsovetskom prostranstve", in Igor' Kondakov, ed., *Sovremennye transformatsii rossiiskoi kul'tury* (Moscow, 2005), pp. 564–603. See also Edward S. Herman and Noam Chomsky, *Manufacturing Consent: The Political Economy of the Mass Media* (New York, 1988).
161. Roland Barthes, "Myth Today", in his *Mythologies*, trans. Annette Lavers (New York, 1973).

mutually exclusive models of the world became firmly established in the popular press and the minds of ordinary Russians. The surge of interest in the supernatural in the 1990s was a product of glasnost and press freedom when state censorship, which had been the monopoly regulator of the media and the instrument for inculcating ideological principles, was taken out of the equation. Mavericks who previously had been able to express their views only within a narrow circle of people they could trust, or through *samizdat*, were suddenly given a public platform. Marginalised trends like occultism, mysticism and other "spiritual practices" were able to emerge from the underground and redefine their status. A plethora of viewpoints and philosophies now reached a wider public, including some stridently at variance with official science. Discourses competed in a way previously unimaginable, and the post-Soviet citizen proved as eager as his Western counterparts to abandon the broad highway of academic science for the narrow, twisting paths of alternative doctrines founded on new and eccentric-seeming courses of treatment, approaches to dealing with problems, and ways of understanding oneself, society and nature.

The main cause was not a badly educated public, let down by Soviet and post-Soviet schools and colleges. It was not disenchantment with dialectical or historical materialism leading people to turn from scientistic philosophy to mysticism. It was not even the social exclusion of a considerable segment of the Russian population which, in a time of traumatic changes in values and culture, was living in a climate of uncertainty and disorientation. No doubt, anomie and disillusionment did at first play a part in stimulating interest in previously taboo or semi-taboo topics. However, the real cause was a long-term trend in the organisation of social rationality, a pluralisation of legitimate social discourse. This tended to reduce the power of academic science, increased competition between different approaches to interpreting society and the natural world, and opened the way to explanations recently considered parascientific or absurd.

In the U.S.S.R., several generations were indoctrinated to have unquestioning faith in the omnipotence of science, in vast scientific projects,

138

from making the rivers of Siberia run backwards to the conquest of the moon or Mars. Now the new cosmopolitan rationality of the emerging Russian middle class (like that of Americans, Germans and the British) cheerfully accommodates familiarity with the achievements of modern technology with reading horoscopes on the back page of an illustrated magazine. Legitimisation of the irrational has become part of the post-Soviet value system, an unanticipated side effect of free speech, democratisation and the emancipation of society from sterile ideology. At the same time it has shown potential as a bridgehead for relaunching authoritarian thinking, nostalgia for a glorious past and the searchings of grassroots nationalism.

APRIL

1 April

Last week, air traffic controllers of Nalchik squadron observed a U.F.O. for twenty-three minutes (*Izvestiia*, 92, p. 4).

2 April

Party publications across the country are rapidly losing circulation, and there are the beginnings of a mass exodus of journalists. By the end of 1990, 50 per cent of the staff of *Leningradskaya Pravda* had been made redundant. Some found jobs at *Neva Times*, a newspaper recently established by the Leningrad City Soviet (*Noveishaia istoriia otechestvennogo kino*).

A unique reading room opens at the Krestovsky Island library in Leningrad, giving readers access to such formerly restricted books as the works of Vladimir Voinovich, Aleksandr Zinoviev, Vasiliy Klyuchevsky, Lev Kopelev, Leon Trotsky and Nikolai Berdyaev, and the periodicals *Kontinent*, *The Country and the World*, *Facets* (*Grani*), *Third Wave* and *Russian Renaissance* (*Izvestiia*, 93, p. 3). "A phone call from the Leningrad Department of Literature and Publishing to the Reserved Collections of the Academy of Sciences Library advised that all the works of Leon Trotsky were to be reclassified for general access" (Kseniia Liutova, *Spetskhran Biblioteki Akademii nauk: Iz istorii sekretnykh fondov* [St Petersburg, 1999]).

5 April

"Activities of any association of citizens, including political parties, public organisations and mass movements aimed at inciting national or racial hostility, hatred or disrespect, the use of violence on ethnic, racial or religious grounds, and also activities directly aiming to forcibly undermine the integrity of the U.S.S.R. as defined by the U.S.S.R. Constitution, of union and autonomous republics, autonomous provinces and regions, is illegal and punishable by law" (*Izvestiia*, 96, p. 1).

6 April

Publication of a new law, passed on 3 April by the U.S.S.R. Supreme Soviet, regulating secession of union republics from the U.S.S.R.: "A decision to secede from the U.S.S.R. is taken by the people of the union republic freely expressing its will in a referendum. The decision to hold a referendum rests with the Supreme Soviet of the union republic, on its own initiative or upon receipt of a request signed by one-tenth of the Soviet citizens permanently residing in the territory of the republic and entitled to vote under the laws of the U.S.S.R."

7 April

Izvestiya reports that the economy continued to decline in March. Manufacturing of goods has fallen by 1.6 per cent in comparison with March of last year (*Izvestiia*, 98, p. 1).

Galina Vishnevskaya, Mstislav Rostropovich, Chingiz Aitmatov, Yuriy Afanasiev, Metropolitan Pitirim, Mufti Muhammad Sodiq Muhammad Yusuf, Vladimir Tsvetkov, Nikolai Shmelyov and Marshal Aleksandr Silantiev become trustees of the international charity Eternal Remembrance of Soldiers (established in December 1989). The foundation will collect information about locations where soldiers are buried, ensuring the provision of dignified graves and memorials, and that they are properly maintained, cared for and available for visiting by citizens of all nations (*Moskovskii komsomolets*, 80, p. 4).

9 April

Deputy Chairman of the U.S.S.R. Council of Ministers Leonid Abalkin holds a conference about transition of the Soviet economy to a regulated market model. Asked at what level the decision was taken, Abalkin replies that the government is an executive body which can propose measures but ultimately only implement decisions of the Supreme Soviet. The Politburo of the Communist Party no longer takes, and would never again take, decisions of this kind. The only possible pattern of decision-making is: the President – Parliament – the Congress of People's Deputies of the U.S.S.R. (*Izvestiia*, 101, p. 1).

A law "Concerning general principles of local self-government and local administration in the U.S.S.R." introduces "normal" local self-government to replace the binary system of soviets and Party committees, under which the former were in reality wholly subordinate to the latter.

The Georgian flag is flown at half-mast as a sign of mourning. The republic commemorates the tragic events in Tbilisi in April 1989, when a violent crackdown in the city centre by assault and interior ministry troops killed, according to various estimates, between sixteen and twenty-three people. Hundreds were wounded or affected by tear gas. A protest demonstration outside the headquarters of the Transcaucasian Military District demands withdrawal of Soviet troops from Georgia. This is followed by a rally many thousands strong at the central stadium, where there are calls for restoration of Georgia's independence (*Moskovskie novosti*, 15, p. 4).

10 April

Mikhail Gorbachev receives the British Foreign Secretary, Douglas Hurd. Gorbachev notes that, despite some problems, Soviet–British relations are basically satisfactory. On one issue, the future of Germany, Gorbachev mentions a recent telephone conversation with Prime Minister Margaret Thatcher and a letter recently received. The position of both countries is, he says, quite close. At the same time, he explains in considerable detail why the U.S.S.R. would consider it unacceptable for a reunified Germany to join N.A.T.O. (*Pravda*, 11 April, p. 1).

11 April

A rally in support of Telman Gdlyan and Nikolai Ivanov in Moscow is attended by about twenty thousand people. Placards urge, "Muscovites and Leningraders! Stand up for your people's deputies!"; "Put the bribe-takers, not the investigators, behind bars!" (*Moskovskii komsomolets*, 85, p. 3). The then Public Prosecutor Aleksandr Sukharev had signed a finding of the Public Prosecutor's Office recommending to himself a criminal investigation and the bringing of charges against Gdlyan and Ivanov, the Public Prosecutor's Office's own serious fraud investigators.

Leningrad meeting in support of Gdlyan and Ivanov, 17 April 1990

An agreement is signed in Moscow between the U.S.S.R. and PepsiCo. By the year 2000 there are plans to build twenty-six plants in the U.S.S.R. for the manufacture of Pepsi-Cola (*Izvestiia*, 102, p. 6).

11–12 April

Eduard Shevardnadze holds talks with Douglas Hurd on European issues. He confirms that the U.S.S.R. favours integrating the reunification of Germany with a positive evolution of Europe, with new security arrangements replacing the confrontation of military blocs. An important element would be a centre to forestall the risk of war in Europe, as proposed by the

U.S.S.R. and supported by several European countries (*Izvestiia*, 11 and 12 April, pp. 1, 3).

13 April

Mikhail Gorbachev meets Wojciech Jaruzelski, President of the Republic of Poland. Both sides emphasise the moral importance of clarifying the circumstances of the death in the Second World War of Polish officers from the Kozelsk, Starobelsk and Ostashkov concentration camps. Papers recently found by Soviet historians suggest that the blame lay with the U.S.S.R.'s Lavrentiy Beria and his henchmen. "We express deep sympathy for the Polish people, families and friends of the victims," Gorbachev says. "Some of our own Soviet people were also killed there, in Katyn. It is our shared tragedy" (*Pravda*, 15 April, p. 1). On the declassifying and reclassifying of documents on Katyn, see Aleksandr Melenberg, "Ne otdadim Katyn'! Ugolovnoe delo prekrashcheno. Dokumenty zasekrecheny", *Novaia gazeta*, 10 (21 March), 2005; http://2005.novayagazeta.ru/nomer/2005/20n/n20n-s27.shtml

15 April

A Leningrad television programme on the night of 6 April shows video materials lasting more than three hours, filmed during Gdlyan and Ivanov's investigation of corruption. In an interview with *Moscow News*, Gdlyan observes that "this broadcast is a breakthrough in an information blackout around us which has lasted almost a year and a half. Tens of millions of our fellow citizens have, for the first time, had an opportunity on the basis of documentary evidence to decide for themselves how much truth there is in the accusations levelled against us. The information we have suggests that the vast majority of viewers who saw the broadcast are now on our side. In spite of all the harassment and defamation, I feel that most people do now trust us" (*Moskovskie novosti*, 15, p. 6).

The staff of the Lenin Library in Moscow were so zealous in performing their task of "ideological guidance" as to what Soviet people read that they had little time left to work on the library's unique holdings, or even to conserve them. Such is the conclusion delivered by a group of independent experts to the cultural commission of the U.S.S.R. Supreme Soviet. The experts found that the library staff constantly reduced the number of people allowed to read there and put obstacles in the way of those wanting to work with manuscripts, especially if they wanted to publish them (*Moskovskie novosti*, 15, p. 2).

16 April

The tax office formed several years earlier is given powers analogous to those of similar services abroad. It is proposed to create a unified Soviet revenue service (*Izvestiia*, 107, p. 2).

17 April

Having exhausted the possibilities of legislative warfare, Moscow resorts to economic sanctions against Lithuania. Economists calculate that leaving the U.S.S.R. would cost the republic $33 billion. Vytautas Landsbergis proposes negotiating a transition period with the U.S.S.R.'s leaders, but Gorbachev demands immediate rescinding of the Declaration of Independence. When Landsbergis refuses, Moscow institutes an economic blockade, cutting off all supplies of oil and natural gas (which provide 95 per cent of Lithuania's energy). The republic's Cabinet of Ministers sets up an anti-blockade commission headed by Algirdas Brazauskas, who, drawing on old contacts, obtains direct shipments of fuel by bartering with other union republics (*Noveishaia istoriia otechestvennogo kino*).

The Association of Book Publishers of Russia is founded.

The U.S.S.R. resolves to join the International Criminal Police Organisation (Interpol) (*Izvestiia*, 17 April).

18 April

There is heated discussion at a meeting of the U.S.S.R. Supreme Soviet considering the case of Gdlyan and Ivanov. People's Deputy Nikolai Tutov attempts to read a message from them to the meeting, but is prevented from doing so (*Izvestiia*, 109, p. 1).

The Supreme Soviet resolves to reject the Public Prosecutor's request to remove the immunity from prosecution of People's Deputies Gdlyan and Ivanov, but, due to the impossibility of their continuing to work in the Prosecutor's Office, agrees to their dismissal from his staff (*Izvestiia*, 110, p. 1).

19 April

The new Nicaraguan government (which replaced the Sandinistas after free elections in February) agrees a ceasefire with the Contras, thus ending the most vicious civil conflict of the 1980s.

A Museum of Psychophysics and Parapsychology opens in Moscow (*Moskovskii komsomolets*, 90, p. 1). It continues to exist as the Museum of Parapsychology until 2002, after which it seems to vanish.

20 April

A presidential decree requires permission to be obtained from the U.S.S.R. Council of Ministers before rallies and demonstrations can be held within the area bounded by the Sadovaya Moscow Ring Road (*Noveishaia istoriia otechestvennogo kino*).

A commemorative evening to mark the 120th anniversary of the birth of Lenin is held at the Bolshoy Theatre. Gorbachev says, "Defending Lenin is not worshipping a god. When we defend Lenin, we are paying tribute to what has been created by generations of Soviet people; we defend our present quest and our socialist future" (*Izvestiia*, 112, p. 1).

22 April

"Reports of sightings of UFOs in the skies above Moscow are being received almost daily by the Soyuz U.F.O. Centre. They seem to be taking a particular interest in the area around the Altufiev Highway" (*Moskovskii komsomolets*, 93, p. 1.)

24 April

At the National Tourist Club, a symposium is organised by Apple Computers and Interproject, a joint venture company. Its purpose is to identify the market for Macintosh computers in the U.S.S.R., and to set up a users' club (*Moskovskii komsomolets*, 94, p. 1).

28 April

In the election for First Secretary of the Leningrad provincial Party committee, 610 of the 1,007 delegates vote to reappoint Boris Gidaspov (*Izvestiia*, 119, p. 2).

30 April

Nobel Prize-winning author Aleksandr Solzhenitsyn is donating all royalties from Soviet publications of his books, approximately 2 million roubles, to the Russian Orthodox Church's fund for restoration of the Solovki Monastery [formerly a prison camp] (*Izvestiia*, 121, p. 4).

In Novokuznetsk, the First Congress of Independent Workers' Movements and Organisations demands the transfer of some of the funds of the Central Trade Union Council of the U.S.S.R. to free trade unions, the removal of all privileges of Party committees in enterprises and institutions, and legal recognition of workers' committees (*Argumenty i Fakty*, 17, p. 1).

THE SHOCK OF IRREVOCABILITY

Hasan Guseynov

My memories of 1990 were quite different from how I have now, sixteen years later, found it to have been after reading documents, memoirs, published diaries and poems written at the time. Even then, however, it was recognised as a pivotal moment. The year 1990 was the penultimate year of the existence of the Soviet Union and of Russia within its old borders. The first issue of *Moscow News*, published on 7 January, 1990, offered forecasts for the coming year, accompanied by analytical commentary. My own prediction began, "Let us mention first what is least agreeable, the disintegration of what is territorially the largest country in the modern world. Symptomatic of this are the mass national movements with their accompanying violence, and the emerging national differentiation within the Communist Party." I seem to have got that right, in that within two years the U.S.S.R. had ceased to exist, but am embarrassed to have depersonalised the historical reality of violence perpetrated by one human being against another, and to have anthropomorphised the state. That unconscious slip strikes me now as crucial, pointing as it does to a breaking of the link between the active and passive groups of the population, and within the professional class, the fruits of which we are reaping today, in late 2006.

In the same centre spread, *Moscow News* printed a note by Galina Starovoytova on the situation in Nagorno-Karabakh and the then current state of the conflict between Armenia and Azerbaijan. My friendship with Galina was strengthened by our shared conviction that any national group was entitled to self-determination when it came to their political system and how, and on whom, they were dependent. In this case, the issue was the right of the Armenian majority in Nagorno-Karabakh to determine its own future and, if it so chose, to secede from Azerbaijan.

Our differences might seem academic. Starovoytova believed that civil society would be built from an ethnos which had achieved statehood. Denis Dragunsky and I had been thinking through these issues in 1988–90 and had co-authored a book which was published in 1990, only to be swept up in the kind of events it was considering. We felt that Starovoytova was mistaken, and that civil society had to be based on universal, not national, values. Soon, however, demands for "Russian sovereignty" rose to the top of the political agenda, and all doubts were simply swept aside as to whether this nation-state, rising from the ruins of an empire, would be capable of putting the national tradition of oppression behind it. Might the new state not, in fact, exacerbate institutional oppression?

It is important, of course, to be clear about who exactly swept these doubts aside. There are always people who will say, "I warned way back when that nothing would change! Plus ça change!" There were also people who failed to recognise quite how radical the changes were until long after others, more agile, had taken risks and profited from them. Far more interesting are two categories of people from different social strata who responded vigorously to the sudden weakening of the regime. What united them was that they wasted no time or energy interpreting what was happening, but embraced it – sometimes in old age, for the first time in their lives! – as a new reality they had created themselves.

Our first category embarked on a practical reorganisation of property relations, creating new institutions and a new social environment. Some former dissidents gained control of the media and saw business enterprise (which was still being called "the cooperative movement") as a tool for restructuring politics. As opponents of the Soviet system with experience of outright opposition to it, they had no illusions about its ability to reform itself. At first sight paradoxically, they were much more fiercely opposed to Gorbachev and the liberal wing of the Communist Party than to local economic managers and bureaucrats.

The second category consisted mainly of liberal intellectuals who saw the task as being to restructure their personal relations with the system. They wanted to move forward into new times while bringing with them the social assumptions with which they were familiar. They believed that a relatively peaceful transformation of the system was possible. There was, after all, an example of prosperous socialism in Yugoslavia. Few foresaw the consequences of the election in 1990 of Slobodan Milošević as that country's president.

Of course, there were also the individuals with a foot in both camps who founded new educational institutions or created new media and industrial corporations. The protagonists of the political system emerging in 1990 were not to know that quite a few of them would be murdered in the coming decade, but they were already moulding their own future.

The last people I remember meeting in the offices of The Twentieth Century and the World (Vek XX i mir) at the very beginning of 1990 were Mikhail Gefter (1918–1995), Galina Starovoytova (1946–1998) and Gleb Pavlovsky (b. 1951). Each had a unique biography, but what I would like to compare are their public careers, their visible social roles, rather than their political and philosophical views. I hope the comparison will contribute to a better understanding of the state of Russian society in 2006–7. At all events, it is something I need to do in order to clarify where my own misunderstandings were of the political and social events of 1990.

For Mikhail Gefter and Gleb Pavlovsky, this "new thaw" was nothing new. Indeed, Gefter had a sense of déjà vu and tried without great success to view the new reality partly through his own Khrushchev-period lenses, partly in the light of the reconstruction of Europe after the Second World War, and also with the aid of some new tools donated by Pavlovsky. In 1992, Gefter briefly visited Bremen, where I was then working, and told me I had been mistaken in the late 1980s in believing that he was the leader and Pavlovsky the sidekick in their intellectual and political partnership. In terms of historical theory he thought that might have been true, but certainly not in respect of practical politics.

The Historically Active Individuals of Odessa was a group that formed around Pavlovsky in the early 1970s. Just the fact of their existence in the rotten, post-"thaw" U.S.S.R. provided Gefter with political support. Pavlovsky satisfied Gefter's longing to create a school of thought, a think tank that would perform the same role as had more or less been played in the 1960s by the Institute of World History of the U.S.S.R. Academy of Sciences. Most importantly, it was Pavlovsky who ultimately legitimated Gefter's eclectic concept of history. This was not an abstract theory of history, but a practical model for possible future political action.

I did not see that in 1990, and thought the dialogues between Gefter and Pavlovsky about Lenin were pretty tame. The way in which they sought to apply political lessons of the late nineteenth and early twentieth centuries to late Soviet politics struck me as frankly tedious. I recognise now, however, that Gefter was the only person, or at least one of few, who understood that Leninism was still an effective political theory deserving of study. In a 1992 letter recently published in *New Literary Observer*, Mikhail Gasparov writes,

> For me, one of the most memorable moments of the past month was a five-minute televised talk by Mikhail Gefter, a dissident histor- ian who seems to have been published more in Europe than in Russia. It came in a round-up of the week's events, which included the anniversary of Lenin's birth. Gefter, a little old man with a tartan blanket, said, very definitely and seriously, straight into the camera, that pouring scorn on Lenin was not the obvious way to come to terms with our history. He reminded us that in the 1920s, some very important people who were not in the least inclined to Com- munism had said that probably the only other person to have had a comparable impact on history was Jesus Christ.[162]

Just like Gefter's generation, people born in the 1940s and '50s knew for a

162. M.-L. Bott, ed., "'Chitat' menia podriad nikomu ne interesno ...': Pis'ma M. L. Gasparova k Marii-Luize Bott, 1981–2004 gg.", *Novoe Literaturnoe Obozrenie*, 77 (2006), p. 181.

fact that this was the last chance history would give them. This was not because of their age, but because they could feel that a society as unstable as ours in the late 1980s could not continue like that for long, and that when it cooled and hardened, they would do better to be somewhere warm where they had influence. For Starovoytova, this was her first crack of the whip, but for Pavlovsky it was the second. His first "personal perestroika" had come when he had confronted the Soviet system fifteen years earlier. He had seen an aspect of the Soviet regime which was virtually invisible in the late 1980s and early 1990s. Pavlovsky had experience both of the punitive side of the K.G.B. and of relative reconciliation with it. At the end of the 1980s he could regard himself as having won a victory through compromise. Starovoytova came to understand the Soviet system only gradually, deciding policy as she went along. Their different experiences were behind their different approaches.

Although they had differing views about what was happening in Soviet society, in 1990 Starovoytova and Pavlovsky seemed to be saying much the same things about the same country, but the events of the next decade were to show that they disagreed about virtually everything, from Russia's geographical boundaries to the potential of its multi-national population. Starovoytova saw what was happening as a living, mass social movement and was inspired by the hundred thousand-strong Moscow rallies of 1989, to say nothing of the national liberation movements which showed an academic ethnographer a changeable ethnic group coming together from the thousands of details of her research to form a single fire-breathing dragon. She decided she could speak to that dragon over the heads of its old master. Recognising the futility of trying to foist herself on the political establishment as a specialist adviser, Starovoytova decided to take up politics herself. She rapidly rose to become an opposition leader, both in the former Soviet republic of Armenia and in the junior capital of the Soviet Union and Russia, Leningrad-St Petersburg.

We met in the summer of 1991 at a St Petersburg conference on the rights of minorities. Civil war had already broken out on the periphery of the former U.S.S.R. Mastering the art of compromise, Starovoytova relied on Democratic Russia as her political base, but was obliged also to interact with bureaucratic cliques which were viscerally opposed to allowing the public to participate in politics. In 1990, public attention had been focused on the "battle for Gorbachev" between the progressive and populist Yeltsin and the conservative and Party-K.G.B. politicians like Ligachov and Gidaspov. The public that supported Starovoytova did not foresee that Yeltsin and his team would also avail themselves of the old Soviet infrastructure, and that ultimately the decisive force in the regime of the first President of Russia would not be representatives of civil society but rather an agglomeration of K.G.B. agents and newly rich youthful members of the Party and Young Communist League. In 1990, however, Starovoytova and those around her were enthused by the prospects for the growth of civil society.

Pavlovsky for his part appeared to be taken aback by the sheer inertia and sluggishness of "the people" when facing the challenge of the times. I believe he saw little sign of promise in the mass of the population, who had never asked Gorbachev to give them freedom in the first place but in whom Starovoytova was putting her trust. In the tectonic fissures of the U.S.S.R. he saw no sign of material from which the new state could be built. One year later, he would name his anti-hero "Byelovezha Man" – a brain-dead, half-democrat, half-conservative mindlessly repeating vacuous slogans about the "collapse of the empire" without the slightest understanding of its consequences.

A group with the dynamism which Pavlovsky hoped would turn the situation round was indeed found by the end of the 1990s, but not where Starovoytova was looking for it. If we can use the language of discussions which took place in 1999–2000 to talk about 1990, Galina had been relying on popular support of her democratic political aspirations, whereas Gleb doubted it would ever be possible to put together a new people for a new country out of the politically illiterate slime (as it was termed in a debate on the polit.ru Internet forum) of Yeltsin's Byelovezha Man. Perhaps this point of disagreement was in fact the point of no return which ruled out further fruitful debate.

Starovoytova was convinced that the time had come to engage in politics in the U.S.S.R., and that, in the interests of political freedom, old historic institutions could be sacrificed. Pavlovsky loathed the idea of Russia becoming a "normal" country. Looking back, I can see his growing frustration with those who, in the last year of perestroika, were prepared to sacrifice the historic values of the Russian Mir for the sake of universal values of freedom. Pavlovsky had never been a great believer in conspiracy theories but from the early 1990s began to be attracted by the idea of creating a grand conspiracy of his own, a conspiracy to save Russian history and even the empire.

In Russia, the ideology of sovereignty is understood rather in the spirit of Carl Schmitt. Since it stemmed directly from the events of 1990, we shall dwell on it a little longer.

To oversimplify, we can say that the "Starovoytova party", with the support of the liberal-democratic segment of the population, wagered its money on the phantom of civil society and lost. The "Pavlovsky party", on the other hand, sided with energetic statist activists in the bureaucracy, government and media – and enjoyed a tactical success. As Mikhail Gasparov crisply remarked, "The government changed its policy from seeking to create a petty bourgeoisie to seeking to create a haute bourgeoisie." At what cost we shall not consider here.

The media in the 1990s were much more interested in institutional changes than in what was going on in people's minds. This was partly because it was now actually possible to introduce new institutions, from cooperatives to commodity exchanges, to turn the professional high schools into lyceums, and to rebuild the Cathedral of Christ the Saviour, dynamited in 1934, on the site of the Moscow open-air swimming pool. The late Soviet media puzzled over the newly available opinion polls the way a monkey might puzzle over a pair of spectacles. Their response in 1990 to the issue of job discrimination against former collaborators with the totalitarian regime was weak, effectively just going along with the official line. The Yuriy Levada Centre began working just before 1990 on their "*Homo Sovieticus*" project. In 2004, Levada reported in a public lecture on the polit.ru website:

> We found we had been naive, and when we analysed our first project in 1989, it was immediately clear that we had the wrong approach. We needed to take a more dispassionate look at the enthusiasms which were affecting many people, including those taking part in our study. We kept running up against brick walls, the wall of the still existent regime, the wall of the customs of that time and a wall coming from the people themselves. We found that many things which seemed now to be allowed were not being taken advantage of. You seemed to be allowed to be free, and all around people were urging you to be free, and yet there did not seem to be much more freedom than there always had been. What you saw was a lot of hoo-ha around cooperative businesses, a first bout of free market economics with all sorts of bizarre and comical accompaniments. The new free citizen, thoughtful and intelligent, was nowhere to be seen. It seemed rather as if freedom was the freedom to rush backwards, not just to yesterday but to the day before. Our free man reverted to the traditional stereotype and started behaving, not just like a pre-revolutionary Russian but like someone from Russia before the age of Peter the Great.[163]

This was understandable. Facts were surfacing at this time which society was simply not ready to assimilate, which meant that it failed to take advantage of a short interval when the repressive apparatus of the government, and the institutions of the Party and K.G.B. in general, were in a state of confusion and relative powerlessness. This was also affected by the fact that the original democratic, late Soviet segment of society had been

163. http://www.polit.ru/lectures/2004/04/15/levada.html

severely culled. Brezhnev, Chernenko, Andropov and Bobkov had simply crushed the human rights movement in the 1970s and '80s. People who had demonstrated their political maturity by, for example, going to prison for their beliefs, and by being capable of thinking of alternative paths along which the Soviet Union might develop, were heart-breakingly few within the "democratic community" which had just been legalised and given its freedom. On the other hand, there were large numbers of representatives of the so-called "competent agencies" in the movement. These people had failed to fulfil their only direct obligation of ensuring the security of the state to which they had sworn allegiance. In 1990 they were ready to swear allegiance to any gang which looked like coming out on top.

That is why the theft of Soviet state property occurred at such breakneck speed and was so little reported in the media. That was not the result of a deliberate conspiracy, but merely a demonstration of the essence of the Soviet system. When had the Soviet government ever given its citizens advance warning that their savings were about to be wiped out, by the financial reform, say, in 1947 or 1961? Now, in 1990, a free market had been declared! The truth about the plundering of state property by the military, Communist Party and Young Communist League officials for whom it was within easy reach was known only to a narrow circle permitted to engage in "business", men who hunted each other like wild animals. The media heard only distant echoes of what was going on, and journalists who made bold to lift the lid on the proceedings were swiftly dispatched to the next world.

Today, it seems – cynical as it may sound – that a little homeopathic terror did save the late Soviet Union and early post-Soviet Russia from all-out civil war. On the periphery of the U.S.S.R., civil war was indeed being waged under the guise of so-called "ethnic clashes": the war between Armenia and Azerbaijan over Nagorno-Karabakh, the conflicts between Moldova and Transnistria, and in Central Asia. In the context of regional history, these were indeed ethnic conflicts, but in the context of the history of Russia and the U.S.S.R., they were just as much part of the war over the Soviet legacy as the deployment of Soviet tanks to Baku and Vilnius and the halting of oil supplies to Lithuania in the spring of 1990. In terms of Hjalte Tin's typology of civil war, we can categorise the dissolution of the U.S.S.R. in 1991 as termination of a civil war between the armed subjects of a single state over redistribution of administrative and political resources.[164] In Yugoslavia, the efforts of the Serbian leaders and League of Communists to halt the collapse of the federation led to the outbreak of civil war, with subsequent international intervention and the replacement of the federation with a number of independent states.

But to return to the careers of our public figures as the U.S.S.R. began to collapse. In 1990, how did they view the dividing up of the Soviet legacy? Undoubtedly, it was seen, in the context of contemporary world events, as a natural process. Some, but not all, thought that the loss of empire in return for freedom was a fair exchange. The independence of the Baltic states, the subsequent declarations of "independence from the U.S.S.R." by the Russian Federation (on 8 and 12 June), by Uzbekistan (on 20 June), and, only a month later, by Ukraine (on 16 July) were equated with such global acts of nation-building and liberation as the victory of the leaders of the black majorities in Zimbabwe and South Africa, and the reunification of Germany.

We need to remember that much more space was given over to world politics in the Soviet media than later in the 1990s. In the *Moscow News* forecast for 1990, nobody foresaw quite how rapidly the U.S.S.R. would collapse. The conspiracy theories came later. "The shock of the irrevocable loss of the old world order", as Andrey Fadin called it, was only really felt by most people three years later, when, for the foreseeable future, national politics was replaced by infighting within Yeltsin's oligarch-dominated bureaucracy and the seeing off of younger potential rivals. It is possible to show how, slowly at first but then by leaps and bounds (for example, in 1993), national politics became less important and undercover infighting more effective. Politics was to be completely replaced by spin-doctoring only in 1996. In 1990 almost no-one had heard of this buzzword of the mid-1990s.

164. Hjalte Tin, *A Typology of Civil Wars*, Working Papers 1997/12 (Copenhagen, 1997).

The inertia of the U.S.S.R.'s global image as the leader of the socialist transformation of the rest of the world alleviated the "shock of irrevocability" for former Soviet citizens. The awarding of the Nobel Peace Prize in 1990 to Mikhail Gorbachev was symbolic of this. Other symbolic acts which split the late Soviet democrats were the election of Slobodan Milošević as the last president of Yugoslavia and of Lech Wałęsa as the first president of independent Poland. If the "Starovoytova party" believed that behind the figurehead of a new, free Russia there should stand European, Roman Catholic Wałęsa, for the "Pavlovsky party" that shadow should be the socialist and nationalist Milošević, the last hero fighting to save Yugoslavia, mini-successor of the Austro-Hungarian-Ottoman empires.

This fissure had widened by the mid-1990s, when Russian society first had to come to terms with the map of the rest of the world. What did it want, political and economic freedom even at the cost of a rapid shrinking of the Russian state within its present borders, or a state able to restore Russia's greatness but at the cost of reducing some of its citizens' rights and freedoms? In 1990 this question was addressed to all "Soviet people". Later it became merely one of the topics discussed in private exchanges between the state's administrators and dynamic new billionaires. A Third Way would have been an accelerated political convergence of the U.S.S.R. with the West, which was urged by Andrey Sakharov, but alas he died just two weeks short of 1990. After the war in Yugoslavia, the motif of a potential threat from the West was again heard in the debating of Russia's national interest. Was I aware of these dichotomies in 1990? Perhaps not.

The month-by-month chronology in this book is particularly helpful because it lists, not the main events of 1990, but only what was reported in the media at the time. Today it is clear that the media did not by any means report all of the most important events. They did not cover what, in the next decade and a half, would prove crucial for the life of Russia in the aftermath of that collapse. Keeping to the standard news headings of the modern press – politics; economics and technology; finance and commodities; sport; culture; property; celebrity gossip; miscellaneous – we readily see that the late Soviet media carried almost nothing about the issues that mattered most: the redistribution of property, the arms industry, misappropriation of assets of the Group of Soviet Forces in Germany, embezzlement of the funds allocated for resettling former Soviet soldiers in the U.S.S.R., the redesigning of the infrastructure of state repression. For understandable reasons, there was no public analysis of the cosying up of organised crime and big business. The formation of national liberation movements in, for example, the North Caucasus was analysed in terms of ideology with almost no discussion of their impact on the Russian economy. This meant that the regime acquired its understanding of these movements only through the medium of open warfare against them.

In 1988–9, all attempts by the professionally qualified to get the ear of the then Soviet leadership were in vain. The basic method for "counteracting the deteriorating situation", as official language put it, was to declare a state of emergency. Rather than "counteracting" the problem, this led, on every occasion, to an escalation of violence. Violence was not just the main political tool of the Soviet leadership but also a kind of constantly reinforced programming in the minds of the passive majority. The regime's agencies to this day regard violence as a cognitive tool. They measure the governability of the society entrusted to their care by its passive receptivity towards signals emitted by the state. This seems to be innate in any system of government and the default attitude of every official. It is the reason why democracy, for all its obvious drawbacks and risks of disorganisation, is essential to enable legislative bodies – a duma, a parliament or a Reichstag – to place obstacles in the way of administrators intoxicated by the technologies of governance. Alas, in 1990 the media had other preoccupations, and the issue of institutional violence was eclipsed by the seeming irrationality of inter-ethnic violence.

At the root of institutional violence lies the notion of sovereignty. This suspect concept was central to the events of 1990 and remains high on the agenda as a means of squaring circles. It is extraordinary that the foreign word *suverenitet* – a real agnonym, frequently used but not wholly understood – should be such a bee in the bonnet of our ruling class. It should refer to a person's right to be responsible for themselves and choose their own destiny, but instead it is used almost invariably to refer to the right to decide other people's destinies. Doubtless, the problem would remain in the unlikely event that Russian speakers all agreed to talk not about sovereignty but about, say, self-determination. We would then have to define which self was to be allowed to determine itself. The trouble in 1990 was the absence of any self. The U.S.S.R. was an empty shell, represented by that internationalist "best friend of the Germans", Gorbachev. Then there was "democratic Russia", represented by the more familiar and populist, but totally non-transparent, Yeltsin.

The chronicle of 1990 testifies that it was then, not during the August 1991 coup attempt, that real power shifted from Gorbachev to Yeltsin. The shift occurred on two levels: that of the government bureaucracy, which, along underground corridors, slipped away from the President of the U.S.S.R. to the President of Russia, and that of the economy, where decentralisation and privatisation were seen as an opportunity too good to be missed.

The fusion of the intelligence agencies with business, which began in the late 1980s, was not considered politically significant. A later striking example was the transfiguration of Filipp Bobkov, former Deputy Chief of the K.G.B. and Director of its Fifth (anti-dissident) Department, into the head of security of Vladimir Gusinsky's "Most" media and banking empire. Security is security. The political implications of the developing love-in of the K.G.B. and big business, which with hindsight we can discern in the events of 1990, were not visible, were not "made public", at the time. When the Russian media in the mid-1990s spotted what was happening to their country, it was already too late to do anything about it.

There was another major dichotomy between personal freedom and the duty of a Soviet citizen, even though the Soviet Union had ceased to exist in law. Among a general public which values national sovereignty more highly than personal freedom, Gorky's formulation "If an enemy does not surrender, he must be destroyed" continues to be regarded as normative, rather like Ayatollah Khomeini's fatwah for the murder of Salman Rushdie, which he never got round to revoking. After the 1990 declaration of Russia's sovereignty, the new country's statist political leaders carried on behaving as if the U.S.S.R. still existed. By choosing to adopt the philosophy of "sovereignty", they implicated themselves in a rerun of the saga of the collapse of the U.S.S.R., only now in new circumstances. For an entire decade, with major milestones in 1993, 1996 and 1999, they remained in ideological denial of the collapse of the U.S.S.R. and furiously resisted attempts to remove the discrepancy between the borders of the Russian Federation and those of a Soviet empire which had stretched "from the taiga to Britannia's oceans".

The concept of "sovereignty" was central also for people in a hurry to reinterpret recent Soviet history from the new perspective of imperial decay. In a 1989 article on "Stalinism" for the *Dictionary of New Thinking*, Gefter describes Stalin as Lenin's successor in destroying the main "sovereigns" of Russia: the sovereigns of the land (the peasantry); the local sovereigns of government (the functionaries of post-1917 Bolshevism l ike Bukharin *et al.*); and the sovereigns of the word (the intellectuals).[165] There is nothing original in this notion, except perhaps for one thing: the price for Russia to exist within its former Soviet borders was total "de-sovereignisation" of its population. So what? The people never asked to be sovereign, neither in 1990 nor in 2006.

The programming I mentioned above is not a metaphor but a term for a set of commands that prompt a particular train of thought which leads to an action. Violence, especially in the form of a professionally committed murder – that is, an act of terrorism – automatically allocates the roles of potential victims and those potentially in a position to commission murder (and, of course, also of potential copycat killers). The former speculate and seek to reassure each other: "We just need to try and work out one thing: who benefits from this murder?" Or, "What can the victim have said or

165. M.Ia. Gefter, *Iz tekh i etikh let* (Moscow, 1998), pp. 414–15.

done that sealed their fate?" Most people just get acclimatised to recurrent violence and see it as natural and inevitable, something which will always exist and which it is useless and dangerous to protest about. That is the perfect breeding ground for terrorism. On 9 September, 1990, "unidentified assailants" murdered the priest and theologian Aleksandr Men. The media talked a lot about it, but it was not seen to symbolise a particular kind of politics, and the ripples from the intelligentsia's moral indignation subsided without producing the slightest effect. The potential suspect offered only one argument to prove his innocence: "That act didn't make me the slightest bit better off. You'd do better to look for the killer where the potential victims are huddled. See what they can tell you."

An instinctive readiness to inflict and endure any amount of social humiliation was also being prepared in 1990. In August 1991, just a few thousand brave men and women averted a massacre in the Russian capital. The death of three Muscovites proved a sufficient sacrifice on the altar of freedom and the rule of law. After 1993, however, and especially towards the end of the 1990s, terror against individuals and entire ethnic groups (ranging from the devastation of Chechnya to the wrecking of the *Beware: Religion!* exhibition) gradually became a familiar and normal part of the life of Russian society. An instinctive readiness to endure humiliation has become one of Russia's key consumer characteristics, and part of the Russian brand image the world over today is unabashed tourists and swashbuckling travelling salesmen.

An interesting gap in the media discourse of 1990 is the absence of any mention of "betrayal", a key concept for those who think the collapse of the U.S.S.R. was the greatest catastrophe of the twentieth century.[166] Contemporaries observed a completely different reality in which force of circumstance saw Nelson Mandela released from prison, Germany reunified, and the declaration by Boris Yeltsin and the parliament of the R.S.F.S.R. that

166. If we disregard debate within the Party about betrayal of Communist ideals, instanced by Nina Andreyeva's renowned letter "I cannot sacrifice my principles". This denounced the betrayal not of the Russian empire but of the ideology of its Soviet hypostasis.

Russia was seceding from the U.S.S.R. In none of these cases was there a conspiracy or any conspirators, betrayal or traitors. In the decade which followed, the discourse of "betrayal" became popular and was used as a universal skeleton key for revealing what was really behind all political events.

This was partly due to the failure of the media, even in the relatively free political environment of 1990, to identify the main source of the administrative threat to the hoped-for democratic transition: the Soviet secret police. It was a fatal mistake, because betrayal is the core business of the secret police. Duplicity is the be-all and end-all of this type of personality, which is capable under particular circumstances of inflicting irreparable damage on any society. Today, there is a big difference between the concentrated fear of uncontrollable mass violence of 1990 and the present fear of highly diffused but pinpoint violence. The main problem is that all the issues to which the U.S.S.R. failed to find answers in 1990 seem still to preoccupy those who, fifteen years later, are trying to ignore the fact that the U.S.S.R. no longer exists. It seems not to matter what point they have reached in their political careers, or which topics today excite our free media.

MAY

30 April–2 May

In Novokuznetsk, Kemerovo province, a congress is held of independent workers' movements and organisations which have emerged in the wake of the 1989 strike movement.

1 May

The official May Day parade through Red Square is followed by a march by political oppositionists, from extreme right-wingers to anarchists with anti-government banners. As soon as the demonstration starts, Gorbachev and other members of the Politburo and Soviet leadership leave the top of Lenin's Mausoleum, from where they traditionally greeted the march past.

"The start", Moscow, 1 May, 1990

Palace Square, Leningrad, 1 May, 1990

Protest meeting on Palace Square, Leningrad, 1 May, 1990

Soviet television cuts the live broadcast from Red Square (later claiming that this was somehow at the request of the Moscow Voters Association). Foreign television companies continue broadcasting the event. The nightly news programme *Time* (*Vremya*) is cancelled. Moscow's City Soviet leaders, including Gavriil Popov and Yuriy Luzhkov, remain in their places on the stand for middle-ranking leaders next to the mausoleum.

Protest march on
Nevsky Prospekt,
Leningrad, 1 May, 1990

"Long live independ-
ent Lithuania!",
protest meeting on
Palace Square,
Leningrad, 1 May, 1990

Team of the former Chairman of the Moscow City Executive Committee, Valeriy Saikin, Red Square, Moscow, May or June 1990

3 May

Lithuania introduces monthly rations of flour, 2 kilograms per person; cereals, 2 kilograms; butter, 2 kilograms; sugar, 2 kilograms (*Izvestiia*, 124, p. 2).

Death of Pimen (Sergey Izvekov), Patriarch of Moscow and All Russia, People's Deputy of the U.S.S.R. Filaret, Metropolitan of Kiev and Galich and Patriarchal Exarch of Ukraine, is elected *locum tenens* of the patriarchal throne (*Izvestiia*, 125, p. 6). See essay below by Nikolai Mitrokhin.

Luciano Pavarotti performs a programme including works by Gluck, Bellini, Rossini and Mascagni at the Bolshoy Theatre. Proceeds are donated to the Foundation for Victims of the Armenian Earthquake (*Izvestiia*, 125, p. 3).

I.M.A. Press Agency conducted a survey of 801 Muscovites for *Moscow News* between 28 April and 2 May:

Should our country move to a market economy?

Yes	58 per cent
No	26 per cent
Don't know	16 per cent

If "yes", when should the transition begin?

Immediately	56 per cent
In 1 year's time	14 per cent
In 2–3 years' time	13 per cent
In 5 years' time or more	9 per cent
Don't know	10 per cent

Do you agree with the claim that under market conditions everybody will have an opportunity to become rich?

Yes	33 per cent
No	58 per cent
Don't know	9 per cent

Will there be more room for creativity and initiative?

Yes	66 per cent
No	23 per cent
Don't know	11 per cent

Some experts believe the introduction of market relations will cause unemployment. Do you think that unemployment is:

Beneficial for society	4 per cent
A normal occurrence	39 per cent
An abnormal occurrence	27 per cent
A tragedy for society	25 per cent
Don't know	5 per cent

How likely is it that you would become unemployed under market conditions?

Very likely	6 per cent
Likely	20 per cent
Unlikely	34 per cent
Very unlikely	29 per cent
Don't know	11 per cent

If the market gave you the opportunity to choose, where would you like to work?

In a state enterprise   35 per cent

In a joint venture with a foreign firm 33 per cent

In a private company   13 per cent

Be self-employed   13 per cent

In a cooperative   7 per cent

Don't know   11 per cent

Do you agree with private ownership of enterprises?

Yes   57 per cent

No   31 per cent

Don't know   12 per cent

Do you agree that our country needs private ownership of land?

Yes   79 per cent

No   13 per cent

Don't know   8 per cent

How do you feel about attracting Western investment in the Soviet economy?

Positive   70 per cent

Negative   23 per cent

Don't know   7 per cent

(*Moskovskie novosti*, 19, p. 10).

4 May

The Supreme Council of Latvia adopts a declaration "On Restoration of the Independent Republic of Latvia". Relations between the Republic of Latvia and the U.S.S.R. would be based on their peace treaty of 11 August, 1920 (*Izvestiia*, 127, p. 1).

5 May

"No matter how much we complain that we do not have enough glasnost (transparency), and we really do not, it is still the only thing we have achieved. It is because of the policy of glasnost that people know how we lived, how we are living today, and what the future may hold if things just carry on as before. A fundamental shift has occurred in public awareness. That has been achieved by Gorbachev, and by us journalists" (Mikhail Poltoranin [member of the U.S.S.R. Supreme Soviet committee on glasnost, citizens' rights and appeals; member of the coordinating council of the Inter-Regional Deputies Group], "The Press Must Be Independent", *Moskovskii komsomolets*, 102, p. 1).

6 May

The U.S.S.R. Council of Ministers abolishes the law enforcement agencies' control over the acquisition, storage and use of copying equipment (*Izvestiia*, 127, p. 2). This removes the most important obstacle to freedom of speech. Previously, interior ministry agencies had kept incriminating samples of the fonts of all typewriters in state institutions. Access to photocopiers had been virtually impossible for private individuals. Xeroxing of *samizdat* (self-published) and *tamizdat* (Western-published) literature had been illegal and punished.

A Urals publisher is the first to risk printing Boris Yeltsin's memoirs, *Against the Grain*, in the U.S.S.R. Written in 1989–90, it had by this time appeared in a dozen other countries (*Moskovskie novosti*, 18, p. 2).

8 May

The anti-blockade commission of the Supreme Soviet of Lithuania declares economic sanctions against the U.S.S.R. and reduces planned deliveries of meat and milk by 10 per cent (*Izvestiia*, 129, p. 3).

The Supreme Soviet of Estonia declares the country independent and rescinds the act of the Estonian Parliament of 21 July, 1940, accepting incorporation into the U.S.S.R. (*Izvestiia*, 130, p. 4).

10 May

A treaty between the ministries of agriculture of Lithuania, Latvia and Estonia comes into effect (*Izvestiia*, 131, p. 2).

11 May

A major charity event, "Into the 21st Century Without Drugs", is organised by the U.S.S.R. Society for Rescuing Children and Teenagers from Drugs (*Moskovskii komsomolets*, 106, p. 3).

Death of Venedikt Yerofeyev (b. 1938), one of the greatest Russian writers of uncensored literature of the twentieth century, a founder of Russian postmodernism and author of the "poem in prose" *Moscow-Petushki* (1970). He dies of cancer [of the throat, resulting from alcoholism].

14 May

Under a new law, publicly insulting or slandering the President of the U.S.S.R. carries a penalty of up to 3,000 roubles or imprisonment for up to two years. For libel in the media, the fine is up to 25,000 roubles or six years in prison. [Most offenders, of whom there are known to have been about twenty, got away with small fines] (*Noveishaia istoriia otechestvennogo kino*).

The renowned Near Caves of Kiev-Pechersk Monastery are returned to the Ukrainian Orthodox Church (*Izvestiia*, 135).

15 May

A U.S.S.R. presidential decree "annuls" the Estonian Supreme Soviet's declaration of independence and declares illegal all actions of official bodies, staff and citizens based on that proposition (*Izvestiia*, 136, p.1). Another decree "annuls" the declaration of independence of Latvia. The Supreme Soviet of Latvia continues its legislative activity (*Izvestiia*, 136, pp. 1–2).

17 May

In Moscow, Stanislav Govorukhin's documentary *This Is No Way to Live* has its premiere. Soviet society is shown as impoverished, degraded and criminalised. In 1991 the film wins in three categories at the Russian Nika Awards. The film's title becomes a commonplace of perestroika journalism.

20 May

According to the Centre for the Study of Public Opinion, the right-wing group Pamyat' and similar associations are supported by no more than 1–2 per cent of the population. In large cities this can rise to 6 per cent. They do not have a presence in the countryside (*Moskovskie novosti*, 20, p. 9). The Chairman of the Federal Assembly of the Czech and Slovak Federal Republic, Alexander Dubček, is received at the Kremlin by Mikhail Gorbachev (*Moskovskie novosti*, 21, p. 15).

23 May

In a long speech between sessions of the First Congress of People's Deputies of the R.S.F.S.R., Gorbachev talks about choosing socialism, condemns attempts to "seize power", and says that anyone who claims to have quick solutions is a political fraud. He criticises Yeltsin for "denying the principles formulated by Lenin on which the Union Treaty of 1922 was based", and says that, while he supports strengthening Russian sovereignty, Yeltsin is reducing the concept to absurdity.

By this time, Gorbachev was never going to have a major impact on the situation at the congress. After it had rejected Yeltsin, the Politburo had made the mistake of failing to make sure there was a credible rival to him at the congress. Gorbachev refused to meet with several influential representatives of Democratic Russia, who had doubts about Yeltsin and wanted to sound out the possibility of their jointly promoting an alternative candidate. Some of Gorbachev's closest associates later believed that his cavalier attitude resulted less from pressure from conservatives in the Party leadership than from a straightforward underestimation of the power base Yeltsin would gain as head of the Russian state (Viktor Sheinis, *Vzlet i padenie parlamenta: perelomnye gody v rossiiskoi politike (1985–1993)*, 2 vols [Moscow, 2005], vol. 1, p. 305).

24 May

In his speech to the U.S.S.R. Supreme Soviet on the government's economic policy, Nikolai Ryzhkov expands on the Abalkin Commission's vision of transition to a regulated market economy. The first stage provides for emergency measures, including reducing the budget deficit from the 93 billion roubles of 1989 to 25 billion roubles in 1992 through price reform. It is proposed to experiment with a doubling of the price of bread. The speech causes an instant panic in Moscow. Rallies are held throughout the country to demand no price rises. Gorbachev, who had several times promised that prices in the U.S.S.R. would remain unchanged, distances himself from the government programme. The U.S.S.R. Supreme Soviet sends the reforms back to the Council of Ministers for further work by 1 September (based on *Noveishaia istoriia otechestvennogo kino*).

26 May

In a third ballot, Yeltsin obtains 503 votes to Ivan Polozkov's 458 votes. Since neither candidate receives more than half the votes, a new election must be held with new nominations (*Izvestiia*, 148, p. 1).

The arrival of mobile shops in 1990, Istra-Senezh Broiler Production Association, Moscow Province

Statements by the candidates:

Ivan Polozkov: "It seems to me this fetishisation of the concept of a market economy is dangerous, especially if it involves private ownership of the means of production, presenting it as a new version of the 'radiant future'."

Boris Yeltsin: "Transition to a market economy would make the entire administrative-command system redundant, and it would effectively wither away" (*Izvestiia*, 147, pp. 1–2).

27 May

Galina Starovoytova: "We are presently witnessing the formation of a new union. It is developing of its own accord. A new Union Treaty may be concluded very soon, bypassing the U.S.S.R. government if it continues to drag its feet" (*Moskovskie novosti*, 21, p. 4).

29 May

Boris Yeltsin is elected Chairman of the R.S.F.S.R. Supreme Soviet (*Izvestiia*, 150, p. 1).

In all three ballot rounds, the bulk of votes for Yeltsin came from the Democrats. Despite reservations about a leader from the top echelons of the Party bureaucracy, they had no alternative.

Yeltsin evidently picked up a number of votes from waverers, no doubt impressed by his infrequent but vigorous and well-crafted speeches to the congress, his openness to different opinions and people, and his ability to calm a rebellious audience. Even more importantly, wavering deputies were aware of the mood prevaling among their constituents, who were rooting for the man the regime was persecuting. The e-voting system at the congress made it possible for citizens to be informed promptly of how their representatives were voting.

There was, however, another factor. Behind the scenes, in full accord with the rules of the games apparatchiks play, people close to Yeltsin were working on potential defectors, promising them positions in the new government bodies. These votes, we may deduce, belonged to members of the Party, Soviet, and military elites and their intellectual advisers, who agreed a deal to secure their slice of the national cake before the crucial vote. The composition of the ruling inner circle, the state administration and the presidential administration, which formed during 1990, confirms this hypothesis.

Once Yeltsin was elected Chairman, there was a man at the helm who by no means saw himself as leader of the Democrats, and who had every intention of keeping his distance from all the factions which had supported him. This was not immediately evident. Yeltsin did not have a stable majority at the congress and was accordingly lavish in the favours he gave to those willing to support him (Viktor Sheynis).

ENDS AND MEANS: INITIAL IDEAS, INSTITUTIONS THAT WIN

Vitaliy Yelizarov

I

The year 1990 was important for Russian political history, and a milestone too in the history of political science. It followed on from the "autumn of the peoples", characterised by Adam Przeworski as "a dismal failure of the predictive power of political science", and is seen as the crest of what Samuel Huntington called "the third wave of democratisation".[167] It was not just that the political upheavals which changed the map of Eastern Europe had proved unpredictable. The further political development of the "new democracies" – countries in which, since the mid-1970s, there had been a transition from an authoritarian to a more democratic regime – forced a reconsideration of the theoretical underpinnings of democratisation studies, primarily "transitology", which had been accepted since then.

Transitology had itself been a reaction against traditional theories of democracy current in the mid-twentieth century. In the 1960s, democracy studies focused mainly on socio-economic factors. Methodologically, they were close to more general theories of modernisation, and they gave grounds for optimism. Strong positive correlations were found between levels of economic prosperity, education, urbanisation and – democracy. This seemed to bode well for a democratic future for the Soviet Union and the countries of Eastern Europe. The question of how these prospects might be realised remained unanswered, as did the question of how poor

167. Adam Przeworski, *Democracy and the Market* (Cambridge, 1991); Samuel P. Huntington, *The Third Wave: Democratisation in the Late Twentieth Century* (Norman, 1991).

countries like seventeenth-century England or modern India were able to be democratic. The situation changed in the early 1970s.

II

The year 1970 saw the publication of Dankwart Rustow's "Transitions to Democracy", an article that earned him the title of "the father of transitology".[168] Rustow proposed separating the issues of the origins and of the existence of democracy, focusing on analysis of political factors which affected democratic development. The only "basic condition" for democracy to appear, he proposed, was national unity, which he defined as a situation in which the vast majority of citizens have no doubt as to which political community they belong to. This definition allows for democracy developing in a pre-modern, pre-national period and with a low level of economic development.

Rustow's model of democracy, founded on that basic condition, comprises the following phases:

1. The *preliminary phase* sees a period of prolonged and inconclusive political struggle between rival forces, usually social classes. The protagonists vacillate between different ideologies, and this phase leads to polarisation rather than pluralism.

2. The *decision phase*. If the conflicting parties find themselves facing stalemate, some of their leaders will opt for plurality in unity, and for institutionalising key aspects of democratic procedures. The choice in favour of democracy results from the interplay of forces. The agreement worked out by the leaders varies according to circumstances, but must be carried through into the rules of professional politics and the institution of citizenship.

3. The *habituation phase*. This comprises three processes:

168. Dankwart A. Rustow, "Transitions to Democracy: Toward a Dynamic Model", *Comparative Politics*, 2/3 (1970), pp. 334–63.

- politicians and citizens place their faith in the new rules, and apply
  them to new issues;
- they confirm their democratic practices and beliefs;
- people become firmly fitted into the new structure by the forging of
  effective links to party organisation.

Rustow's model assumes there is a sequence, from a sense of national identity (a precondition for political identity), through struggle, compromise
and "habituation", to democracy. Acceptance of the new rules is part of the
transition process rather than a prerequisite. Success in applying his principles to a number of Latin American "transitions" was taken as confirming
that transitology's basic postulates were correct. Researchers focused
mainly on the notion that democracy is a possible product of political
struggle. This led to most attention being paid to the decision phase of
democratic transition, the arrival at a consensus to play by democratic
rules.

Until the late 1980s, Rustow's methodology was tacitly accepted by
most researchers. They believed they had an adequate theoretical tool for
analysing the political changes which, in the second half of the twentieth
century, were faced by countries in many parts of the globe. That is, until a
number of transitions to democracy in the late 1980s and early 1990s
(mainly in Eastern Europe and the former U.S.S.R.), and the way in which
these new democracies developed politically, aroused controversy over
whether transitology's theoretical foundations were sufficiently robust.
The scholarly consensus collapsed and transitology became a field in
which new empirical data might be analysed using any of a variety of
approaches.[169] This was seen as a defeat, and nowadays transitology
occupies a place in the history of political science little grander than that

---

169. See Przeworski, *Democracy and the Market*; Valerie Bunce, "Should Transitologists Be
Grounded?", *Slavic Review*, 54/1 (1995), pp. 109–27; Petr Kopecky and Cas Mudde, "What
Has Eastern Europe Taught Us about the Democratisation Literature (and Vice Versa)?",
European Journal of Political Research, 37 (2000), pp. 517–39.

which the theory of phlogiston occupies in the history of chemistry. The vagaries of democratisation in Russia contributed in no small measure to its demise.

Transitology was attacked on three main counts. First, the uncertainty of outcomes of political interaction was so high as to preclude accurate prediction, and the political deals struck by no means always advanced democratisation. The problem was not wholly unexpected and could be resolved. Political agreements which led to the formation of a one-party system in Mexico (which outlived the U.S.S.R.) were already known.[170] Additional models were developed, from simple two-dimensional schemes[171] to complex constructs employing the mathematical tools of games theory, to accommodate uncertainty as a key characteristic of transition.[172] Second, and far more troublesome, were the national and institutional aspects of democratisation. The "basic condition" of national unity was not everywhere in evidence. For all the differences in the political trajectories of the U.S.S.R. and Yugoslavia, the absence of political unity was directly linked to national issues and a lack of consensus (both in the elites and in a large proportion of the population) in respect of the civic identity of national communities. Third, it proved impossible to study the political development of the new democracies without taking full account of the institutional context of political interactions.[173] The institutional legacy of the old regime, and also the new institutions which emerged in the course of political transformation, largely determined the political actors' strategic behaviour.

170. Alan Knight, "Mexico's Elite Settlement: Conjuncture and Consequences", in John Higley and Richard Gunther, eds, *Elites and Democratic Consolidation in Latin America and Southern Europe* (Cambridge, 1992), pp. 113–45.

171. Terry Karl and Philippe Schmitter, "Models of Transition in Latin America, Southern and Eastern Europe", *International Social Science Journal*, 128 (1991), pp. 269–84; Gerardo Munck and Carol Leff, "Modes of Transition and Democratisation: South America and Eastern Europe in Comparative Perspective", *Comparative Politics*, 29/3 (1997), pp. 343–62.

172. Gary Marks, "Rational Sources of Chaos in Democratic Transition", *American Behavioral Scientist*, 35/4–5 (1992), pp. 397–421; Josep Colomer, *Strategic Transitions: Game Theory and Democratisation* (Baltimore and London, 2000).

173. Rustow himself gives a mixed assessment of institutional factors. On the one hand, focusing on the structure of political conflict and the interactions between political actors,

III

When considering Russia's version of democratic transition and examining its political development in the late 1980s and early 1990s, political scientists are in general overall agreement. Limited liberalisation in 1985–8 extended political and civil liberties. The initial buzzwords of "glasnost" (transparency), "renewal" and "acceleration" were soon replaced by the rhetoric of "perestroika" (restructuring), a term Mikhail Gorbachev, who instigated the reforms, used as a linguistic weapon against the conservative wing of the Communist Party elite to mark an ideological shift in his political position.

This phase culminated in the constitutional reform of 1988 and the first, relatively free, elections of 1989, which marked the birth of democratic politics in Russia. The years 1989–91 saw abolition (or, at least, revision) of Article 6 of the Constitution which had enshrined the Party's right to a monopoly on political power, and the first free, post-U.S.S.R., elections (to the Russian Federation's Congress of People's Deputies and a number of local soviets), as well as adoption of a Declaration of Sovereignty of Russia. The Communist Party lost its monopoly on power, new political parties gained legal status, and disagreements between the U.S.S.R.'s centre and the Union's republics intensified. In 1991–3 there followed the attempted coup by conservative Communist elements of 19–21 August, 1991; the collapse of the U.S.S.R.; Russian President Yeltsin's moratorium on elections in the autumn of 1991; the 1992 economic reforms, which

he refers to the "danger of throwing away the political baby with the institutional bathwater" (*Transitions to Democracy*, p. 344). On the other hand, he stresses the importance of the institutional context for the emergence of democracy, describing the design of the electoral and party systems as essential elements for successful completion of the habituation phase. In 1970 Rustow had needed to distance himself from the earlier institutionalism (which he called "sterile legalism") which assigned greater weight to formal rules than to the actions of political players. The debate around the institutional legacy of the new East European democracies strengthened the position of neo-institutionalists and showed up the deficiencies of a model that reduced the political process to a succession of conflicts. Rustow's paraphrase came back to bite him.

relaxed price controls and created hyperinflation; and the confrontation between Yeltsin and the Russian Federation's Supreme Soviet which led to his shelling of the parliament in Moscow (the "White House") in October 1993. The outcome of this period was adoption of the present Russian constitution, establishment of an electoral system[174] and the first elections to the Russian parliament. Irrespective of how one evaluates the events of August 1991 and October 1993, they represented resolution of political conflict by a resort to violence and what has been described as "imposed transition".[175] This was an outcome in which the victorious side made its own rules and crushed its political opponents.

This article will restrict itself to the events of 1990, so we shall not attempt to assess whether the political vicissitudes of the perestroika period led to success or failure of democratisation. Irrespective of what kind of democracy, if indeed it is a democracy, resulted from the perestroika period, for present purposes we shall seek only to demarcate and describe the institutional context of political developments of the time.

Politicians are primarily interested in maximising their power. This is characteristic of the species, and, to the cynical eye of the political scientist, a democrat is little different from a Communist. In this respect, all political animals are equal. This does not mean that politicians are ideologically omnivorous, but merely identifies one of the factors of the process of political selection. When considering alternatives, the politician selects those which will contribute to advancing his political career, and uses whatever tools he needs and can access to achieve the tasks he has set himself. The electoral system, political parties, the parliamentary arena and the presidency are all components in the institutional arsenal politicians can use to achieve their career goals and to implement their ideological programme.

Some obvious facts suggest themselves as the baseline for the political

174. The electoral reform of 2003–4 altered the structure of contestation at both the central and regional levels of Russian politics, as well as abruptly curtailing the scope of electoral politics in the constituent territories of the Russian Federation.

175. A term coined by Charles Schmitter in "Models of Transition in Latin America, Southern and Eastern Europe", pp. 269–84.

history of 1990. The partially free 1989 elections to the U.S.S.R. Supreme Soviet were used by the reformers to put pressure on conservatives on the Communist Party's Central Committee. They used the electoral mechanism as a weapon in a struggle within the elite. Whatever goals and interests had guided the authors of the 1988 constitutional reform and the subsequent 1989 election, the consequences were evidently very different from what they intended.

The 1989 elections are a perfect fit for Samuel Huntington's description of elections sponsored by an authoritarian regime, conducted under its control, neither completely free nor fair, which lead unexpectedly to the overthrow of the regime.[176] Elections, which until then had been a ritual for legitimising the Communist regime, introduced political feedback, and from then on contestation was embedded in the political system. New political protagonists opposing the old Party elite were able to use the election campaign to acquire political "start-up capital". This was demonstrated most strikingly by the "democratic" career of Boris Yeltsin, who, for all his charisma and popularity, had until 1989 no real way to challenge the old elite. Within a year, he was dominating the political scene. The 1989 elections extended genuine political participation and installed an electoral mechanism for contested politics.

These two aspects were fundamental to the success of the new political system.[177] The institution of elections became a key, but not the crucial, element of Russian politics. The effectiveness of elections as a means for organising public contestation and putting citizens' participation on the political agenda depends on the creation of a system of elected government and political parties. In general, if democratisation occurs under a civil regime, then, no matter what the alignment of political forces, the government institutions resulting from "founding" elections (i.e., the first fair,

176. Samuel P. Huntington, *The Third Wave*.
177. Robert A. Dahl identified political participation and public contestation as crucial elements of democratisation. See his *Polyarchy: Participation and Opposition* (New Haven, 1971).

free and competitive elections held after a country has rejected authoritarianism) get on with their business of governing. Since founding elections
are a contest between parties, the elected government bodies are formed on
a party-political basis. This applies principally to the parliament, although
in fact the presidents of most new democracies have party affiliations too.
At this point, the nature of parties changes. If previously ideology was the
primary motivation of party activists, once a party is a channel for recruit-
ing members of a government and, more broadly, of a political elite, career
incentives assume a more important role in its further development.[178]

This was the scenario in most cases of post-Soviet democratisation. Irrespective of which parties came to power in founding or later elections, political contestation continued in the form of competition between parties. This
was true of countries like Poland and Hungary, where new parties arose on
the basis of social networks of dissent which had existed semi-legally under
Communist rule. It also applied to countries without a strong tradition of
dissent, like Bulgaria and Mongolia, where the successors of the former
ruling parties succeeded in dominating the political scene.[179]

Russia developed quite differently. No robust party system developed
in the early 1990s. Instead, the U.S.S.R. broke up and in 1993 the president
declared a moratorium on elections in the now sovereign Russian Federation. Much scholarly attention has been devoted to the problematical
relationship between the U.S.S.R.'s centre and the union's republics, as

178. Angelo Panebianco's "collective" and "selective" incentives. Although these overlap,
the theoretical distinction is widely used to analyse the stages of development of political
parties and levels of participation. See his *Political Parties: Organisation and Power* (Cambridge,
1988), p. 50.

179. The case of Mongolia is particularly interesting. The weakness of Russia's party
system is often blamed on Soviet political culture. This explanation does not address the
examples of Ukraine, Georgia and Moldova, let alone the Baltic republics. It seems even
less convincing when applied to Mongolia (and, indeed, Bulgaria) which has never been
accused of having an overly democratic political culture. Nevertheless, after an election in
1996, the former ruling party ceded power to a democratic coalition. Four years later, the
ruling party regained its position, again as the result of elections, and has since been
obliged periodically to enter into coalition agreements with the democrats.

well as to ideological and organisational aspects of the early stages of developing a party system. There has been less study of the link between federalism and party-building.

The other country where early experimentation with party politics aggravated federal problems was Yugoslavia. There, as in the Soviet Union, the national aspects of democratisation raised a host of institutional problems. The Soviet federal model common to both disintegrated in much the same way. If for the U.S.S.R. the year 1990 was the culmination of "the parade of sovereignties",[180] for Yugoslavia it was the year when nationalists won the elections in every republic of the federation. The integrity of its existing state was an acute problem also for the German Democratic Republic and Czechoslovakia, but in both these cases, founding elections were held before nationalist ideologies started being used as political weapons. As a result, the issues of reunification and partition that followed were dealt with as technical matters, within a legal framework and following parliamentary procedures.[181]

Enough has been written about why Yugoslavia and the U.S.S.R. fell apart. Our interest is in how the institutional legacy of Soviet federalism affected the development of Russia's political party system. The country's experience was in many respects unique, and for us 1990 is the most revealing year.

IV

Extension of political participation and public contestation continued in 1990. The proportion of constituencies fielding unopposed candidates in elections to the Russian Federation's Soviet of People's Deputies fell from

180. Republican declarations of sovereignty will be found in A. I. Doronchenkov, ed., K Soiuzu suverennykh narodov: Sbornik dokumentov KPSS, zakonodatel'nykh aktov, deklaratsii, obrashchenii i prezidentskikh ukazov, posviashchennykh problemam natsional'no-gosudarstvennogo suvereniteta (Moscow, 1991).

181. The inter-ethnic dispute between Czechs and Slovaks bears no comparison with the depth of the ethnic conflict already visible in the results of the Yugoslav elections of 1990. Even Czechoslovakia, founded in 1989 and considered a classic example of a "bi-federal" democracy (a loose federation of two autonomous republics with the power of veto) split in 1993.

23 per cent in 1989 to 3 per cent in 1990.[182] Moreover, whereas in 1989 the average number of candidates competing for election to the U.S.S.R. Soviet of People's Deputies was around two per seat, the following year there were some seven contenders per parliamentary seat in the Soviet of People's Deputies of the Russian Federation.[183] The free elections in 1990 to Russia's new parliament were a first experience of electoral campaigning, with legally registered political parties.

Right up until 1990 there had been no legal basis for parties other than the Communist Party to exist. The financial and organisational resources of the Communist Party were still vastly greater than those of any other political associations, no matter what their ideological orientation, and which, describing themselves as parties or political movements, fielded candidates against those of the regime.[184] This situation changed during the pre-election campaign for the Congress of People's Deputies of the Russian Federation. The electoral contestation consisted entirely of a growing challenge by the democrats to the Soviet regime and its ruling Communist Party. Voters' clubs and associations sprang up all over Russia and provided the opposition's institutional infrastructure. The most efficiently organised was the Moscow Voters' Association, formed in the late summer of 1989 as a coalition of voters' clubs. Its objectives were succinctly defined: the exchange of information between voters' clubs, coordination of the organising of rallies and demonstrations, and the drafting of oppositional legislative proposals for elected deputies. Their campaign strategy included drafting a programme of radical political, economic and constitutional reforms, and inviting democratic candidates from Moscow and the provinces to discuss and adopt it.[185]

182. Viktor L. Sheinis, *Vzlet i padenie parlamenta: Perelomnye gody v rossiiskoi politike (1985–1993)*, vol. 1 (Moscow, 2005), p. 265.
183. *Ibid*. See also Nikolai Biriukov and Viktor Sergeev, *Stanovlenie institutov predstavitel'noi vlasti v sovremennoi Rossii* (Moscow, 2004), p. 509.
184. A considerable selection of ideological alternatives to Communist ideology had already formed by the mid-1980s and included not only liberal but nationalist varieties of dissent.
185. Yitzhak M. Brudny, "The Dynamics of 'Democratic Russia', 1990–1993", *Post-Soviet Affairs*, 9/2 (1993), p. 143.

As the new political movements became more organised, their proposals became more radical. On 20–21 January, 1990 the Democratic Russia voters' bloc held its founding conference and declared,

> Democrats cannot be only a body supporting reforms undertaken by the country's leaders. They can and should become an independent political force. In some instances they will provide support for the reformers, but on other occasions they should criticise half-heartedness, shortcomings, political errors and economic miscalculations. There will also be occasions when they should propose their own alternatives.[186]

This time too, though, constitutional reform was initiated by reformers within the Communist Party. On 11 March, 1990 a plenary session of the Party's Central Committee agreed to propose to an Extraordinary Third Congress of People's Deputies of the U.S.S.R. "Amendments and Additions to the Constitution (Fundamental Law) of the U.S.S.R. on the Political System (Articles 6 and 7 of the Constitution of the U.S.S.R.)".[187] The congress convened on 12 March and approved the amendments, thereby giving citizens the right to join not just "public societies" but also political parties.[188] This took place between the first and second ballots for the Congress of People's Deputies of the Russian Federation, with the result that demands in most of the voters' associations' manifestos were passed into law even before their campaign had concluded.

The Communist Party's constitutionally enshrined monopoly of power was abandoned at the same time the post of President of the U.S.S.R. was

---

186. "Predvybornaia programma 'Demokraticheskoi Rossii'", *Ogonek*, 6 (1990), pp. 17–18.
187. Biriukov and Sergeev, "Stanovlenie institutov predstavitel'noi vlasti v sovremennoi Rossii", p. 151.
188. "Zakon Soiuza Sovetskikh Sotsialisticheskikh Respublik 'Ob uchrezhdenii posta Prezidenta SSSR i o vnesenii izmenenii i dopolnenii i Konstitutsiiu (Osnovnoi Zakon) SSSR", *Vneocherednoi Tretii S"ezd narodnykh deputatov SSSR. 12–15 marta 1990 goda: Stenograficheskii otchet*, Moscow, vol. 3 (1990), pp. 193–4.

established. When, on 15 March, 1990, Gorbachev was elected President of the U.S.S.R., he retained the post of General Secretary of the Communist Party.[189] By seizing the initiative and repudiating a constitutional monopoly of power which had become a political liability, the reformist wing of the Party hoped to bolster its institutional position at the highest level of state power. However, while still only discussing the feasibility of a presidency, Gorbachev was surprised by the reaction from the heads of the union republics.[190] Nursultan Nazarbayev, First Secretary of the Communist Party of Kazakhstan, remarked approvingly on the timeliness of the proposal and went on to suggest that there should be not just a President of the U.S.S.R. but one of each of the Soviet republics: "The quest for sovereignty was given a powerful impetus as the disintegration of the U.S.S.R. was provided with a legal framework."[191]

V

Political consequences of the reform of the constitution by the Third U.S.S.R. Congress in March 1990 and the new pre-election campaign for what would now be the Russian Republic's First Congress of People's Deputies in May were not long in coming. By the end of the latter, the institutional map of Russian politics had been redrawn. The May congress gave institutional form to a trend which had been emerging during the campaign. The contestation by individual politicians and political movements shifted from the realms of inter-party rivalry to that of political

189. Gorbachev was elected President by the congress, which was at odds with the newly adopted constitutional amendments: "Article 127¹ of the Constitution (see Section II of the Law 'Establishing the post of President of the U.S.S.R.') provides for the election of the President 'by Soviet citizens on the basis of universal, equal and direct suffrage', while Paragraph 1 of Section III of the same Act states that 'the first President of the U.S.S.R. is elected by the Congress of People's Deputies of the U.S.S.R.'" (Biriukov and Sergeev, *Stanovlenie institutov predstavitel'noi vlasti v sovremennoi Rossii*, p. 155).

190. Mikhail Gorbachev, *Zhizn' i reformy* (Moscow, 1995), vol. 1, p. 485.

191. Rudol'f G. Pikhoia, *Moskva. Kreml'. Vlast'. Dve istorii odnoi strany: Rossiia na izlome tysiacheletii, 1985–2005* (Moscow, 2007), p. 169.

confrontation, made possible by the institutional structure of the U.S.S.R.

The First Congress of People's Deputies of the R.S.F.S.R. convened on 16 May. The main items on the agenda were election of a chairman and vice-chairmen of its Supreme Soviet, election of deputies to the Supreme Soviet, and the issue of state sovereignty for Russia. It was immediately apparent that the electoral success of oppositional forces, despite having a major ideological impact, was quite limited in administrative terms. Democratic Russia gained nearly a quarter of the seats, about the same as the conservative opposition's Communists of Russia, which meant that no faction had an absolute majority. Yeltsin, the most popular politician at the time, scraped in as chairman, with the support of Democratic Russia, by just four votes.[192] The Democrats failed to have their candidates appointed as vice-chairmen: "Even Ruslan Khasbulatov, a compromise candidate, was elected first vice-chairman only on a second ballot."[193] In the Supreme Soviet itself, the Democrats were more secure, but not dominant. All the contention faded away, however, when the Declaration of Sovereignty of Russia was put to the vote.

Once again, this was a change instigated by the reformers inside the Communist Party. Indeed, the proposal of sovereignty was put forward on the congress's first day by none other than Aleksandr Vlasov, outgoing Chairman of the R.S.F.S.R. Council of Ministers, and Vitaliy Vorotnikov, whose position of Chairman of the Presidium of the Supreme Soviet of the R.S.F.S.R. was being abolished. The move had been approved by Gorbachev,[194] the reformers evidently failing to foresee the use their main opponent, Yeltsin, would make of Russian sovereignty for his own ends. Vadim Medvedev, a Gorbachev supporter, recalls, "It was only at the First Congress that Yeltsin himself seized on the notion of Russian sovereignty. Before that he had never commented on the relationship between the Union centre and the republics."[195] Vlasov and Vorotnikov tried to use the

192. Precisely 50 per cent plus one vote of the constitutional number of 1,068 deputies (Biriukov and Sergeev, *Stanovlenie institutov predstavitel'noi vlasti v sovremennoi Rossii*, p. 313). 193. Ibid., p. 314.   194. Pikhoia, *Moskva. Kreml'. Vlast'*, p. 179. 195. From an interview given on 28 June, 2004 by Vadim A. Medvedev to Viktor L. Sheynis, in Sheinis, *Vzlet i padenie parlamenta*, vol. 1, p. 305.

issue of Russian sovereignty in their own campaigns to become Chairman of the Supreme Soviet by winning over the congress delegates, not doubting that a majority would favour the idea.[196] They were right about that. The declaration was passed with an overwhelming 907 in favour and 13 against, with 9 abstentions.[197] Those who instigated the Declaration of Sovereignty got their tactics right but their strategy disastrously wrong. The reformers in the Communist Party got the declaration through but failed to retain the chairmanship. Yeltsin was helped to victory by the unity of his supporters and the disunity of his opponents, who failed to put up a single, authoritative candidate against him.[198]

The Declaration of Sovereignty of Russia and the election of the main opponent of the leaders of the U.S.S.R. as Chairman of the R.S.F.S.R.'s Supreme Soviet did not mean that Russia became an independent state or that Yeltsin became a puppet-master pulling the strings in Russia's government. Opposition from Communists of Russia and their supporters often meant that he was constrained in the appointments he could make. Indeed, until the failed coup, the opposition in the Supreme Soviet attempted constantly to unseat him as chairman. The struggle between Gorbachev and Yeltsin and the conflict between the Union and republican governments have been described in detail elsewhere.[199]

196. In his speech Vitaliy I. Vorotnikov commented, "I do not see among the deputies anybody implacably opposed … and I think we are sufficiently united to adopt a document which clearly and definitely expresses the desire of the peoples of Russia for independence and sovereignty" (*Pervyi s'ezd narodnykh deputatov RSFSR: Stenograficheskii otchet* [Moscow, 1992], vol. 1, p. 563).
197. *Pervyi s'ezd*, vol. 4, p. 251. The only disagreement came during the voting article by article. Five hundred and forty-four deputies voted in favour of the primacy of Russian law over that of the U.S.S.R., with 271 against, and 30 abstentions. Even here, the supporters of sovereignty had a very convincing majority.
198. The Russia fraction, which united "national patriot" opponents of Democratic Russia, voted, as did most Communists, together with the Democrats in favour of Russian state sovereignty.
199. Notably, in Pikhoia's *Moskva. Kreml'. Vlast'*, and Zigmund Stankevich, *Istoriia krusheniia SSSR: politiko-pravovye aspekty* (Moscow, 2011). Despite their differences, both authors agree on the main causes of the "institutional divorce" of the Russian Federation from the U.S.S.R.

Nevertheless, despite being almost irreconcilable ideological opponents, the rival parliamentary factions invariably came together sufficiently
to obtain the necessary majority to pass legislation which bolstered the
R.S.F.S.R.'s institutional autonomy. The "War of Laws" broke out on the
last day of the congress with the adoption of a decree entitled "Demarcation of the Functions of Management of Organisations in the R.S.F.S.R.
(Basis of a New Federal Treaty)". The decree removed the Council of Ministers of the R.S.F.S.R. from subordination to the U.S.S.R. government. Eight
U.S.S.R. ministries retained direct control over Russian organisations,
enterprises and institutions, including the Ministry of Defence and the
K.G.B. This was qualified, however, by a note that the Russian republican
Interior Ministry would "interact" with the U.S.S.R. Ministry, and it was
envisaged that a Russian republican K.G.B. would be created in due course.
The State Bank of the R.S.F.S.R. and Bank of Foreign Trade gained auton-
omy and were now subordinate to the Supreme Soviet of the R.S.F.S.R.

Just one month after the congress ended, Yeltsin announced, at the
Twenty-Eighth Congress of the C.P.S.U., that he was resigning from the
Party on the grounds that he could not carry out his duties as Chairman of
the Supreme Soviet of Russia while remaining under the constraints of
Communist Party discipline: "Yeltsin resigned from the Party Gorbachev
had tried to expel him from in October 1987, from the Party where he had
vainly sought support at the Nineteenth All-Union Communist Party
Conference in July 1988. Now it was his turn to reject the Communist
Party."[200] Yeltsin no longer needed the Party. He and his supporters had a
new institutional base where others could no longer dictate the rules. Now
they could lay down the rules their opponents would have to follow. The
R.S.F.S.R. was becoming autonomous, a process that underlay all political
conflicts until the unsuccessful coup attempt of August 1991 gave Yeltsin
victory over the supporters of the U.S.S.R.

The virtual unanimity over the matter of the sovereignty of the Russian
republic did not mean that anyone underrated the serious nationalistic

200. Pikhoia, *Moskva. Kreml'. Vlast'*, p. 192.

passions confronting the U.S.S.R. in the late 1980s or that they were all pursuing the same goal. Most knew that the declaration was constitutionally questionable:[201]

> The disorganised, spontaneous power of widespread nationalist sentiment was becoming organised. Militia squads were being set up and illegally armed. The militants, armed or unarmed but ready for action, were numbered in tens of thousands. In order to contain and neutralise ethnic conflicts, and also to prevent power from being seized by national fronts, a state of emergency had been declared in several regions and the army sent in.[202]

This quotation is from a book Boris Kurashvili sent to the printers in March 1990. One of the Communist reformers, despite his gloomy view of the situation, he had no doubt at that time that the U.S.S.R. remained viable. Neither, irrespective of their ideological affiliations, did most of those who voted for the Declaration of Sovereignty doubt it or have any wish to destroy the U.S.S.R.

Political rivalry between the supporters of different ideologies intensified throughout 1990, but from this moment on the main schisms and alliances occurred in the context of confrontation between the U.S.S.R. Party and state elite and their Russian republican counterparts. Fragmentation of political parties occurred along just the same lines as those along which territorial regions of the state were breaking away. On 19 June, 1990, a week after the Declaration of Sovereignty, a conference was held of delegates from the regions of Russia to the Twenty-Eighth Congress of the U.S.S.R. Communist Party. On 20 June, it proclaimed itself the founding congress of the Communist Party of the Russian republic. The new party was formed to counter the reformers within the Communist Party and adopted a hard-line conservative stance in respect of democratisation,

201. Sheinis, *Vzlet i padenie parlamenta*, pp. 318, 322.
202. Boris P. Kurashvili, *Strana na rasput'e* (Moscow, 1990), pp. 24–5.

replicating the split between the U.S.S.R. centre and the Russian republican Supreme Soviet.

Throughout the second half of 1990, the U.S.S.R. leadership was losing control of the levers of state administration. A law on "Property in the R.S.F.S.R." came into effect on 1 January, 1991, and on 22 January the R.S.F.S.R. Council of Ministers approved a statute governing procedures for transition of the control of enterprises from Union to Russian jurisdiction.[203]

The U.S.S.R. government's unsuccessful attempt at military suppression of Lithuanian independence in January 1991 underlined the ongoing institutional collapse of the Soviet Union. Whether or not the armed clashes in Vilnius between pro- and anti-independence groups were inspired by orders from the U.S.S.R. government or resulted from a lack of clear instructions and its administrative collapse, it became apparent as events unfolded that the U.S.S.R. was no longer a state functioning as, in Max Weber's definition, an entity able to claim a "monopoly on the legitimate use of force" in territories over which it claimed jurisdiction. In January 1991, by Weber's definition, the U.S.S.R. ceased to exist as a state. After the events in Lithuania, negotiations between Russia, Kazakhstan, Ukraine and Belarus, begun in late 1990, were resumed. Their aim was the signing of agreements between four independent states which would make redundant the Union Treaty being prepared by the government of the U.S.S.R.[204]

VI

The sidelining of political parties is an important feature of Russia's political history in the second half of the 1990s. Parties which seemed only recently to have demonstrated their effectiveness in galvanising political activism were found to be dispensable. They had been set up to win elections but found themselves becalmed in the wake of elections to the repub-

203. Sheinis, *Vzlet i padenie parlamenta*, p. 321; Pikhoia, *Moskva. Kreml'. Vlast'*, p. 235.
204. Pikhoia, *Moskva. Kreml'. Vlast'*, p. 251.

lican and local soviets. It was unclear what prospects were held out by free elections, so that working for one of the new parties seemed no guarantee of a successful political career. Not the least of the problems was that such leaders of the democratic movement as Yeltsin (who became President of Russia), Anatoliy Sobchak (who became Mayor of St Petersburg), and Gavriil Popov (who became Mayor of Moscow) gained their popularity and standing without the support of any of the parties. They accepted that parties were needed, but in practice did not see the newly apparent organisations as a significant power base. Matters were not helped by the parties' aversion to the strict discipline that typified their main opponent, the Communist Party. This had an impact on their ability to organise effectively.[205]

Given the institutional weakness of a struggling party system which had only recently become legal, as political conflicts escalated, public contestation developed within the framework of U.S.S.R. federalism. Republican parliaments took over the function of parties. One of the first acts of the People's Deputies after the Declaration of Sovereignty of Russia was to consider how best to disseminate information about its activities. On 18 June, 1990, the most authoritative institution of the R.S.F.S.R., a majority of whose members opposed state interference in the media, conferred on the Supreme Soviet and the Russian Council of Ministers the right to create a Russian republican mass-media network and to publish a government newspaper, *Sovetskaya Rossiya*. A resolution on "Mass media of the R.S.F.S.R." was passed on 21 June.[206] This was entirely sensible, given that the leaders of the U.S.S.R. still had a monopoly of power, including the power to control the mass media. It served to bolster the independence of the Russian parliament. The U.S.S.R. centre for its part took the same approach, attempting to mobilise public support electorally by resorting to

205. Grigorii Golosov, "Proiskhozhdenie sovremennykh rossiiskikh politicheskikh partii, 1987–1993", in Vladimir Gel'man *et al.*, eds, *Pervyi elektoral'nyi tsikl v Rossii* (Moscow, 2000), pp. 77–105.
206. *Sovetskaia Rossiia*, 22 June, 1990.

a referendum. During the referendum campaign to decide the future of the U.S.S.R. and the creation of the post of President of the R.S.F.S.R., both the Union and the Russian republican leaderships acted like political parties, appealing to their supporters for votes. The institutional conflict was resolved by the Russian presidential campaign of June 1991, in which political parties played a purely ancillary role.

The Russian republic was neither the inventor of this new form of political contestation nor the first standard-bearer in the "parade of sovereignties". All the republics of the U.S.S.R. were experiencing similar upheavals. Indeed, in the mutinous Baltic republics, the national parliaments, which one might have assumed to be made up of Party functionaries loyal to the leaders of the U.S.S.R., set about seceding no less enthusiastically than the popular-front parties.[207] The institutional framework they chose after finalisation of the "U.S.S.R. Divorce" played a decisive role in the fate of the party system in the union republics.[208] Researchers suggest, however, that, in the case of Russia, the event that dealt the final blow to the development of a democratic party system was the moratorium on elections following the August 1991 coup attempt.

According to Adam Przeworski, "Democracy is a system in which parties lose elections", not a system in which democrats, having won an

207. In November 1988, Dainis Evans, Chairman of the Popular Front of Latvia, declared, "There is no political force in Latvia, and I say this very seriously, capable of causing Latvia to secede from the Soviet Union" (Vladimir V. Sogrin, *Politicheskaia istoriia sovremennoi Rossii (1985–1994): ot Gorbacheva do El'tsina* (Moscow, 1994), pp. 46–7. That same month, the Supreme Soviet of the Estonian Soviet Socialist Republic passed a constitutional amendment which read, "The Supreme Soviet of the Estonian SSR has the right to suspend or limit the application of legislative or other statutory deeds of the U.S.S.R." (Ibid., p. 47).

208. The earlier a republic declared its national sovereignty and held founding elections, the more viable its party system proved. The link is, of course, complex and in many respects self-regulating. The more time political parties had (including successor parties to the former republican Communist parties) to build institutions, the greater their role in the new institutional model. Where political parties had time to become significant challengers, the choice was usually in favour of a parliamentary system. This was most clearly the case in the Baltic republics. Where the development of party politics was blocked, as in the Central Asian republics, a presidential system was selected.

election, cancel further elections if they find it politically expedient. For all its drawbacks, the great advantage of contesting parties is that a party, having suffered total defeat in one electoral race, has the prospect of taking its revenge in the next one. This is why the party form of political contestation makes it possible to implement long-term strategies. This was precisely the prospect denied to the newly legalised Russian political parties.

For all their early shortcomings, the political parties' electoral potential remained considerable. When the moratorium on elections was introduced, Democratic Russia was the largest non-Communist political organisation in Russia. It estimated that it had between three and four hundred thousand active members. Surveys conducted in March 1991 indicate that 53 per cent of Muscovites trusted Democratic Russia, whereas only 11 per cent trusted the Communist Party. Holding "founding" elections on a party-political basis would have been the natural way forward after the Belavezha Accords between Russia, Belarus, Ukraine and Kazakhstan, but the instinct of institutional self-preservation proved too strong. Having received, after the failed conservative coup of August 1991, carte blanche to carry out their policies, neither the president nor the Supreme Soviet of Russia was prepared to expose themselves to the risk of electoral contestation, even though they had every prospect of winning.

The new political parties suddenly found themselves redundant and, at this most vulnerable stage of their development, were in no fit state to pull through undamaged. Even mighty Democratic Russia was forced to resolve its problems through organisational collaboration with the state bureaucracy, which led to its disintegration as a viable independent party when Russian parliamentary elections were next held in 1993.[209] By the autumn of 1993, the institutional field for party contestation was scorched earth. Many who voted for the Russia's Choice party in December 1993 genuinely believed they were supporting the successor institution to, and leaders of, Democratic Russia. Ideologically not wide of the mark, politically this was

209. For full details, see Brudny, The Dynamics of "Democratic Russia", 1990–1993, pp. 141–70.

far from being the case. Only 7 per cent of those on the electoral list of the "party of power" in 1993 were members of former democratic organisations which had been incorporated. Indeed, one of its leaders, Vladimir Shumeyko, announced that Russia's Choice was "the ruling party" even before the elections.[210]

It was not the case that declaring a moratorium on elections could abolish political contestation. The moratorium of late 1991 merely reinforced a trend which had become evident in 1990 whereby, in the absence of party politics, political contestation took the form of confrontation between institutions of governance. The conflict between the Supreme Soviet of the Russian republic and its president now replicated the institutional logic of the preceding 1990 conflict between the leaders of the U.S.S.R. and R.S.F.S.R. During the new stand-off, both sides again appealed directly to the population for support, arrogating to themselves functions which, in a system of contested elections, would have been performed by political parties.[211] The April 1993 referendum on whether the electorate had confidence in Yeltsin and/or in the Supreme Soviet, which opposed him, precisely mirrored the logic of the U.S.S.R. leaders' referendum campaign in March 1991.

VII

We said at the beginning of this essay that 1990 was a momentous year both for Russian history and for political science. The main surprise for political

---

210. Vladimir A. Kolosov, "Sdvigi v politicheskikh orientatsiiakh izbiratelei i geografiia golosovaniia za partiinye spiski", in V. Kolosov, ed., Rossiia na vyborakh: uroki i perspektivy (Moscow, 1995), p. 18.

211. Despite many claims to the contrary, the Supreme Soviet of the Russian Federation was an entirely functional legislative body. The political standoff between the presidency and the Supreme Soviet in 1992–3 was an institutional confrontation due to lack of clarity in defining the powers of the two institutions. See Joel M. Ostrow, "Institutional Design and Legislative Conflict: The Russian Supreme Soviet – A Well-oiled Machine, out of Control", Communist and Post-Communist Studies, 29/4 (1996), pp. 413–33; idem., Comparing Post-Soviet Legislatures: A Theory of Institutional Design and Political Conflict (Columbus, 2000).

scientists was a tangle of national (relating to a sense of political identity) and institutional factors influencing democratisation which transitology failed to take into account. In Russia's case, this manifested itself in an intensification of federative problems and the direction in which the political party system developed.

In 1990 there was still everything to play for. No possibilities had yet been ruled out. It was a year in which new ideological boundaries were laid down, new institutions established, new political strategies developed. Political opponents were building institutional fortifications against each other. Politicians were looking over new ideologies, mobilising organisational reserves, preparing institutional capacity. This was as true of party politics as of the confrontation between the U.S.S.R. and Russian republic camps. Democratic parties which had been put together virtually from scratch in a single year became capable of political action. Political leaders, including the future "non-communist" victors, could not do without political parties, which were one of the most effective tools of contested politics. In return, parties deployed the political authority of these leaders as their most powerful electoral and organisational asset.

This was the last year of the "perestroika period", when the institutional (selective) incentives in Russian politics not only survived but were strengthened at the expense of the institutionalisation of new political parties. Active participation in party politics ceased to be merely a means of achieving ideological solidarity and identity. "Selective" incentives of party activity, the prospect of a political career, were no longer the province of a ruling Communist Party. Other career paths were opening up in the political system. The deputies (including those from the Democratic Russia party) elected to the R.S.F.S.R. Supreme Soviet experienced this at first hand. Party politics might already have appeared in Russia, but in 1990, Russian politics were not yet party politics. Neither was that the case in 1991.

There were many more ideological ends in 1990 than available institutional means, and having a voice in the Russian parliament was a more effective institutional weapon than relying on the political parties with their limited resources. Although divided by personal and ideological disagreements, the people's deputies of the Russian republic acted as one whenever the institutional powers and competencies of Russia's Supreme Soviet were under debate. Their motivation can by no means be reduced to ideological cynicism or mercenary careerism, even if there were elements of both. Pragmatic political action was determined by the institutional framework. No politician can operate in an organisational vacuum, and the institutional power of Russia's parliament proved a more effective tool for achieving ideological aims than did the political parties. The framework of public contestation was provided by the institutional stand-off between the U.S.S.R. centre and the R.S.F.S.R. Supreme Soviet, and inter-party conflicts were subordinate to that.

In 1990, political opponents did not resolve their differences through compromise, but there was as yet insufficient determination, or a lack of resources, for the use of force. The main factors affecting political choices were escalation of political tensions, limited institutional resources and a dearth of relevant information. The players opted for tactics against strategies, reducing the political process to a zero-sum game which culminated in the failed coup of August 1991.

In 1990, however, as we have said, there was still everything to play for. Politicians could argue about ideas and ideals, split into parties and parliaments, weave intrigues and calculate moves. And, of course, be caught out by surprises. A hopeful journey had begun and, as is so often the case, for some of its participants it proved far more interesting than arriving.

JUNE

30 May–4 June

Mikhail Gorbachev visits the U.S. and Canada. A major result of the trip is that the U.S.S.R. de facto agrees to the future possibility of a united Germany becoming a member of N.A.T.O. Agreements are signed, inter alia, on trade relations between the U.S.S.R. and the U.S.; the non-production of chemical weapons, destruction of existing stockpiles and facilitating of a multilateral conference on banning chemical weapons; developing the peaceful use of atomic energy; and expanding exchanges of university students.

An independent association of terrestrial, satellite and cable television providers is founded in the U.S.S.R., with American participation (*Izvestiia*, 153, p. 7).

2 June

Founding documents of the Moscow Commodity Exchange, with Yugoslav and Italian participation, are signed (*Izvestiia*, 155, p. 2).

In Moscow, an unauthorised rally is held by the Moscow Student Club to mark the first anniversary of the massacre of students in Tiananmen Square, Beijing (*Novyi khronograf*).

Relics of the Solovki saints Savvatiy, Zosima and German are returned to the Russian Orthodox Church, having been taken from the Solovki Monastery in 1939.

Saudi Arabia's King Fahd sends a million copies of the Koran to the U.S.S.R. The first batch of a beautifully produced edition (in Arabic) is received in Moscow, Kazan and Ufa (*Moskovskie novosti*, 22, p. 2).

4 June

The Supreme Soviet of the Kirghiz S.S.R. declares a state of emergency in the city of Osh and several nearby villages after a conflict between Kirghiz and Uzbeks (Izvestiia, 158, p. 2; http://www.welcome.kg/ru/history/nz/). According to the U.S.S.R. Public Prosecutor's Office, casualties on both sides in the cities of Osh and Uzgen and in villages in Osh province total almost three hundred people. Unofficial estimates put the total several times higher.

5 June

In 1988–9 and the first half of 1990, some one million citizens were politically "rehabilitated", taking the total to over two million. Rehabilitation was denied to 21,333 persons who had betrayed their country during the Second World War; been involved in reprisals; been Nazi criminals, members of nationalist gangs or their accomplices; or been former employees of administrative bodies found to have fabricated criminal cases; and to individuals who had committed premeditated murder or other serious crimes (Izvestiia, 157, p. 2).

6 June

As of 6 June, there are thirty-two groupings of deputies in the Congress of People's Deputies of the R.S.F.S.R. Among the larger groups are Democratic Russia, Communists of Russia, the Agrarian group, an Independent Deputies group, the Glasnost journalists' group and supporters of the Democratic Platform within the C.P.S.U. (Argumenty i Fakty, 23, p. 2).

The Supreme Soviet of Moldova, as Moldavia has been renamed, declares acts of administrative insubordination in the Transnistrian region unconstitutional and rules that any "independent" decisions taken there are illegal (Izvestiia, 158, p. 2).

Moscow City Council decides to rebuild the demolished seventeenth-century Kazan Cathedral on the approach to Red Square (Izvestiia, 158, p. 6).

7 June

In Kiev, a two-day Organisational Council of the Ukrainian Autocephalous Orthodox Church elects as Patriarch of Kiev and All Ukraine Metropolitan Mstislav (Skrypnyk), who is residing in the U.S. Thus he is elected in absentia.

The Fifth Congress of Muslims in the European Part of the U.S.S.R. and Siberia opens in Ufa, Bashkiria (*Izvestiia*, 159, p. 2).

8 June

A General Council of the Russian Orthodox Church elects as Patriarch of Moscow and All Russia Aleksiy, Metropolitan of Leningrad and Novgorod (in the world, Aleksey Ridiger). The new patriarch is sixty-one and was born in Tallinn, Estonia (*Izvestiia*, 160, p. 1).

Mikhail Gorbachev holds a joint press conference with British Prime Minister Margaret Thatcher, who is visiting the U.S.S.R. Responding to a question about the future of the Warsaw Pact and N.A.T.O., Gorbachev says,

> The East European countries are well able to see the positive things our partners in the West do. We view representatives of the West not as adversaries but as partners in building new relationships in Europe. A new situation may arise where both these blocs will become open and declare themselves willing to admit any other European state. As our aim is pan-European institutions and pan-European security, we must increasingly interact with all Europeans (*Pravda*, 10 June, 1990).

9 June

The Sixth Congress of U.S.S.R. Cinematographers announces that it is moving onto a republican basis. The new federation of independent film associations would not be subject to decisions taken by the U.S.S.R. government.

10 June

Yegor Yakovlev, editor of *Moscow News*, interviews Boris Yeltsin:

Yakovlev: "Could you, perhaps aphoristically, express your vision of the future of Russia?"

Yeltsin: "All right. Through crisis to stabilisation and rebirth."

Yakovlev: "Will it be possible, even in the first stage as we struggle through the crisis, to maintain living standards?"

Yeltsin: "I am aware of alternative proposals. They provide for a mechanism to prevent living standards from falling. It is important not to confuse two concepts: prices and living standards. Prices can be increased providing living standards are safeguarded" (*Mosvkovskie novosti*, 23, p. 7).

In an interview with the B.B.C., Mikhail Gorbachev announces for the first time that he is in favour of a U.S.S.R. in which the republics delegate rights to the central government (*Komsomol'skaya pravda*, 24 June, 1990).

11 June

The Soviet–American International Cultural Initiative (Soros Foundation) and the Soviet Culture pavilion of the U.S.S.R. Exhibition of Economic Achievements spends half a million roubles on mounting the *Archives Come to Life* exhibition. Documents are provided by eight state archives. Unofficial organisations, the People's Archive documentation centre and Memorial are also invited to participate. Admission costs 1 rouble (*Izvestiia*, 163, p. 3).

The Cultural Initiative and its successor the Open Society Institute did a vast amount to support Russian science, arts and civic organisations over the following decade.

11–13 June

The founding congress of the U.S.S.R. Peasants' Union, a social and political association of collective farm chairmen and state farm directors, takes place in Moscow (*Sel'skaia zhizn'*, 27 July; *Komsomol'skaia pravda*, 24 June). In his speech at the congress, Yegor Ligachov confirms that he firmly favours giving priority to public ownership of land and explains failures in agriculture as being due to the weakening of the influence of Party committees on the economy. Boris Yeltsin says he believes that the land-owning peasants are the foundation for developing the agricultural sector, and that they should own not only the means of production but also the land. They also should be guaranteed a free choice of how they farm the land, and Party organisations should not interfere. The congress applauds both speakers (Izvestiia, 166, p. 1).

11–15 June

In Donetsk, the First Congress of Miners adopts resolutions on the socio-economic situation and ways of introducing market relations (Argumenty i Fakty, 25, p. 2).

12 June

The Congress of People's Deputies of the R.S.F.S.R. adopts the Declaration of Sovereignty of Russia by a landslide majority of 907 in favour and 13 against, with 9 abstentions (Izvestiia, 164, p. 1). This is actually a declaration of independence of the R.S.F.S.R. government from that of the U.S.S.R. and, as such, is a major milestone in the drawn-out disintegration of the U.S.S.R.

The U.S.S.R. law "Concerning the Press and Other Mass Media" would take effect from 1 August. By 1 January, 1991, all existing mass media would be required to register, "every one of them, including the oldest and most 'central'" (Moskovskii komsomolets, 134, p. 1). This law, for the first time in the history of the U.S.S.R., provided a legislative, rather than merely a declarative, basis for freedom of the press.

17 June

In Moscow, the Second U.S.S.R. Conference of the Democratic Platform of the C.P.S.U. appears to be favouring complete secession from the rest of the Party. The real sensation is a speech by K.G.B. Major-General Kalugin, who retired in March. He speaks of the dangers for a democratising society, which, in his opinion, are continuing to emanate from the state security services. The total number of their employees, he points out, is more than that of the intelligence services of America, Europe and Asia (possibly excluding China) combined. He calls for the depoliticisation of the agencies, cutting their staff by at least 50 per cent, renouncing political surveillance, renouncing the services of informers, and immediately dismantling the institutions for disseminating disinformation in the U.S.S.R. and abroad (*Izvestiia*, 169, p. 2).

19 June

The South African Parliament abolishes racial segregation in public places, a law first introduced in 1953.

Representatives of France, Germany, Belgium, the Netherlands and Luxembourg sign a convention in Schengen Castle, Luxembourg to facilitate cross-border movement of citizens of those countries.

19–20 June

The Russian Party Conference of 2,768 delegates from Russia to the Twenty-Eighth Congress of the C.P.S.U. turns into the founding congress of the R.S.F.S.R. Communist Party. Mikhail Gorbachev supports the proposal for a Communist Party of Russia (*Pravda*, 20 June, 1990).

20–22 June

The fifth Tynyanov Readings are held in Rēzekne and Daugavpils, Latvia (*Piatye Tynianovskie chteniia: Tezisy dokladov i materialy dlia obsuzhdeniia* [Riga, 1990], pp. 3–4).

21 June

The U.S.S.R. government adopts a regulation on public companies and securities. A section is devoted to transforming state enterprises into joint stock companies, which would be a shared decision of the employees and the competent ministry (*Izvestiia*, 173, p. 2). This is one of the most important laws promoting deregulation of the media and of numerous industrial and commercial enterprises.

22 June

The R.S.F.S.R. Congress of People's Deputies discusses a draft resolution "Concerning demarcation of functions in the management of institutions on the territory of the R.S.F.S.R.". Prerogatives of the U.S.S.R. ministries and agencies remain, for the time being, the provision of defence, state security, operation of the railways and civil aviation, and the navy (*Izvestiia*, 175, p. 2).

23 June

Ivan Polozkov is elected First Secretary of the R.S.F.S.R. Communist Party (*Izvestiia*, 175, p. 1).

24 June

In collaboration with Italy's Fiat car company, the U.S.S.R. intends to increase production of cars by nine hundred thousand units per year (*Izvestiia*, 176, p. 4).

29 June

Stores in Moscow are given the right to assume complete economic independence. The Moscow City Soviet resolves that any state shop whose staff so wish can be granted autonomous status in law. It can open a business account with state or other banks, and become administratively independent of the R.S.F.S.R. Ministry of Trade (*Moskovskie novosti*, 27, p. 2).

The Moscow City Soviet passes a number of major resolutions. From 1 July, 1990 ". . . all non-residential, detached buildings, as well as non-residential premises within state-owned residential blocks" will be declared communal property of the City Soviet. It resolves to transfer state-owned accommodation into the private ownership of Muscovites who wish to receive it, free of charge, within the established norms of entitlement and in compliance with the principles of social justice (*Izvestiia*, 182, p. 1).

In June 1990, 512 people in the U.S.S.R. were registered as HIV positive (*Argumenty i Fakty*, 29, p. 5).

THE BEGINNING OF THE END: NOTES OF AN EYEWITNESS, EDITED BY AN HISTORIAN, BEING THE SAME PERSON

Marietta Chudakova

These are not memoirs, athough I began 1990 by remarking in an interview that it was imperative for all of us to write about ourselves:

> All my hopes rest on my contemporaries' memoirs, but by that I mean not just autobiographical prose but real memoirs of the kind which were such an important part of Russian literature in the nineteenth century. The memoirs of a Pavel Annenkov or Pyotr Vyazemsky are exemplars of Russian literary prose, and I believe this is our path to self-discovery. We will need to search for the right form because we currently lack the words needed in order to give an honest account of ourselves. They have been worn away and it will be no easy matter to formulate thoughts which are genuinely our own. We talk a lot about pluralism, but for pluralism each person must have their own viewpoint on the events occurring around them. Until then, we are on thin ice. We need to start with a bold, "My name is So-and-So and I want to remember what life was like for me."[212]

What mattered back then, and still does today, is for people not to be afraid to have an opinion about what happened, and that can only be built on the basis of what we think about ourselves and our past life.

People who lived a substantial part of their lives in the Soviet period,

212. "Put' k sebe", *Literaturnoe obozrenie*, 1 (1990), p. 36.

and that is who I was addressing, did not generally take much interest in themselves. Notable exceptions, in my opinion, were *Just a Life*, the memoirs of Sarra Zhitomirskaya, who was in charge of the Manuscript Department of the old Lenin Library in Moscow from 1952 to 1976, and the reminiscences of Aron Gurevich and Rafail Ganelin. Naum Korzhavin wrote two tomes in which he speaks with incredible honesty about the "bloody enticements of the era", admitting that he was one of those enticed, and for many years seduced. Others have stayed silent, and only those imprisoned in the Gulag are still telling us their stories. This fear of ourselves is one reason why everything has come to be the way it is today.

I shall try, despite the paucity of memoirs, to reconstruct that special year of 1990 from my memory, my diary and some notes by Aleksandr Chudakov. He and I had similar views on what was occurring.

From my diary:

31 December, 1989, 23.50 hrs
Gorbachev begins his New Year address with a grave, almost tragic expression. "No matter how difficult this year has been, we bid it farewell with feelings not only of regret . . ." For an instant, fear, almost horror, shows in his face. What does he see ahead? What does he sense?

His eyes light up again, the eyes of Gorbachev the optimist, by outlook and heredity. He talks again about the future, with that sense of hope so traditional in our afflicted land. "The post-war division of Europe is a thing of the past . . . solidarity . . . harmony."

The Kremlin chimes ring out. For the first time in many years, a choir actually sings the words of the national anthem! "Glory to thee, our great homeland of freedom . . ." Good. At last that doesn't ring false. But then, oh dear: "Bulwark unfailing of peoples united . . ." That jars! Neither do we need the view of Lenin's mausoleum, or the words about his Party leading us forward to the triumph of Communism.

What will the '90s hold for us?

I

By the start of 1990, an increasingly free press had created a new and quite singular scene in Russian literature, mediated mainly through the literary journals. In that interview for *Literaturnoe obozrenie*, I had said,

> There was a time when the journals printed new work. The author wrote his final full stop and sent his piece off to the journal. Sometimes, indeed, the novel started appearing in print while that final full stop was still a distant prospect. That was true not only in Dostoyevsky's days but also in in the 1920s and 1930s. Today, when you open a journal you have to wonder what you are looking at. Was it written half a century ago? Seventy years ago? Is it something which for decades has been gathering dust unread in the archives, or something the whole world read, assimilated and forgot long ago, and which is brand new only for us?
>
> The reading public is divided sharply into those who in the past quarter-century have read and reread *Doctor Zhivago*, and those who are reading it now for the first time. For some, the prose and poetry in today's journals were the banned books they read in their youth, while for others they are the live context of current literary life. Genuinely new works are being offered to readers in quite different literary contexts, which is a very unusual state of affairs. How difficult it is, too, to be published today next to Pasternak, Platonov and Rozanov! Difficult but, I believe, fruitful. How sad, after all, to be only the best of a bad bunch.
>
> If we open a new issue of one of the journals, we can expect to find works in one of three categories: those from the first decade of the twentieth century, some from the 1960s and 1970s, and genuinely new works. Good, bad or indifferent are not immanent

qualities in writing, and there are different kinds of "good".

At present we are bringing sunken ships back to the surface, and immediately deciding which we can still sail in and which would be better dispatched to a museum as an important artefact representative of its period. Mayakovsky's metaphors are coming to life: "... happening upon iron lines of poetry, you finger them respectfully, like an old but deadly weapon ..." In our age, the real revelations come when the language of literature reacts to the language of everyday, and in turn affects it. That was the foundation of Mikhail Zoshchenko's innovation and the literary revolution he brought about. He was more actively aware than other writers of the language of the new Soviet society.

Listen to the language of some of the leading figures of our state today. You can't help noticing huge numbers of stylistic errors, and that is because the language of the U.S.S.R. was totally unprepared to deal with the realities that confront it now. It is crumbling before our eyes. I do not laugh at their errors but listen to them avidly. They are a great improvement on the faultless speech of the past. They are evidence that our language, totally stultified for the past twenty years, has finally come back to life. Yevgeniy Polivanov, an outstanding linguist in the Stalin era, wrote about the "the revolution's Church Slavonic language". This was "correct" language, as opposed to the incorrect language used by a Petrograd worker who "at an outdoor rally began almost every sentence with the words 'Looking at it the right way ...', but omitted to say what way that was". It's like the deputies in the Supreme Soviet today who talk about "the most optimal path".

These errors Polivanov contrasted with such "monstrously disciplined speech" as "the predatory sharks of imperialism", "the hydra of counterrevolution", "establish contact with ..." These, Polivanov noted, were not incorrect in terms of logic or accepted usage. On the contrary, it was precisely because of their linguistic correctness that they "have become such common currency and turned into clichés".

The clichés of the recent past are breaking down even as we watch, and the writer who will forge ahead is whoever succeeds in catching that changeover and running with it.

A lot of this is due to the lack of passion in literature today. I believe those who are presently writing "scurrilous" fiction will shortly find a passion to light up life. People will be reminded that life is a gift. Today we have lost that awareness because of all sorts of dreadful deeds. It was difficult for it to be borne unscathed through the horrors of what is now the distant past, and through the ghastly tedium of the recent past. It has to be found anew in every age. Mikhail Bulgakov had that awareness. He subtitled *A Theatrical Novel* "A Dead Man's Memoir".

Intellectual life is growing with a giddying speed that can be compared only with the rate at which the economy is moving in the opposite direction. Perhaps this is why, when our authors start trying to write about the present, they prove so unequal to the task. This is the greatest challenge facing our literature. The path back to yourself is one of the most difficult to find, but today it is the only path we have.[213]

II

Two men, Andrey Sakharov and Natan Eydelman, died in late 1989. They were incommensurable, but each of great importance to Russia.

The importance of Sakharov's death, both at the time and later, was clear to everyone. Today, both are forgotten, no matter how great the efforts to deny it, as regards Sakharov at least. I wrote about Eydelman in March 1990, about the events of those times and his involvement in them, which had a considerable impact on the mood of many people in 1990. Here is the

213. Ibid., pp. 33–4, 36.

last part of that article:

> In his angry 1987 letter to the renowned writer Viktor Astafiev, Eydelman grasped an electric wire with his bare hand, like a thoughtless child. The wire had long been live, and at his touch it became red hot. There were weaknesses in Natan's first letter. Aleksandr Chudakov and I warned him about them even before Astafiev's reply, which everybody found shocking.[214] Natan, as a specialist in Russian history, really shouldn't have been surprised.
>
> It would no doubt have been better if Natan had sent his correspondent a short treatise on the Jews in Russia, on the multi-national empire which the Bolsheviks inherited and willingly accepted, and on their overconfident attempt to restructure an imperial state. It is a pity that he didn't, but for a historian he was too close to the issue of anti-Semitism. From the early 1970s, subterranean stirrings, which came into the open in all their ugliness only in the final years of his life, had taught him to fear anti-Semitism. At the same time, Eydelman underestimated how dangerous it was, perhaps because of his amicable and unassertive personality, and how intractable, because of the kind of historian he was. The Astafiev correspondence somehow narrowed his public following, which became very polarised. This distressed him, and he remained much more open-minded than his supporters, who became embattled.
>
> After living through Stalin's "struggle against cosmopolitanism" in his youth, Natan's spirits had revived in the more buoyant Khrushchev years. Now, alas, he saw in the latest, unprecedentedly radical upturn, a new, dark groundswell which emanated not from the government but from hitherto unsuspected nooks and

214. Many remember the change that came over Viktor Astafiev in the wake of this ill-starred correspondence. Shortly before his death, he read Yuliy Krelin's memoirs of Natan, which Krelin had sent him, and told me over the phone from Krasnoyarsk that he had known nothing about Eydelman, but that if he had, he would never have written to him in those terms. He asked me to convey this to Krelin.

crannies. He seems not to have anticipated the visceral outburst of anti-Semitism we have all seen in recent years.

It was a constant torment in the last year of his life. He would become depressed but then cheer up, hoping things would get better. In the spring, while lecturing at Stanford University, he and I talked a lot about these matters. I sensed that he was increasingly heavy-hearted. In his own country of Russia, people were beginning to treat him, the best Russian historian for decades, with a churlish hostility, as someone who belonged to a different tribe.

The new era took him, like most of us, by surprise. The "cosy brutality" ended, and the ecological niches dug out with such effort were destroyed. The straightforward relations with a regime which had left its terrorist phase behind, ended. The straightforward relations with the public at large also ended. Glasnost produced an uncompromising differentiation.

In the period that was over, he had felt an unsatisfiable desire for action, to be able to exert influence on his country, perhaps even on its current history. Academic research was not enough. A nagging sense of being prevented from participating in the country's future, of being destined forever to wait in port for a favourable wind, ate away at him far more painfully than for most of his fellow citizens. Additionally, his ambition and dignity were constantly being trampled on in those years by continual refusal of permission to travel abroad, where archives were waiting for him which no-one else had touched. He was worn down by the times. He was tormented by having to renounce the topics of greatest interest to him. One of his colleagues speculated recently that, under different circumstances, Natan would have written not about Sergey Muraviov-Apostol, the aristocratic leader of the 1825 Decembrist Revolt, but probably about the more radical Pavel Pestel and the rootedness of the notion of a utopian state in Russia's history. Natan was forever meaning to work up the diary entries he had kept all his life, but was instead obliged to publish research to preserve his reputation.

It was a time when his most important projects had to be put off because they were unlikely to pass the censor. The general reaction that began in 1962, the state's grinding into reverse gear, also delayed his major reinterpretation of Russian history and the mentality of its protagonists, which barely manages to peep out from the pages of *Revolution from Above*.

In that book, Natan, in order to understand what was happening and to forecast possible futures, drew on his knowledge of the Russian autocracy and court circles, the government and the opposition, and the revolutionary intelligentsia. The next step, I believe, would have been to broach a topic long placed off limits by official Soviet historiography, social circumstances and popular prejudice. This was the unpredictable, national and nationalistic relationship between the intelligible and the irrational; the burden of historical destiny; the weight of the past, of slights and grudges which suddenly unbalance the life of modern nations. That would have been his next, urgent task, but it was one that fate did not allow him to address.[215]

From my diary:

Sunday, 7 January, 1990, Orthodox Christmas Day
How difficult the end of last year was, and how many people are afraid of what the immediate future holds, but so far, so good! I look into it without fear, although I have a physical sense of how rapidly we are being carried – whither? Out to the open sea?

Aleksandr and I went to the Herzen Museum today to remember Natan on the fortieth day since his death.

215. "Eshche ne vspominaia – pomnia", *Tynianovskii sbornik: Chetvertye Tynianovskie chteniia* (Riga, 1990), pp. 332–4.

III

27 January

On 18 January, the April writers' society was holding an open microphone evening in the Main Hall of the Central Writers' Club. I was in the Little Hall lecturing on Bulgakov to eleventh-grade students. From time to time we could hear public announcements, ". . . The meeting is being adjourned . . ." It was a minor annoyance.

Apparently, however, the Main Hall had been invaded by people in black shirts with megaphones who, before the meeting could start, began yelling, "Take yourselves off to Israel! Now we're in charge here!"

They showed a clip on *Viewpoint* on television yesterday. If the incident can't be brought to court (and the prosecutor spoke in a disgraceful manner, with an anti-Semitic smirk he didn't bother to conceal), their aim of scaring people away from public meetings and of setting off a "Russian revolt" will be achieved. It's a shameless invocation of the peasant masses and boundless expanses of Russia, as if these people are their serfs, to be deployed at will. [. . .]

There are attempts to reconcile Armenia and Azerbaijan. In Stankevich's opinion the troops were deployed too late, and too little effort was made to find political solutions (as usual). Yesterday, I suddenly recognised that we are now in a post-revolutionary phase, similar in some respects to the 1920s.

The threat from the Russian nationalists is not so much of pogroms (I hope it won't come to that) as of their managing to dumb everything down. Before we know it (I reckon within five to seven years), even if the current level of democracy is preserved (the term is an artificial construct, so let's say "the current level of press freedom"), we will be back back under the authority of new [Soviet-style academic authorities like] Ovcharenko and Metchenko.

28 January

On Tuesday, there is a meeting at the Art and Literature Archive on Pasternak. I've no doubt there will be many new, interesting papers, but who is going to turn up? I don't anticipate much of an audience. The cultural supply now greatly exceeds demand.

What's going on?

What is going on is seemingly just the standard process of the laying down of an "occupation layer", the stratum of cultural detritus from which a civilisation can be identified and dated. People write in journals, give reports at meetings. They don't go to every event, they don't read everything that is printed, but this layer may later provide the soil from which a normal civilisation can grow. Today's primary schoolchildren will draw sustenance from this soil, on which their roots will feed naturally, not having to strain to suck up nutrients from artesian depths the way we had to.

These two opposed processes – dumbing down as against accumulating a cultural foundation – were proceeding in 1990, rapidly and simultaneously, and in combination with many other, less plainly identifiable or even completely hidden tendencies.

Some people focused their attention mainly on the first process, the strategy of forcing down standards, often accompanied by overtones of menace. That combination blighted Natan Eydelman's last years. It was particularly influential in 1990 in affecting the way those people decided their future. "Don't you understand? They say crosses are already being chalked on people's doors!" my closest friend told me, her eyes as large as saucers. "So what?" "So they will come and ransack those apartments." "Have you never seen a certain four-letter word written on a fence?" I shouted. "Do you think that means you are going to get raped if you go there?" She laughed and took the point, but the fear continued to grow, and not only the fear of a pogrom. People lost confidence that they would be able to count on obtaining normal medical care, at least for their children. The son of that friend had a kidney disease and her Russian husband demanded imperiously of her, a Jew, "Just tell me what you think we're going to do if he urgently needs dialysis and there are thirty-five other people in the queue?" Eventually, under pressure from him, they emigrated. For the first year in Israel, she was terribly homesick, but then she never looked back or doubted they had taken the right decision.

Others focused on the second process of contributing to the country's cultural capital, deciding to devote their future to that and try to advance it.

IV

Most people continued to speak and write the old Soviet language, weltering in its dishonesty and phoniness. "More socialism!" People repeated that futile phrase after Gorbachev for several years. He at least did think about socialism constantly, but these were people in the arts and humanities, who had long ago ceased to care a fig about socialism. By 1990 that particular incantation had ceased to be heard.

In the years before Bukharin was fully rehabilitated, people invariably carried on referring to him as an "honest Soviet person". It was the same formulation that had been used in rehabilitation certificates issued to people many years before.

In the following year, by now no longer living in the U.S.S.R. but in Russia, I described the events which had just taken place and their main protagonists, the "'6os generation" who supported Gorbachev. They seemed now unable to recognise victory when it was handed to them. ("They would have made a better fist of accepting defeat.") These were the same people who in the early 1960s, after Solzhenitsyn's *One Day in the Life of Ivan Denisovich* had been published (which you would have thought left little room for doubt about the nature of Communist rule), decided to join the Party in order to fight for a "return to Leninist norms". A few years later they were expelled from that very Party for taking reform too seriously.

After that, they were swallowed up in the fog of the 1970s. They sat at home, wistfully drinking toasts "to the victory of our lost cause". An aura of doom and gloom became the hallmark of a "decent" individual. Perestroika caught them with their pants down. They had hurriedly to think through things they had omitted to think through in the previous three decades. "Onwards! . . . Onwards! . . . Onwards! . . ." we heard from the stage and the pages of the press. Onwards, to that far distant and most error-free of socialisms!

The torrent of documents reprinted in newspapers, magazines and journals, and presented in exhibitions and on television, completely ruled out any prospect of a "continued advance towards socialism". Our blood-soaked history rose out of the mire and the filth and spilled from our television screens and over the glossy pages of *Ogonyok*. Faith in the old ideology was destroyed for good and all, leaving a vacuum in people's minds.

What did those accustomed to holding sway in a literature-centred society offer in its place? They replaced Stalin with Bukharin. A full four years passed during which the writers bumbled through a mental evolution which any writer worthy of his salt should have undergone long before or, if he hadn't, he should never have taken up the pen. All this in public, in front of millions of people desperate for a totally honest telling of the truth, or at least deserving of honest introspection and a frank admission of not knowing it.[216]

The way those crucial years of 1987–90 were spent by those paid to provide the public with journalistic insight could only instil dismay and grim foreboding, not least as to what and who would displace the virtual "Bukharin" from the pedestal he by no means deserved.

No doubt the language of journalism was influenced by outmoded "left wing" terminology which had the allure of the West and Euro-communism (Cohen). No new political language had evolved in Moscow kitchens in the

216. "Tiagost' uspekha beznadezhnogo dela", *Strannik: literatura, iskusstvo, politika*, 1/3 (1992), p. 4.

1960s or in the newspapers and television of the late 1980s. That was when we really felt the lack of that lost generation of people born in the 1890s, and murdered under Stalin.

V

The mood of the year among people other than the intelligentsia is captured by our crime novelist Nikolai Leonov in the thinking of one of his characters who makes the transition from a pilfering Soviet retail manager to a full-blown present-day mafioso:

> In those days, he had cursed the bringers of perestroika, endowing them with every mortal sin. In a civilised world you didn't start bombing without a declaration of war. There was a way of doing things, there was an understanding, tacit but binding, about who was allowed to get away with what. There was a way of life which ensured that what was right got built, decisions were taken, voting occurred, reports were made; but then suddenly, in broad, peaceful daylight, they had opened fire. Epaulettes went flying, Party membership cards, ranks. Whole corporations were torpe-doed which were way above his, Yuriy Petrovich Lebedev's, level. That wasn't on. It was immoral! There should have been a warning. He wasn't being hypocritical. His anger was totally sincere. Over the previous twenty years a commonwealth of permissiveness and personal enrichment had taken root and flourished. Where were you then, comrades, with your flamethrowers? On the factory floor? Out in the fields? Untrained footsloggers on a route march? No! You were in there among all the others who turned a blind eye to the establishment of a businessmen's mutual aid society. For two decades you saw no evil and now, today, you stigmatise those happy years as "the period of stagnation" and set out to destroy our effective alliance. At the very least there should have been a warn-

ing. He, Yuriy Lebedev, for example, had never been aware of living in a "period of stagnation" which, incidentally, had seemed little different from any other period.[217]

From my diary:

29 May

Watching the R.S.F.S.R. Supreme Soviet on television, I find the faces in the hall completely fascinating and scrutinise whoever is speaking. No, this is not yet a body representing the whole of Russia, only one or two segments of it. There are no genuine peasants. (Have any survived, or have the last of them been sovietised?) There is no real rustic sage, an engineer, perhaps, or a teacher. These are people riding the crest of a wave. They sit, sometimes, at a tense moment, staring open-mouthed. They are not quick-witted. At one moment they will exultantly applaud power, the next applaud venerable weakness. For all that, this is Russia, emotional, volatile, moody, strong on hindsight. Yesterday, many people were asking what need there was for them to meet when 95 per cent of Russian voters support Yeltsin. Aleksandr phoned and said he had heard on the radio that Yeltsin has been elected. Is this the beginning of a new phase in Russia's history? Our so-called national sovereignty has been approved. From whom, pray, are we now independent, I several times wondered as I listened to the deputies. From whom does Russia aspire to be independent? The polar bears? Perhaps it's just a strange, warped way of clambering out of our warped, ahistorical national life of the last several decades.

VI

In June, on my way to the Fifth Tynyanov Readings, the participants talked on the train more about social than scholarly concerns. On 1 July, already

217. Nikolai Leonov, *Eshche ne vecher* (Moscow, 2004), pp. 175–6.

back in Moscow, I noted down some comments which unfortunately had initiated not a debate but an emotional exchange:

"Aren't you concerned, Marietta, when a flood of works by Father Sergey Bulgakov is unleashed by *Novy mir* on its two million subscribers?"

"After all," N. chimed in, without his usual irony, "who's to say what a person might be capable of, what deeds he might be prompted to undertake on a surfeit of S. Bulgakov?"

Such was the lofty view of a sophisticated, highly knowledgeable intellectual (who had read his Sergey Bulgakov long ago) of the undifferentiated mass of his fellow countrymen. One might have hoped he would be proposing to collaborate with them to build a civil society on a site already fairly clear of the rubbish left behind by the Soviet Union. Instead, he seemed keener to snobbishly restrict their access to Russian philosophy, which for seventy years had been safely locked away out of their sight. Today, many years later, this "debate" is tacitly continuing, only by now from different continents.

At those readings, I gave a paper in which I attempted to define the current situation in scholarship in the humanities, in literature and in society. I recalled the mid-1970s, when Russian literature was at the height of its importance in the Soviet Union. A group of scholars equipped a collection of Yuriy Tynyanov's articles with a dense critical apparatus, and succeeded with superhuman efforts in forcing it through all the levels of the 1977 censorship. This process took up far more time and nervous energy than the work itself. Imagine their amazement when they subsequently found it on the home bookshelves of physicists, chemists and mathematicians, together with other demanding volumes of literary analysis. This was the time when those I called in my talk "philologists of the third phase" were obtaining their academic education, a generation born in the 1940s which was soon to become the backbone of Slavonic studies in Russia and throughout the rest of the world:

From the early 1970s any work of genuine literary scholarship which managed to get into print became a significant event, a substitute in the minds of a large educated public for the social change they desired. This kind of significance was not restricted to literary works by contemporary authors, or even to works of literature. To an even greater extent it attached to "cultural heritage" texts about the past, including literary history. Scholarly writing about literature, from commentary on an article to an explication of a poem, began to take on the same significance, assuming the status of an event not only for the authors themselves and their colleagues but for a readership more extensive than one can imagine in any other country. Highly educated people outside the humanities developed a taste for fact-laden commentaries written in dry, scholarly language and set in small print. Physicists and chemists were drawn to academic philology, firstly, no doubt, as a source of information about literature, but secondly as a source of definitive language, free from demagogy, a rare and precious commodity in the ocean of the contemporary bastardised printed word; and finally, for want in the U.S.S.R. of sociological, political or economic printed matter closer to their needs, or of memoirs written with any integrity. These readers satisfied their intellectual and social interests indirectly, by taking a diversion through philology. They were pleased to make contact with something oppositional and prestigious.

In the fifth year of perestroika, one of the least superficial consequences of change has occurred: Russian society is ceasing to focus on literature.

One of the first signs of this entirely new situation was a change of attitude towards the publishing of literary or quasi-literary texts. They have lost the special cachet that attached both to publishers and published who got work past the censor. Today, that old feeling of having been in luck and having won an important victory attaches, instead, to the successful commercial operation of a journal or a publishing house.

Philologists of the third phase suddenly found themselves in a radically different situation. Until recently, they had been secure in the knowledge, although they would hardly have articulated the thought, that in Russia working in literature was highly prestigious. Moreover, they were working in the part of it which was persecuted. Finally, they were working on its most precious materials.

Such victories as getting work through to publication relatively unscathed, and such defeats as seeing the text severely truncated or even the printing plates completely broken up, were no mere shadow-boxing. A real fight was on to preserve the cultural tradition, to maintain a set of values which lay outside the confines of Soviet literary and social life with its obligatory ideological meetings and appointments at Ostankino with loyal literary functionaries like Pyotr Proskurin or Aleksandr Chakovsky. Scholars of the third phase not only maintained these values but had them ready to produce when the time came and they were needed. They were, however, to face serious psychological problems over their place in society.

The generation from which these philologists of the third phase were recruited had faced a choice in the latter part of the 1960s which became an inescapable decision in the early 1970s. Some emigrated, others became dissidents and went on to imprisonment and/or emigration. Yet others, rejecting both these options, dedicated themselves to working in solitude at their profession and adopting a stance of unwavering, mute opposition.

The very beginning of perestroika saw the sudden widespread adoption of their values, the loss of their personal link with their specialised readers, the loss of their status in society, marginal but familiar and in its way rewarding. To make matters worse, this was accompanied by scholarship finding itself in a spotlight that revealed weaknesses in its methodology and the concepts with which it operated.

The revision of values, which now preoccupies the whole of society, applies also to philology. No longer is it viewed through a veil of deference. It is treated like any other academic discipline, which is an unfamiliar situation for it in Russia, and not particularly comfortable.

A scholar no longer enjoys reflected glory from the subject of his researches ("He is studying Tsvetayeva! Mandelshtam!"). He answers for himself and for the quality of his scholarship. Many aspects of society today make demands on him: politics, economics, public life expect a literal rather than a metaphorical response, and will no longer take no for an answer. Dogged renunciation is dismissed as the dullness or eccentricity of an old gentleman.

The philologist finds his credentials being questioned by a more demanding public, and to some extent already by a more demanding scholarly community. He is not used to this, does not like it and may possibly be unable to find an answer to it.

For a time, historical fact-finding elbowed literature aside, but it too is slowly moving away from centre stage to a more natural, specialist niche. Articles on economics and politics have legitimately taken their place in the press, and memoirs no longer have to be fictionalised to placate the censor. Somewhat querulously, literary criticism and literary history have followed literature itself, or perhaps even preceded it, down to a less prestigious but condign level.

To some extent, today's thirty- to thirty-five-year-olds, replacing the philologists of the third phase, have also been poisoned by the old focus on literature. In previous years, they could aspire to be published only in duplicated university collections of papers, or at best in the *News of the Academy of Sciences' Department of Literature and Language*. Now, instead of heaving a sigh of relief and settling down to honest academic toil without being harassed by outsiders, they are skittishly trying to find their place in the sun by battling their way onto the pages of literary journals. An all-too-human proclivity to want now all the things they didn't have in their past decade of scholarly endeavour is deforming the discipline's language even before it has become established. Quite needlessly, they are trying to adapt it (as in years gone by) to the tastes of a mass readership. Let us hope that the generation after this one, today's graduate students, will be free of all these temptations and complexes.

The departure of literature from centre stage in Russian life will affect everyone who sees themselves as part of the scholarly community. Apart from anything else, they will need to take their place in society, get themselves registered within the profession, and sign up to one of the political parties or deliberately decide not to. Some will face those same choices of the early 1970s.[218]

As the Bolsheviks liked to say, no-one will be allowed just to sit it out.[219]

VII

From my diary:

24 June

Back yesterday morning from the Tynyanov Readings. The Russian Communists' congress is over. For the first time, Gorbachev, replying to written questions from the audience, looks browbeaten.[220]

218. Within two years, one of the Readings' participants had emigrated to Israel and a few had become professors at American universities. They nearly all remained regular participants of the Readings, however.

219. "Tynianovskie chteniia: avtopolemika", *Piatye Tynianovskie chteniia: Tezisy dokladov i materialy dlia obsuzhdeniia* (Riga, 1990), pp. 324–8.

220. This was because it was the Russian republican (R.S.F.S.R.) congress, not the U.S.S.R. Party Congress. It had been dreamed up by his enemies a few years earlier, and was outside his control.

I understand the anxiety of a Party man facing the Party majority, which is the main player in its hierarchy. Whether that majority is being manipulated by a skilful or just a super-strong individual, or whether it is organising itself is neither here nor there. It is an anxiety that is instinctive for any top functionary or Party activist, fear of a monster of whose nature they all are fully aware. It is one thing for Gorbachev to face a heterogeneous audience, some of them intelligent, some of them weak, a mixed bag,[221] quite another when he knows every member of the audience has that little red Party card in their pocket, uniting them all into a single fist, a single hammer, ready to come down on the head of anyone who steps out of line. He stood at the podium and felt in his water the history of his Party, a history in which many have walked from that podium without their trousers, and quite a few without their heads.

28 June

The country's future is on a knife edge. Even the West, to judge from yesterday's television, has put its relations with us on ice and is waiting to see what will happen at the Twenty-Eighth Communist Party Congress.

Everyone feels that this is a dangerous time. The Russian Communist Party is demanding that the U.S.S.R. Communist Party congress be postponed until autumn (to give it time to gather its strength). I no longer perceive Gorbachev as a human being. He has become elusive, politics personified, and his politics too have become elusive, almost no more than temporising. Previously, that was a means of implementing his strategy. Yeltsin wants the congress now.

Everything is coming unstuck. The Russian people seem baffled by having two leaders. It goes against our national mentality.

For all that, I have a surprising feeling that there has been

221. I was referring to the earlier Congress of People's Deputies of the U.S.S.R.

enough time for something positive to have taken root. The train has been so heavily freighted during the perestroika period that now it is moving forward under its own inertia, despite the bumpiness of the track.

2 July

At 10.00 this morning, the Twenty-Eighth Congress of the Communist Party of the U.S.S.R. opened. Soothing tones and silly smiles from Gorbachev. Visiting my mother in No. 16 Hospital, I talked to two of the doctors. They said as one, "He should be ashamed of himself! People need to have something they can believe in! All that lying has got to stop. They need to say, 'Yes, it was our fault!' and then the people will trust them. You can't just go on pretending!"

That is how ordinary, educated, professional people see the situation.

3 July

Aleksandr and I visited Lev Kopelev yesterday. I said, "All right, this is a press conference. Two questions. One: Is it acceptable that a significant part of the country is emigrating?" "Unfortunately, yes. They are frightened." "Do you think their fear is justified?" "No, I don't."

I repeated my views on the lack of justification for emigrating. "None of them are brave enough just to say they want a better quality of life because you only live once." Here N.N. interjected that the country was collapsing. (We had recently crossed swords on this subject: "Russia is finished anyway." "No, it isn't!") There had been a social experiment on a scale exceeding anything imaginable, she said. "I can't think of anything comparable in the entire history of humankind." "Mm," I said. "Perhaps some time before Ancient Egypt?" "It's obviously too late to salvage anything." "So should everyone just emigrate under a banner reading, 'Sauve qui peut!'?"

"Tell me, Marietta," she protested. "Do you just want to stick a label on the situation or try to understand it?" "Both. Why are those who are emigrating so reluctant to label what they are doing? They are evidently embarrassed."

My next question to Kopelev was, "What can be done right now? Is there a party capable of taking over power from the Communist Party without an interregnum?" "If I were in Gorbachev's place just now, I would declare a brief military coup. I would expel the Party from wherever I found it and keep troops in the streets until new parties could be formed."

"We've already had one brief coup which became permanent . . ." "You're right, but to be honest, I can only hope for a miracle." "A perfectly reasonable hope in Russia."

I should explain that what touched a raw nerve with me was people resorting to false causality: "We are emigrating *because* we can't stay here, and anyway there is no point." Later, in Chicago in 1992, I spoke to a colleague who had emigrated long before: "Boris, why do you keep telling me how bad everything is in Russia and how it can never get better? Even if things do get better in Russia, you will still be all right here!"

How, though, could I not also understand B., a Muscovite I spoke to yesterday? Without the benefit of higher education or even, as far as I know, higher vocational education, he seemed able to accomplish very successfully anything he put his mind to. When, later, business entrepreneurship began to be legal, he decided to emigrate to America. I asked him, "Why you? This is your time. You of all people can't be worried!" His reply was short and to the point: "I'm fed up. We meet foreign partners at the airport, they've hardly set foot on the tarmac, and instantly, before any business can be discussed, people are trying to get money off them. I'm ashamed for us. And pogroms? I have a daughter." "There aren't going to be pogroms in Russia," I said. He spelled it out for me, syllable by syllable: "I am fed up with lying in bed night after night wondering whether or not there will be." I said, "Okay. You are right. No more questions."

I was sure we would not have pogroms, but he was right in not wanting to gamble on our Russian backwoodsmen. I hope he is able to sleep soundly in Los Angeles.

7 July

N. is evidently going to emigrate to Germany. That's fine, but I don't see why he has to go around prophesying the ruin of Russia and the imminent day of the pogrom thug. His wife would have talked him into leaving anyway, even if everything in Russia were improving exponentially. It's obvious that whatever happens we aren't going to reach the German standard of living for decades, but wouldn't it be more honest just to say, "I'm leaving because Gorbachev has given us the opportunity to travel and emigrate?"

But then . . . It has occurred to me in the last half hour to wonder why we get so het up about this, both those who are leaving and I myself. Life is short. I should be happy that someone has a chance to change their destiny and the will to do it.

So my attitude should be: I'm sorry they're leaving, but let them leave without recrimination.

On the other hand, there is the point that perestroika is helping N. to emigrate, and in return, by emigrating, he is putting a spanner in the works by depleting the reserves of intellectual energy in Russia.

[. . .]

The congress shambles slowly towards the cliff edge . . . Aleksandr said today, "No, we will probably soon see that Gorbachev knows what he is doing and has the measure of his villains. He knows you can't leave them alone together in a room." It is better for him to stay with them, not to resign, otherwise they will just shift to the right. So he will stay on and contain them until new institutions can form.

13 July

Yesterday was the crucial moment at the Party congress. In the morning they announced the results of the vote for Deputy General Secretary. Ligachov picked up just 776 votes, with 3,642 against him.

This is evidently due to the Communists' main characteristic: you can never rely on them. I can imagine that before the congress they looked, not just to us but to each other, like a mighty single-minded horde ready to topple Gorbachev and turn back the wheel of history, or their part of it, at least. But then gradually, sensing the power emanating from Gorbachev (which is the only thing they respect), they took a step back, then another, retreating, retreating.

What flair! Gorbachev intuited that, by conducting a secret ballot rather than a roll call, people would dare to express their honest preference and he would be able to chuck Ligachov out on his ear. Then, precisely because they saw how easily, by snapping his fingers, the General Secretary got his way and took Ligachov out,[222] and saw how many were against Ligachov, Gorbachev was home and dry. They saw how the scales were weighted and did not unite to fight. Actually, they haven't known how to do that for years. They are only afraid of each other. They retreated in disarray.

Having that early vote was important, because Gorbachev was able to rub Ligachov's face in the dirt and kept him on tenterhooks. Among this gang of criminals that counts heavily against a candidate.

For the past ten days or so I have been glued to the television,

222. Gorbachev wanted to get rid of Ligachov and had taken a snap decision the previous day to have an early vote on his candidacy. In my diary I was trying to explain how advantageous that decision was, based on Gorbachev's understanding of his party.

intently watching the thrashing tail of a great evil creature shuddering in its death agony: the Communist Party, which has ruled this land for so many decades. I didn't think I would live to see it, although on more than one occasion Aleksandr and I dreamed that this day would come.

15 July

I am putting the finishing touches – I hope – to my postscript to Mikhail Bulgakov's *Selected Works* for Enlightenment publishers.[223] I quote an editorial from the *Historical Herald* in 1917: "Our country has embarked upon a new stage of history . . . let us call forth its creative powers which for so long have been under the yoke of the old regime." Russia "must reveal the treasures of its spirit and give voice to the new word it was not hitherto allowed to utter but which the peoples of the world have long awaited."

How like our own times, except that no-one is awaiting anything from us other than that we may at last enjoy a more or less normal way of life and become a more or less respectable member of the international community. They are, of course, glad that the roaring monster has sloughed its skin and now appears in a different form. But is even this what we genuinely look like, or do we ultimately look different under this skin? That is what the "peoples of the world" are really wondering.

And what about us? Does our nation really believe it has a new word to reveal? No. It believes in nothing whatsoever, and what good can come out of such total indifference?

VIII

In July 1990, the Fourth World Congress for Soviet and East European Studies was held in Harrogate in England. Given that the previous one had been

223. Mikhail Bulgakov had just been included in the school literature syllabus and I was asked to compile a one-volume collection.

held in Washington, D.C. in 1985, you can imagine the euphoria of the participants, some twenty-five hundred of whom descended on the United Kingdom!

There too, the future career of many Russian academics in the humanities took shape. "It's a meat market!" one ecstatic colleague kept repeating.

It became clear not only that many Western institutions were more than willing to sign long-term contracts, but, even more importantly, that the situation had changed dramatically, and nobody was quite sure how. Before this, anyone planning to leave Russia had had to make a final, irrevocable decision. Now it seemed clear that there was no decision to make. You could come to work in the West and go back to Russia in the vacations.

A lot of people did. This took away any need to justify emigrating ideologically. It was no longer necessary to cite the overall hopelessness of the situation in Russia, with the concomitant sense of imminent cataclysm (although, even subsequently, there was no shortage of that). People could go abroad without seeming to emigrate. Naturally, colleagues who left and became professors in the West, completely (or half or three-quarters) dropped out of the country's so-called public and civic life (including elections), in which the mediocrities who didn't leave participated ever more eagerly. Bright, highly educated colleagues probably weren't particularly interested in Russia's civic life anyway. At least they were able to participate fully in the academic life of the planet, and in any case Russia's destiny was never going to be decided in university departments and faculties.

Aleksandr Chudakov and I spent a considerable part of 1990, as of the preceding and subsequent years, abroad. It was only in 1994, after spending the spring semester in Geneva, that I told my foreign colleagues that in future I would spend no more than two or three months a year outside Russia. The time had come to decide whether one lived there or not. J. Douglas Clayton, who had invited me to spend a semester in Ottawa in 1995, managed at my request to fit my teaching into two months. Chudakov, who before Gorbachev had never been allowed out of Russia to attend a single symposium, taught the spring semester of 1990 at the University of Michigan. I went to visit him there for a month and went on to a number of other universities. We shared a long autumn semester at the University of Southern California, and attended a number of conferences in other countries.

Even there we could find someone with whom to mull over Russian affairs. Aleksandr talked by phone nearly every day to Naum Korzhavin, who lived in Boston. Their deliberations about Russia fill many pages of his diary that year.

From the diary of Aleksandr Chudakov:

23 November

Korzhavin: Gorbachev is a colossal politician, but he has lost touch with the situation. Stalin well remembered earlier times, when the Russian people were not sheep. (Three revolutions!) He feared them and took his own special kind of precautions. Gorbachev, however, is a Soviet-style Party functionary and thinks the people can be manipulated at will.

Me: The people have shown wisdom and forebearance. All sorts of things could have kicked off long ago.

Korzhavin: Of course, but Gorbachev does not trust them. You see, I'm a little tired. "If Russia is no more, what kind of captain am I?" At the end, plaintively, "You aren't going to do a bunk to the West, then?" "Why do you ask?" "Everybody else is." "We will be last in the queue. Only if it comes to firing squads."

On 12 October 1990, after a four-month trial of the culprits of the January nationalist fracas at the Central Writers' Club, K. V. Smirnov-Ostashvili was sentenced to two years' imprisonment, to be served in a medium-security labour camp. I said at the time, and repeated later, that the sentence was a clear and important signal from the state that governmental anti-Semitism was a thing of the past in our country. (The day-to-day aggravation was another matter.) Few people agreed.

It was in 1990 that many people who were intellectually well able to think about Russia's future decided they couldn't be bothered. They chose to give priority to their own scholarly and personal lives.

In this year too, at the scene of the crime, so to speak, through the efforts, I suspect, of some high-calibre minds, the unwise and harmful idea of Russian grandeur surfaced, not as a topic for historiosophical musing (which might have been quite constructive, given the abrupt decline in the ideological constituent of Russia's atmosphere), but as a literal priority of social policy.

From my diary:

28 November

R. on the subject of Barabanov's article in *Problems of Philosophy* (as paraphrased by Aleksandr Nosov): "He is no Christian! Because if he were, he would know that history has a beginning and an end! You have all betrayed the Russian Idea! You want to arrange everything in accordance with some standard European model!"

I said, "Yes, it would be good to let even just a few generations enjoy life!"

Nosov told them, "I have just come back from West Germany. When I see the kind of life people with disabilities live there, I wonder whether we shouldn't scale back our glorying in the Russian soul a little, when disabled people in Russia are stuck at home soiling themselves."

I retorted, "You're becoming left-wing! And what a monarchist you used to be!"

As if that weren't enough, we were treated to V. N. yesterday on The Word channel, hysterically, sanctimoniously, wringing his hands and ranting on about Christianity and our God-given Father the Tsar. Then, after we've seen him at his desk, the camera zooms in on him standing looking like a repentant demon at the doors of a church. It was truly nauseating! Exactly what caused Russian intellectuals to run a mile from the Church at the beginning of the twentieth century.

On television there was already talk about the threat of fascism, while the more educated ones informed us that "Mussolini was not a racist" and suggested that it was time to start discussing National Socialism. They reminded us (I quote from my diary entry for the day) that "in 1919 the N.S.D.A.P. had only four thousand members, and that in 1933 Hitler came to power by democratic means".

[. . .]

Who are a majority of Russians prepared to follow today? To my horror, Gorbachev has started resembling Brezhnev. I can just see our mafiosi glancing furtively at the television screen and saying, "Go on your travels, my precious, to your Paris. Enjoy the French cuisine and shoot your mouth off there, just as long as you leave us alone in the meantime to grab everything in Russia we can lay our hands on!"

Yesterday at the Central Writers' Club, I saw Ilya Konstanti-novsky. He gave me his book about Tolstoy. He is just back from Vienna. He had watched people in Germany making up food parcels for us. (I cried yesterday at the sight of an old woman in Leningrad who had been on the front line during the war, weeping at the humiliation of receiving an aid parcel from defeated Germany. What are we to make of it? Reparations continuing even to the present day? Time stood still for a moment, and there was my brother sending us a parcel in 1945 from defeated Germany. [Today I can add: to a starving family with two soldiers at the front. – M. C.]) He too has misgivings about the future. How long ago was it that we were pleased at the sight of Gorbachev?

"Yes, he hasn't turned out to be very clever." "Too uneducated?" "No, it's just that a sow can have very different looking piglets, but all of them have been born to a sow. It's the same with him. He was born to the same sow as the rest of them."

He's right. At moments of stress, Gorbachev displays precisely those archetypal hereditary characteristics.

3 December

Recently, a bright young taxi driver remarked, "Gorbachev should have resigned as General Secretary of the Communist Party last summer. The whole country would have admired that. Now, though, when people march on the Party district committees in the spring, he may well be hanged with the rest of them."

"Why do you think it will happen in the spring? When the bread runs out?" "No, it's nothing to do with bread running out. That sort of thing just generally gets going in the spring."

Gorbachev at the C.P.S.U. Congress, and particularly at a meeting with the cultural intelligentsia a few days ago (what was that in aid of? Nobody has the faintest idea), declared that he was opposed to private property. You feel like asking, "Well, why did you stir everything up in the first place? You might as well have left things as they were!" Secondly, he declared, "I cannot renounce what both my grandfathers believed in" (both having been imprisoned, as he himself said, for no good reason!) "and my father – the ideal of socialism!"

A dispiriting impression. What is he trying to hold together with all this? Or was my father-in-law right when he used to say, "Tut-tut, doesn't know his ABC." I often think of Pavel Ivanovich now.

[. . .]

In the evening, a report from the R.S.F.S.R. Congress of People's Deputies.

The deputies are very worked up, arguing loudly, almost shouting, about private property. Here it is again, the issue of land ownership! The issue of power, what else? A constitutional amendment on private property is passed, placing it on an equal footing with any other form of property.

The deputies were saying openly that deputies who are Communists had been called in for a pep talk at the Central Committee today! A day of triumph for Yeltsin and many others, followed by his press conference, which went extremely well. Everybody was talking about the making of history. A pre-revolutionary promise has come to pass. The decades of Bolshevik deceit are at an end.

IX

12 December

Yesterday I was at the Seventh Congress of Writers of the R.S.F.S.R. [Nobody yet knew that all these congresses were the end of the line, the Twenty-Eighth of the C.P.S.U., the Seventh of the R.S.F.S.R. writers. – M.C.] Bondarev's reports ("Stalingrad", "The Wave", etc., the rage of a man losing his clout in the new climate), Prokhanov – my first sighting of this Soviet Superman. The audience swooned when he told them firmly that now "we must learn how to make money for our Union", and his demeanour suggested he would teach any laggards the hard way.

For two days, I sat in the audience as a delegate representing the critics and literary historians of Moscow, and became increasingly persuaded that I had to stick it out to the end. It was a bacchanalia. People (including Vladimir Rasputin) were running on to the stage completely beside themselves. A certain Vladimir Arro tried to chide them: "What are you talking about? Remember the law on freedom of the press has been approved! That is effectively the end of censorship!" Nobody was the least bit interested!

I saw only too clearly what our "focus on literature" looks like in action, and how terrible, and no less spectacular than those of the Party, were the convulsions accompanying its demise. They had had the carpet pulled

from under their feet – "And all you can think about is freedom of the press
..." At that I decided I needed to write about this grisly end for *Literaturnaya gazeta* and bring it to the notice of a broader public than the Tynyanov Readings would reach.

Excerpts from the article:

> An important admission was made in the editorial in the first issue
> of a new newspaper entitled *Day*, which was distributed free to
> delegates: "The writer has been pushed out of politics, ideology
> and public life. Other people who are not artists lead the crowds,
> lead the marches, study, organise and arm our peoples. The writer,
> his hopes (of what?) disappointed, retreats in dismay to his desk
> where a neglected sheet of paper lies, and does not know what
> words to write."
>
> Reader, admit that in the years of stagnation people did not
> write that coherently and movingly, or in a manner so menacing
> and plaintive.
>
> What were the writers who came to the platform one after the
> other complaining about; whom were they menacing and why?
>
> Aleksandr Prokhanov in his speech expressed himself less
> fulsomely than in the newspaper he edits: "Suddenly the people
> seem no longer to need the books we write." Absolutely true.
>
> It seemed those days would never end. Our readers are patient
> and tenacious, and for twenty years went on reading, in the ever
> more dimly lit carriages of the metro and overground trains, much-
> thumbed copies of *Girdle of Rock* [a trilogy by Yevgeniy Fyodorov],
> *The Siege* [a trilogy by Aleksandr Chakovsky] and other novels by
> several of those who gathered in December in the auditorium of
> the Soviet Army Theatre.
>
> Why they were really there was to debate the impact of the
> unexpected granting of press freedom. The two main effects of this
> collided and formed a vortex in the auditorium. The first was one

everybody already knew about: today's new reader is reading books by quite different authors from the delegates to this congress. The second, far less obvious, effect is that our literature has come adrift from its long-standing mooring and sailed away, taking with it bad, average, quite good and actually very good writers. The sensation of drifting and heaving was profoundly unsettling for this audience, but none of the speakers told its members the truth.

The truth, as I have no hesitation in asserting, is that literature has suddenly become marginal to Russian society. Since the time of Pushkin, it had occupied a central place in our culture which, for good reason, it retained in post-revolutionary Russia. We are witnessing a momentous process. For the first time in almost two centuries, literature has ceased to be a central pillar of our society.[224]

The spiritual authority of writers who refused to mediate official ideology, and paid for that by forfeiting their literary careers, sometimes indeed paying with their lives, provided a pedestal for other writers who never produced anything not readily publishable in the press of the time. Today's members of the Writers' Union presume to speak on behalf of two centuries of Russian literature, but how many of them are fit to take their place in the "normally" developing literature of a free society, without censorship but also without the feeding trough, without state tutelage but also without patronage from public funds?

The prevalent reaction was petulant rage at the loss of rights which seemed to have been conferred for life, and a determination to get them back at any cost, including putting history into reverse.

Literature is vacating its place at the centre of Russian culture just as the spoken word is taking off, primarily in public speaking, which for many years was frozen in the canonical forms of written reports. Now it has come to life and can be heard everywhere, at

---

224. "Ne zasloniat'sia ot real'nosti", *Literaturnaia gazeta*, 1 (5327), 9 January, 1991, pp. 1, 10.

rallies, congresses and meetings. At one extreme is loud, "expressive" reading from a prepared text, supersaturated with imagery. This "literary" speech, a kind of hyper-writing, is an out-of-season blossoming of literature at a time when its decline is obvious. You cannot grasp what exactly the author is trying to say, as meaning becomes blurred and is replaced by motifs, intentions and aims.

At the other extreme is the political spoken word as practised by today's politicians. Here we find minimalism, a complete absence of grandiloquence, an obvious departure from the legacy of their predecessors. It is the politicians who have led the way in freely speaking out in the new era, while writers continue to chisel away at their set pieces of literary rhetoric.

"So, guys, here's the next issue we need to decide our position on . . . What we've been exchanging our views on up to now . . . We have been devoting considerably less attention to the spiritual sphere . . . It was highlighted about this at the plenary session . . ."

This too is dysfunctional language, but of a quite different kind. At the "literary" extreme, it is the exquisite fashioning of the discourse that ties the tongue in knots, while here there is undoubtedly real meaning behind the words, political reality. The language, however, is completely detached from the literary tradition, following its own bureaucratic and chummy syntax, with its own orthoepy, and following it with a curious persistence. One can hardly believe that grown men and women in the past five years of liberated public speaking have been unable to learn the correct pronunciation of frequently recurring words. And yet real meaning, political realities, are nevertheless behind these maimed words. Unfortunately, they are behind the words and seem to exist in parallel with the flow of the speech. At the beginning of perestroika, today's major political figures, in full public view, learned to speak without clichés, searching for new words to express new thoughts and a new reality. They seem now to have given up looking. Instead of a word that precisely conveys a thought, we hear oblique speech and faulty syntax, and have already grown accustomed to it.

The origins of this go back to the early 1920s, indeed to the 1918 Constitution, which deprived people from the "exploiting" – i.e., educated – classes of a public platform. The plough churned the layers of soil and up to the surface of public life came people who did not understand most of the words and phrases used in the speeches and articles of the "fathers of the revolution". Not understanding, they were still obliged to speak this new language. What was supposedly "their" language, born of the habitual use of only half-understood words, from the utterance of inherently impenetrable thoughts, received official support. It was handed down from generation to generation and was the only language officials spoke for seventy years in the airless environment of district and provincial Party committees closed to the public, and on the floors above. What is more, they appeared to understand each other perfectly well.

Today's language is like a high, exposed riverbank on which you can clearly see the strata laid down in different geological periods. Of course, we feel the tragic closeness to us of the works currently being published in our journals which our compatriots wrote long ago and of which we had never heard. They remind us of the appalling, recently exposed layers of mass graves of the multitudes executed by the Communist regime. Nevertheless, these are not bones but voices which still speak to us, and how different they are from our present speech and the way our present writers and politicians use language. They seem as incompatible as oil and water. They do not soak into our soil but run off its caked crust. It is, however, that very contradiction which holds the promise of a new and better Russian language in the, possibly not too distant, future.

The average Soviet writer cannot look forward to a smooth road ahead. He faces disruption no less traumatic than what confronted his predecessors in the early 1920s, only in reverse. Back then, writers who already had an established reputation and readership in pre-revolutionary Russia were forced, if they stayed on in Soviet Russia, to agree to new rules. At first, these were not onerous, but the writers had increasingly, as time went by, to adapt to censorship. Today's writers face a different future. Their tacit contract with the reader has gone. Until recently the reader knew, subconsciously but with certainty, what he could not expect to find in a new work by a famous writer. Censorship affected them both. The reader formed his judgement of the book within that framework.

Today, the framework has been smashed, and earlier assumptions no longer hold. The field for comparison has expanded, and the more courageous writers, fully aware of what is happening, recognise that they are no longer able to claim the status of real professionals. The path to even the kind of commercial success which books by Agatha Christie and Georges Simenon enjoy in the Western world is closed to them, and neither of those Western authors, we should note, ever claimed intellectual dominion over their readers.

Now may be a good time for ex-writers to find a major and desperately needed role in their own land and among their own people, just as the writers of Teleshov's generation did in past revolutionary times, as directors of museums or as guardians of libraries. Discarded writers could become thoughtful chroniclers of the present state of the country in conscientiously documented essays. Will they have the courage to scale back their ambitions and drastically alter the course of their biographies?

From the diary of Aleksandr Chudakov:

31 December
A sense of exhaustion. A period in our history has ended. Democracy, although one was reluctant to believe it but as might have been expected, has proved weak. We are veering further and further to the right. May Gorbachev himself be behind this change of direction?

Sat up till 3.00 in the morning on 8 January, 1991 at *Literaturnaya gazeta*, keeping a close eye on the printing of my article. Early in the morning, Yuriy Tsivian phoned from Riga and cheerfully announced, "It's clear now that they're turning back the clock, so at least we know where we stand again." (He was referring to the military assault on the Baltic States etc.) We can carry on with the Tynyanov Readings.

Shortly before, Yuriy had been lamenting how hard he was finding the times and suggesting, only half-seriously, of course, that he might not mind going back to the old days when you could at least predict how people were likely to behave.

"Well, fine," I said. "Just do nothing and you'll be a good person, because at least you won't be doing anything bad."

X

The first months of 1991 changed everything for me. It started with the tanks and paratroopers in Vilnius. Up till then, all my writing, as in previous decades, had been about literary history. Even the interview for *Literaturnaya gazeta* was about the Russian language. During the entire perestroika period, I kept right out of public affairs, having had quite enough of battling sundry administrators and censors and generally making a nuisance of myself in earlier years. I was really glad there were so many broad-shouldered "foremen on the perestroika building site", and that I could finally write (and get published) work that had been off limits.

I had been sitting at my desk getting on with my academic work when the radio obliged me with news of the invasion. Now, I suddenly found I couldn't go on until I had somehow responded.

On 11 January (as I recorded on 20 January), I "started writing a letter about Lithuania. Phoned Sergey Bocharov, who said he would definitely support it. I called Sergey Averintsev. 'Of course, Marietta, I am just getting ready to speak on Echo of Moscow radio myself.'"

We gave the letter the title of John F. Kennedy's resounding, "Freedom Is Indivisible!" It was the first declaration by Russian scholars and writers to be read on Lithuanian radio during the crisis:

> A sense of personal involvement in what is happening at this time in the Baltic republics obliges us to take up the pen.
>
> The generation to which we belong might seem able to deny responsibility for the events of 1940, but we have nevertheless felt guilty for many years over the Soviet Union's occupation of the Baltic States. The pronouncements in recent times about those events relieved us in some measure of the burden of that guilt. The dramatic advance of the Baltic republics to independence has implications for the future of many people, and we support it. We believed that through patient negotiation, with essential guarantees of the rights of all the peoples inhabiting those lands, reasonable and humane solutions could be arrived at.
>
> The events in Vilnius and the loss of life have changed our understanding of the situation.
>
> We protest against the actions of those who today, by now in our name, have dared to take the criminal decision to use military force against Lithuania and who are threatening to unleash it against the other Baltic peoples. We call on all who read this letter to do everything possible to stop violence again becoming the only

way our state communicates with human beings.

Marietta Chudakova, Sergey Averintsev, Sergey Bocharov, Mikhail Gasparov, Fazil Iskander, Sergo Lominadze, Oleg Chukhontsev

The new year ushered in a genuinely new era. On 20 January, Aleksandr and I addressed a rally in Manège Square protesting against Gorbachev's actions.

29 January

I have begun almost to hate this man who is so cloddishly ruining and wrecking everything he himself initiated. I see him now as a peevish tyrant who is increasingly cutting himself off from everyone and who trusts no-one except such faithful servants as Yanayev. A decree about patrolling the streets . . . If it is directed against rapists and robbers, why the armoured personnel carriers?

2 February

The big freeze we have had for a week entirely reflects the dire chill in the political climate. There are joint patrols of the army and Interior Ministry on the streets of major cities. The faces of senior officers on television seem already to bear the imprint of the past five years and their embarrassment at being used for this kind of repression. I phoned Lidiya Chukovskaya. She is being stifled by her workload which is, as always, vast. She is depressed, as I am, that all the intellectuals have decamped to the West and "in pursuit of a video-cassette recorder are prepared to shut their eyes to everything that is happening in their own nation. When things are bad in any country, its citizens head back to help. We do the opposite."

Events of the summer and autumn of 1991 turned all this into history. They left unanswered questions about the relationship between personal, human qualities, aspirations, actions and expectations – and other factors:

the age-old question of the role of the individual. These events soon divided thinking citizens into those who were seriously concerned and others who totally rejected the "human factor", arguing that everything that had happened and was happening now was because of oil, gas and the like. Human beings were just pawns in the hands of impersonal circumstance, and if they did act, they did so purely for direct, selfish gain.

The most important feature of 1990 was something unheard of. Within four or five years, a particular set of freedoms had formed and become established. They had become firm enough beneath your feet to take your weight. We had grown used to them, despite their being so different from the conditions that had obtained until recently. At the same time, we could not help feeling that we were hurtling along on a downward trajectory. And there was a continual sound of rustling from every direction. It was the Communist Party, aware in its infallibility that the game was up, hastening to grab and squirrel away everything it could, and everything to which it had no business helping itself. This all took place with the connivance of a wholly passive Gorbachev. It is completely obvious that the real looting took place in 1990 rather than later.

People's assumptions mattered. Some had taken the view ever since 1986–7 that perestroika was no more than a blip, just another short-lived "thaw". "Strike while the iron is Gorbachev!" they exclaimed. Now they could confidently assert that they had been right, although in fact they were not. Others said and wrote that the past would not return, that we had moved on, and that they were preparing to prevent any attempt to turn the clock back.

Might it in 1990 have been possible to do one vitally important thing, which has not been done to this day and which underlies all that is worst about present-day Russia: to create civil society? Or is that mere fantasy?

The fact that there was no civil society at the time (as we would do well to remember today) was the result of deliberate policy on the part of the Communist Party, from the early days of its seizure of power up to and including Gorbachev. He failed to resolve this issue for himself, fearing any sign that society was organising itself, any channelling of social energy that was not under the Party's control. In 1990, he already resented anyone who moved in the direction of self-organisation.

How could people do this to him when it was he, Gorbachev, who had transformed the Central Committee of the C.P.S.U., beating down Ligachov and the others? Who, he wondered, was "slipping in" (a favourite expression) the idea that a society could be created which was not under the control of his new, liberal Kremlin? In just the same way, he could not understand why Lithuania should want independence. There is unforgettable television footage of Gorbachev in Vilnius, surrounded by Lithuanians. He is red-faced and angry and trying to persuade them how good and right it is for everyone together to build an improved Soviet Union under his leadership. A tall deputy, Eduardas Vilkas, is looking at him with a gentle smile. On his face and the face of every other Lithuanian there we see plainly something Gorbachev was oddly unable to see: "Dear Mikhail Sergeyevich! Do you really think we are going to let slip a unique, unbelievable, historic opportunity for which we have been waiting for half a century?"

This was why educated citizens of the U.S.S.R. had every reason in 1990 not to have faith in Gorbachev. In contrast to the early years of perestroika, many people no longer wished to lend their energy and intelligence to efforts to renovate a society which, they now believed, had little prospect of being overhauled sufficiently radically to stop it from still being Soviet. They feared that the renovation would only bring to the surface dark and openly murderous forces.

No-one could, or can, foretell the future, especially of a nation like Russia. It was just that some people bought into the project in the belief that it was not hopeless. Others chose to go for something more predictable and closer to the interests of their family and the only life they had. This is not the place to hand down judgements, let alone categorical and harsh judgements. In Arthur Miller's play "The Price", which I once saw in a wonderful production at the Bolshoy Drama Theatre in Leningrad and which made a lasting impression on me, one brother abandons his old, sick father and has a distinguished career as a doctor. The other brother stays at home looking after his father and succeeds only in becoming a policeman. After the father's death, the brothers meet in the house and the situation proves to be much more complicated. The two men have done what they did, their lives have passed, and there is little more to be said.

So was there something more we could have attempted, something more we could have achieved?

In theory, yes, if in 1990 the mutual antagonism between the various segments of late Soviet society had not been so extreme. It was to become even more extreme, but by then in the circumstances of post-Soviet Russia.

JULY

1 July

The new law on property, which the U.S.S.R. Supreme Soviet passed in March, comes into force. Many economists see it as merely declarative, allowing for the possibility of different forms of ownership in the Soviet economy, but providing virtually no mechanisms for moving towards them (*Izvestiia*, 184, p. 1).

A rally many thousands strong is held in Palace Square, Leningrad, in support of democratic change and a multi-party system. There are warnings of the real danger of a counter-attack by conservative forces. No C.P.S.U. members are among the speakers (*Izvestiia*, 184, p. 2).

A chartered flight brings 118 residents of Vilnius, Kaunas and other Lithuanian cities to Tomsk. They are family members of people exiled to Siberia during Stalin's repressions and have come to reclaim their relatives' remains. The costs are borne by charitable organisations and enterprises in Lithuania (*Izvestiia*, 183, p. 4).

Tom Stoppard's "Rosencrantz and Guildenstern Are Dead" (1966), translated by Iosif Brodsky, is produced at the Mayakovsky Theatre by Yevgeniy Ariye (*Izvestiia*, 26, p. 30).

3 July

Mikhail Gorbachev addresses the Twenty-Eighth Congress of the C.P.S.U. on "The way ahead with Perestroika":

> The Stalinist model of socialism is being replaced by a civic society of free people. The political system is being radically transformed, and real democracy is being reborn. Conditions are being created in the economy for free competition between socialist producers,

and the old relations of production which alienated workers from their property and the results of their labour are being dismantled. A hyper-centralised state is being transformed into a true federation. Ideological diktat is giving way to free thinking and glasnost, to public disclosure of information. In foreign policy there is renunciation of confrontation. The U.S.S.R. has become a country open to peace and cooperation, regarded not with fear but with respect.

We inherited a very unhappy legacy. The U.S.S.R. was declining at increasing speed into a second-class state. By the early 1980s, it was clear that the country's apparent prosperity was based on barbaric misuse of natural and human resources.

Gorbachev declares that now one of the most serious brakes on perestroika is active opposition to change from a layer of bureaucracy in government bodies, and the vested interests which are backing them (*Izvestiia*, 185, p. 1).

"Experts in black and white magic, poltergeists and hypnosis have a new centre for the study of anomalous contacts, financed by Agafo, a Soviet–American joint venture" (*Izvestiia*, 185, p. 6).

5–6 July

In London, the Council of N.A.T.O. adopts a declaration whereby affiliated states pledge not to be the first to use nuclear weapons. This marks the beginning of an extended dialogue between N.A.T.O. and the Warsaw Pact.

6 July

The Supreme Soviet of Ukraine unprecedentedly recalls deputies of the Ukrainian parliament from the Twenty-Eighth Congress of the C.P.S.U. to attend to domestic issues (*Izvestiia*, 189, p. 2).

11 July

Mikhail Gorbachev is re-elected C.P.S.U. General Secretary, with 3,411 delegates voting in favour and 1,116 against. The other candidate, Teymuraz Avaliani, Secretary of Kiselyov City Party Committee, obtains 501 votes. For the first time since the assassination of Kirov in 1934, election to the highest office in the Party is, at least formally, contested (Izvestiia, 193, p. 1).

A one-day political strike is held by miners in Donbass and Kuzbass to demand the resignation of the U.S.S.R. government (Moskovskie novosti, 29, p. 6). See essays below by Sergey Turkin and Sergey Khramov.

12 July

Vladimir Ivashko is elected Deputy General Secretary of the C.P.S.U., with 3,109 votes in favour and 1,309 against. Yegor Ligachov gains 776 votes in favour, but has 3,642 against (Izvestiia, 194, p. 1).

In Moscow, the Sinbad cooperative sets up an organisation with the unassuming title of "Protection Division". This private agency can provide protection for anyone in need of it. Selection of employees is rigorous, with only one applicant in ten accepted (Moskovskii komsomolets, 157, p. 1).

13 July

During the nomination process of candidates for membership of the Party Central Committee, Boris Yeltsin asks for the floor and announces his resignation from the C.P.S.U. He explains that under a multi-party system it is unlikely he would be able to comply with the wishes of any one party, as he is committed to serving all the people. He would cooperate with all parties and public bodies. Yeltsin then walks out of the congress (Izvestiia, 195, p. 1).

The leaders of the Moscow and Leningrad City Soviets, Gavriil Popov and Anatoliy Sobchak, announce that they are resigning from the C.P.S.U. because the Twenty-Eighth Congress "had demonstrated the C.P.S.U.'s total inability to propose a realistic programme" for transition to a market economy, respect for universal human values and a determination to implement thorough-going democratisation of the Party (Izvestiia, 196, p. 2).

14 July

A meeting of the workforce of the Gas Research and Development Institute in Krasnodar decides by ninety-three votes to three to nominate ex-K.G.B. Major General Oleg Kalugin as its candidate for People's Deputy of the U.S.S.R. (*Moskovskie novosti*, 29, p. 2).

Mikhail Gorbachev signs a decree "Concerning the democratisation and development of television and radio broadcasting in the U.S.S.R." Despite the liberal-sounding title, the decree is intended primarily to rescue the failing monopoly over broadcasting of the State Committee for Television and Radio.

The R.S.F.S.R. Supreme Soviet declares Kaliningrad province a free enterprise zone (Iurii Zverev, "*Kaliningradskaia oblast' Rossii v novoi sisteme geopoliticheskikh koordinat*"; http://poli.vub.ac.be/publi/etni-2/yzverev.htm).

15 July

A rally in Manège Square in Moscow is organised by Democratic Russia; the Moscow Voters' Society; the People's Front of Moscow; Shield: the Union for the Social Welfare of Servicemen and Their Families; the Free Democratic Party of Russia; the Democratic Platform of the C.P.S.U.; Memorial; and the Sodruzhestvo (Fellowship) Foundation, Leningrad. The slogans include "Down with the Communist Party!" and "U.S.S.R. Government – Resign!" (*Izvestiia*, 198, p. 6). This manifestation of democratic forces is the largest anti-government and anti-Communist protest in Moscow between 1988 and 1991. There is no conflict over it with the city authorities, and the organisers claim that four hundred thousand people have participated. Yuriy Lyubimov proposes moving the statue of the K.G.B.'s founder, Feliks Dzerzhinsky, into the Lubyanka central prison and painting that sinister building black, as a monument to dark times (*Moskovskie novosti*, 29, p. 6).

The Moscow City Soviet resolves that Muscovites will become owners of their current apartments, able to freely buy and sell them. The transfer of

Postage stamp from Ukraine,
released in 1991 after the adoption of
the Declaration of State Sovereignty

property rights will begin in the first half of 1991 (*Moskovskie novosti*, 28, p. 2).

A mass grave of victims of Stalin's purges is discovered at Kilometre 239 on the Moscow–Yaroslavl highway, in woods near the village of Selifontovo (*Izvestiia*, 197, p. 4).

16 July

Deputies of the Ukrainian parliament adopt a Declaration of Sovereignty (*Izvestiia*, 199, p. 2).

Grigoriy Yavlinsky is appointed Deputy Chairman of the R.S.F.S.R. Council of Ministers, a post he later describes as "Deputy Revolutions Tsar" (see his biography at http://www.yabloko.ru/Persons/YAVL/ yavl-biog.html).

17 July

The U.S.S.R. Prosecutor's Office institutes criminal proceedings against K.G.B. Major General Oleg Kalugin on the grounds of disclosure of state secrets (*Izvestiia*, 206, p. 8).

20 July

From 12 to 22 July, members of Shield conduct a thorough investigation into the events of January 1990 in Baku. Their commission concludes that a war crime was committed, and they demand that criminal charges be brought against the Minister of Defence, Dmitriy Yazov, who personally commanded the operation, and other persons (*Moskovskie novosti*, 32, p. 15). The Public Prosecutor's Office did not open a criminal case.

21 July

An appeal from the U.S.S.R. Supreme Soviet to the peoples of Lithuania, Latvia and Estonia reads, "For the first time we have an opportunity to arrange our mutual relations in a democratic and neighbourly manner, so that each nation should fully enjoy the benefits of cooperation, integration, stability and security. These are achievable objectives" (*Izvestiia*, 203, p. 1).

22 July

The city authorities close the Lvov branch of the National V. I. Lenin Museum and turn it into a community and cultural centre (*Moskovskie novosti*, 29, p. 2).

24 July

The U.S.S.R. Council of Ministers gives permission for the sale of alcohol in the mornings and on weekdays. The anti-vodka campaign had caused irreparable damage to the reputation of Mikhail Gorbachev (who was lampooned as "the Mineral Secretary" and "General Softdrinkery") by a population which believed him to have introduced it. After five years of systematic destruction of the alcohol industry, the counters of wine and spirits shops were bare. Sales of liquor were permitted only after 2.00 p.m., and had been rationed since 1989 (*Noveishaia istoriia otechestvennogo kino*).

"Tobacco!", Leningrad, summer 1990

25 July

A "Serb parliament", convened in Croatia, passes a Declaration of Sovereignty and Autonomy of the Serb nation in Croatia.

A presidential decree, "Concerning amendments to the practice of foreign trade by the U.S.S.R.", directs that from 1 January, 1991 trade with other Comecon countries should be based on world prices and settled in freely convertible currency (*Izvestiia*, 207, p. 1).

Cigarettes disappear from sale, in the wake of sugar and soap, and ration coupons are introduced. On the black market, old women and spivs sell cigarettes at between 3 and 5 roubles a pack, and even cigarette butts are traded at up to 3 roubles a jar. A wave of "tobacco riots" sweeps the country. The crisis is finally resolved only at the end of 1991, when Philip Morris exports more than twenty billion cigarettes to Russia and deliveries of relatively cheap Polish cigarettes begin (*Noveishaia istoriia otechestvennogo kino*).

The C.P.S.U. Central Committee opens a press relations centre at the October Hotel (*Izvestiia*, 207, p. 2).

26 July

A presidential decree is published, "Concerning prohibition of establishing armed groups not authorised under U.S.S.R. legislation, and the seizure of weaponry in cases of illegal possession" (*Izvestiia*, 208, p. 1).

At a meeting with media chiefs, Vladimir Boldyrev, head of the Glavlit censorship board, reports that "the prohibitory functions and pre-press monitoring of the media are being discontinued" (*Moskovskii komsomolets*, 169, p. 1).

27 July

Mikhail Gorbachev, Boris Yeltsin, Nikolai Ryzhkov and Ivan Silayev sign a mandate for the development of a coherent programme of transition to a market economy as the basis for the economic provisions of a future federal treaty (*Pravda*, 12 August). The programme is developed during August by a group of economists under Stanislav Shatalin and Grigoriy Yavlinsky, and comes to be known as the 500 Days programme (replacing the earlier 400 Days programme).

The Byelorussian Supreme Soviet passes a Declaration of Sovereignty (*Izvestiia*, 211, p. 1).

28 July

Moscow City Soviet restores Gorky Street's historical name of Tverskaya (*Izvestiia*, 210, p. 3).

30 July

The first Conference of Leaseholders and Entrepreneurs of the R.S.F.S.R. is held in Leningrad (*Izvestiia*, 212, p. 1).

The workforce of Vasyuganneft, the largest oil and gas company in the Central Ob region, resolves to withdraw from the regional Tomskneft Association and become a fully independent company, cooperating on a contractual basis with other enterprises, in order to exploit the region's natural resources more effectively (*Izvestiia*, 212, p. 2).

A "Communiqué of a meeting of the chairmen of the Supreme Soviets of the Latvian, Lithuanian, and Estonian Republics and of the R.S.F.S.R.", signed by Anatolijs Gorbunov, Vytautas Landsbergis, Arnold Rüütel, and Boris Yeltsin, announces their intention to prepare bilateral treaties without delay (*Izvestiia*, 212, p. 2).

Also in July

"Jesus Christ Superstar", by Andrew Lloyd Webber and Tim Rice, was directed by Pavel Chomsky at the Moscow City Soviet Theatre (*Noveishaia istoriia otechestvennoi kinematografii*). The musical was a huge success.

First Gallery used the latest communications technology during the organising of an exhibition in the course of which works by artists were transmitted between New York and Moscow by fax (*Noveishaia istoriia otechestvennogo kino*).

IDEOLOGICAL CONSTRUCTION OF A PARTY SPECTRUM: THE FALSE START OF 1990

Vadim Goncharov

In June 1990, one of the activists of Moscow's unofficial socialist movement, Boris Kurashvili, speculated as to how a party system might evolve in the U.S.S.R. over the coming decade. In his scenario, ". . . three socialistically inclined parties ultimately emerged out of the Communist Party: one moderately left wing; one centre-left, and one centre-right."[225] The moderate left-wing party would continue to call itself the Communist Party; the centre-left party would call itself the Democratic Socialist Party; and the centre-right party would choose the title of Social-Democratic Party. Kurashvili predicted that in the election in 2000, ". . . the centre-left party [would] have a decisive lead with about 50 per cent of the vote, while the other two [would] have roughly equal support at around 20 per cent of the vote each and [would] live in hope of better times."[226] A stable 5 per cent of the vote would go to a Liberal Democratic Party advocating complete denationalisation of the economy, while the remaining 5 per cent would be divided between Green parties and parties representing the national republics.[227]

To give Kurashvili his due, the forecast, if we compare it with the actual results of the Russian parliamentary elections of 1999 and 2003, was not far off the mark. He did not, of course, foresee the coming disintegration of the U.S.S.R. or the formation of unprincipled, paternalistic "parties of power", but the situation towards the ends of the party spectrum is not too far from his predictions.

225. Boris P. Kurashvili, *Strana na rasput'e: Poteri i perspektivy perestroiki* (Moscow, 1990), p. 164.
226. Ibid., p. 166.   227. Ibid., pp.. 169–71.

Interestingly, Kurashvili uses the terms "right-wing" and "left-wing" in the sense that became usual in Russia somewhat later. In 1990, for journalists and the public in general, "left" mainly referred to the supporters of radical reforms in the economy and politics, while "right" meant opponents of the reforms who advocated a return to Soviet values along the lines of 1984. According to social surveys, the shift whereby economic issues came to dominate political positioning, which resulted in "right" and "left" changing places, occurred between 1993 and 1996.[228]

By far the most interesting aspect of this prediction is the fact that Kurashvili had no doubt that in the near future systematic electoral contestation would appear in the U.S.S.R. and a stable party system would offer a limited set of clear ideological alternatives to voters. If that had indeed happened, Russia's democratic transition would have been different. A political system might have emerged with parties succeeding each other in power in accordance with the results of competitive elections and being held to account for implementing policies readily identifiable in familiar ideological terms. In the first half of 1990 that seemed a likely outcome.

Grounds for such expectations were provided by the pre-election campaigning to choose delegates to the Congress of People's Deputies of the R.S.F.S.R. and local soviets. The main struggle in the 1990 elections was between representatives of two ideological camps: Communists and democrats. The confrontation was less than straightforward, because the vast majority of those in the democratic camp were also members of the Communist Party. In the context of the electoral politics of 1990, this did not matter too much: the electorate had little difficulty in recognising the situation and voting either for Soviet values or against them.

In fifty or so Russian cities, the Democratic Russia electoral list gained half or more of the seats.[229] Local soviets divided along ideological lines.

228. Geoffrey Evans and Stephen Whitefield, "The Evolution of Left and Right in Post-Soviet Russia", *Europe–Asia Studies*, 50/6 (1998), p. 1028.
229. V. N. Berezovskii *et al.*, "Novye obshchestvenno-politicheskie organizatsii i dvizheniia RSFSR (opyt analiza i klassifikatsii)", *Rossiia: partii, assotsiatsii, soiuzy, kluby. Spravochnik*, vol. 1, pt 1 (Moscow, 1991), p. 6.

An analogous division was evident in the political make-up of the newly elected Russian legislature. The struggle for the post of Chairman of the R.S.F.S.R. Supreme Soviet was between candidates from Democratic Russia and Communists of Russia. Foreign observers commented that, "Democratic Russia and Communists of Russia both behaved at the First Congress like Western parties, attempting to organise the agenda, nominate their candidate for chairman, and enact their special programmes."[230] This rivalry reflected the ideological polarisation of Russian society at the time.

At the beginning of the campaign, U.S.S.R. and Russian republican law did not yet allow for official registration of political parties, so Democratic Russia was an umbrella organisation. It was anticipated that out of Democratic Russia parties with different ideological orientations would emerge after the task of democratising Russia was complete. That is in fact what happened, but none of these parties of the next generation were as successful as Democratic Russia was in the spring of 1990 in providing electoral guidance for voters. Sergey Mitrokhin rightly observed that "organisations which officially consider themselves to be parties are nothing of the sort. At best they can be classified as proto-parties. Conversely, a broad coalition of very varied forces (including proto-parties), which more or less satisfies the criteria, does not call itself a party but the Democratic Russia movement."[231] Democratic Russia as it was in 1990–91 failed to become the ruling party, but it came closer than any other post-Soviet organisation, with the exception, perhaps, of the Communist Party in 1996. At all events, its organisational capabilities were impressive. During the 1991 election campaign for the presidency of Russia, the movement mobilised some 150,000 activists to campaign for Boris Yeltsin.[232]

230. Jerry F. Hough, *Democratisation and Revolution in the USSR, 1985–1991* (Washington, DC, 1997), p. 304.
231. Sergei Mitrokhin, "Fenomen protopartii", *Vek XX i mir*, 10 (1991); http://old.russ.ru/antolog/vek/1991/10/mitroh.htm
232. Geir Flikke, "From External Success to Internal Collapse: The Case of Democratic Russia", *Europe–Asia Studies*, 56/8 (December 2004), p. 1209.

The example of Democratic Russia would seem to show that it was possible for mass ideological parties to be created and operate successfully in Russia, and the lack of any other successful examples is readily explained by the peculiarities of Russia's institutional design after adoption of the "super-presidential" Constitution of 1993. Events in 1990 provide the perspective for an alternative interpretation of the subsequent development of Russia's electoral politics, in which ideology came to be in demand while real political parties did not.

In the late twentieth century, Russia had a highly educated population which had demonstrated its ability to participate actively in political life as soon as the threat of repression was lifted. In February 1990, open-air meetings held by a coalition of democratic organisations on Manège Square in Moscow were attracting more than a hundred thousand people. The ideological competence of Russian voters was also not in doubt. The Soviet regime put a great deal of effort into familiarising its citizens with ideological concepts. Some researchers even consider that the mechanism of mass indoctrination, with its educational bonus, was a more significant feature of Soviet politics than the content of the dull official ideology being indoctrinated. In 1966, Alfred Meyer defined Soviet ideology as "a body of doctrine which the Communist Party teaches all Soviet citizens, from school children to the higher party leadership".[233] Of course, behind the Iron Curtain, Soviet citizens' knowledge of other than Marxist ideological concepts was very limited, but, from the introduction of glasnost, the information deficit was quickly remedied. Even more importantly, the electoral preferences of Russian voters as revealed in the free election campaigns of 1989 and 1990 had a clear ideological structure. Voters in major Russian cities – particularly in Moscow and Leningrad, when choosing their representatives for the Congress of People's Deputies of the U.S.S.R. in March 1989 – mostly supported radical advocates of greater economic and political freedom.

233. Alfred Meyer, "The Functions of Ideology in the Soviet Political System", Soviet Studies, 17/3 (January 1966), p. 273.

Voters need ideology in order to lower the "costs" of gathering and processing information. Democratic politics is mass politics, but political issues are complex and voters' cognitive abilities are limited. Far-left critics of capitalist society enthusiastically use the metaphor of "one-dimensional man" suggested by Herbert Marcuse.[234] The fact is that one-dimensional man does exist in nature. He is a voter. He lives in a one-dimensional political world and easily identifies his position on a one-dimensional scale running from left to right. This is confirmed by polls of public opinion undertaken as part of the World Values Survey. As of 2004, the vast majority of citizens in the countries studied had little difficulty placing their politics on a scale where '1' indicated extreme left-wing and '10' extreme right-wing views.[235]

There are two main theoretical approaches to the question of using ideology in electoral campaigns. The spatial model is based on the notion that ideology is a means of lowering information-processing costs for the voter.[236] Its proponents believe that virtually every voter is capable of recognising an elementary ideological scale, of differentiating between "right-wing" and "left-wing", of placing themselves on the scale, and of voting for the candidate or party closest to their ideological preferences. Political parties and candidates tend to try to position themselves where the majority of voters are concentrated. In two-party systems this is usually a notional "centre".

Some researchers challenge the spatial model and favour a "saliency" model which, in their view, is better suited to the conditions of modern electoral campaigning.[237] By "saliency" they mean identifying the most

234. Herbert Marcuse, *One-Dimensional Man* (London, 1991).
235. Russell J. Dalton, "Social Modernisation and the End of Ideology Debate: Patterns of Ideological Polarisation", *Japanese Journal of Political Science*, 7/1 (2006), pp. 1–22, 7.
236. Melvin J. Hinich and Michael C. Munger, *Ideology and the Theory of Political Choice* (Ann Arbor, 1994).
237. David M. Farrell *et al.*, "Parties and Campaign Professionals in a Digital Age: Political Consultants in the United States and Their Counterparts Overseas", *International Journal of Press/Politics*, 6/4 (September 2001), p. 15.

topical issues which need to be addressed by candidates and parties in the election campaign. The ideological straight line is done away with, and in its place are salient issues in the media spotlight and dark, desolate spaces between them. The public is no longer required to attempt systematic, ideological thinking. Clearly, the second model requires political actors to move more nimbly and with greater sophistication than the first. Mass parties cannot change their position quickly to accord with the latest demands of voters, so they are replaced by "electoral-professional parties".[238]

A political party is a strange organisation. For an aspiring politician seeking elective office, it can offer resources to promote his career. For citizens whose interest in politics is less self-serving, it can be a club for discussing political issues. Grass-roots activists have few opportunities to influence the formulation of party policy because, as in any large-scale organisation, power is soon concentrated in the hands of a small, permanent professional staff.[239] Nevertheless, their incentives are fairly clear.

The main question is rather what use a political party is to rank-and-file members who are not activists, and to party leaders who have their eyes on governing the state. In the mid-twentieth century, leaders relied organisationally on their party during electoral campaigns, and rank-and-file members gained symbolic capital in the eyes of their immediate social circle because they had access to arcane information and could occasionally shake hands with leaders whom the man in the street knew only from newspaper photographs. With the advent of television, academics began talking about the decline of political parties.[240] Nowadays, a party membership card does not bring a voter any closer to the leader or make them uniquely privy to internal information. Access is provided by television.

238. Angelo Panebianco, *Political Parties: Organisation and Power* (Cambridge, 1988).
239. This thesis, proposed in the early twentieth century, is known as "the Michels-Ostrogorsky iron law of oligarchy".
240. Per Selle and Lars Svasånd, "Membership in Party Organisations and the Problem of Decline of Parties", *Comparative Political Studies*, 17 (1991), pp. 35–79; Harold D. Clarke and Marianne C. Stewart, "The Decline of Parties in the Minds of Citizens", *Annual Review of Political Science*, 1/1 (1998), pp. 357–78.

Without getting off the couch, you can watch lively political debate and don't need to pay a membership fee to do so.

The democracy movement had no shortage of volunteers willing to work without pay in the election campaigns of 1990, distributing leaflets and joining protests, but this upsurge in political participation was due to its novelty and proved a transient phenomenon. The 1990 activists were predominantly middle-aged professionals with higher education who found it interesting to participate in politics.[241] Financially, they were fairly well off, and had time on their hands and little opportunity to convert it into money. That situation was not to last.

In 1998 the survey results were published of a cohort of people who had been active participants in the election campaign of 1990, lived in the Moscow area and had worked as volunteers for the "democrats".[242] In 1990, the vast majority had been employed in white-collar work, and most (43 per cent) were members of the technical intelligentsia. Over the following eight years, their social status altered markedly. Many were obliged to change their occupations, some becoming small businesspeople. By December 1993, only about 40 per cent had still been participating in election campaigns, and by the 1995 parliamentary elections, 94 per cent of respondents were participating only as voters.[243]

The role of ideologically motivated volunteers was important in 1990, but even then not crucial. Television was already a more reliable channel of communication. The role of a political leader changes depending on how they connect with voters. While the intermediaries were middle- and lower-level party supporters, the leaders' most important quality was organisational ability. When television became the intermediary, the leaders became actors or television personalities.

In 1990, Russia's political leaders were already television personalities.

241. Marc Garcelon, "The Estate of Change: The Specialist Rebellion and the Democratic Movement in Moscow, 1989–1991", Theory and Society, 26/1 (February 1997), pp. 47–9.
242. Aleksandr Golovkov, "Kuda delis' demokraty?", Nezavisimaia gazeta, 11 June, 1998.
243. Ibid.

They became celebrities when the congresses of people's deputies began to be broadcast live. As Yuriy Levada observed, "Unlike Western M.P.s, our parliamentarians are not trying to convince each other but to address voters directly from the television screen."[244]

One of Democratic Russia's most effective electoral techniques was to get a T.V. star to lend a little of their fame to a less high-profile candidate in the struggle against the Communist partocracy: "The facsimile signature of a popular leader like Yeltsin, Travkin or Stankevich on a standard propaganda leaflet worked like a charm every time."[245]

The symbolic capital of being a T.V.-star deputy vastly exceeded the value of controlling a grassroots organisation of political activists. For months, the democratic majority of the Leningrad City Soviet was unable to choose a leader, until Anatoliy Sobchak, a charismatic orator from the Inter-regional Deputies Group, was offered the throne. He was hastily elected to one of the few remaining seats in the soviet and became Chairman immediately. Not surprisingly, there was soon friction. Sobchak felt under no obligation to the deputies of the democratic majority. It was television, not they, which had made him leader.

Among the democrats' television stars, one undoubtedly outshone all others. By early 1990, Boris Yeltsin was the acknowledged leader of the democratic movement in Russia. Initially, his aims and those of Democratic Russia coincided, but even at that stage Yeltsin baulked at formalising his relations with the organisation, preferring to keep his options open.[246] In 1987–8, the clash between him and Gorbachev had been the most absorbing aspect of Russian politics for millions of television viewers. The relationship between the two men developed like the plot of a Brazilian soap opera, alternating between war and peace. Their conflict

244. Iurii A. Levada, "Chto zhe dal'she? Razmyshleniia o politicheskoi situatsii v strane", *Izvestiia*, 10 April, 1990.

245. Sergei Mitrokhin, "Fenomen protopartii".

246. See the interview with Vyacheslav Igrunov, "O stanovlenii politiki na rubezhe vos'midesiatykh i devianostykh"; http://www.igrunov.ru/cat/vchk-cat-bibl/interv/all_interv/vchk-cat-bibl-interv-mdg_92.html

was one of the few stable elements in Russian politics right through until December 1991.

When, on 29 May, 1990, Yeltsin was elected Chairman of the R.S.F.S.R. Supreme Soviet by a small margin, he became less dependent on the organisational support of Democratic Russia. From then until the present day, political parties in Russia have had to content themselves with a very subsidiary role. They have been no more than an optional ritual setting for a political regime with a strong leader. The transition to a personalised political regime may have culminated in 1993, with the adoption of a new Russian constitution, but by mid-1990 Yeltsin had already taken the first steps in that direction. Jockeying for power, he dramatically changed the agenda.

Adoption of the Declaration of Sovereignty of Russia and the beginning of the "war of laws" between the U.S.S.R.'s central leadership and the Russian Federation pushed aside the contest between democrats and Communists. The ideological party-political spectrum collapsed before it could gain a foothold in everyday politics. From being a democratic champion fighting the Communist Party establishment, Yeltsin was instantly transformed into the leader of a national liberation struggle against the dictatorship of the U.S.S.R.'s bureaucracy. A charismatic leader has more capacity for nimble-footed manoeuvring than a political party, as Yeltsin was to demonstrate repeatedly. He regularly outwitted his opponents by switching the electorate's attention from one "salient" issue to another. There was nothing particularly malign about this. For Yeltsin it was just a logical and effective political strategy. Populist leadership requires that the leader constantly shifts to adopt the stance currently most appealing to the community. Later, when unconditional victory had been won against the institutions and Communist establishment of the U.S.S.R., Yeltsin found a new enemy in the parliament of the Russian Federation. Institutional contestation became a recurrent element of Russian politics, which never did develop into ideologically based party politics.

FREE FLIGHT: THE REBIRTH OF SOVIET AERONAUTICS

Svetlana Koroleva

Balloons are like the air of freedom. The more of them there are, the
more advanced and free the country. Balloons appear when enslavement disappears. Balloons appeared in Ukraine in 1990.

Vyacheslav Gardashnik, Chairman of the Ukrainian Federation of
Hot Air Ballooning [247]

The year 1990 was a major anniversary for Russian aeronautics. On 14 July,
1890, the Russian Minister of War approved the establishment of an Aeronautical Department and Aeronautical Training Park. From then, and
almost until 1990, the production of craft lighter than air was subordinate
to the needs of the military. To this day, many people associate twentieth-
century aerostats primarily with the tethered barrage balloons that floated
above Moscow during the Second World War. Manned aerostats and
airships invariably served military purposes. Today specialists often remark
that, if everything had not been so shrouded in secrecy, the Soviet air
force in the 1930s could have boasted of lighter-than-air craft which
stood comparison with the best in the world. The development of even
military manned aerostats came to an abrupt end in the U.S.S.R. in 1940,
however, consequent upon the catastrophic crash on 6 February, 1938 of
the U.S.S.R.-V6 airship *Osoviakhim*. This was on a test flight to check the
performance of its materials in polar conditions, and the intention was
that, if the results were positive, the airship would be sent from Murmansk

247. "V Kieve prokhodit festival' 'Vozdushnoe bratstvo'", Kiev city server, 21 July, 2006;
http://kiev2000.com/news/view.asp?ID=227030&Part=10

to retrieve a Soviet research team working on drifting ice floes in the Green-land Sea. The airship crashed into Mt Neblo in the Kola Peninsula. It is difficult now to establish the exact cause of the disaster.

In the late 1930s, after a succession of high-profile catastrophes, the construction of dirigibles was severely reduced throughout the world. In the Soviet Union, however, not only military development of airships was curtailed but also, more generally, any kind of flying as a sport. Even in the 1930s, the focus of Soviet aeronautics was on setting world altitude records using stratospheric balloons. Clearly, free, uncontrolled flying around in hot air balloons was incompatible with a country cut off by an Iron Curtain. None of the experts on flight whom I interviewed knew of an explicit prohi-bition in the 1970s on constructing balloons, but there was a tacit under-standing that any attempt to do so would be very unwise.

This situation, like much else in the country, began to change shortly before 1990. In 1988, several organisations in the U.S.S.R. began almost simultaneously to design hot air balloons. The initial stimulus was the appearance of two Hungarian balloons in Lithuania, then a constituent republic of the U.S.S.R., and a presentation in Moscow by a British firm, Cameron Balloons, in partnership with the Collaboration (Sotrudni-chestvo) cooperative. Despite many difficulties, a balloon inscribed "The First Montgolfière Made in the U.S.S.R.", entirely designed and manufac-tured in the U.S.S.R., rose into the Moscow sky at Tushino Aerodrome on 28 July, 1989. Funding for the balloon's development came from the Insti-tute of Evolutionary Morphology of the U.S.S.R. Academy of Sciences, which intended to use it to monitor the development of flora and fauna.[248] "We called our first montgolfière Aerovek, 'A Century of Flight', to empha-sise the revival of aeronautics in our country," says Aleksandr Komissarov, one of its creators. "It was guaranteed to be safe and splendid because so many splendid people put their hearts and souls into working on it."[249] "When a boom in hot air balloons began in our country, the chief engineer

248. A. V. Talanov, *Vse o vozdushnykh sharakh* (Moscow, 2002).
249. Quoted in the journal *Vozdukhoplavatel'*, 2 (16) (1999).

called me in and said, 'Design one!' That was in December 1989," says Mikhail Naidorf, who worked at the Dolgoprudny Automation Design Centre. The only institution in the U.S.S.R. working on lighter-than-air craft, needless to say for military purposes, the centre had been set up in 1955–6 after N.A.T.O. started making extensive use of hot air balloons for aerial photographic reconnaissance.

An experimental civilian hot air balloon, the TA-1, had its first flight in November 1990, and in the same year the first aerostat took to the sky above Irkutsk. It had been imported from Czechoslovakia by Leonid Kachev, where it had been manufactured to order by Kubíček Balloons. In 1990, Interavia began the small-scale manufacture of hot air balloons, and new means of acquiring them began to appear. You could buy a share in one, and some

The International Aerostat
Festival, Leningrad, 1990

269

people traded Russian cars for balloons with their colleagues in Eastern Europe.

On 11–17 May, 1990, Ryazan was the venue for the Sky of Russia Hot Air Balloon Fiesta, which gained an entry in the *Guinness Book of Records* as the first-ever balloon festival in Russia. It was attended by aeronauts from Great Britain, Norway, Germany, Yugoslavia and Australia. There was just one balloon from the U.S.S.R. A week later, 23–7 May, a better-attended event was the International Hot Air Balloon Fiesta held in Leningrad, with forty-one crews, several of which were from the U.S.S.R. These two festivals saw the first free flights in Soviet airspace of Soviet and foreign aeronauts.

The year 1990 was when people's desire to be allowed to fly freely, and their efforts to create the necessary technical and other facilities, began to yield results, and by 1991 it was possible to hold the first U.S.S.R. Hot Air Balloon Championship from 7 to 15 September. We conducted a survey among the staff of one of Russia's leading balloon companies, and also talked to aeronauts, in order to find out how 1990 is remembered by today's enthusiasts and those who design and manufacture hot air balloons in Russia.

Many of those who were to become designers and balloonists had dreamed about it in earlier decades, but had seen no prospect of realising their aspirations. When they sensed that an opportunity might be arising, they first approached military manufacturers and, after the inevitable rejection, started looking around for alternatives. Some working at secret military establishments had little choice but to resign and move elsewhere. Others were able to add ballooning to their existing work, as was the case for staff at the Dolgoprudny Automation Design Centre. People who before had been working on anti-aircraft defences, devising ways of destroying airborne objects including aerostats, now moved over to creating them, and for many the transition was difficult both technically and psychologic-ally. Other members of the ballooning community, however, knew nothing in 1990 about the history of airships and had no idea that ballooning would become part of their lives, saying things like "I never imagined that in our day and age anybody was still interested in airships" or "All I knew was what we were taught at school in physics about the Montgolfier brothers and what I read in Jules Verne's *Around the World in Eighty Days*" or "I had only ever seen hot air balloons on television."

Most future balloonists were already sports enthusiasts, and almost invariably their sports were associated with freedom of movement and visiting remote areas of the country. One might be a keen mountain climber, while another loved white-water rafting. Many rated the expeditions they went on in 1990 as, for them, the most important events of the year.

Other respondents remember 1990 for events which led directly to their current fascination with ballooning. Many who today are friends and colleagues knew nothing of each other's existence back then. One balloonist who lived in Moscow never heard about the fiesta in Ryazan, and its organisers had no knowledge of him or his balloon. Manufacture of balloons started quite independently in several parts of the Soviet Union at virtually the same time. For many of those who took part in the early competitions and fiestas, these were their first encounters with the international ballooning community, in other words, with the free world. One respondent considered the major event of 1990 to be participation by a Soviet team in a hot air balloon festival in France.

We have mentioned that what was claimed to be the first hot air balloon to be manufactured in the U.S.S.R. owed its appearance in the Moscow sky to Cameron Balloons. Donald Cameron, a British sportsman and entrepreneur, was the protagonist of the outstanding flight of 1990. Not one of the respondents of our modest survey had any recollection of Cameron's flight, yet it deserves a special mention. It would have been impossible in previous decades, but it would also have been more problematical in the years since 1990.

On 4 October, 1990, the newspaper *Soviet Latvia* reported the appearance in the sky of an Unidentified Flying Object.[250] However, the Object that landed on 3 October near a Latvian village, though Flying, was not

250. P. Man'ko, "Vstrecha s NLO v forme shara", *Sovetskaia Latviia*, 4 September, 1990.

The Soviet hot-air balloon prepares for take off, International Balloon Festival, France, 1990

Unidentified. It was the Doctus hot air balloon, piloted by Donald Cameron. His co-pilot was Gennadiy Oparin from Leningrad. The balloon had taken off from Cardington near London, and it had been agreed with the Soviet authorities that it should cross the Soviet border at a strictly defined point before landing in Leningrad.

Cameron Balloons is one of the largest companies in the world for the manufacture of aeronautical devices. At that time, Cameron's aerostats were, and today still are, considered to be among the best and most reliable in the world. Hearing about the changes in the U.S.S.R., Cameron himself wanted to donate one of his famous balloons to Soviet enthusiasts. He wrote a letter to the cosmonaut Gherman Titov, who he had heard was an influential figure in aviation, space and sport. Titov replied that he would come to England, but the visit never took place. "In the 1980s, somebody in D.O.S.A.A.F., the voluntary trust that supported the Soviet armed forces, told me about a crank who was constantly writing letters and offering to donate a balloon and train pilots to fly it. He invariably received the reply that we did not engage in bourgeois sports in the U.S.S.R. I was intrigued by his letter and wrote to him," Gennadiy Oparin related many years later.[251]

The main difficulty for balloonists was getting permission to cross the Soviet border. Here's how it looked from the other side of the English Channel: "I have no idea how Gennadiy managed to get permission for the flight! I know only that he had to go to Moscow several times and visit several ministries (including, it was rumoured, the K.G.B.) and embassies and make many phone calls. The written permission we eventually received stipulated unambiguously that we must land at Pulkovo Airport for customs inspection!"[252]

No doubt Cameron was mindful of the incident in 1983 when Soviet fighter jets shot down a South Korean airliner (with all its passengers) that had flown into Soviet airspace. Under Article 53 of the U.S.S.R.'s 1983 Aviation Code, which was still in force in 1990, "An aircraft in violation of the rules for crossing the state border of the Russian Federation or of the regulations governing use of the airspace of the Russian Federation will be deemed an intruder and compelled to land." Additionally, on 1 March, 1983 a law adopted by the Supreme Soviet "Concerning the state border of the U.S.S.R." came into effect. Article 36 of this Act reads: "The Air Defence Forces in protecting the state border of the U.S.S.R. may, in cases where termination of the violation or detention of intruders cannot be achieved by other means, employ armaments and other military technology."

Attempts to fly over the Iron Curtain were very dangerous and ended tragically not only in the U.S.S.R. but in other Warsaw Pact countries. There were, however, a few successful attempts. Among the exhibits of the Berlin Wall Museum is a balloon used on 16 September, 1979 in one of the most daring escapes from East to West Germany. Eight intrepid escapers built it out of umbrella fabric using blueprints from popular science magazines. Lacking essential technical knowledge, they were able to gain the requisite lift only by increasing the balloon's size, and so built the largest balloon in

---

251. Interview with G. I. Oparin, in *Smena*, 9 (2003).
252. D. Cameron, "UK to USSR", *Aerostat: The Journal of the British Balloon and Airship Club*, 21/5 (October 1990), p. 19.

the history of post-war Europe. The major change in 1990 which enabled Cameron and Oparin to make their flight was that, while military institutions and the K.G.B. remained highly secretive, it became feasible to address a request to them with some hope of reaching an agreement. At the cost of a great deal of time and effort, official permission to fly from England to the U.S.S.R. was eventually received.

Today, Russian balloonists who are planning flights taking them beyond the borders of the Russian Federation still have to consult many departments and spend a lot of time explaining to representatives of the state security services (without whose permission any form of flight in most parts of the country is out of the question) that establishing in advance exactly where they will land is impossible. In most cases, they do get permission, but until the late 1980s that was unimaginable. It would simply never have occurred to anyone to apply to the K.G.B. for permission to fly a hot air balloon. The Aviation Code and the State Borders Act had not changed, so the changes were in people's attitudes. Some individuals realised, or intuited, that it was now possible to apply to the relevant bodies, while the officials there felt obliged to consider their requests seriously and even to negotiate in order to reach an accommodation.

Those responsible for taking the decision on Cameron's application were doubtless also unaware that a balloon, unlike an airship or plane, cannot be required to comply rigorously with official instructions. Balloons follow the wind. A balloon can be piloted to the extent that the height it is flying at can be adjusted, enabling it to follow the direction of the airstream at that particular height, but the direction of the wind cannot be controlled. The representatives of state security proposed that the balloon should land at an airport. Any pilot knows, in the first place, that in order not to encounter aircraft at a major airport a balloon would need to land precisely on time, which is not always possible, and, secondly, that a slab of concrete is not the ideal surface for a soft landing. It also seemed likely that getting the balloon cleared by Soviet customs would be a major problem. Cameron nevertheless decided to accept all the conditions put forward.

The weather forecast on 1 October, 1990 was favourable and Doctus took to the skies. At first, it was accompanied by a British helicopter, but then the balloonists were on their own. For two days they flew over the North Sea and passed the coasts of Holland, Germany, Denmark and Sweden. Over Estonia the wind rose, and this was followed by an unfavourable weather forecast for Leningrad. The balloon was obliged to rise to a height of around 5,000 metres. It became clear that they were not going to be able to land as agreed as the wind carried the balloon in the direction of Latvia.

Cameron's flight was getting extensive coverage in the world press and the whereabouts of the balloon was continuously reported by journalists in the countries over which it was passing. We have no information as to whether the balloon was being tracked by Soviet air defences. At all events, they did not attempt to shoot it down, and, when the balloon did land, nobody was waiting for it. The landing occurred in a potato field, a much more agreeable surface than an airport. It is difficult to imagine the reaction of the Latvian peasants to the appearance of an enormous globe bearing a portrait of Aristotle, or to the beings clad in orange flying suits that climbed out of the gondola. Cameron relates that he accidentally left the flying boots he had bought specially for the flight at home, so he was wearing a pair of stylish British shoes. Rigans recall subsequent reports in the local newspapers about the landing of foreign spies.

After their initial alarm, the villagers offered assistance to the travellers and a place to sleep. In the middle of the night, however, after the balloon had been packed up and the pilots had been fed and retired to bed, the K.G.B. arrived claiming to have information that a huge sphere with foreign writing on it had appeared in the village and that a gun battle had ensued. The latter, of course, was pure invention. The pilots were, nevertheless, obliged to comply with the authorities' instructions and were taken to Pulkovo Airport, bringing their balloon, now classified as luggage, along with them.

A week after the trip, the Independent newspaper proclaimed Don Cameron the first man to fly non-stop in a balloon from England to the

U.S.S.R., and quoted him as saying of his delayed return home, "I really began to think it would be faster by balloon."[253] No-one has yet made the flight in the opposite direction. After the trip, Prince Andrew presented the pilots with the British Balloon and Airship Club's Salomons Trophy, a cup fashioned in 1910 by Fabergé, for an outstanding performance in a British-built flying device. The flight lasted 45 hours 55 minutes and covered a distance of some 2,200 kilometres. It was a good result for the time, but the balloonists did not set any new records. David Morgan of the British Balloon and Airship Club supposed that in sporting terms the flight was not a major event. It was considered interesting but soon forgotten other than by people with a particular interest. By 1990 the international balloon-racing community was already fairly blasé about flights across borders or over the sea. The first transatlantic flight had taken place in August 1978, and there had been many flights from the U.K. to other countries.

This, however, is to miss the point. Just a few years before this historic flight, nothing of the sort could have been envisaged. In 1990 a pilot who lived in Bristol and another who lived in Leningrad decided that the time had come when it could.

Hot air balloons were soon to become a symbol of freedom. One rose above Vilnius in Lithuania as a symbol of independence, while another took to the sky during the Orange Revolution in 2004 above Maidan Independence Square in Kiev, Ukraine. In Russia, too, hot air balloons are seen as symbols of freedom for the individual if not for the citizen. It is to the credit of 1990 that, ever since, people in Russia have continued to build and fly balloons.

"When I was a child," Boris Slavin has written, "I remember how, to celebrate the 800th Anniversary of Moscow, a balloon in the form of a glowing cube with a portrait of Stalin flew over Moscow. Visible from every direction, it was a gigantic three-dimensional icon of a man-god."[254] That balloon, however, was firmly tethered to the ground.

253. D. Cameron, "UK to USSR", p. 20.
254. B. Slavin, "O sotsializme, svobode i totalitarizme"; http://www.alternativy.ru/en/node/225

Since the mid-1990s, ballooning has been the province not only of sport and recreation but also of business and marketing. It has become a way of life for a substantial number of people, for whom their greatest joy is again and again to experience the sensation of flying free. Japanese balloonists called this "*satori*", enlightenment. For them, communing with the essence of the elements is tantamount to freedom.

The first balloon fiesta in Ryazan, 1990

TRADE UNIONS IN 1990: AN INVOLVED OBSERVER'S VIEW

Sergey Khramov [255]

Many terms like "trade union", "worker", "the labour movement" and "strike" had different meanings when used in Soviet propaganda from what they meant in other languages. The term *worker*, for example, is generally applied by the International Labour Organisation to mean anyone who is employed and receives a wage or salary, but in the Soviet Union the word *rabochii* meant a worker who was defined as a worker in the U.S.S.R. classification of jobs and professions, as distinct from a *sluzhashchii*, or state employee. The logic behind this classification scheme was far from clear. For example, a civil aviation pilot, whose job unquestionably required higher education, was a "worker", while a nurse in general practice, whose job required far less training, was a "state employee". A "trade union" as understood by the I.L.O. is an organisation set up by workers on their own initiative to stand up to an employer in negotiating the employment relationship. It independently decides its own rules and regulations, elects representatives and chooses to join or not to join a confederation of trade unions. In the U.S.S.R., however, a trade union meant a body subordinate to the ministry of an industrial sector, or the welfare department of an enterprise. It had no choice but to be subordinate also to the U.S.S.R. Central Council of Trade Unions, an institution which had replaced the People's Commissariat of Labour in 1932 and which, among other things, set industrial standards for the state.

On the other hand, in the U.S.S.R. a worker was a member of the "hege-

255. Sergey Khramov, from 1989 to 2008 leader of Sotsprof, a confederation of independent trade unions; in 1990 and subsequently, an active participant in the workers' movement, human rights activist and expert on labour law issues.

monic class". The social status of a miner or a worker at a major military factory was far higher than that of a nurse, a teacher or, during perestroika, the owner of a cooperative selling home-made pies at the entrance to a mine.

I contend that those pies, or at least the myth that the small-time entrepreneurs selling them at the mine entrance were making more money than "the most important workers in the U.S.S.R." – the miners who provided the country with coal – were the spark that ignited the miners' strike on 11 July, 1989. Only the spark, mind, but a spark that was fanned into a major conflagration by the mines' directors. We can deduce this from the forty or so demands put forward by the strike committees at the time. These included such management issues as the delivery of equipment and mine props, an adequate supply of freight wagons, state funding of social services, and, of greatest importance to the management, the granting of economic independence to each mine and allowing the management to apply its profits at their discretion. (To this day, most mines remain divisions of mining conglomerates like Vorkuta Coal or Chelyabinsk Coal.)

Ever since 1989, the assertion has been repeatedly made in scholarly journals and journalism that this was the time when the miners started playing politics. To my mind, it was on the contrary in 1989–90 that the politicians started playing politics with the coal miners.

The excitement began on 11 July, 1989, with a protest action when several dozen miners in Mezhdurechensk refused to come back up to the surface. The same form of protest had been used by miners of Section 9 of the North Mine in Vorkuta in the spring of 1989, but that action had had no political impact. The men who protested in Vorkuta and Mezhdurechensk were heroes who did not know what to expect: a new wave of shootings such as quelled the workers' uprising in Novocherkassk in 1962, dismissal from their jobs, or something else? In July 1989, those who gathered in the squares of mining towns had, nevertheless, a fair idea that the political situation was now very different. For many, taking the platform at a protest meeting then was the prelude to a career in politics.

In June 1989, for example, Yuriy Boldyrev, an activist of the Donetsk miners' movement, came to see me in Moscow. I was then the leader of the newly established Sotsprof association of free trade unions and tried to persuade him of the need to establish free trade unions for miners, but he only wanted me to obtain justice for him in Moscow by having him reinstated as a member of the Communist Party.[256] In July, he became a member of the Donetsk strike committee of two representatives from each of twenty-one mines. Within a year, half of those forty-two were people's deputies in city or provincial soviets. A good number were chairing committees of the old Soviet trade union, and only five were still members of the strike committee. Boldyrev went on to become a People's Deputy in the Ukrainian parliament, the Verkhovna Rada.

There was good reason why Soviet politicians so loved the miners. They were, and still are, relatively few in number. The nature of their work and their traditions mean that they form a coherent social group. In Soviet times and in the 1990s, the regime and journalists conferred on them the status of "the most important representatives of the working class". It was far easier for the U.S.S.R. authorities and their rivals, the politicians of the Russian republican government, to pose as friends of the people by conceding the demands of three hundred thousand miners and promoting their spokesmen to be deputies than by getting to grips with the problems of two million textile workers or five million teachers.

In May and June 1989, there was the grand televised political spectacular of the First Congress of People's Deputies of the U.S.S.R. and the beginning of the campaign to nominate and elect candidates for various levels of soviets. These elections took place in late 1989. Perhaps that is why, although they were not ignored by the media, protests in the spring of 1989 by air traffic controllers, miners in Vorkuta, bauxite miners in the North Urals, staff at the Lenin Library in Moscow, and workers at the Komsomol Automotive and Ordzhonikidze Machine Tools Factories in Moscow had little political impact.

256. I was unable to help him there because I had never been a member of the Communist Party. At the time I was one of the leaders of the Russian Social-Democratic Party.

Three trends were evident in the labour movement in 1989–91. Supporters of the first believed that all problems could be solved by new, free elections in the primary, factory-level trade union committees, retaining the Soviet-style Central Council of Trade Unions. This trend was supported by some of the leaders of the C.C.T.U. It was fleshed out at the C.C.T.U.'s September 1989 Plenum and at the Nineteenth Congress of Trade Unions of the U.S.S.R. in October 1990. It was supported by the founders of the Russian Federation of Independent Trade Unions in March 1990. The C.C.T.U. actively promoted this policy at miners' congresses.

The second trend favoured developing a non-trade union, politicised "workers' movement". This was to consist of regional and factory-based workers' clubs, strike committees and workers' committees whose membership would be restricted to "workers" according to the Soviet definition. They would be advised by academic economists, sociologists and political scientists, and it was hoped that this would parallel the impact of Solidarity in Poland in the early 1980s.[257] This trend culminated in the setting up in May 1990 of the Labour Confederation (*Konfederatsiia truda*).[258] The movement's ideologists were often at different ends of the spectrum on

257. A spontaneous strike in 1979 at the Lenin Shipyard in Gdansk, Poland was led by Lech Wałęsa, an electrician who had lost his job there in 1976. The political platform of Solidarity, the workers' association created by the strikers, was provided by the dissident Polish intellectuals Tadeusz Mazowiecki, Adam Michnik and others. This explains why Solidarity was not a traditional trade union based on a particular industry sector but, effectively, a political party based on regions. It had its committees based in Polish provinces, just as the ruling Polish United Workers' Party had provincial committees.

258. The ideologists of the Labour Confederation (*Konfederatsiia truda*) were Leonid Gordon, Galina Rakitskaya, Ilya Shablinsky, Viktor Komarovsky and, a little later, Lyudmila Alekseyeva. The present Russian National Confederation of Labour (*Vserossiiskaia konfederatsiia truda*) and Labour Confederation of Russia (*Konfederatsiia truda Rossii*) have no institutional relationship with the Labour Confederation. The Labour Confederation of Russia was formed on 12 April, 1995 on the initiative of the Russo-American Trade Union Research and Education Fund. Originally created as a trade-union association uniting free industrial trade unions, but opposing Sotsprof, the Labour Confederation of Russia subsequently split, as a result of which, in August 1995, the Russian Independent Trade Union of Miners, five industrial trade unions of Sotsprof and four regional trade-union associations formed the Russian National Confederation of Labour (*Vserossiiskaia konfederatsiia truda*).

other political issues. Similar views informed the Councils of Labour Collectives (introduced by the government in 1987 to raise the efficiency of industry), which sought the right for workers to participate directly in managing their enterprises.

The third trend, articulated by the present writer, envisaged setting up new trade unions with no genetic link to the C.C.T.U. It made use of trade union rights under existing legislation to represent the labour and welfare interests of workers (as defined by the I.L.O.) and to safeguard their rights. The hope was that, if the new trade unions were able to conclude agreements with enterprises, this would enhance the social status of workers and encourage the growth of a huge class of skilled workers. That would in turn lead to a more educated electorate. Alongside the setting up of new unions, 1989–90 saw more specialised free trade unions separate out from the old-style C.C.T.U. unions. Trade unions of this kind were successfully created for air traffic controllers, civil aviation pilots, dock workers and seamen.

Relations between these various trends could be strained. The first free miners' trade union was created by Sotsprof at the Abakumov coal mine in Donetsk in November 1989. Its leader, Sergey Naidyonov, was ostracised by other members of the strike committee for setting it up. Sotsprof trade unions were formed in December 1989 at two other mines in Donetsk, but Workers' Movement supporters were concerned to preserve the hierarchical system of qualifications detailed in official Soviet job descriptions and suspicious of trade unions of any sort. Worker-deputies of the R.S.F.S.R. Supreme Soviet[259] were adamant in the drafting of the Law on Collective

259. Their subsequent careers are interesting. Aleksandr Lugovoy, head of the working group on drafting the Law on Collective Bargaining Agreements, went on to become Deputy Head of the State Labour Inspectorate. The miner Ivan Shoshviashvili later became an activist in a minor political party led by Sazhi Umalatova; Aleksandr Kosopkin who, until his election, drove a locomotive, later became Director of the President's Office for Russian Domestic Policy and, from 2004, representative of the President of the Russian Federation in the State Duma. After October 1993, Sergey Andropov was head of the Moscow regional State Labour Inspectorate. Vladimir Makhanov was Chairman of the Duma Committee on Property and Privatisation.

Agreements, which became law in May 1992, [260] that an enterprise had three distinct elements: the management, the trade union committee, and the workers. My efforts to persuade them that in a normal situation a trade union consisted of workers produced a compromise formulation referring to the "trade union or other representative body of employees". Strike committees and workers' councils refused categorically to cooperate with the free trade unions emerging in parallel with them. [261] It was not unknown for more than one strike committee to be set up in the same region. In Vorkuta there were two, one set up by the management of Vorkuta Coal.

Two kinds of trade union, one Soviet and the other free, clashed at the First and Second Miners' Congresses in Donetsk in June and October 1990. The official C.C.T.U. had lost face during negotiations between the U.S.S.R. Council of Ministers and the miners when the official trade union leaders sided with the government. To make amends and as a damage limitation exercise, it now provided organisational support for the congresses. It had a further aim of diverting protesting miners away from the free trade unions. The delegates to these congresses, "representatives of the vanguard of the working class", had in any case no wish to turn their workers' movement into a trade union. This would have obliged them to become involved in meticulous legal paperwork and to be accountable to each miner for decisions affecting his vital daily interests. Delegates from American trade unions who were present at the first congress expressed amazement that

---

260. The law of the Russian Federation "Concerning collective contracts and agreements" came into force in May 1992. It was amended in 1995 but superseded in October 2006 with the introduction of a new edition of the Labour Code. The "Collective contracts and agreements" law laid the foundations for genuine reform of labour relations in Russia, but was obstructed by the Russian Federation of Independent Trade Unions (*Federatsiia nezavisimykh profsoiuzov Rossii*). Getting the law repealed was the main aim of the Labour Code, for which Andrey Isayev, a leader of the government's United Russia party, lobbied. The Labour Code was first adopted in 2001 and renewed in 2006. I am proud to have drafted and written the law on "Collective contracts and agreements" and its 1995 amendments.

261. They were, however, willing to listen to the views of advisers from the Academy of Sciences' Institute for International Economics and International Relations, its Institute of the International Labour Movement and the like.

mass miners' strikes were taking place in the U.S.S.R. without the existence of an independent miners' union.

In November 1989, Pavel Kudyukin[262] and I organised a meeting between miners from the government's commission to implement Resolution 608 of the U.S.S.R. Council of Ministers and representatives of Solidarity, and in January 1990, nine members of miners' strike committees travelled all over the U.S. at the invitation of the A.F.L.-C.I.O. federation of unions to see for themselves how the American miners' union worked. Despite this, the setting up of a free trade union was repeatedly postponed. The culprits were evidently academic consultants jealously guarding their anticipated monopoly as channels for foreign aid. Finally, on the last day of the second congress, at the request of Anatoliy Malykhin and 135 delegates, an Independent Trade Union of Miners was finally founded, giving organisational shape to the Workers' Movement. The new organisation decided, however, to remain aloof from other free trade unions.

For the miners' movement, 1990 differed from 1989 not least because the political struggle was replaced by a sense of euphoria at the perceived achievement of democracy and a belief that law had replaced the system of Party appointments from above. This climate galvanised the incipient free trade union movement. Under the aegis of Sotsprof alone, trade unions were established for refrigeration workers; restaurant musicians; journalists; welders; sailors of the Pacific Fleet; the Moscow police; Moscow metro workers; public transport drivers in Tula, Vladivostok and Moscow; steelworkers in Angarsk, Lysva and Moscow; workers at the No. 1 and No. 2 Watch Factories in Moscow; workers at Lublin Foundry; medics in Moscow, Orekhovo-Zuyevo and Nizhny Novgorod; workers at the Likhachov and Komsomol Automotive Factories; workers in the defence industry in Orenburg; builders in Moscow; staff at the pilot factory of the Siberian Branch

262. Pavel Kudyukin, historian, human rights activist and essayist. In 1989–90, he founded and was one of the leaders of the Russian Social-Democratic Party. An acknowledged expert on the history of foreign trade unions and their methods of conducting strikes, in 1991 he became deputy to the Minister of Labour, Aleksandr Shokhin.

of the Academy of Sciences; temporary oil workers in Surgut; and workers at the Oktyabr Pigment and Electrical Appliance factories in Tambov. Strikes were organised of the conductors of Kievan post-office railway carriages, and of the drivers at Bus Depot No. 16 in Moscow.

All these events gained far less press coverage than the miners' strikes and protests because they were undertaken by the workers themselves and not in the course of more newsworthy political conflicts. In reality, there never was the much vaunted "dual power", with strike committees challenging Soviets, as many journalists claimed after visiting the mining towns in 1989. When politicians wanted to portray themselves as taking decisions in the interests of the workers, the miners' movement was put on a pedestal and hyped in the media. On 1–2 March, 1991, a national strike was organised by the new Independent Trade Union of Miners. Sotsprof supported it, and I wrote a letter to the then Soviet Prime Minister, Valentin Pavlov. Initially the strikers' demand was very specific: they wanted a general pay agreement for the mining industry. On 6 March, however, Anatoliy Malykhin, who was leading the protest in Moscow, turned it political by calling for Gorbachev to resign. This caused a great stir in the press and attracted worldwide attention. But the strike had been needed to resolve an economic dispute; turning it into a political strike served quite different ends. Important as the political issue might have been, the upshot was that the pay agreement was forgotten and the miners lost out. On the bright side, however, the miners' union leaders got their political careers off to a great start: Malykhin became Yeltsin's presidential representative in Kemerovo province[263] while Mikhail Kislyuk became Governor.[264]

By no means all of the free trade unions which sprang up in 1989–91

---

263. Anatoliy Malykhin (b. 1957), miner, economist; retired from the post of representative of the President of Russia in Kemerovo province in 1997; for a time, was a member of the Union of Right Forces party; currently Director-general of the not-for-profit partnership, the Association of Energy-Producing Cities.
264. Mikhail Kislyuk (b. 1951) was initially a mine finance officer and then, until 1990, Chairman of the Executive Committee of the Russian National Confederation of Labour. He is currently a businessman who also manages the Trade Union Centre N.G.O.

managed to survive. Today, of all those created in every sector of the economy in the enthusiasm of perestroika, the ones which survive are mainly in the coal industry, aviation and other forms of transport. In 1989–91 trade union confederations could be formed in two ways. On the one hand were associations like Sotsprof, envisaged from the outset as an umbrella organisation, within which new overall trade unions could be set up to cover all industries, and specialist trade unions within sectors (for example, metal workers, civil service accountants or textile workers) which subsequently amalgamated into industry-wide trade unions. The second approach was for a movement first to take shape among the workers of a particular sector, and then for these specialised trade unions to unite in larger associations. For example, shipping trade unions came together in the Confederation of Russian Workers. The Russian National Association of Civil Aviation Trade Unions brings together such aviation-industry unions as air traffic controllers, pilots and radar specialists. There is a different Russian Federation of Trade Unions which includes the Russian Federal Trade Union of Air-Traffic Controllers and the Trade Union of Aviation Workers in Radar and Communication Systems. Some unions, like the Russian Federal Trade Union of Air-Traffic Controllers, are simultaneously members of several associations, including international ones.

For independent trade unions, 1990 was both a good and a bad year. The movement grew up and, in effect, trade union leaders began to understand what a trade union ought to be doing. They were not a department of a company's management, but neither was it obligatory for them to participate directly in national politics. Among the unfortunate results of the year was the fact that, through the joint efforts of the media and politicians, the public gained a very distorted picture of the trade union movement, which continued throughout the 1990s and endures to this day.

In advanced industrialised countries, the workers' movement and the trade union movement are virtually synonymous. For the media and post-Soviet public opinion in Russia, they are almost antonyms. The workers' movement is seen as being involved in strike action, which journalists present as defence of workers' rights. Trade unions are considered far less interesting and important, because defending workers' rights is seen in purely political terms, without a legal dimension. This is wrong and dangerous. Human rights, including workers' rights, need primarily to be a matter for the law.

This is well understood by those who today make an informed choice to join the new trade unions, as also by those who work in the trade union movement every day. It is, unfortunately, something journalists, politicians and employers have a tendency to forget. Back in 1990, that kind of "forgetfulness" was already too much in evidence.

AUGUST

2–4 August

Iraqi troops invade Kuwait on the orders of President Saddam Hussein. The U.N. Security Council calls for immediate withdrawal and, on the same day, the U.S., Britain and France freeze Iraqi assets in their banks and impose an arms embargo. On 3 August, U.S. Secretary of State James Baker flies to Moscow, where he is assured that the U.S.S.R. supports the embargo. On 4 August, China announces that it has ceased to supply arms to Iraq (A. Semenov, "Tri voiny Saddama"; http://historiwars.narod.ru/Index/XXv/saddam/saddam3.htm).

Boris Yeltsin speaks in the Latvian parliament: "We would like to be among the first to conclude a treaty between Russia and Latvia, before the

Celebrating Assault Troops Day, Park of Culture, Moscow, 2 August, 1990

Celebrating Assault Troops Day, Park of Culture, Moscow, 2 August, 1990

U.S.S.R. Treaty and before the new constitution is adopted. That is, within one and a half months" (*Izvestiia*, 215, p. 2). The agreement was signed in Tallinn, not "within one and a half months" but only on 13 January, 1991. It provided for protecting the rights of the Russian-speaking population in Latvia and was ratified by the Latvian parliament. The R.S.F.S.R. Supreme Soviet, and later the Russian State Duma, refused to ratify it (Igor' Vatolin, "Rossiia ne zashchitila svoikh", *Chas* [Riga], 16 January, 2006; http://www.russkie.org/index.php?module=whatwritten&id=20).

Yevgeniy Primakov reports that a working group has been set up to "prepare an outline U.S.S.R. programme for transition to a market economy as the basis of a new U.S.S.R. treaty". This has been agreed by Mikhail Gorbachev, Boris Yeltsin, Nikolai Ryzhkov and Ivan Silayev. The work will be supervised by Gorbachev and Yeltsin (*Izvestiia*, 216, p. 2).

4 August

Levon Ter-Petrossian, leader of the Armenian National Movement, is elected Chairman of the Armenian Supreme Soviet (*Izvestiia*, 218, p. 2). He thereby becomes the first non-Communist leader of a Soviet republic.

The U.S.S.R. Council of Ministers adopts a decree on measures to create a foreign exchange market (*Izvestiia*, 220, p. 1).

The Vainakh Democratic Party, founded on 5 May, 1990, holds a rally in Grozny demanding the status of a sovereign union republic for Checheno-Ingushetia (*Novyi khronograf*, 13 [1990]; http://www.panorama.ru/gazeta/newchr/nc13.html).

5 August

According to the U.S.S.R. Interior Ministry, twenty-three thousand Russian-speaking refugees have left Tajikistan since the beginning of the year (*Izvestiia*, 218, p. 2).

Ten years after the death of Vladimir Vysotsky, the Moscow City Soviet agrees to establish a museum and cultural centre, Vysotsky House on Taganka. It is not to be a typical, stuffy museum, but open to everyone, especially poets, musicians and actors (*Moskovskie novosti*, 31, p. 2).

For the first time in the history of the U.S.S.R., the legendary anthology *Vekhi* (Milestones: A Collection of Articles about the Russian Intelligentsia) was reprinted by A.P.N. Novosti in an edition of fifty thousand copies (*Moskovskie novosti*, 31, p. 2).

6 August

Boris Yeltsin arrives in the Tatar Republic at the beginning of a working visit to the Volga region, the Urals, Siberia and the Soviet Far East (*Izvestiia*, 220, p. 2).

9 August

The U.S.S.R. Council of Ministers adopts a decree on measures to create and develop small enterprises (*Izvestiia*, 222, p. 1).

Lithuania, August 1990

Vilnius, Lithuania, August 1990

10 August

The beach under the bridge near Sportivnaya metro station, Moscow, August 1990

11 August

The Kemerovo Provincial Soviet decides to compile an inventory of Party property. The bureau of the provincial Party committee declares the decision illegal and advises the soviet's (Communist) Chairman, Aman Tuleyev, to have it reconsidered (*Izvestiia*, 224, p. 3).

12 August

August 1990 is the peak of the so-called "Coupon Economy". Ration coupons rapidly find a niche in the economy. They are bought, sold and traded. As they are issued to every living adult, drinkers are happy to avail themselves of the vodka which the authorities have thoughtfully put aside for teetotallers, and pensioners exchange vodka coupons for meat coupons while alcoholics do the reverse (Kirill Kobrin).

The Crimean provincial executive committee adopts a plan for resettling Crimean Tatars returning home after having been deported in 1944. Five

A typical scene during the "Coupon Economy"

thousand families are to be resettled in 1991 in almost every region, but every city and region, including Sevastopol, will have a quota (*Moskovskie novosti*, 32, p. 2). Refat Chubarov, one of the Crimean Tatars' leaders, suspected that this even distribution was to prevent them from becoming a democratic political force. The plan also provided for no Tatars to be allowed to settle on the southern coast of Crimea. The Tatars, however, wanted to return to their former homes (Refat Chubarov, "Esli by ne avtoritet i davlenie Prezidenta, krymskotatarskaia problema voobshche ne reshalas' by . . .", *Den'* [Kiev], 27 January, 2004).

14 August

In Moscow, the U.S.S.R. State Committee on the Press issues the first registration certificates to newspapers and magazines. No. 1 is issued to *Izvestiia*. 124 applications have so far been received, and more than a hundred are for new titles. Twenty applications are from private individuals who are planning to publish sixteen magazines and three newspapers (*Izvestiia*, 227, p. 1).

The journalists of *Smena* ("Next Shift") in Leningrad go on hunger strike, demanding that it should be registered as independent of the Young Communist League (*Noveishaia istoriia otechestvennogo kino*).

A presidential decree "Concerning the restoration of the rights of all victims of political repressions in the 1920s to 1950s" (*Izvestiia*, 227, p. 1) is

Hunger strike by staff of *Smena* ("Next Shift")

the final admission of the state's crimes against its citizens during the Stalin era. (But no earlier. The decree did not apply to those persecuted during the 1917 Revolution and Civil War.)

Casinos Austria International open their first casino in the U.S.S.R. in Riga (*Izvestiia*, 227, p. 8).

15 *August*

Viktor Tsoy (b. 1962), one of the most charismatic stars in the history of Russian rock music, dies in a car crash, apparently after falling asleep at the wheel due to overwork (http://www.vsesmi.ru/news/34608/82746).

16 *August*

Soviet citizenship is restored by presidential decree to twenty-three people, including Aleksandr Solzhenitsyn, Vasiliy Aksyonov, Vladimir Voinovich, Valeriy Chalidze, Viktor Korchnoy, Oscar Rabin, Lev Kopelev, Georgiy Vladimov, Yuriy Orlov and Valeriy Tarsis (*Izvestiia*, 229, p. 1).

There was no restoration of citizenship for Vladimir Bukovsky or Iosif Brodsky.

17 August

The workforce of *The Banner* (*Znamya*) resolves at a general meeting to take over the journal, in full conformity with U.S.S.R. law, and apply for registration (*Izvestiia*, 230, p. 3; http://magazines.russ.ru/znamia/history/ hist. html).

16–17 August

Armed clashes between the Croatian police and the Serbian population in Croatia sees the start of an openly secessionist movement in Knin Krajina, an area of Croatia predominantly populated by Serbs.

22 August

The border conflict between Armenia and Azerbaijan erupts again with extreme violence. There is sustained shelling of territory by both sides (*Izvestiia*, 235, p. 1).

In Moscow's Danilov Monastery, a Synodal Commission of the Russian Orthodox Church studies proposals from the Synod of the Ukrainian Orthodox Church to give it greater independence in light of numerous religious and administrative problems in the republic (*Izvestiia*, 236, p. 3).

"Iosif Brodsky at Fifty" is the theme of an exhibition at the Anna Akhmatova Museum in Leningrad (*Izvestiia*, 235, p. 3).

Echo of Moscow, the first radio station independent of the State Committee on Television and Radio, begins broadcasting. It was the first mass-media business to be registered on 9 August and broadcasts daily from 19.00 to 21.00. Its owners are the Moscow City Soviet, the Radio association, *Ogonyok* and the Faculty of Journalism of Moscow State University (*Moskovskii komsomolets*, 191, p. 1). A stake in the company was later acquired by Gazprom Media.

23 August

The Armenian Supreme Soviet declares independence (*Izvestiia*, 237, p. 2).

24 August

The Russian writer Sergey Dovlatov dies in New York (see obituaries by Natal'ia Kuznetsova, Lev Losev and Mikhail Lemkhin in *Russkaia mysl'*, 3843, 13 August, and at http://www.sergeidovlatov.com. Natal'ia Gorbanevskaya).

25 August

The Supreme Soviet of the Abkhazian Autonomous Soviet Socialist Republic passes a Declaration of Sovereignty and renames itself the Abkhazian Soviet Socialist Republic. On 26 August a further resolution claims that, as a result of the Georgian Supreme Soviet's decision to declare null and void all Soviet national arrangements since February 1921, the incorporation of Abkhazia in Georgia no longer has any legal basis.

26 August

With an impressive margin over his twenty rivals, former K.G.B. Major General Oleg Kalugin wins a second round of balloting to become a People's Deputy of the U.S.S.R., polling, according to preliminary data, 46 per cent of all votes cast (*Moskovskie novosti*, 34, p. 5).

Half a million people each year applied to the Department for Visas and Registration (O.V.I.R.) to emigrate from the U.S.S.R. During the previous six months, however, only 203,000 had left, because there was no legal right to emigrate from the U.S.S.R. other than "to be reunited with close relatives". If a new law on entry and exit allowed unrestricted emigration, the U.S.S.R. Interior Ministry estimates that six hundred thousand citizens will emigrate immediately. O.V.I.R. explains that the visa regime is being democratised, and émigrés from the U.S.S.R. are even allowed to return. So far, however, only a few hundred have done so.

28 August

The five permanent members of the U.N. Security Council approve a peace plan for Cambodia. On 11 September the plan is accepted by the four

Cambodian parties which, in various shifting alliances, have been fighting each other (Natal'ia Gorbanevskaya).

29 August

Mikhail Gorbachev and Boris Yeltsin discuss the economic situation, transition to a market economy, strengthening economic ties of the republics and creating a single U.S.S.R. market (*Pravda*, 31 August.) The competing programmes for combating the economic crisis and integrating the economies of the republics of the U.S.S.R. on a new basis are also considered.

Vitaliy Ignatenko, newly appointed press secretary of the President of the U.S.S.R., a forty-nine-year old professional journalist, holds his first briefing for Soviet and foreign journalists at the press centre of the Soviet Foreign Ministry (*Izvestiia*, 243, p. 2).

30 August

A commission of people's deputies of the Kharkov City Soviet, set up at the request of voters, identifies eighty-four cases of abuse by staff at the provincial committee of the Communist Party of Ukraine in allocating apartments (*Izvestiia*, 243, p. 3).

30–31 August

A joint meeting of the Presidential Council and the U.S.S.R. Soviet of the Federation agrees to submit to the U.S.S.R. Supreme Soviet a single, consolidated economic reform project based on the programmes of Abel Aganbegyan, Stanislav Shatalin, Grigoriy Yavlinsky and Leonid Abalkin. During a heated debate, serious complaints are made about the attitude of the U.S.S.R. government and there are calls for Nikolai Ryzhkov to resign. At a press conference after the meeting, Gorbachev remarks, "We should probably give some thought to the possibility that the power of the president needs to be strengthened and that it needs to function more effectively" (*Pravda*, 2 September, 1990). In fact, Gorbachev was publicly threatening to take over Ryzhkov's powers in retaliation for the latter's efforts to thwart market reforms. The U.S.S.R. Supreme Soviet subsequently failed to approve a programme to stabilise the economy. In September 1990, the R.S.F.S.R. leadership adopted the 500 Days programme, but they too failed to implement it.

The Supreme Soviet of the Tatar A.S.S.R. adopts a Declaration of Sovereignty and renames itself the Tatar Soviet Socialist Republic (*Izvestiia*, 244, p. 2).

Also in August

The U.S.S.R. Statistics Committee confirmed that industrial production in August 1990 fell by 1.7 per cent, compared with the corresponding period in 1989 (*Izvestiia*, 257, p. 1).

The Moscow City Soviet, led by Gavriil Popov, founded *The Capital*, a social and political magazine, and *Chimes* (*Kuranty*), a newspaper. The publications rapidly became very popular (*Noveishaia istoriia otechestvennogo kino*), and subsequently gave strong support to Yeltsin's campaign to become President of Russia.

An armed group of eleven individuals hijacked a TU-134 at Chulman Airport in Yakutia. The authorities met all the terrorists' demands and the plane was flown to Pakistan. There, the terrorists surrendered to the local authorities, evidently expecting to be hailed as heroes. Instead, the government of Pakistan punished them severely. Two months later, Igor Suslov, one of the hijackers, hanged himself in a Pakistani jail. Aviation terrorism assumed catastrophic proportions. In 1990 there were thirty-three hijackings (*Ibid.*).

Vladimir Naumov's film *Ten Years Without Correspondence Rights* was released. After the Second World War, the hero, Mikhail, returns to Moscow to take revenge on Zavyalov, whose false denunciation in 1937 had led to Mikhail's father being shot. As the truth of the matter is so obvious, Mikhail makes no secret of what he is doing and kills Zavyalov. He waits calmly for the arrival of the N.K.V.D., whom Zavyalov had managed to phone.

Thought publishing house brought out a two-volume collection of works by Friedrich Nietzsche, edited by Karen Svas'ian, which has been recognised as a definitive Russian edition (Ibid.).

THE FUNERAL OF FOOD, OR THE SOVIET SHOPPING BASKET IN 1990

Sergey Karnaukhov

Two parodies, one on television and one in a newspaper, characterise our period. The programme Bingo! (Oba-na!) was broadcast in early 1991, but had clearly been made earlier. It parodied the succession of funerals of C.P.S.U. general secretaries, which everyone remembered from the first half of the 1980s, except that now Soviet citizens were sorrowfully bidding a last farewell not to a political leader but to food. In December 1990, the Leningrad newspaper Next Shift (Smena) put on its front page a parody of Surikov's nineteenth-century painting showing Boyarina Morozova being whisked away on a sleigh to exile for her Old Believer religious views. Here, however, it was not the doughty matriarch but condensed milk, coffee, vegetables and fruit which were being whisked away.[265] Every month of 1990 saw further grocery items making their last journey: salt, matches, washing powder, men's socks . . .

In 1990–91, shortages of basic goods unquestionably peaked, but in many Russian cities they had been commonplace since the late 1970s. The legendary "sausage trains" leaving Moscow with newly provisioned shoppers from neighbouring provinces have now even got into Wikipedia.[266] Living with a constant shortage of produce, which was said to be "tossed out" randomly to shops (or had to be "acquired", or "got by pulling strings"), was something which the provinces, and even major regional centres, were obliged grudgingly to put up with. The National Food

265. Smena, 300, 30 December, 1990.
266. See http://ru.wikipedia.org/wiki/Товарный_дефицит_в_СССР In the early 1980s, the present author used to travel every two months from Tula province to Moscow to buy food and clothing.

Programme, inaugurated in May 1982 and intended to run until 1990, was, if little more than vacuous rhetoric, at least an acknowledgement of the seriousness of the problem facing the U.S.S.R.

By the 1980s, ration cards, euphemistically called "invitations" or "coupons", were being introduced in some provinces.[267] At the 19th Party Conference in June 1988, Yegor Ligachov reproached Yeltsin for having, as First Secretary in Sverdlovsk, "put the whole province on coupons". Rationing of certain foodstuffs was clearly forced on local authorities by circumstances, and they did it surreptitiously and piecemeal in order belatedly to pacify the population. Quite what was rationed by the time perestroika began can only be discovered by sifting through Soviet Executive Committee and Party archives. There was no standardisation across regions. A big change in 1990 was the creeping transformation of this ad hoc rationing as a partial solution to localised shortages of certain foods into the main way in which most of the population was fed. For the first time since Khrushchev's failures in the early 1960s, food shortages affected the U.S.S.R.'s major cities. Typically, rationing covered the basics of meat, sugar and alcohol, but the list grew steadily longer.

WHAT DID PEOPLE OUTSIDE THE CAPITAL HAVE IN THEIR SHOPPING BASKETS IN 1990?

Soviet statistics relating to food supplies recorded only the official (and often falsified) "volumes".[268] As a result, we have had to resort to estimates and extrapolation from incomplete data. We deliberately restrict ourselves to attempting to describe what food went into shopping baskets in 1990 in

267. Examples of these are collected by "tesseristics" enthusiasts. On coupons in the Urals and Vologda from 1970 to the 1980s, see http://www.bonistikaweb.ru/URALSKIY/makurin.htm, http://www.bonistikaweb.ru/VOLOGODSKIY/vologodskiy-2.htm (with illustrations), as well as Vladimir Rudenko's 1990 article, "Talon dlia tesserista", Ural'skii sledopyt, 1 (1991), pp. 78–80.

268. On the extent to which Soviet statistics misrepresented the real situation in the economy, see Grigorii I. Khanin, Dinamika ekonomicheskogo razvitiia SSSR (Novosibirsk, 1991).

Irkutsk, Leningrad and Tiksi, a small port on the shores of the Laptev Sea in the Soviet Arctic. My respondents in Irkutsk province and Leningrad were predominantly from the Soviet urban middle class and its upcoming generation of university and college students, which further reduces the representativeness of the sample.

One of two main sources of food was extensive mandatory deliveries from state and collective farms throughout the U.S.S.R., supplemented by purchases from the rural population. These included meat and dairy products, sugar and confectionery. This produce was centrally distributed in accordance with the state plan to the various republics, to provincial, municipal and district food-distribution centres, and even to particular food shops. Levels of pilfering, misreporting and shortages soared as the state's centralised supply system fell apart. In 1990, the managers of collective and state farms, those of provinces, and even the leaders of republics were trying every trick in the book to divert food away from mandatory deliveries to the state, because its rates were far below those which could be obtained in the marketplace. The main cause of a universal food crisis was the increasing unworkability of a system in which those at lower levels in the supply chain could only sell (or steal, or pass out through the back door) what they were allocated by those above them.

The second major source of food was the "Moscow Provision". These were deliveries directly controlled by agencies in Moscow and they passed through far fewer intermediate levels. They covered a small number of privileged towns and cities which were considered strategically important to the national economy and national security.[269] The process of distribution was monitored much more strictly, with the result that a lot more produce actually arrived where it was supposed to.

Apart from these two centralised sources, the contents of the family shopping basket depended on an ancillary economy of networks of friends

269. On the extent of the "Moscow Provision" in a particular town environment, see N. V. Mel'nikova, *Fenomen zakrytogo atomnogo goroda* (Ekaterinburg, 2006) ("Ocherki istorii Urala", 42).

and family, personal initiative, skills and abilities. For example, although Irkutsk was the provincial capital, its supply of food and goods fell far behind that of nearby Angarsk. In Angarsk the major enterprises were petrochemical plants and installations for processing uranium, and it was included in the Moscow Provision. In 1989, a system of rationing had been introduced in Irkutsk, Angarsk and all the towns in the province. Initially, the coupons in both cities were the same: 1 kilogram of meat, 800 grams of sausage or 2 tins of stew; 300 grams of butter (a second 200-gram pack had to be cut in half); 1 kilogram of sugar; tobacco and matches; one bottle of vodka or two of wine. However, you could buy better-quality and more varied products with your coupons in Angarsk than in Irkutsk. Enterprising residents of Irkutsk would accordingly go food shopping in Angarsk. "You had to get there in the morning. Most people from Irkutsk only arrived in the afternoon, but before that goods were removed from the shelves to stop them buying everything up" (male, aged forty-five in 1990, Irkutsk).[270]

It was considered great good fortune for an enterprise to get itself included in the Angarsk (i.e., Moscow) Provision. An Irkutsk geological enterprise whose dispatch office was located in a nearby village achieved this feat by arguing that it was prospecting for and mining uranium. Twice a week the geologists' empty truck would depart for Angarsk and return laden with goods and produce in short supply. This was then distributed among the inhabitants of the village in return for ration coupons. On these days, people would drive to the village from Irkutsk and head for the Geology store: "A busful would arrive from town. We had socks and sausage and butter in the shop. You needed coupons, but at least the stuff was available" (female, aged thirty-eight, Ust-Kuda). In order to protect itself from this invasion, the company introduced its own coupons, which were issued only to local people. The enterprise's managers even had to lift the Soviet ban on private farming, which it had previously been held would constitute a threat to law and order in the village.

270. Respondents' ages are given as they were in 1990.

In 1990, residents of Irkutsk province had to make do with one newspaper published by the provincial Party committee and soviet, an official "youth" newspaper, and two or three innovative but ephemeral independent newspapers. East-Siberian Pravda devoted considerable column-inches to the food supply. In the spring and autumn almost every issue included "News from the Fields", with reports on the extent of the area sown and the harvest. In mid-September 1990, the mayor gave instructions that potatoes and other vegetables should be sold directly from delivery trucks in order to shorten the path from producer to consumer and, presumably, to reduce opportunities for thieving and selling to middlemen.[271] The newspaper called for agricultural output to be increased and stored more efficiently. It also demanded tighter control over distribution and recommended allowing more private enterprise shops to open.

Soviet Youth, published by the province's Young Communist League, evidently felt more free to criticise, but, as in East-Siberian Pravda, most 1990 reports focused on berating the system for rationing alcohol with coupons. To judge solely on the basis of newspaper reports, one might suppose the population of Irkutsk province subsisted mainly on wine and vodka during this period.

In Soviet times, Leningrad always had preferential provisioning in comparison with other provincial capitals.[272] There, rationing was introduced almost a year later than in Irkutsk. The initial restriction was that food could only be bought by people registered as resident in Leningrad. Proof of this required production of what the authorities elegantly called a "business card", a term the populace took to, perhaps because of its Western connotations.

Ration coupons were introduced for alcohol and sugar only on 1 July, 1990. One coupon entitled a shopper to one bottle of vodka and two of wine. People in Irkutsk had to choose which one they preferred. Perhaps because of this comparative generosity, alcohol coupons were soon not

271. Vostochno-Sibirskaia pravda, 211, 14 September, 1990.
272. See Nikolai Smirnov, ed., Peterburg: Istoriia torgovli, 2 vols, vol. 2 (St Petersburg, 2002).

only being traded on the black market in Leningrad but assiduously coun-
terfeited: "820,000 litres more wine and spirits have been sold than
planned. Ration coupons are evidently being forged or reused a second and
third time."[273] The going rate on the black market was between 5 and 7
roubles for a coupon.

By 1 December, 1990, the coupons being introduced in Leningrad were
intended to ensure every resident a minimum selection of produce each
month. People were entitled to buy 1.5 kilograms of meat, meat products or
chicken; 1 kilogram of sausage; half a kilogram of butter; 250 grams of
sunflower oil; ten eggs; 1 kilogram of cereals and/or pasta; and half a kilogram of flour.[274]

A special announcement was made that bread would not be rationed.[275]
Leningraders took to calling the coupons "kartochki", a deliberate allusion
to rationing during the Siege of Leningrad. Officially they were called
"ration-book coupons" and could be exchanged only at the time a salesper-
son tore them out of the book. Loose coupons were supposed to be invalid.

The first problem with the new coupons was that few people were
exchanging them, preferring to save them up for celebrating the New Year.
Shops were obliged to let people buy sausage for the last three hours before
closing time without coupons, because it was low quality and wouldn't
keep. Leningraders were warned that if they hoarded their coupons, there
might not be sufficient of some products to satisfy the New Year rush.[276]

FOOD SOVEREIGNTY, AUDITS AND CHECKS

Back in January 1990, the only method the authorities could think of
initially for improving Leningrad's food supply was to introduce restrictions. Rationing was one measure, but they also introduced checks at the
province's "borders" to prevent "exporting" of goods. There was tighter

273. *Leningradskaia pravda*, 284, 12 December, 1990.   274. *Leningradskaia pravda*, 268, 22
November, 1990.   275. *Leningradskaia pravda*, 265, 17 November, 1990.
276. *Leningradskaia pravda*, 284, 12 December, 1990.

reporting, and even raiding by workers' control squads.

In an interview for *Evening Leningrad*, S. G. Petrov, Secretary of the Leningrad City Party Committee, called for the sealing of channels for exporting meat products to other regions. "Today," he explained, "all the provinces around us are operating a coupon system of rationing. This obliges Leningrad and our province to take appropriate action."[277] Yu. Maksimov, Chairman of the Leningrad agricultural committee, supported Petrov with an article titled "Business Cards? The Only Solution!"[278] The authors of a regular satirical column in *Evening Leningrad* reported that "In the city of Zalepukhinsk it has recently become possible to buy even newspapers only on production of a passport or business card."[279]

The new regulations did create a welcome source of revenue for Leningraders: "passport hire", whereby savvy citizens rented out their passports to visitors. *Leningradskaya Pravda* blamed the visitors: "Unduly enterprising guests are willing to pay 5–7 roubles to use a resident's registration document in a shop."[280] Some residents reacted positively to the new arrangements. Z. Khokhlova wrote to *Leningradskaya Pravda*, "Leningrad is being plundered by people from other parts of the country. They buy up goods in huge quantities. We will have more goods on the shelves now, I'm sure. Everything that is produced here will stay here."[281] Not many people agreed. The youthfully challenging newspaper *Next Shift*, for example, published a selection of letters from Leningraders outraged by the new measures, which they considered immoral and in violation of the rights of residents of neighbouring provinces.[282]

Under the circumstances, the Democrats newly elected as deputies to the City Soviet could hardly maintain their free-market stance and had no option but to accept rationing as an unavoidable temporary measure. *Next Shift* changed its position in January, proposing the even more radical measure of introducing comprehensive rationing to guarantee

277. *Vechernii Leningrad*, 5, 6 January, 1990.   278. *Leningradskaia pravda*, 14, 18 January, 1990.   279. *Leningradskaia pravda*, 10, 12 January, 1990.   280. *Ibid.*
281. *Leningradskaia pravda*, 17, 21 January, 1990.   282. *Smena*, 14, 17 January, 1990.

Leningraders a varied diet every month.[283] Many politicians in Leningrad and Leningrad province saw the move from Soviet to free market trade with the Baltic republics as responsible for the food shortages. The Baltic republics did sharply reduce their deliveries of food and substantially increase their prices. *Leningradskaya Pravda* published a list of products which Latvia had banned from export,[284] but Leningraders cheerfully visited Latvia and Estonia to buy meat, dairy products and clothing: "Yes, we went there in busloads, through our trade union" (male, aged forty-five, Leningrad).

A similar attempt to establish "food sovereignty" was observable in Siberia. Newspapers had reported that in 1989 126,700 tonnes of meat, 737,000 tonnes of milk and 103,000 tonnes of vegetables had been produced in Irkutsk province.[285] Here too an attempt was made to monitor the movement of food and goods more closely by carrying out systematic raids and inspections. In *East-Siberian Pravda*, the head of the provincial department of statistics advised in early 1990 that, of sixty perfume and cosmetic products which were supposed to be available in the region, fifty were nowhere to be found. Virtually all that was available was henna, compressed face-powder and pine concentrates. The newspaper's conclusion sounded little short of derisive: "But do not despair! Soviet woman is always beautiful, even without cosmetics. Perfumery products are only a luxury."[286] More seriously, the newspaper went on to report that, "Of 229 categories of foodstuffs in the list, inspections have found no sign of 125, including certain varieties of cheese and dairy products; smoked, raw and roast beef, pork, lamb; all varieties of sausage, by-products, semi-prepared products; tea and coffee; cakes and pastries."[287]

Officials again blamed a leakage of goods out of the province, noting later in the year that, "Only 20 per cent of the pasta products and confectionery allocated remain in the province; 2 per cent of tea; 3 per cent of

283. Smena, 11, 13 January, 1990.   284. Leningradskaia pravda, 231, 6 October, 1990.
285. Sovetskaia molodezh', 27, 6 March, 1990.   286. Vostochno-Sibirskaia pravda, 3, 4 January, 1990.   287. Ibid.

yeast; 10 per cent of knitwear; 16 per cent of footwear; and 40 per cent of felt boots."[288] The shortage of goods and produce was also seen as being artificially created by speculators and "saboteurs". The provincial directorate of the K.G.B. provided a telephone number which citizens could call to report rail wagons being unloaded and "traders".[289] The local youth newspaper regularly published statistics to inform its readers of how much food was being produced or brought in for the province. It reported that the Department to Combat Theft of Socialist Property had detected 291 violations of the law and discovered concealment of goods valued at 22,000 roubles.[290] (At the time, a bottle of vodka cost 9 roubles 10 kopecks.[291])

Coupons were issued each quarter in Irkutsk and were colour-coded to indicate not only the quarter they related to but also the district. By compartmentalising the city's and province's residents, who could not buy meat or sugar outside their own district, the authorities hoped to bring distribution of goods under control. Only people in possession of a residence permit for the province were permitted to sell goods, and by late 1990 improvised checkpoints had been set up at borders to prevent goods being exported out of the province.[292] Similar checkpoints were introduced in the autumn of 1990 on internal borders in the south of Russia. If these measures were intended to frustrate speculation in goods in short supply and to ensure distribution of them in accordance with official plans, they were not, if local newspapers are to be believed, very effective. East-Siberian Pravda is full of reports and readers' letters about speculation in wine and spirits and coupons for alcohol. The finger of suspicion was pointed at Gypsies, taxi drivers and babushki, old women who usually did not drink themselves but who eked out their pensions with this "biznes".

An attempt was made to combat forgery by validating coupons with the imprimatur of Soviet district committees, but this proved impractical, and the only validation was by having coupons stamped by the residence

288. Vostochno-Sibirskaia pravda, 230, 4 October, 1990.   289. Vostochno-Sibirskaia pravda, 290, 18 December, 1990.   290. Sovetskaia molodezh', 105, 6 September, 1990.
291. Sovetskaia molodezh', 27, 6 March 1990.   292. Sovetskaia molodezh', 141, 8 December, 1990.

committees and other local bodies which issued them. These counter-measures met with little success: "Under the new system, in addition to 426,000 valid coupons, a further 220,000 forged coupons were redeemed."[293] People had to stand in two queues, first to obtain coupons, then to redeem them. As a result, the black market price rose from 3 to 10 roubles.[294] Queues for alcohol, especially on the last days of the month when coupons were expiring, become enormous, sometimes leading to a riot. *Soviet Youth* reported one such disturbance in Irkutsk. Only the "coincidental" presence of a police team prevented serious trouble by pacifying the crowd and ordering the shop to stay open until the last customer had been served.[295] Public dissatisfaction with the level of provision in general and in respect of tobacco in particular led to open revolt in Leningrad, where, in August, Nevsky Prospekt, the city's principal thoroughfare, was blocked by smokers. (In an interview, Marina Salier, Chairwoman of the Leningrad City Soviet's food commission, described the incident as a deliberate "provocation".)[296]

Leningrad newspapers carried reports throughout 1990 of the finds resulting from checks and raids on warehouses and shop storerooms. For example, *Leningrad Worker* wrote of massive concealment of cereals, meat, confectionery, sausages and chocolate.[297]

Inspections and raids were not confined to shops. A raid was mounted on the suppliers of produce to the Leningrad Soviet, Leningrad City Executive Committee, Leningrad Provincial Executive Committee and the K.G.B. The fight against unfair privileges extended to Party and government officials. An inspection found that the canteens of these institutions were provided with "300 kilograms of red caviar, 55 kilograms of black caviar, 6,100 cans of sprats, 25 tonnes of superior-quality smoked meat products, and 204 tonnes of chippolata and saveloy sausages". The report went on to note that "The official allocation of superior-quality smoked

293. *Vostochno-Sibirskaia pravda*, 178, 7 August, 1990.   294. *Vostochno-Sibirskaia pravda*, 160, 17 July, 1990.   295. *Sovetskaia molodezh'*, 101, 4 September, 1990.   296. *Sovetskaia molodezh'*, 220, 24 September, 1990.   297. *Leningradskii rabochii*, 12, 23 March, 1990.

meat products for the entire city of Leningrad is 20 tonnes." As a result, a tongue-in-cheek decision was taken to sell 75 per cent of the caviar and 100 per cent of the smoked delicacies through retail stores under the brand name of "Smolny Delicatessen". Proceeds would be allocated in the proportions of 30 per cent to modernising delicatessen factories and 70 per cent to social welfare organisations.[298] Plundering these four privileged cafeterias could hardly have fed the whole of Leningrad, but an example was made by removing feeding privileges from officialdom when provisioning of the population at large was deteriorating at a disastrous rate.

The U.S.S.R. government had added fuel to the fire. On 24 May, Prime Minister Nikolai Ryzhkov talked about transition to a "regulated market" and, more to the point, about the need to raise prices (in, of course, a staged and measured manner). The citizenry took this as an announcement that prices were about to rise. Ryzhkov's speech was blamed by the Chairman of the standing committee of the Leningrad Soviet for Trade and Consumer Services for a massive rush to stock up on food: "Everything is being grabbed from the shelves. Stricter controls are planned, so do not be surprised if you are asked to present your business card more frequently. Certain checks will be put in place on the roads to prevent food supplies from being spirited out of the city by speculators."[299] *Leningradskaya Pravda* reported that, whereas in Leningrad the usual daily sales of flour totalled 59 tonnes, on 25 May the total was 115 tonnes.[300] *Rush Hour* (*Chas Pik*) had different data, suggesting that on 24 May, following Ryzhkov's speech, in Leningrad 447 tonnes of flour were sold, the amount usually sold in a month; also 230 tonnes of salt instead of 27, and 400 tonnes of cereals as against a normal daily total of 80.[301] This was the background to the holding in Leningrad in August 1990 of *Inrybprom-90*, an international exhibition showcasing the

298. *Leningradskii rabochii*, 182, 9 August, 1990. 299. *Leningradskii rabochii*, 123, 29 May, 1990. 300. *Leningradskaia pravda*, 129, 5 June, 1990.
301. *Chas pik*, 15, 4 June, 1990. Nancy Ries, an American anthropologist, writes about the hoarding of salt, sugar, cereals and pasta by Muscovites in early 1990 and their disappearance from the shelves. See Ries, *Russian Talk: Culture and Conversation During Perestroika* (Ithaca, NY, 1997).

achievements of the Soviet fishing fleet and fish-processing industries. It was lambasted by almost all the Leningrad newspapers.

It was traditional each autumn for townspeople to be conscripted to help state and collective farms bring in the harvest. *Leningradskaya Pravda* and *Evening Leningrad* duly displayed photographs on their front pages showing the "helpers from the city" and deploying the familiar Soviet clichés: "the battle for the harvest", "the People's Deputies' team did a great job . . ." and so on.[302] It was obligatory to show that survivors of the Siege of Leningrad were involved. Relations between the city's institutions and the farms were changing, however, from patronage to barter. In return for help with the harvest, city enterprises received a proportion of the vegetables to sell to their employees.

Unofficial "expeditions" to state- and collective-farm fields were not uncommon. Sometimes this spontaneous self-service went beyond people stealing provisions for themselves (see below) and was plainly commercial, well organised and semi-criminal. *Evening Leningrad*'s correspondent reported angrily that "they are not only filling bags and rucksacks but whole trucks". One farm complained that "almost 100 tonnes of vegetables a day are being taken from the fields without payment and half the crop has been carted off".[303]

Another consequence of the restrictions was that a previously secret privilege bestowed from above on an elite few became a standard survival technique for nimble managers. An extension of the Soviet practice of negotiating direct ordering of produce (*prodovol'stvennyi zakaz*) enabled businesses, hospitals and schools to contract with shops to supply produce in exchange for appropriate services. The correspondent of *Evening Leningrad* expostulated, "Has it not occurred to hospital staff that giving medical priority to care workers in the commercial sector does not accord very well with the concept of social justice?"[304]

302. *Leningradskaia pravda*, 217, 20 September; 221, 25 September; 224, 28 September; 226, 30 September, 1990.   303. *Leningradskaia pravda* , 233, 8 October, 1990.
304. *Vechernii Leningrad*, 20 December (No. 291), 1990.

During 1990, a decline in agricultural output in north-western Russia was noted in all sectors except alcohol production, which in the first half of 1990 increased in cash terms by 30 million roubles against the same period in 1989.[305] In June, an economist pointed out that there were now shortages in 95 per cent of all categories of goods.[306] In October it was reported that crop areas had been reduced, and that there was a fall in production of meat by 2.6 per cent, of milk by 4.1 per cent and of eggs by 2.8 per cent, and a 12 per cent decline in stocks of manufactured goods.[307] By November, the crisis had escalated to the point where the authorities in Karelia, Leningrad and Leningrad province, Novgorod, Pskov and Vologda province had to appeal to Mikhail Gorbachev and Boris Yeltsin for help in restricting transportation of goods out of the north-west.[308] An unforeseen decline in state deliveries forced the Leningrad authorities to introduce further extensive food rationing.

No controls, whether ration coupons or inspections or armed guards in the fields and at regional borders, could be more than a palliative. They could not address the underlying problem, which was the absence of market mechanisms of supply at a time when the old system had effectively collapsed. The state still regulated the price at which food and manufactured goods were bought and sold, but could no longer force suppliers to sell their wares to it in the quantities it dictated. In Leningrad, one result was the surprisingly slow unloading of goods wagons bringing food into the city. Reports about this read like communiqués from the front line: "Three hundred wagons full of meat have been standing for a long time at the city's goods stations!"[309] or "Two hundred wagons containing meat have yet to be unloaded at the city's goods stations!"[310] They were probably being held back by officials of the local distribution network who wanted to sell them at market prices.

305. *Vechernii Leningrad*, 124, 28 July, 1990.   306. *Vechernii Leningrad*, 134, 11 June, 1990.
307. *Vechernii Leningrad*, 250, 30 October, 1990.   308. *Leningradskaia pravda*, 263–4, 17 November, 1990.   309. *Vechernii Leningrad*, 41, 17 February, 1990.   310. *Vechernii Leningrad*, 53, 3 March; 103, 3 May, 1990.

"YOU HAD TO GRAB WHAT YOU COULD GET"

Getting food with your coupons is something people laugh about today: "I remember for a meat coupon they would give you not 800 but 850 grams of sausage. If the sales assistant didn't cut it right, she would shave off a few grams more. If that still wasn't enough, she'd do it again" (female, aged thirty-two, Irkutsk). There was only really a problem "if a visitor arrived and we had to prepare a meal" (male, forty-five, Leningrad). A certain amount of wizardry became essential: "We were inventive: we added berries, raisins and apple to curd cheese" (female, thirty-two, Irkutsk). News that vodka, sausages or butter had been "tossed out" in a nearby shop spread instantly through apartment blocks: "My mother would drop everything and go and buy it" (female, thirty-two, Irkutsk).

The choice of produce in the shops was meagre, and a queue formed immediately anything was delivered: "You had to grab what you could get" (male, forty-five, Leningrad); "To be able to buy enough sausage for the whole family, I had to queue several times, change my hat, wrap my scarf round me. If I took several loaves of bread, people would shout "Speculator!" at me. What was I supposed to do? I had three men in my household!" (female, thirty-five, Leningrad). The famous "George Bush's legs" from America were rapturously received: "The plump chicken legs, compressed into blocks, seemed to come to life and fly to the hands of excited housewives."[311] In 1990, new delicatessen shops brought some relief with semi-prepared food items: "They were popular. The quality was very average, but better than in the state shops" (female, sixty-five, Leningrad). A tour guide was able to take advantage of the situation: "I found myself in different districts, so could see what was being sold where and snap it up" (female, thirty-eight, Leningrad).

It was a rare treat to stumble upon an official presentation package of food: "You could only buy them if you were in the right place at the right time, if you had business in one of the district committees of the Party"

311. Smena, 166, 20 July, 1990.

(male, forty-three, Leningrad). The price was low, but you could only buy them in district committees or political-education clubs. You needed a pass to gain access to these institutions, so you did not get in very often. Only a few Leningraders were able to benefit from this privilege. An equally rare treat was a visit to a foreign currency Beryozka shop to buy cigarettes, tinned goods and confectionery. This was only possible if foreign friends came to visit; they tended to buy goods in the Beryozkas because "they knew our food products were iffy" (female, thirty-two, Irkutsk). Sometimes foreigners who considered themselves cognoscenti of Soviet life brought all their own food with them because of doubts about the quality of local produce: "Some Americans came with their own water and brought their own cookies. They were very suspicious of what my wife cooked for them" (male, forty-five, Leningrad). Diets were supplemented as usual by mushrooms and berries: "I would get on the train with my brother and we would go off to the woods. Our dad knew just where we could find mushrooms. We dried them, and made jam with the berries" (female, twenty-three, Leningrad); "We bought some ingredients, crushed cranberries and made fruit juice" (male, forty-seven, Leningrad).

The situation was particularly difficult for babies and their parents, whether they lived in Irkutsk or Leningrad. You had to get up early to go to the free dairy centre for baby food: "My father-in-law got up at 6.00 in the morning, went to the babies' food centre and collected the supplies. He brought them home and went off at 7.00 to work. If you got there any later there would be nothing left" (female, thirty-two, Irkutsk); "You had to leave at 6.00 in the morning to get your place in the queue for the shop, which opened at 7.00. Then there would be enough milk for you. You had to stand outside in the frost. There were huge queues everywhere" (male, forty-five, Leningrad).

Coupons for wine and spirits made even people who didn't drink, or who drank infrequently, feel obliged to battle through to their entitlement of liquor. One respondent said, "Selling coupons was considered wrong in our family, so bottles of wine and spirits stood unopened in the cupboard.

We only used them up at New Year or on birthdays. But for the coupons, we wouldn't have bought vodka so often" (male, thirty-two, Irkutsk). Alcohol also became a common "liquid currency" for paying tradesmen. They started being reluctant to accept cash, and alcohol coupons became a kind of substitute. They could also be exchanged for food: "I went to the market. I felt ashamed and embarrassed and didn't know how to suggest it, but then I did and they quickly worked everything out. I bought mushrooms, grilled them and bottled them in jars. Later on we served them with potatoes" (female, thirty-two, Irkutsk).

Members of the Soviet middle class, engineers, scientists and the like, rarely visited the market in Irkutsk. One interviewee recalled going there when she was pregnant "only to get cherries. I had a great craving for them. We didn't buy meat. It was too expensive" (female, thirty-two, Irkutsk). In Leningrad also the market was "just too expensive" (female, sixty-five, Leningrad). This perception is hardly surprising: the total value of a month's coupons was only 10 roubles. At Kuznechny Market, the prices reported in Leningradskaya Pravda in the autumn of 1990 were: 400 grams of sour cream, 8 roubles; a kilogram of liver, 60 roubles; perch, 20 roubles; pickled gherkins, 8 roubles; pork, 20 roubles; grapes, 8 roubles; dried apricots, 12–18 roubles. Eggs were 7 roubles for ten.[312] In fact prices at Kuznechny Market were rather lower than in other Leningrad markets because of competition from an official store there run by the Markets Association, which kept prices down. Leningradskaya Pravda's reporter pointed out, however, that in general, despite the paucity of customers, market traders kept their prices high, confident that they would be able to sell their goods to "southerners" and foreigners.

Our Leningrad respondents, who were mostly between thirty and forty years old in 1990 and often had small children, got a lot of help from parents, who could always be relied on for a meal, a loan, a food parcel, or berries and vegetables from their garden: "Sometimes we were short of money and borrowed from my husband's parents. It was always 50

312. Smena, 246, 25 October; 275–6, 1 December, 1990.

roubles. I think they kept 50 roubles aside specially for us. Whenever we asked for a loan my mother-in-law always brought it" (female, thirty-two, Irkutsk); "My husband often dropped in on his parents for lunch, and they always had a pack of *pelmeni* Siberian dumplings waiting. He is very partial to them. My mother sent apples from Alma-Ata. She would pay the guard 3 roubles and send them by train. She sent us dried fruit as well" (female, thirty-two, Irkutsk).

Dachas in the countryside were one of the main sources of food in Irkutsk.[313] Most vegetables, berries and fruit came from dachas. Even people who had no gardening experience, unless from helping with the harvest when they were students, got themselves an allotment, grew vegetables and started canning. The geologists' village already mentioned had only one canning machine and people would queue up at it. The geologists had yet to learn how to make winter salads: "Only Tamara had a canning machine, so we borrowed hers. We would agree among ourselves who would have it when" (female, thirty-eight, Ust-Kuda). Irkutsk students living in hostels did not have dachas but received regular parcels from home, with meat, dripping and eggs if they came from the countryside, or coveted canned food from the city, like tinned stew or condensed milk, and tea and coffee. Students from other towns were discriminated against; the Irkutsk Council of University and College Rectors decided not to allocate them coupons for alcohol. This was represented as being part of the struggle against alcoholism, but coupons could be readily bought in any wine shop. Alternatively, if the students could get hold of yeast, a jar would appear on their radiator with a rubber glove stretched over the top.

Other Leningraders who did not have dacha plots or preferred to use them as places to relax rather than for growing vegetables compensated by pilfering: "I had just started medical school, and we were taken to sort potatoes at a vegetable warehouse. They kept a close eye on us, but of

---

313. By 1990, 8.5 million families had garden plots and 5.1 million had communal allotments. See Tatyana G. Nefedova and Judith Pallot, *Russia's Unknown Agriculture: Household Production in Post-Communist Russia* (Oxford, 2007).

course we helped ourselves. One time we hid there until the bus left without us, and hitch-hiked home. A truck took us as far as Shushary. While we were waiting for the train we went over to a field. What cabbages! Not the kind of rotting garbage they had in the shops. We helped ourselves and came home fully laden" (male, fifteen, Leningrad); "My brother and I took rucksacks and went to the state farm fields. In the old days every inch of land around Petersburg was cultivated. We filled two rucksacks with potatoes and carrots and that kept us going for two or three weeks" (female, twenty-three, Leningrad). Another way of getting round the lack of a dacha plot or vegetable gardens was, on the spur of the moment (and sometimes in a more organised manner), to raids fields near the city:

> Our faculty and the freshmen were, as usual in September, digging up potatoes. It was the last year, or the one before last, at a place up in Karelia. We always went to the same Soviet farm. We were third years but some of us lads went as "supervisors", with the approval of the Dean's office, of course. One time, my friend and I went there on our own initiative, just to see how the freshers were getting on, like, just for a visit, with flasks, of course, and, more to the point, with rucksacks. We chatted to them for half a day, poked around in the fields conscientiously, and in the end, of course, went home with our rucksacks full. At the end of the harvesting the freshers went home with full sacks too" (male, twenty-four, Leningrad).

Networks of family and friends were important: "Dad had a friend. They had fought in the war together. He was forever bringing us produce from his dacha, a rucksack full. Mum's sister sent us dripping from Smolensk. Not much, but I remember how good it tasted!" (female, twenty-three, Leningrad). "Knowing the right people" (blat) was very important at that time, although many of my interviewees did not. Through contacts you could get hold of anything: "My friend emigrated and left me some papers, including a notebook. It was all in alphabetical order, not of surnames but of what you could get or who you could get it through. For example: Tolya – tickets; Valya – pharmacy. The whole book was full of names like that" (male, forty-five, Leningrad). And:

> My friend worked in the supplies department at a factory. He phoned me and said, "Coffee, but a sackful." The beans were green and needed to be roasted, but everybody knew how to do that. We discussed recipes: whether to add garlic or something else, how to turn the beans. He repeated, "But a sackful." A sack was 15 kilograms. The price was lower than in the shops, and in any case there wasn't any in the shops. It was cheap, but 15 kilograms! I was running all over the institute trying to find people to buy it. We clubbed together and got one sack. Then he phoned again and said, "Sugar, but a sackful, 50 kilograms." Sugar was 90 kopecks in the shops, but I was getting it for 50. "A tanker of brandy has turned up." He offered me as little as 2 litres, but I took more, because everyone wants brandy. There were adverts in toilets telling you who was selling what. I did that once. A woman I knew asked me to sell an enormous quantity of calico, about a hundred metres. People came to see me at the institute and I would measure it out (male, forty-five, Leningrad).

Despite all these ploys, and contrary to how people think now, many interviewees, especially those in higher education, had not regarded food problems as particularly catastrophic: "The material side of life wasn't that important. People didn't make a big thing about food. We bought what was available" (male, forty-five, Leningrad). In 1990 there was still a great boom in books and magazines. Previously banned films were available on videocassettes. Large amounts were spent not on food but on books and films: "My husband began to be better paid. Salaries were increased, and as a senior academic he began to receive more. In the past we had never had much to spend on books, so now he went wild and bought everything he could lay his hands on" (female, thirty-two, Irkutsk); "We didn't queue in shops. We bought whatever was available, and we exchanged vodka coupons for pasta or cereal" (female, twenty-three, Leningrad); "Public debate was very lively then and we weren't too interested in food. Our daughter had just been born and we only went to the market to buy milk for her" (male, forty-five, Leningrad); "I can't really remember much about the shops. I had just defended my dissertation and was constantly travelling to Moscow. What I do remember is the consternation of staff at the institute in Moscow when they forgot to bring a bottle on the day vegetable oil was being distributed. Two hundred and fifty grams, I think we got" (female, thirty-six, Irkutsk).

While I was writing this essay, I obtained a book recording the income and expenditure of an Irkutsk family with above-average means. Entries were made almost every day in June 1990. The family consisted of a husband, wife and baby daughter. Their total income for the month was 1,057 roubles and expenditure was 680 roubles. The husband's earnings enabled him not only to support his family on coupons but also to buy some produce (mainly fruit and vegetables) at the market and to spend substantial amounts on books and videocassettes. They bought meat and meat products (liver, heart or poultry) in the state shops in return for ration coupons. Most of the money spent on food (the notebook also records expenditure on goods like light bulbs, shoes and clothing) went on bread, vegetables (tomatoes, onions, radishes, fennel, cabbage), fish, eggs and dairy products. Sausage and minced meat figured only at the beginning (6 June) and end (30 June) of the month. It was probably difficult to buy them in the middle because of the supply shortages mentioned in the local newspapers.[314]

In 1990, then, interviewees in both Irkutsk and Leningrad filled their shopping baskets with food from state shops (mostly rationed), produce

314. See *Raskhody Irkutskoi sem'i letom 1990 goda*, in Sergei Karnaukhov, "Pokhorony edy", *Novoe literaturnoe obozrenie*, 84 (2007), pp. 651–2.

from gardens outside the city (most often belonging to parents), foraging in woods or fields near the city,[315] and trips to the countryside and other, better provisioned, towns. In a few cases, this was supplemented by purchases at the market or from commercial shops and, in rather more cases, through unofficial contacts.

AN OASIS OF SOCIALISM

While the shopping basket of a Leningrader contained, as in Soviet times, more diverse produce than that of a resident of Irkutsk, it bore no comparison with the variety of produce a run-of-the-mill resident of Tiksi could afford.

Tiksi, "the ocean gateway of Yakutia", is a northern port which was also an important air force base on the Soviet border. The year 1990 was the last time military aircraft delivered the customary autumn airlift of fruit and vegetables to the settlement.[316] The main supplies, the "Northern Run", came up the River Lena or via the northern sea route. Tiksi was supplied not only with essentials but with products which would make the eyes water of a resident of the capital of the Yakut Autonomous Soviet Socialist Republic, to which the port was nominally subordinate. Raw smoked sausage, top-quality tinned meats and fruit (usually from Bulgaria or Hungary), and condensed milk, which by 1990 had vanished from the shelves of many cities, were taken as a matter of course by the residents of Tiksi.

Barter between the native population and the townspeople played an important part in enhancing their diet. Native peoples of the region paid

315. According to Novosibirsk sociologists, approximately one quarter of the U.S.S.R.'s gross agricultural output in the early 1980s was being produced on private plots. See Zemfira Kalugina, *Lichnoe podsobnoe khoziaistvo v SSSR: Sotsial'nye reguliatory i rezul'taty razvitiia* (Novosibirsk, 1991).

316. In 1989 the Yakutia Maritime Transport Association (of which the port of Tiksi was a member) was permitted to engage in independent foreign business activity. In 1990, in addition to overseas freight transportation, the Tiksi fleet shipped 311,000 tonnes of cargo on coastal trade and intra-Arctic shipping lanes, its best result ever. See http://www.tiksi.ru/index.php?sec_id=4&id=94&PHPSESSID=73157011c1dd15a69d4ed6effec8co8e

for services with venison and fish. People could also catch fish themselves: many port employees would throw a fish trap into the sea on their way to work in the morning and pull it out full of fish on their return in the evening. However, in this unique and isolated world, extended networks of family and friends also provided support. If a family member happened to receive bartered venison or fish, they would commonly share it within their circle. There was neither a market nor commercial shops in Tiksi.

What 1990 brought to Tiksi, however, was ration coupons, whole sheets of them. Meat products were listed individually: cooked sausage, smoked sausage, pork, beef, stew. Each kind of cereal had its own coupon, as had, needless to say, sugar, condensed milk and alcohol. There were coupons for virtually everything. For the inhabitants of Tiksi, who were not accustomed to stinting themselves and who expected to take their summer holidays on the Black Sea coast, ration coupons came as a nasty shock. They were accompanied by the similarly unprecedented phenomenon of queues in the state shops. The present author arrived from Irkutsk at about this time, and to an outsider the settlement appeared to have everything you could dream of and plenty of it. Ration coupons were the most import-ant provider of food for the Tiksi shopping basket. This abundance was, however, the last of the goods from the Northern Run. By 1991, the provision had dwindled greatly and become less reliable, not only in terms of food but even of coal. The workers of Tiksi soon began leaving for the "mainland".

Comparing these interviews and the newspaper reports, we can see that in 1990 there were considerable differences in the contents of the shopping baskets of citizens of the U.S.S.R. (despite the similarities between Irkutsk and Leningrad). There were differences not only between regions but also within them. What was available on the urban fringe and in villages differed from the provision in towns. How much of what went into the basket was still heavily dependent on such state agencies as the depart-ments of the Ministry of Trade and the State Agricultural Committee, which produced and distributed food throughout the country. From the earliest Soviet times allocation had been patently hierarchical, and already in 1990 economic freedoms were allowing enterprising people to make sufficient money to buy food at the market or in commercial shops.[317]

The year 1990 saw the writing of Alla Pugachova's elegantly titled, but now largely forgotten, song "Chomp". It was something of a hit, featuring on television in the main Christmas show and even being performed at a concert at Luzhniki Stadium to mark the first hundred days of Yeltsin's presidency in September 1991:[318]

> If you're sad and the wife's run away
> Go over and open the fridge.
> Lift out the gammon and
> Take out the salmon,
> And pig yourself, *burzhui*, no call for dismay.
>
> Chomp-chomp-chomp-chomp . . .
> Forget about the wife
> Chomp-chomp-chomp-chomp . . .
> Pretend this is the life.
>
> That was all very well, but today it's sheer hell.
> Go on now, go open the fridge.
> Take out the ration book and put it on to cook,
> A pinch of salt – pretend you're doing well.

317. Changes in the 1990s, as against the late 1980s, are described by Vladimir Vagin, mainly on the example of Pskov, and by Vyacheslav Glazychev, on the basis of extensive data relating to the Volga region. See Vladimir Vagin, "Russkii provintsial'nyi gorod: kliuchevye elementy zhizneustroistva", *Mir Rossii*, 6/4 (1997), pp. 53–88; Viacheslav Glazychev, *Glubinnaia Rossiia 2000–2002* (Moscow, 2004).
318. Music by Vladimir Kochulkov, lyrics by Margarita Marchukova, album *Eto zavtra, a segodnia …*

Chomp-chomp-chomp-chomp . . .
Not much of a dinner.
Chomp-chomp-chomp-chomp . . .
But at least we're getting thinner!

Chomp-chomp-chomp-chomp . . .
Now we've all stopped fretting.
Chomp-chomp-chomp-chomp . . .
Time for giving and forgetting.

Okay, comrades? What comes next? Hey!

What came next was worse. Alyona Apina's 1993 hit was titled "Two Measly Sausage Slices". In the memories of interviewees, my friends and acquaintances, and indeed myself, 1990 was nothing in comparison with the two years which followed. The food crisis was replaced by late payment of salaries, payment in kind and galloping inflation. But that's another story.

— Это не листовки, это талоны на манну небесную!

"They aren't leaflets, they're coupons for manna from heaven!"
Cartoon from the the satirical magazine *Crocodile*, 1990

SEPTEMBER

1 September

The conflict over registration of the journals *The Banner* (Znamya), *The Spark* (Ogonyok) and *Literaturnaya gazeta* is not over yet. The claim to ownership of *The Banner* by its workforce is disputed by the Board of the U.S.S.R. Writers' Union and Pravda, the publishing company of the Central Committee of the C.P.S.U. (*Izvestiia*, 246, p. 2). The claim to ownership of *Ogonyok* is disputed, again by Pravda, and that of *Literaturnaya gazeta* again by the Board of the U.S.S.R. Writers' Union.

In the first September issue of *Ogonyok*, its editor, Vitaliy Korotich, published an open letter:

> We are being nailed to the wall, using the subscription campaign for next year, by having the price of the weekly ratcheted up to over 46 roubles. On the one hand, of course, this is only the cost of two bottles of fairly indifferent Soviet brandy, but it makes it difficult for us to reach the democratic reader. We make too much money for the System to be left in peace. Our former masters, ignoring all laws and regulations, are ordering us to carry on working for a piggy bank we no longer wish to fill. The System has given up on logic. They don't even attempt to refer to the laws on the Press in their discussions with our management team (*Ogonek*, 36, p. 3).

3 September

In the rerun of elections on 2 September in the Krasnodar region, Oleg Kalugin is elected U.S.S.R. People's Deputy by a large margin, gaining 57.9 per cent of the vote (*Izvestiia*, 247, p. 2).

5 September

Starting on this day, Leningrad grocery stores will serve customers only on presentation of a "business card" identifying them as a resident of Leningrad city or province (*Izvestiia*, 249, p. 2).

The governments of the R.S.F.S.R. and the Republic of Armenia sign an agreement on economic and cultural cooperation (*Izvestiia*, 249, p. 2).

6 September

The propaganda film *Boris Yeltsin: Portrait of a Fighter* is banned from release in Frunze, the capital of Kyrgyzstan (formerly Kirghizia) (*Izvestiia*, 250, p. 2).

7 September

According to Gavriil Popov, the tobacco and bread crises, and the reactions to them of the U.S.S.R. government, are proof of its incompetence. Popov calls for the R.S.F.S.R. Supreme Soviet to demand the resignation of the U.S.S.R. Council of Ministers (*Izvestiia*, 251, p. 2).

In Arkhangelsk, Nika-T.V. is registered as an independent limited-liability television company to rival state-run television. Its owners are ten Arkhangelsk enterprises, the City Soviet and Nika-T.V., an independent company. Broadcasting will be on two new channels, one of which will be at the disposal of the City Soviet. The other will be a commercial entertainment channel (*Izvestiia*, 251, p. 2).

9 September

Aleksandr Men, a renowned liberal Orthodox priest, theologian and public figure, is murdered. His body is found between his home and the railway platform at Semkhoz in the Zagorsk district of Moscow province. The cause of death is loss of blood after a blow to the head (*Izvestiia*, 254, p. 6). The investigation team insisted that the murder was thoroughly investigated over a period of many years, but it remained unsolved despite direct orders to find the killer from two heads of state: first Mikhail Gorbachev, and later Boris Yeltsin. See the articles above by Hasan Guseynov and below by Nikolai Mitrokhin.

> Kennedy's assassination devastated and purified the soul of Americans. The murder of the Polish priest Jerzy Popiełuszko by state security officers caused outrage in Poland which permanently alienated Poles from their "people's" government. The U.S.S.R. did not even shudder. So much the worse for the U.S.S.R. Citizens standing in queues found other things to talk about. So much the worse for those citizens. We are mired much more deeply than our brothers in the socialist camp. It will take us much longer and be more terrible to extricate ourselves. We did not rebel. We were not outraged. We did not demand the immediate resignation of the authorities responsible for the deaths of women murdered by sappers with shovels. Nobody, not even a criminal general, got punished. And now, an axe blow to the head. This is a turning point in our history (Aleksandr Minkin, "Ne rydaite obo mne", *Ogonek*, 39, p. 33).

10 September

The fourth session of the U.S.S.R. Supreme Soviet opens. One of the most notable events is a speech on behalf of the Interregional Group of Deputies by Anatoliy Sobchak. Rejecting the agenda proposed by the Presidium, he says,

> We propose that a first priority should be to consider the changing role and functions of the highest bodies of the state in the light of the declarations of sovereignty adopted by the republics. We want to hear, not just another programme from the government, but an assessment from the President and the Prime Minister personally of the country's economic situation, in order to see how realistically and critically they are evaluating the present situation. The Supreme

Soviet simply does not have the right to allow a government to remain in power which has demonstrated its inability to rescue the country from crisis.

Reacting to criticism of Prime Minister Nikolai Ryzhkov's programme, Politburo member Gennadiy Yanayev, entirely out of order, takes the floor and directs a torrent of abuse at the Chairman, Ivan Laptev, Head of the Soviet of the Union, accusing him of "unreasonable tolerance" and demanding that he should intervene "when the Party is being insulted, along with a number of people whom the present assembly ought not even to be discussing" (Izvestiia, 255, pp. 1–2).

The valves of the Kazakh gas-compressor station in Azerbaijan, closed since 20 August, are reopened, restoring the supply of gas to Armenia, where the economy has been in a catastrophic state (Izvestiia, 254, p. 2).

11 September

Nikolai Ryzhkov gives a report to the U.S.S.R. Supreme Soviet. In the ensuing discussion, many deputies, including Anatoliy Sobchak, Ella Pamfilova and Erkin Yusupov, remark that the people who wrote the report seem entirely disconnected from the queues for sugar and bread, or the fact that agriculture and entire industries are being destroyed. There are repeated proposals to suspend the session to give deputies an opportunity to familiarise themselves properly with the government and Shatalin programmes. The President intervenes in an attempt to restore order, asking deputies not to jump the gun and to lower the temperature of the debate. Gorbachev comments that he personally is more impressed by Shatalin's plan (Izvestiia, 255, p. 1). In the ensuing debate, people's deputy Nikolai Ivanov proposes that the session should consider demanding the resignation of Gorbachev and Lukianov. The Chairman has no option but to put this to the vote, and it is rejected. Neither is there support for a proposal from Aleksandr Obolensky to call for the immediate resignation of the Ryzhkov government (Izvestiia, 256, pp. 1–2).

Before a vote at the R.S.F.S.R. [not the U.S.S.R.] Supreme Soviet, Yavlinsky addresses the deputies:

The phrase "500 days" applied to this programme means two things. First, that all the actions taken during the transition must be synchronised and fitted into a relatively short period of time. Taking too long and implementing them in an uncoordinated manner will have negative effects and make it impossible to act sensibly.

Second, after five hundred days of implementing the programme there will be an economy guaranteed to free people from the economic slavery we have today, and which will provide all the necessary preconditions for economic progress.

Will we be able to make the transition to a market economy? Yes, but it is an extremely difficult thing to do. It will be difficult and painful. Is it possible to devise a programme that avoids hardship? No. That is because we have inherited a disaster. We will implement this programme as the first step on the road to a future without further disasters and to economic freedom.

Replying to questions from members of the R.S.F.S.R. Chamber of Nationalities, Yavlinsky says,

We have very little time left. The U.S.S.R. government has had good reason to be saying ever since last year that the situation is alarming and something needs to be done. The programme adopted at the Second Congress of People's Deputies of the U.S.S.R. failed. In May they failed to adopt any programme at all. Now we have two. I do not want to rush you, but it is important that you are aware that the crisis is worsening. There is almost no time for further deliberation (*Izvestiia*, 255, p. 2).

By an overwhelming majority of 213 in favour, 2 against, and with 6 abstentions, the R.S.F.S.R. Supreme Soviet approves the programme for transition to a market economy presented by the working group of Stanislav
Shatalin and Grigoriy Yavlinsky (Izvestiia, 256, p. 1).

The newly created R.S.F.S.R. Union of Journalists declares its intention of
being an economically and institutionally independent non-governmental
organisation (Izvestiia, 255, p. 2).

The revived Makarius Fair in Nizhny Novgorod will be held in its traditional location from 21 to 27 September (Izvestiia, 255, p. 2).

14 September

At a joint meeting of the commissions and committees of the U.S.S.R.
Supreme Soviet, deputies question the underlying premises of the Shatalin
programme. On the issue of who would bear responsibility, Yavlinsky says
that everybody would bear responsibility, both those who devised the programme and those who approved and voted to accept it (Izvestiia, 259, p. 2).

Before the morning session of the R.S.F.S.R. Supreme Soviet, deputies
are presented with a draft resolution of no confidence in the U.S.S.R.
government. Yeltsin proposes that the resolution be considered in the
Soviet's commissions and committees before being put to a vote. This is
supported by a majority of deputies (Izvestiia, 158, p. 2).

15 September

In the Medvedkovo woods, where political prisoners from Oryol prison
were executed, a memorial to the victims of repression is unveiled (Izvestiia,
259, p. 2).

In the town of Shuya in Ivanovo province, a joint Soviet–West German
computer factory is being constructed which is expected to produce a
hundred thousand high-quality computers per year (Izvestiia, 260, p. 1).

16 September

There is particularly heated discussion in the Constitutional Commission of the R.S.F.S.R. Supreme Soviet over whether Russia should have a powerful president, as in the U.S., or a parliamentary republic in which the president does not head the executive branch of government (*Izvestiia*, 260, p. 2).

Twelve leading experts from five countries, under U.S. financier George Soros, analyse the draft programmes for transition to a market economy devised by the U.S.S.R. government and Academician Shatalin's group. Soros expresses the following opinion:

> The U.S.S.R. government intends to carry out an administrative reform of prices. It wants to continue to do what the Soviet government did for decades. In the meantime, the crisis has reached a critical stage. In order to gain credibility, which it currently lacks, the government needs to promise the people an immediate improvement in the economic situation. It cannot do this unless it introduces tough economic measures. As regards the document from Shatalin's group, having read it, I view the future with greater optimism. This is a decisive break with the past, specific and comprehensive, rather carefully thought through and elaborated, but not yet a finished plan. Some problems remain, and they are political. If they can be removed, implementing the ideas of the Shatalin group could be the beginning of a new era (*Moskovskie novosti*, 37, p. 4).

17 September

"Society is entering a crucial phase. New outlines of the state are forming. A new correlation of forces at every level is crystallising. The role of the union centre is being transformed. Multi-polarity is appearing. Not only the appearance of the regime and its structure are changing but also its nature. The main thing now is not to disrupt this peaceful process, not to be gulled by provocations and not to allow the chaos to spread. How and when this process ends will depend on whether the democrats become the major force behind it" (Liliia Shevtsova, "Krizis vlasti", *Izvestiia*, 261, p. 3).

18 September

Aleksandr Solzhenitsyn's article, "Rebuilding Russia: Reflections and Tentative Proposals", is published as a supplement to *Komsomolskaya pravda*, with a print run of twenty-two million. According to his wife, Solzhenitsyn was attracted by the prospect of addressing it to the whole of Russia. It was reprinted shortly afterwards as a supplement to *Literaturnaya gazeta*.

Maksim Sokolov commented:

> The "unconditional rejection of a malignant Marxist-Leninist utopia which was blind from birth" trumpeted from Vermont and the call to "give scope to healthy private initiative" would have been far more helpful to Yeltsin six months ago. Today these ideas have become commonplace.
>
> Both Solzhenitsyn's critics and his supporters agree that he is a great writer and was a great political figure. That "the clock of communism has chimed its last" is largely due to him. Today, this great writer is no longer a great politician. It is largely thanks to him that Russia has entered a new era of bourgeois democracy, but he has remained behind in his own era. You cannot step into the same river twice, and it is probably equally impossible to return to 1970s Russia (Maksim Sokolov, "Aleksandr Solzhenitsyn: vtoroe 'Pis'mo k vozhdiam'", *Kommersant*, 38, 1 October, 1990).

The morning session of the U.S.S.R. Supreme Soviet begins with economists Aganbegyan, Shatalin and Abalkin replying to deputies' questions. The leader of collective and state farm managers, Vasiliy Starodubtsev, categorically rejects Shatalin's programme and describes privatisation of land as a step backwards: "Why is there not a single word in the programme about socialism or a socialist approach? Is this not backsliding from socialism and its values?" Deputy Leonid Sukhov berates Gorbachev for "betraying the ideals of the Party" and for being overenthusiastic about glasnost (*Izvestiia*, 262, pp. 1–2).

19 September

In Moscow, the founding Congress of Trade Unions of the R.S.F.S.R. concludes. Its main result is to have finally established a Federation of Independent Trade Unions of Russia. Ivan Polozkov, First Secretary of the Russian Communist Party, speaks at the congress. His active support immediately raises questions about how independent the Federation is likely to prove (*Izvestiia*, 263, p. 2).

20 September

By an overwhelming majority of 164 in favour, 1 against, and with 16 abstentions, the R.S.F.S.R. Supreme Soviet resolves to propose to the U.S.S.R. government that it should resign: "The RSFSR Supreme Soviet declares that the U.S.S.R. government is incapable of leading the country out of the present extremely severe economic crisis, is not fit to fulfil its constitutional duty of protecting the sovereignty of the R.S.F.S.R., has lost the confidence of the R.S.F.S.R. Supreme Soviet and does not command the support of the population at large" (*Izvestiia*, 264, p. 1).

21 September

"Boris Yeltsin, Chairman of the R.S.F.S.R. Supreme Soviet, was involved in a traffic accident in Moscow, at the intersection of Tverskaya Street and Gottwald Street. A medical examination revealed concussion and several bruises, but the victim's condition does not give cause for medical concern" (*Moskovskii komsomolets*, 218, p. 1).

24 September

The U.S.S.R. Supreme Soviet adopts what many feel is an indecisive resolution: on the one hand, to proceed further with the economic reform proposals initiated by Gorbachev and Yeltsin, but on the other hand, to incorporate all that is best in the draft submitted by the U.S.S.R. government. Stanislav Shatalin comments, "I remain convinced that the risk to the country of transition to a market economy is less than the price to be paid for procrastination" (*Izvestiia*, 268, p. 1).

A law is also passed "Concerning additional measures to stabilise the economic and political life of the U.S.S.R." This gives Gorbachev additional powers as President of the U.S.S.R., including the right to summarily issue statutory decrees which accord with the U.S.S.R. Constitution and to issue instructions in respect of property relations, the organisation of economic management etc. It also confers the right to set up agencies and other government bodies to expedite the formation in the U.S.S.R. of a nationwide market, and to ensure the cooperative involvement for these purposes of the union and autonomous republics (*Argumenty i Fakty*, 39, p. 1).

The Supreme Soviet of Latvia adopts a declaration in which it "unequivocally condemns the genocide perpetrated against the Jewish people during the Nazi occupation of Latvia". Over eighty thousand Latvian Jews and more than two hundred thousand Jews from other European countries were murdered in Latvia during the Second World War (*Izvestiia*, 267, p. 2).

An "Appeal to the servicemen of the U.S.S.R.", signed by forty-four R.S.F.S.R. people's deputies, urges soldiers not to obey unconstitutional or criminal orders they might receive in the event of the introduction of direct presidential rule.

26 September

At a session of the U.S.S.R. Supreme Soviet, Deputy Erkegali Rahmadiev enquires about Gorbachev's reaction to Solzhenitsyn's article, "Rebuilding Russia". Gorbachev replies,

> After reading the brochure twice and pondering these matters, I was overwhelmed, and am still overwhelmed, but by very mixed

333

feelings. As a Russian, I respond to the pain and concern for the destiny of the Russian people and the Russian nation. At the same time, however, as a Russian, I cannot agree with Solzhenitsyn's position in respect of other peoples. I would go so far as to say that these political views are objectionable (Izvestiia, 269, p. 1).

30 September

In Kiev, a rally and vast protest demonstration is held by supporters of Rukh, the people's movement of Ukraine, and a number of new political parties and organisations which have arisen out of it. The demonstration attracts tens of thousands of participants (Izvestiia, 273, p. 1).

Also in September

Prior to the crisis in the Persian Gulf, the oil price was $20 a barrel. By early September it had risen to $28, and at the end of the month stood at $41 a barrel (Argumenty i Fakty, 41, p. 8).

THE RUSSIAN ORTHODOX CHURCH IN 1990[319]

Nikolai Mitrokhin

The year 1990 set the agenda of the Russian Orthodox Church for the next decade and a half. Although the freeing of the Church from the tutelage of the Communist Party and Soviet state had already begun, it was in 1990 that the process became irreversible. For the first time in the Soviet period, the Church had a sense of independence, clearly saw where its interests lay and knew how it could promote them. This was bolstered by the first election in decades of a head of the Church without interference from the regime, and the steps he was able to take. The murder of Archpriest Aleksandr Men, the Church's most popular missionary, had far-reaching consequences and irrevocably divided Russian Orthodox intellectuals into two camps. Finally, it was in 1990 that a schism in Ukraine led to fundamental changes in the Moscow Patriarchate's policy towards the Soviet republic (today an independent country), which, second only to Russia, was of greatest importance to the Church.

WHAT WAS THE CHURCH IN 1990?

Social Structure

By 1990, the mainstay of the Church for three decades had been the

319. This essay was written as part of a project on "Influence Groups Within the Russian Orthodox Church Today and Their Economic Activity", financed by the programme of the Federal Chancellor and the Alexander von Humboldt Foundation, Germany. The research was supervised by Prof. Thomas Bremer, Director of the Ecumenical Institute of the University of Westphalia (Münster). The author is grateful to the directors of Forschungsstelle Osteuropa, University of Bremen and personally to Gabriel Superfin for the opportunity to work in the library and archives of the centre.

babushki, elderly female pensioners in the countryside or who had moved to the cities. They made up more than 80 per cent (in many places a full 100 per cent) of regular churchgoers.

This was a state of affairs common to advanced industrial societies in the 1960s–80s, but it was also due to some specifically Soviet factors. Among the former were urbanisation and a dramatic increase in levels of education, the spread of new leisure activities and the technology behind them (television, portable radios, tape recorders, personal ownership of cars, the trappings of tourism). The social role of churches also changed, as many of their previous functions were "usurped" by such other institutions as governments, political parties, trade unions, the media, universities and charities. People developed new intellectual and cultural aspirations, and were able to satisfy them without recourse to churches or, at least, to the traditional churches. Among the specifically Soviet factors were the physical destruction by the secular authorities of most of the Russian Orthodox Church's infrastructure (diocesan offices, religious schools, parishes and monasteries); the killing of clergy and laity (until Stalin's change of policy in 1943); the imposition on the entire working population of long hours of toil every day, leaving no time for the observance of religious rituals; the blocking of the careers of anyone openly practising their faith; the atheistic basis of school and higher education; and atheist propaganda among the adult population.

Khrushchev's "Assault on Heaven" anti-religious campaign in 1958–64 stymied the Church's efforts to harness the widespread post-war interest in religion.[320] Most importantly, Khrushchev finally broke the link with its largest and most important support group, the higher-earning segment of

320. For example, in 1953, according to the Council for Russian Orthodox Church Affairs of the U.S.S.R. Council of Ministers, 150,000 people attended Easter Matins in the thirty-six churches of Moscow. Eighty per cent were women, 20 per cent were men, and 15 percent were young. The same pattern was noted in other cities. In Kiev, some seven thousand people attended the services at St Sophia's Cathedral alone. In some regions of Central and Western Ukraine, up to half those attending were young people.

the lower class, ordinary workers and peasants who had not yet reached retirement age.

The *babushki* to be found in the churches in 1990 had mostly been born and spent their youth in agricultural areas of the provinces where, until the late 1930s and even later, Orthodox traditions and religious family education survived. As adults, however, these women tended to ignore the Church and returned to it only after retirement, when "that was allowed".[321] Coming back to God, they were not only capable of fiercely resisting attempts to close their churches but saw them as a private club where people from other social groups were not particularly welcome. The priest had no absolute authority over them, especially if he failed to support local traditions, including some rooted in "folk Orthodoxy".[322]

The situation was much better in regions which escaped the two waves of anti-religious militancy and the murdering of active believers. Western Ukraine, Western Byelorussia and Moldavia retained a high level of religious culture, with regular church attendance, widespread knowledge of basic doctrine, donations for church needs, respect for priests and a tradition of churchgoing. By Russian standards, a huge number of churches were functioning, and the gender and age profile of believers was significantly different.[323] In the 1970s and '80s, one sixth of all Russian Orthodox churches were located in just seven provinces of Western Ukraine.[324]

As a result, the fortunes of the Russian Orthodox Church in the 1970s were tied to these distant regions, a situation which by 1990 was even more evident. They provided not only revenues but also clergy. A considerable

321. Such a biography is described in Viacheslav Medushevskii, *Pomianite moiu liubov'. O staritse skhimonakhine Antonii* (Moscow, 2004).

322. Aleksandr Panchenko, *Narodnoe pravoslavie* (St Petersburg, 1998).

323. For a detailed comparison of Orthodoxy in different regions of the former U.S.S.R., see Nikolai Mitrokhin, *Russkaia pravoslavnaia tserkov': sovremennoe sostoianie i aktual'nye problemy* (Moscow, 2006), pp. 35–43, 479–580.

324. For more information on the situation in Western Ukraine, see Nikolai Mitrokhin, "Khudshee, konechno, vperedi: Russkaia pravoslavnaia tserkov' na Zapadnoi Ukraine", *Ukrainskaia greko-katolicheskaia tserkov': preodolenie mifa. Materialy seminara* (Moscow, 2002), pp. 106–34; http://religion.gif.ru/ukr/mitr.html

proportion of the priests ordained in the 1960s–80s had grown up in the villages of Transcarpathia, Volhynia, Galicia and Polesye. Networks of such priests from Western Ukraine developed and became powerful, not only there but in dioceses thousands of kilometres away.

A journalist working for a Syktyvkar Orthodox newspaper in the Komi Republic wrote in 1998:

> The fact that most priests up here in the North have come from outside, and indeed from as far away as Western Ukraine, is not that surprising. "Nobody ever destroyed our churches," Mother Anna [the priest's wife in the remote taiga village of Troitsko-Pechorsk – N.M.] told me. "We only had the Soviet regime after the war, but before that we were under Poland. My parents were taught the scriptures when they were at school. Immediately after the war, nobody had time to go around wrecking churches; the main thing was to rebuild all the things that had been destroyed. So the faith was never crushed there. There are people who have been priests for almost sixty years.
>
> We have two churches in our village. One, dedicated to the Archangel Michael, was built at the beginning of the twentieth century. In 1962, when the Communists were going at it hammer and tongs, a miraculous image of the Mother of God appeared on one of the windows. People came from all the surrounding villages to see it. The Communists tried to lure people away by putting on a film show next to the church. They took out the window with the Blessed Virgin Mary and washed it, but still people came. Now the whole iconostasis in the church is gilded with gold leaf.[325]

In the 1970s, a large number of urban young people with higher education

325. E. Suvorov, "Troitsk nad Pechoroi", *Vera-Eskom*, 1998; http://vera.mrezha.ru/10/87.htm

were coming to religion; it was a global trend.[326] University graduates in the U.S., Britain, Germany and the U.S.S.R. discovered dimensions of spirituality they had not known about. The difference was that, in the West the starting point was rejection of the doctrines and practices of the dominant Christian churches in favour of new religious movements; in the U.S.S.R., the official Communist ideology was rejected in favour of all sorts of other religious ideas, including Orthodoxy, which they also had not known about.

The Infrastructure

The number of Russian Orthodox parishes registered with the government increased rapidly from 1987, and by 1 January, 1989 totalled 7,549.[327] The same applied to monasteries, which almost doubled between the beginning of 1987 and the end of 1989, from eighteen to thirty-five.[328] It has to be remembered, however, that this was an increase from the Church's lowest baseline since 1946.

After Khrushchev's campaign, which saw the closure of 40 per cent of churches functioning in the U.S.S.R. in the late 1940s and 1950s, the numbers continued to decline. The main reason was the regime's refusal (with rare exceptions) to permit churches to reopen, let alone to permit new ones to be built in places where there was a perceived need. The rapid depopulation of rural central Russia and the Russian North also took a toll, leaving parishes unviable.

The statistics do not fully reflect the Church's infrastructure in the years before perestroika. In addition to the parishes and monasteries that officially existed, and in addition to the priests registered and controlled by

---

326. Hugh McLeod, "The Sixties: Writing the Religious History of a Crucial Decade", *Kirchliche Zeitgeschichte*, 14 (2002), pp. 36–48. See also Robert Wuthnow, *The Restructuring of American Religion* (Princeton, 1988).

327. Nathaniel Davis, *A Long Walk to the Church: A Contemporary History of Russian Orthodoxy* (Boulder, 1995), p. 66. If in 1987 sixteen new parishes were registered, in 1988 the figure was just under eight hundred.   328. *Ibid.*, p. 155.

the regime, there were many other individuals who played an important part in disseminating and supporting Orthodoxy.

Alongside the legally functioning communities were a considerable number that were unofficial. Not all of these were affiliated to the communities of True Orthodox Christians or the True Orthodox Church. This had been formed back in the 1920s in opposition to the Moscow Patriarchate [which in 1927 was subordinated to the Soviet authorities], but accepted some of its sacraments. Many unofficial groups, as well as secret monasteries, considered themselves loyal to the Russian Orthodox Church but avoided official registration out of concern for their safety; others were hoping to be permitted registration at some future time.[329]

Secretly ordained nuns were a common feature in parishes. The quiet pensioners assisting the priest during services or in practical matters were often nuns, illegally ordained by an authoritative priest or bishop. In the 1960s–80s there were a number of secret monasteries, consisting mainly of nuns but also of monks from houses closed in the early 1960s. In the mountains of Abkhazia, a whole network of secret *skete* communities existed for several dozen monks living in hermit-like conditions of poverty, to whom believers from all over the U.S.S.R. came for spiritual guidance.[330]

Orthodox believers turned for spiritual advice not only, and perhaps not primarily, to priests but to elders (*startsy* and *staritsy*) they knew of, who often had no official standing. Some of the elders were monks in monasteries, but most of them lived and received visitors (sometimes thousands each year) in ordinary city apartments or rural log cabins.[331]

329. Mikhail Shkarovskii, *Russkaia Pravoslavnaia Tserkov' pri Staline i Khrushcheve: Gosudarstvenno-tserkovnye otnosheniia v SSSR v 1939–1964 godakh* (Moscow, 2000), pp. 217–83.
330. G. Chiniakova, ed., *Zhizneopisanie startsa ieroskhimonakha Stefana (Ignatenko)* (Moscow, 2002); *Podvizhniki blagochestiia XX veka. Skhiarkhimandrit otets Feodosii Pochaevskii*, pt 3; "Za istinu" website, http://www.zaistinu.ru/articles/?aid=350
331. The *staritsa* Antoniya, for example, lived with an "open door" in a cramped apartment at Aviamotornaya metro station, receiving a dozen visitors a day (Viacheslav Medushevskii, *Pomianite moiu liubov'*).

The organising of Orthodox funerals in the countryside and, in particular, readings from the Psalter (and coordinating such local rituals as extended leave-taking of the dead) was the job of wise-women who formed a kind of sisterhood. The *babushki* from a local church would act as mediators for the discreet baptising of infants, weddings or, more rarely, funeral services at which Soviet citizens were afraid to be seen entering a church themselves.

Throughout the U.S.S.R., there survived traditional Orthodox families who were not scared away from the Church by the repressions of Stalin or Khrushchev. In the 1960s–80s such families formed an inter-regional network, actively involved in responsible work for the Church. This network provided many candidates for the priesthood and many priests' wives.

Finally, by the 1980s, the urban Orthodox intelligentsia had formed its own network, which included facilities for printing and distributing uncensored literature, *samizdat* periodical literature, clandestine seminars and even Sunday schools. From the early 1980s, this network had close links with the legal Orthodox clergy, not only in Moscow, Leningrad and Kiev but also deep in the provinces.

Relations with the Regime

For decades, the Russian Orthodox Church was under tremendous pressure and controlled by the C.P.S.U. Central Committee, which implemented its policies with the aid of the K.G.B. and other government agencies. The Church was permitted activities such as the preaching of sermons only within the confines of a church. It was also allowed to manufacture, in very restricted quantities, "religious items"; to engage in minimal publishing activity; and to train priests to a quota deliberately set well below what was needed. The international and interfaith activities, the "ecumenical links" of the Church, were directed mainly towards furthering foreign-policy objectives of the regime, although they did to some extent help to preserve the Church and enable it to grow.[332]

During the Brezhnev era, the attitude towards the Church began to soften. Immediately after becoming the country's leader, Leonid Brezhnev put a stop to harsh anti-clerical repression, which never resumed. From 1972 on, for the first time in fifteen years, new parishes were allowed to register. From the late 1970s, indeed, for a variety of reasons which included the holding of the Olympic Games in Moscow in 1980, with its attendant influx of foreigners, and preparations over many years to celebrate the 1998 millennium of the Christianisation of Rus, the Russian Orthodox Church began receiving more substantial concessions.

First, a secret twenty-year ban on ordaining as a priest anyone with higher secular education was lifted, enabling many Orthodox intellectuals not only legally to practise but also openly to profess their faith. In 1979, the Church's Publications Board was granted permission to make its own publicity films. In 1980, Sofrino was founded, an enterprise owned by the Church which had modern equipment for relatively large-scale production of candles and church plate. In the same year the punitive taxation of the income of clergy was halted.[333] In 1983, for the first time in nearly forty years, the Church regained possession of the Svyato-Danilov Monastery, a large monastic complex in the centre of Moscow.[334] It was allowed to

332. For example, through making possible the receipt of literature from the U.S. and Western Europe; visits to the U.S.S.R. by foreign clergy, who were able to meet clergy opposed to the regime; and the preservation and maintenance of a number of Orthodox institutions in the U.S.S.R. so that they could be visited by foreigners.

333. In response to concern expressed by the Board of Religious Affairs, in June 1980 the Presidium of the U.S.S.R. Council of Ministers resolved "to change arrangements for payment of income tax and rent by the clergy", despite an annual cost to the state budget of up to 3 million roubles. Until then, "those servicing religious cults" were deemed to receive an officially fixed salary, which was then taxed at between 25 and 80 per cent. For a priest receiving 200 roubles monthly, the tax was 70 roubles. Rent was charged at four times the rate charged to ordinary citizens. See Irina Maslova, "Sovet po delam religii pri Sovete ministrov SSSR i Russkaia pravoslavnaia tserkov' (1965–1991 gg.)", *Otechestvennaia istoriia*, 6 (2005), p. 56.

334. The Patriarch was informed of the decision to return the Svyato-Danilov Monastery on 17 May, 1983 at the Board of Religious Affairs. See *Zhurnal Moskovskoi Patriarkhii*, 8 (1983), p. 2.

construct several administrative buildings[335] and to establish a number of parishes in large cities. The decision was taken in 1984 to turn the thousandth anniversary of the Christianisation of Rus into a national celebration.

Behind this benign facade, local representatives of the Board of Religious Affairs were still engaging in an all-out struggle with the bishops, who were administratively subordinate to them, to close churches down, often on the false pretext that they were non-viable. Even in the 1970s, many, if not most, of these officials were receiving regular bribes from bishops.[336] The Board of Religious Affairs stayed neutral, and local Party and government officials usually could not be bothered to campaign vigorously against "vestiges of religion".

From the late 1970s, it became apparent that the central government was beginning to recognise the Russian Orthodox Church as its preferred religious partner, not only because of its size and influence in terms of the number of believers but also because it was more malleable and helped with a wide range of tasks. As Konstantin Kharchev, Chairman of the Board of Religious Affairs, put it in March 1988, "Catholics, Protestants, Baptists, Evangelicals, Adventists and many others have their headquarters and administrative institutions beyond the reach of the Soviet authorities, so their rapid expansion is fraught with unpredictable consequences."[337] An obvious example of a "statist" attitude towards the Russian Orthodox Church is seen in the granting of permission in the first half of the 1980s for new Orthodox churches to be opened mainly in border areas with a substantial Russian population: "along the Chinese border", and in Kalin-

335. At least, in Moscow (within the Danilov Monastery) and in Minsk.

336. In 1985, Major A. M. Khvostikov, a K.G.B. agent in Rostov engaged in "counter-intelligence activities relating to the Russian Orthodox Church", was shot for taking bribes in 1972–84 in return for helping the clergy with their problems. See "Chekisty ... v riasakh (interv'iu o. Georgiia Edelshteina)", *Argumenty i Fakty*, 36 (1991).

337. "Religiia i perestroika", in G. Shtriker, ed., *Russkaia pravoslavnaia tserkov' v sovetskoe vremia: Materialy i dokumenty po istorii otnoshenii mezhdu gosudarstvom i Tserkov'iu*, 2 vols (Moscow, 1995), vol. 2, p. 217.

ingrad province. This was doubtless done to back up the Slavic population in these areas and to fight back against Protestant denominations, which were burgeoning, it was felt, because of a lack of Orthodox churches.[338]

Relations with the regime began to improve at breathtaking speed in 1987.[339] Atheist propaganda was halted. The Board of Religious Affairs was transformed from the Church's implacable enemy into an institution that went out of its way to facilitate solutions to its problems, from procuring a prestigious ZIL limousine for the Patriarch[340] to issuing permits for the establishment of new parishes and the transference of entire monastery complexes back to the Church.[341] In closed meetings with Party propagandists, Kharchev lamented that he could not consent to introducing chaplaincies in hospitals because Catholics and Protestants would immediately dominate the niche. The Russian Orthodox Church "in its present downtrodden state lacks the resources to perform this function".[342]

In 1986, for the first time in forty years, a prominent member of the clergy, Metropolitan Pitirim (Nechayev), Director of the Patriarchate's Publications Board, was appointed to the semi-governmental position of board member of the Soviet Cultural Foundation, set up by Raisa Gorbacheva, and

338. This trend was noted by a *samizdat* author (evidently a priest), writing under a pseudonym: K. Golovin, "Griadet den' ...", *Materialy samizdata. Arkhiv samizdata radiostantsii "Svoboda"*, 13 March 1977 3, vyp. 7/87. AS No. 5889. The document is also quoted in *Russkaia pravoslavnaia tserkov' v sovetskoe vremia*, vol. 2, p. 203.

339. Of fundamental importance was a speech by Konstantin Kharchev, Chairman of the Board of Religious Affairs, to the bishops of the R.O.C. on 9 July, 1987 in which he announced the lifting of most of the "Khrushchev" restrictions, including on the ringing of church bells, allowing priests to be members of their church committees, not needing to be "authorised" to take services by the committees' chairmen, and not requiring parents to present their passports before a child could be baptised in church. The speech has not yet been published but is mentioned in Pimen (Khmelevskii), *arkhiepiskop*, *Vsegda s Bogom* (Saratov, 2000), pp. 186–7. 340. Konstantin Kharchev, *Dar liubvi* (Moscow, 2003), p. 192.

341. In 1987, the territory and buildings of the Kozel'sk Vvedensky Optina Pustyn' (Kaluga) and Tolga Svyato-Vvedensky Monastery (Yaroslavl') were restored to the Church, as, in May 1988, were some of the religious relics kept in state museums. So too, somewhat later, was part of the complex of the Kiev-Pechersk Monastery.

342. *Religiia i perestroika*, p. 218.

started accompanying her husband on certain visits abroad. In 1989, three Church leaders became official members of the country's governing elite as people's deputies of the U.S.S.R. [343]

With the consent of the regime, a General Council of the Church was held in 1988. Although formally convened in connection with the millennium of the Christianisation of Rus, it was in fact a council where the Church sought to engage with its changed situation. Its new charter, drafted by one of its rising stars [eventually to become Patriarch], Archbishop Kirill (Gundyayev) of Smolensk, registered the Church's hopes to advance into the areas opening up for it. The council was a kind of precursor of the Congress of People's Deputies of the U.S.S.R., in that delegates from the regions, from venerable bishops to hitherto little-known priests, tried in their speeches to draw attention to all the trials they were facing. For the first time, they had an opportunity to air publicly problems which had been building up for decades. The Publications Board and its Director came in for particular criticism, as did the system of religious education.[344] It was soon clear that the Church needed extensive reform and was proposing to pursue it without government intervention. All it wanted from the government was that it should return property it had confiscated in the past, legalise and permit what it had previously made illegal and persecuted.

As the new year of 1990 came in, the Church had three main priorities. First, it wished to expand its infrastructure by establishing new parishes, monasteries and dioceses, and increasing the number of seminaries. Second, it needed to resolve the question of internal authority: whether to retain or reform the existing system of governance, both in terms of institutions and of individuals, particularly at parish level. (Part of the problem

---

343. Patriarch Pimen (Izvekov) and Metropolitans Alexiy (Ridiger) and Pitirim (Nechayev).
344. A heavily edited transcript was officially published two years later. See *Pomestnyi sobor Russkoi Pravoslavnoi Tserkvi, Troitse-Sergieva Lavra, 6–9 iiunia 1988. Materialy* (Moscow, 1988), pp. 385–428. A fairly detailed account appeared almost immediately in Church *samizdat*: "Iubilei", *Vybor*, 6 (October–December 1988), pp. 19–45.

was to find a place for Russian Orthodox intellectuals and to incorporate the associations they had formed into a modernised Church structure.) The third priority was something completely new: to decide the Church's policy towards separatist and schismatic movements in border regions, particularly in Ukraine.

These issues had to be resolved in the context of root-and-branch reforms in every area of the U.S.S.R.'s social, political and economic life – a rapidly changing environment which was becoming increasingly unstable – and the ever-growing opportunities opening up for the Church.

DEVELOPING THE INFRASTRUCTURE

Massive Registration of Parishes

The main way in which the infrastructure expanded was by groups of believers applying to have churches transferred to them. Some of these applications were at the initiative of clergy, but many came from the laity themselves. Having, as a rule, obtained the priest's blessing and the approval of the diocesan board, a group of believers from a village or urban district with an old church which was empty or little used and not too badly damaged would apply to the local authority to have the constitution of their community registered and to have the building they had their eye on transferred to them. It was usually argued that believers in their village or district had a long and difficult journey to the only functioning church, and that when they got there it was overcrowded. Both things were usually true.

The groups rarely got what they wanted without a struggle. The next stage, which invariably took several months and could take more than a year, involved bringing pressure to bear on the local authority. Despite the fact that officials well knew that returning Church property was national policy, they were frequently obstructive. Only sometimes were there genuine problems, like finding alternative accommodation for organisations being evicted. Many officials acted in the light of their atheist upbringing and engaged in passive resistance to the U.S.S.R.'s increasingly liberal leaders.

Their resistance could be overcome if believers persevered; they soon recognised the effectiveness of taking to the streets to protest. Regular open-air services in the vicinity of their favoured church, pickets and hunger strikes outside administrative buildings, and appeals for help to the liberal media rapidly caught on and proved effective. One of the most famous incidents was a [sixteen-day] hunger strike in March 1989 by four women in Ivanovo, demanding registration of their community and the reopening of the Vvedensky Church [which had been used as a K.G.B. archive]. The episode was colourfully described by a liberal Orthodox journalist with *Ogonyok*, to show the lengths to which believers were prepared to go in their campaigning.[345]

This widely discussed article did not give the full story, however. In fact, clandestine nuns in Ivanovo were trying to obtain legal status. Their community had formed in the first half of the 1980s around Abbot Amvrosiy (Yurasov), who was already becoming prominent.[346] The priest gave the limelight to the hungering women but was himself directing the process. The community was soon registered and ownership of the church transferred at Easter of 1990. Under Abbot Amvrosiy's direction it was to become a very rich, if controversial, fundamentalist Orthodox nunnery.

This tale illustrates a process that was taking place within the Church after 1988. Most members of the clergy took advantage of the new Church charter to try to accumulate all the power, not only spiritual but also administrative, in their parishes. In long-established parishes, they often encountered resistance from parishioners and church supporters. These people did not agree that all elders in the Soviet period had been bad, just as not all priests were administrative geniuses or entirely without avarice. Accordingly, although under the new charter the holy father was no longer debarred from the "twenty", the parish's governing body, it was by no means certain

345. Aleksandr Nezhnyi, "Strasti po Krasnomu khramu", *Ogonek*, 28 (1989), pp. 17–19.
346. *Amvrosii (Iurasov), arkhimandrit* (Ivanovo, 2001).

that he would replace the existing elder and be handed the keys to the safe.

Where new parishes were created, often on the initiative of clergy, the priest became the administrative elder. Indeed, there was such a shortage of staff that priests of new parishes typically gained immediate control of two or three parishes. This inhibited parishioners' involvement and tended to block lay initiatives.

After the Democrats' Victory in the National and Regional Elections

The transfer of property to religious institutions accelerated significantly after the March 1990 elections. These resulted, in many regions of the U.S.S.R., in the return to republican and local government institutions of democratic or national-democratic candidates who actively supported the idea of religious freedom. There was a general sense that action needed to be taken immediately to "revive spiritual life", although what exactly that meant was understood very differently by different political groups.

In such republics as the Baltic States, Transcaucasia and Moldova, and in such regions as Western Ukraine, national democrats bent on rooting out the Communist past saw ethnic and religious factors as closely related. Once in power, they instituted full-scale restitution of Church property. In Russia, Ukraine and Byelorussia, individuals who considered themselves spokespersons for the Orthodox population were elected to their various supreme soviets and played a prominent role in them. In the Russian S.F.S.R.'s Supreme Soviet, deputies of this complexion entered the de facto ruling coalition.

By the autumn of 1990, differences between the authorities of individual republics and the U.S.S.R. centre had become evident. Their confrontation resulted in a "war of laws", including a clash between those relating to the work of religious institutions. The R.S.F.S.R.'s law "Concerning freedom of religion", drafted by priests of the Russian Orthodox Church elected to the parliament and by other deputies supportive of the Church, was passed by the Supreme Soviet on 25 October. It closely resembled laws on the same issue in Europe, but significantly contradicted the comparable U.S.S.R. legislation, which had been passed on 1 October, 1990. The U.S.S.R. law excluded the possibility of religious education in secular schools and any alternative to military service, and retained the Board of Religious Affairs as an information provider, specialist and advisory body.

Even the U.S.S.R. law had been directly amended by the Church. The Moscow Patriarchate's lawyer recalls:

Alexiy, Patriarch of Moscow and All Russia, was invited as a guest of honour to the meeting of the U.S.S.R. Supreme Soviet at which the law was adopted. Before the opening of the session, Anatoliy Lukianov, Chairman of the Soviet, approached the Patriarch. After greetings had been exchanged, the Patriarch requested that he should add to Article 7 a clause stating that "a confederation of religious organisations is also recognised as a legal entity". The amendment was accepted.[347]

This clash between the laws can also be seen in the Patriarchate primarily defending its own corporate interests in the U.S.S.R. parliament, where it had influence, while the rank-and-file priests represented in the Russian republican parliament were more concerned to make life easier for their parishes.

The influence of the Russian Orthodox Church in government agencies grew during 1990 to the extent that, by the year's end, the Patriarchate had moved from polite requests to insistent demands. On 20 December, Patriarch Alexiy II urged Boris Yeltsin, as Chairman of the R.S.F.S.R. Supreme Soviet, to declare Christmas and Good Friday public holidays in Russia for the first time in more than seventy years. He based this request on the newly adopted Russian law "Concerning freedom of conscience".[348]

347. Viktor Kalinin, "Obzor zakonodatel'stva o religii", *Prikhod*, 9 (2006), p. 47.
348. "Pis'mo Sviateishego Patriarkha Aleksiia II Predsedateliu Verkhovnogo Soveta RSFSR B.N. Eltsinu ot 20.12.1990", *Zhurnal Moskovskoi Patriarkhii*, 6 (1991).

The Church's successes were facilitated by an upsurge of support for religion, which began in 1988 and lasted until 1994. The vast majority of Soviet citizens, who had never been inside a church or who, baptised in infancy, had never been back to church in their years of discretion, began to discover Russian Orthodoxy, not without the involvement of the state-controlled mass media. Their first steps were to go as sightseers into functioning churches, to be baptised as adults or to get married in church (these were mostly people who had long before been through a civil marriage ceremony). There was less participation in church services than in mass rituals like the consecration and distribution of Epiphany Water on 18 January and Easter processions. Natalia Sokolova remembers this period in the parish of Grebnevo near Moscow:

In all the churches, the number of people wanting to be baptised in the early 1990s was unusually large, so that two groups of about fifty people had to be christened one after the other. I heard people who were being baptised say, "It's a complete nightmare! So stuffy in there, babies yelling, you can't hear the priest. I thought I was going to faint!" An hour before the priest arrived, I began talking to those who were to be baptised. Twenty or more people gathered round me. I was sad to discover that they hadn't the first idea about the sacrament of Baptism, knew nothing about the creed and had never held a copy of the Gospel. Many of them thought you weren't allowed to go into a church before you had been baptised. I began my talk with the creation of the world, original sin, and generally explained the creed in straightforward language. People listened eagerly to every word, but nobody asked any questions. After forty minutes my strength gave out and I handed over to a woman who explained to those being baptised how to undress, where to put their shoes and so on. Meanwhile, I was answering practical questions because nobody asked religious ones. People wanted to know whether they could drink vodka on the day they had been baptised, whether a blue shirt would do instead of a white one and so forth. When they went into the church, the poor things were given no understanding of anything sacred. They were just tired and frightened by the overcrowding and jostling, which they had to endure for an hour or even two. They were brought to the church, given Communion, received into the church, but no-one explained what was being done or why.[349]

Human Resources

The rapid increase in the number of parishes revealed a drastic shortage of clergy. Already in the first half of the 1980s, 15 to 20 per cent of parishes had no priest. The liberalisation of state policy made it possible to increase the numbers enrolling in existing seminaries, but given that from 1989 the number of parishes was increasing by 20 to 30 per cent annually, this fell far short of solving the problem, especially since the course of study at a seminary lasted four years. The obvious solution was for the Church to open new schools, and primarily theological colleges. Their priority was to give a future priest, who had grown up in an atheistic environment and had usually received an atheistic education, the necessary modicum of knowledge to practise his profession. The first colleges opened in 1989,[350] but 1990 was the year they mushroomed, initially offering a one- or two-year training course.[351]

These schools could impart only modest knowledge. As a rule, the lecturers were the few priests in a diocese who had graduated from the Theological Academy, and often included the Bishop himself. He would turn to teaching not because of any great enthusiasm for pedagogy but because there was no-one else to teach the Old Testament or patristics for

349. Natal'ia Sokolova, *Tserkov' sela Grebnevo v gody gonenii* (Moscow, 2006), pp. 90–91.
350. For example, in Stavropol, Tomsk and Chernigov.
351. In Vladimir, Vologda, Kolomna, Kostroma, Kursk, Omsk, Ryazan, Tashkent and elsewhere. The colleges in Vladimir and Vologda were founded on the basis of catechism classes for adults set up a few months previously.

several hundred kilometres around. It took a number of years (less in large cities, more in the provinces) for better-educated scholars to appear in a diocese, a teaching staff to form and essential books to be bought. Only then did the colleges begin to turn into seminaries with a four-year degree programme. For many priests of the "1990 generation", theological college was to provide the only religious education they received.

Despite the new opportunities to open colleges and seminaries, and push a fairly large number of potential priests through them at the expense of educational quality, there remained an acute shortage of clergy in the dioceses. Bishops had no option but to continue, and even expand, the practice of ordaining as a priest literally any pious layperson they could find. Even that was far from easy. Despite the great increase of interest in religion, few men with no obvious physical or mental deficiency regularly attended church. Almost all those who did, if they attended services for a few months, were invited to be ordained, irrespective of their profession or educational level.

People in Church circles talk openly about tractor drivers who, without leaving their jobs and without any religious education at all, became priests. Let us consider the biographies of two secretaries of diocesan boards, who are nominally second in command after the Bishop himself. I noted down one during a visit in 1998 to the diocese of Lutsk in Volhynia, Western Ukraine.

Archpriest Aleksandr (Kolb) was brought up a Christian from child-hood. In 1985 he completed ten years of schooling in Dubno, Ukraine. In 1985–7 Aleksandr worked as a lathe operator on a collective farm in his native village. In 1987–8 he studied in the preparatory department of the Ukrainian Institute of Water Resources Engineers in Rovno, and in 1988–9 he enrolled on a construction course there, leaving after his ordination. On 19 July, 1989 he was ordained as a deacon by the Archbishop of Volyn and Rovno, and on 2 August, 1989 he was ordained as a priest and sent to minister at the Pokrovsky Church in the village of Novorechitsa. In 1991–5 Aleksandr studied as an external student at the recently opened Kiev

THE RUSSIAN ORTHODOX CHURCH IN 1990

Theological Seminary, and since 1996 he has been teaching liturgics and homiletics at a seminary opened in his diocese. In that same year, he was appointed Diocesan Secretary.[352]

A model biography of a priest from a non-Christian family is that of Archpriest Vyacheslav (Bachin), Abbot of the Svyato-Pokrovsky Cathedral in Krasnoyarsk and Secretary of the diocesan board.[353] In 1987, he graduated from the Political College of the U.S.S.R. Interior Ministry and, more specifically, its military department, which trained deputy commanders of political education for troops of the Interior Ministry. He worked for three years as a political officer, resigning in 1990. In 1991, he was baptised and then, on 4 December, ordained as a deacon, and as a priest four days later.

The Church is only now beginning to overcome the consequences of the critical lack of professional knowledge of many of the priests ordained in 1990–95. The explosive growth in the number of parishes has now fallen to less than 3 per cent per year, the network of theological colleges has been expanded, priests are no longer being ordained without a seminary education, and there is an influx into the colleges of a younger generation brought up as Christians, who were able as childen to attend church and Sunday school, and had free access to religious literature. In dioceses like Grodno and Ryazan, where bishops are acutely aware of having large numbers of uneducated clergy, priests have been obliged in recent years to acquire a theological education. A battle is sometimes waged, with variable results, between village priests who see no point in travelling to town for two years in pursuit of a diploma which they regard as no more than a piece of paper, and bishops who are weary of non-canonical "miracles" performed by their subordinates.

352. Recording of an interview with Archpriest Aleksandr (Kolb), Lutsk, 3 August, 1998. Digital archive of the author.
353. The biography is posted on the cathedral's website. See "Nastoiateli i sviashchennosluzhiteli", website of Pokrovskii kafedral'nyi sobor, Krasnoyarsk; http://www.pokrov-sobor.ru/history3.shtml

New Orthodox Initiatives

Already in 1988, the Church began to extend its influence in society, primarily through the mass media and politics. Priests began to make regular appearances on television and in the press, and clergy were appointed to leadership positions in semi-official charitable organisations and, from 1989, in politics. They were present in official bodies – we have mentioned that some were elected people's deputies of the U.S.S.R. – and were also active in opposition movements.

It is only really in 1990, however, that we can speak of a whole-hearted engagement by the Church with the world: the beginnings of religious ministry in education, law enforcement, the prisons and armed forces, and wide availability of religious literature. Before this time, access to these areas had been firmly barred, not only by legal prohibitions but because professional communities would not countenance any involvement of the clergy. For the Church itself, the challenge of preaching outside the church walls was unexpected, and the vast majority of priests saw no need for it.[354] Already overwhelmed with work and ministering to those who came to the Church of their own volition, semi-educated and not particularly competent preachers were in no rush to face a university or military audience.[355]

The expansion of the Church's sphere of influence and the move into

354. Natalia Sokolova who, by the Church's standards at that time, was an energetic catechist, remarks, when talking of her "sermons", "To our relief, there was not a single instance of anyone starting to argue or express disbelief." See Sokolova, *Tserkov' sela Grebneva*, p. 90.

355. Inability to preach from the pulpit does not mean a priest is incapable of drawing people to the Church. The Russian Orthodox Church lays great store by the majesty and solemnity of the liturgy: the ability to move elegantly and confidently, to sing well, to recite the prayers and invocations clearly, to wear the appropriate vestments correctly throughout the service, and perform such other rituals as sprinkling the holy water gracefully. The combination of a service's powerful aesthetic effect and a skilfully handled taking of confession can have more impact than an articulate sermon. In the Soviet period, a visitor dropping in to a church might then begin to attend regularly from sheer delight at the beauty of the service.

missionary activity in previously closed areas came about through the efforts of active laypeople, particularly members of the intelligentsia who had joined the Church in the 1960s–80s. Eager to see Soviet society become anti-Communist, they supported the idea of an evangelising Church and tried to encourage not only priests from their own ranks into missionary activity but also more traditional and conservative clergy. The major activity was organising lectures in the workplace which were in fact missionary evenings. Liberally-minded institutions were naturally more open to this. Priests had been giving talks at universities from the autumn of 1988, but the Moscow State Institute of Historical Archives was the first higher-education institution to host, in 1989, a series of evangelising lectures by Orthodox clergy under the title "The History of Religions".[356] Father Aleksandr Men, a liberal ideologist of Orthodoxy and unofficial leader of many Orthodox intellectuals, gave the first lectures, later to be replaced by the now no less well-known Orthodox writer Deacon Andrey Kurayev, who in those years was also on the liberal wing of the Church.

Archpriest Boris Pivovarov, sentenced to four years' imprisonment in 1983 for *samizdat* activity, recalls:

In 1990, when the first Orthodox parish in Akademgorodok was being established, in late September when literally only the foundations of the parish church had been laid, the Sunday school opened. As the parish had no accommodation at all, the first classes were held in the largest lecture theatre of Novosibirsk University. They were held on Sundays, and children of different ages came to them. Sometimes mothers would come with babies in their arms; lecturers would bring their students. Between 250 and 300 people might attend, and there would be people standing or even sitting in the aisle, such was the interest in everything to do with the Church. The majority were not churchgoers but wanted to hear about the

356. Iu. Afanas'ev, "Nauka o religii v universitete"; http://www.yuri-afanasiev.ru/humana/tom5_2.htm

Church, about Christ and God. There was no great pedagogical innovation. The classes lasted less than an hour. We chose twelve topics: The Christianisation of Rus (the Millennium had been celebrated just two years previously and people were very interested); the Cross; the Gospel; prayer; fasting; repentance; God's Church, God's commandments. There wasn't the abundance of technology around then which we see nowadays, and the most enthusiastic churchgoers would type up a brief summary of the priest's talk and hand the texts out as people were leaving. We retain what we read better than what we hear, and when they got home, those who had attended the lecture could read these two or three sheets and assimilate it better.

Slides were shown, there was music, and the regular attendance was around two hundred. At that time, people were only beginning to be baptised and go to church. There were no Bibles available yet, but it was the autumn of 1990, the Communist regime was finished, and everybody wanted to hear about God.[357]

In 1990 the U.S.S.R. began gradually to allow priests into the prisons to offer spiritual guidance to prisoners and suspects. The most famous priest was Father Gleb Kaleda, who taught in Moscow's Butyrki prison until his death in 1994.[358] He was a typical representative of the underground Church, just then in the process of becoming legal. Father Gleb had been secretly ordained in 1972 by a Bishop of the Moscow Patriarchate, had completed a doctorate in geology in 1981, and held services at home for his family and a narrow circle of traditional Orthodox intellectuals.[359] He only emerged from his underground existence in 1990, immediately taking on a

357. S. Arkhipov, "Pravoslavnaia gimnaziia v Akademgorodke. Interv'iu s protoiereem Borisom Pivovarovym", 17 March, 2005; http://www.pravoslavie.ru/guest/050317144609
358. Gleb Kaleda, protoierei. Ostanovites' na putiakh vashikh ... Zapiski tiuremnogo sviashchennika (Moscow, 1995); http://www.miloserdie.ru/index.php?ss=20&s=21&id=161
359. Gleb Kaleda, "Bog stuchitsia v serdtsa chelovecheskie ...", Nashe nasledie, 38 (1996), p. 103.

completely new role for a Russian Orthodox priest.[360] And in December 1990, sixty-year-old Konstantin Chernetsky became the first priest of a hospital church, at the Moscow Sechenov Medical Academy. Ordained as a priest in 1969, he and his wife came from families of hereditary clergy.[361]

It is difficult to say exactly when the first talks by clergy to the military took place, but a lecture was given by Pimen (Khmelevsky), Archbishop of Saratov and one of the Church's most enlightened and influential figures. A protégé of Patriarch Alexiy I, friend of Mstislav Rostropovich and Galina Vishnevskaya, Pimen spoke on 9 December, 1990 on "ideological issues" to officers of strategic aviation who had come from all over the country to a conference in the city of Engels in Saratov province. On 25 December, he again addressed a surprising audience, this time at the Communist Party University in Saratov, answering many questions. The title of the talk was "Folk Medicine".[362]

Also in 1990, the first of the annual Church and Society "Readings" took place. These were officially about aspects of education and history; the participants were priests, churchgoers and other interested intellectuals. The first such reading took place in Tomsk, a provincial but university town, and was organised by Leonid Kharaim, a former teacher of philology at the Rostov Pedagogical Institute who had been ordained in 1984.[363] From 1992, annual readings, by now on a national basis, began in Moscow on the initiative of the Synodal Department of Religious Education and Catechesis, and almost simultaneously they started up as diocesan initiatives in several other cities. Since the mid-1990s, they have become established in over half the dioceses of Russia, ranging over issues relating to church life

360. Chronologically, the first case I know of a priest visiting a place of detention was on 15 April, 1990, when, immediately after the Easter service, Pimen (Khmelevsky), Archbishop of Saratov and Volgograd, accompanied by the provincial Director of Interior Affairs, visited one of the Saratov penal colonies and spent half an hour talking to a group of prisoners. This did not lead on to regular contacts, however. See *Pimen (Khmelevskii), arkhiepiskop*, p. 204.   361. T. Kholodilova, "Khram na Devich'em pole", *Vera-Eskom*, 514 (April 2006); http://vera. mrezha.ru/514/10.htm   362. *Pimen (Khmelevskii), arkhiepiskop*, p. 207.   363. Father Leonid's biography was posted on the Internet in a currently missing version of the directory *Kto est' kto v Tomskoi oblasti* (Tomsk, 1996).

and church–state relations. They have thus become a kind of substitute for the general and episcopal councils which are conspicuously absent from the life of the present-day Orthodox Church.

Churchgoing intellectuals were also behind the booming Orthodox press, in which diocesan publications were prominent. Before 1989, the Church published only three titles for the general reader, the *Journal of the Moscow Patriarchate*, *Orthodox Herald* (for parishes in Western Ukraine) and the Berlin *Stimme der Orthodoxie*.[364] In 1990, several dozen new publications appeared almost simultaneously, mostly the diocesan magazines and newspapers which had not been seen during the decades of the Soviet period.

In the autumn of 1990, the Radonezh Brotherhood in Moscow, which consisted of Orthodox intellectuals, opened Yasenevo, the first Russian Orthodox classical grammar school in the U.S.S.R., under the "spiritual patronage" of Abbot Amvrosiy (Yurasov). It took over the premises of School No. 1106. Similar, but more modest, initiatives began to appear in the provinces. Although to date Orthodox grammar schools have been only moderately successful – there are just a few dozen of them and, with few exceptions, they are quite small – those which opened in 1990 were the harbingers of a significant development in the history of the Church.

The first religious charitable institutions also reappeared – for example, the St Kseniya of St Petersburg diocesan charity hospital was founded in Leningrad. Now that the dust has settled, it has to be admitted that this was the least thought out if much anticipated example of the Church's initiatives. The Church found it could not afford the maintenance of such institutions, or pay properly trained staff, if the hospitals were run on a non-paying basis. Today there are no more than five, and they care for only a very few patients.

---

364. The print runs were so tiny that these publications were effectively only available to (by no means all) priests and better-educated church elders. A couple of exclusive publications, *Informatsionnyi biulleten' OVTsS (Otdel vneshnikh tserkovnykh sviazei)* and *Bogoslovskie trudy*, were effectively available only to bishops and an elite circle of senior clergy.

REDISTRIBUTION OF POWER WITHIN THE CHURCH

The Election of a New Patriarch

Pimen (Izvekov), Patriarch of Moscow and All Russia, died on 3 May, 1990. The Church's new leader was elected, not just without delay but with indecent haste, on 6 June. Almost one and a half years had passed between the death of Patriarch Alexiy I (Simansky) and the enthronement of Pimen as his successor. On this occasion not even the traditional forty days of mourning were observed.

The rush was due, not so much to a rapidly developing crisis in Ukraine (see below) as to a consensus within the episcopate that an effective central authority was urgently needed. After a car accident in 1972, Patriarch Pimen had hardly left his apartments. He also dramatically reduced the little contact he had with the outside world. With time, word went round that many administrative problems, including problems in the Synod, could be best resolved through the Patriarch's nurse. The lady, whose name means "hope" in Russian, came to be known as "Nadezhda, Hope of All Russia".[365]

In the 1980s, another influential group formed around the Patriarch and took control of all the financial and economic affairs of the Moscow Patriarchate. It was led by Serapion (Fadeyev), Archbishop of Vladimir and Suzdal from 1980 to 1987, who in 1984–5 was Director of the financial board of the Patriarchate. In 1987 he became Metropolitan of Kishinev, one of the largest and richest eparchates.[366] There he imposed monstrous exactions on the clergy. His boorishness and declared intention of russifying Moldavian Orthodox life did not meet with approval from his subordinates. Their dissatisfaction chimed with the interests of the Moldavian national

365. E. Komarov, "Favoritka iz Chistogo pereulka", *Novye izvestiia*, 13 June, 1999.
366. Its incumbent, Metropolitan Ionafan (Kopolovich), retired voluntarily. Six more bishops retired in 1987–9 in what resembled the purge of inactive old-timers from the C.P.S.U. Central Committee.

revival movement unleashed by perestroika, with the result that, in May 1989, after a service, Metropolitan Serapion was obliged to flee from his cathedral, pursued by a booing crowd armed with axes. It is said that among those who spat into his departing car were a number of priests.[367]

In July 1989, the somewhat chastened metropolitan occupied the see of Tula, less prestigious, but closer to Moscow. His pupils and helpers were high-ranking church administrators, but not members of the Holy Synod. They exploited their unofficial proximity to the Patriarch to control the Patriarchate's "revenue streams" and, in 1989–90, attempted also to seize administrative power in the Church. They were supported in this by Kharchev, the head of the Board of Religious Affairs, in whose view the actions of members of the Synod were "not in the Church's best interests".[368] Serapion's group accordingly proposed to Anatoliy Lukianov, Chairman of the U.S.S.R. Supreme Soviet and the member of the government responsible for issues relating to the Church, that the Holy Synod should be "renewed". The bishops suggested that, as the nation was undertaking a radical purge of all the secular elites, the elite of the Church, most of whom were appointed to their posts in the 1960s, should also be replaced. This suggestion was not well received by the U.S.S.R.'s political leaders: "After dinner, the permanent members of the Synod went to see Lukianov. We were there for a long time. Lukianov said that Mikhail Gorbachev respected the Russian Church, trusted us and would do everything he could to help us. We could contact him directly through Lukianov, and did not have to go through the Board."[369]

After the election of the new Patriarch, the first meeting of the Holy Synod (whose membership they had been seeking to "renew") on 20 July,

367. Author's notes taken on trips to the Chişinău Metropolitanate in 1997–8.

368. Archbishop Pimen (Khmelevsky) of Saratov wrote in his diary on 21 July, 1989 of a conversation with Kharchev, "Later, he complained he had opened three thousand churches, only to be fired from his job because members of the Synod complained to the Central Committee about his interference in Church affairs. His interference had been, he said, for the good of the Church" (Pimen [Khmelevskii], *arkhiepiskop*, p. 199).

369. Diary entry for 28 September, 1989 (Pimen [Khmelevskii], *arkhiepiskop*, p. 202).

1990 dispatched Metropolitan Serapion's favourites to remote and far from prestigious sees: Tashkent in Uzbekistan, Alma-Ata in Kazakhstan, and Tobolsk in Siberia. Only Metropolitan Serapion held on to his see in Tula, never again to exercise influence on Church policy.[370]

The failed rebellion of the favourites was, however, peripheral to the redistribution of power within the Church leadership in 1990. The hierarchs associated with Metropolitan Serapion had no standing with the bishops and could not expect to win the secret ballot to elect a new Patriarch without lobbying for the intervention of the secular authorities. The three serious contenders were all permanent members of the Holy Synod: Alexiy (Ridiger), Metropolitan of Leningrad and Novgorod, who in 1963–86 had been Administrative Director of the Moscow Patriarchate; his successor in that post from 1987, Vladimir (Sabodan), Metropolitan of Rostov and Novocherkassk; and Filaret (Denisenko), Metropolitan of Kiev and Galicia since 1966.

The first appeared to have no support group but, as later transpired, managed to secure the support of most of the [liberal, ecumenical] "Nikodimites" voting at the General Council.[371] The second was himself a Nikodimite, and had administrative levers of control at his disposal. The third was counting on the support of the numerous Ukrainian bishops, most of whom he had consecrated. After the first ballot, however, the hopes of Metropolitan Filaret of Kiev and Galicia were dashed. His characteristically dictatorial management style and blatant violation of his monastic vows doubtless contributed to his receiving only sixty-six votes out of nearly three hundred.

We have a witness, perhaps the only person to have left memoirs about

370. Iliyan (Vostryakov) declined the appointment to Tobolsk and retired on 27 October, 1990. After his exile in Alma-Ata, Alexiy (Kutepov) in 2002 was appointed to the Tula bishopric, vacant after the death of Metropolitan Serapion in 1999.

371. Pupils of Nikodim (Rotov), Metropolitan of Leningrad and Ladoga, who was influential in the 1960s and 1970s. A whole group of prominent Church leaders emerged from under Nikodim's wing and went on to remain in close contact with each other. They took from him not only a desire to be actively involved in social issues but also a belief in the need for close cooperation between Church and State.

the election, which are important for understanding the future direction of the Church:

> I was at the General Council of 1990 at which the new Patriarch was elected (not as a participant but as a member of staff). I will never forget some of the bishops, after the final ballot to decide whether Metropolitan Alexiy or Metropolitan Vladimir would ascend the throne of St Peter, coming out past the altar of the refectory church of the Trinity-Sergius Monastery to get some fresh air while waiting for the result. There walked silently past us: Metropolitan Filaret (Vakhromeyev), deep in thought; impassive Metropolitan Iuvenaliy; Metropolitan Filaret (Denisenko), white with rage after being excluded in the previous round; and Metropolitan Vladimir (Sabodan), on the contrary, red as a lobster. Only Metropolitan Alexiy (Ridiger), appearing completely unfazed, stopped beside us on his way to the altar and asked, "Are you tired?" He added, "Can't be helped. It is hard for all of us." The effect was electrifying, Heaven knows! This prince of the Church with his human, indeed beguiling, expression! We could imagine the effort he must have been making to appear so calm at the moment when his destiny was in the balance.
>
> After a short break, the "metropolitburo" resumed their seats and the results were announced: Metropolitan Alexiy – 166 votes, Metropolitan Vladimir – 143. It was far from a landslide. I believe that 166/143 divide made a profound impression on our Primate, and that he developed a decided allergy to the words "General Council". As he accumulated more and more real power within the Russian Orthodox Church, and became increasingly persuaded of his personal infallibility, the more remote the possibility became of his convening another General Council.[372]

---

372. [bytopisatel (pseud.)], "Mina iuridicheskogo deistviia. Part 1", entry in an online diary on the "LiveJournal" website on 26 June, 2006; http://bytopisatel.livejournal.com/5943.html # cutid1

The New Generation of Bishops

The elevation of Alexiy II to leadership of the Church brought about a major change in its policy towards its priests. By and large, he supported the line of Alexiy I: no internal debates within the Church; no clearly defined groupings; supreme ecclesiastical authority resting with the bishops, who had extensive powers. The new age expanded the Church's opportunities even as the issue of systemic change within the Church was taken off the agenda. Patriarch Alexiy I's prediction had been proved correct. The institution he formed had outlived the Soviet regime and was now in a position to take advantage of the ensuing freedom. Unfortunately, implementing his principles under the new circumstances unexpectedly lowered the intellectual and moral level of the episcopate rather than raising it.

The new Patriarch's first task was to continue to consecrate more bishops. They were needed to fill new and restored sees, to repair the damage inflicted by Khrushchev's "storming of heaven" and then as far as possible to enable the Church to grow. Also, of course, to replace bishops of earlier generations who had gone to a better world. In 1990, in addition to Patriarch Pimen, seven bishops died, including three who were still in post.

Who were the candidates for these positions? The new Patriarch had no ready-made support team within the Church,[373] but that did not mean that he was going to rely on the Nikodimites who had backed him in the election, even though there was a whole reserve of Nikodimite priors and abbots who had been passed over for chirotonia.

In retrospect, we can see that Alexiy II chose his bishops not on the basis of people close to him in spirit (as Alexiy I had), but in order to create a system of checks and balances. Accordingly, he promoted monks from

373. At the Synod's first meeting after the election of the new Patriarch, his childhood friend Vyacheslav (in the monkhood, Korniliy) Jacobs, a respected priest of the Tallinn diocese, became Bishop (now Metropolitan) of Tallinn and All Estonia. This one bishop, together with Arseniy (Yepifanov), a permanent assistant to the Patriarch who was made a bishop a year earlier and is now an archbishop, were the sole members of the Patriarch's "team".

the Trinity-Sergius Monastery and their pupils, conservative provincial clergy trained in the theological colleges of Moscow. This was the source from which he began in the second half of 1990 to ordain new bishops, and he continued that policy until 1997. It was only when it became clear that many of the neophyte bishops were disinclined to accept the Holy Synod's views (some indeed supported a fairly open opposition that emerged within the Church)[374] that the Patriarchate's policy on human resources again abruptly changed.[375]

The Intelligentsia and the Church

The development of relations between the Soviet intelligentsia and the Church was not as straightforward as one might suppose from reading the existing literature. This describes the appearance of priests willing to speak to the intelligentsia in their own language, the receiving into the Church of a few intellectuals in the early 1960s, a Russian religious renaissance in the 1970s and early 1980s, and, finally, the mass conversions of the late 1980s and early 1990s. In fact, by the end of the 1970s, the most active and enterprising representatives of the first Soviet (in education and training) generation of intellectuals to turn to Orthodoxy were warning of a crisis in relations with the Church.[376] The Church's traditionalist majority was prepared to accept intellectuals only on condition that they gave up independent thinking on religious issues, and any remotely political activity.

374. Nikolai Mitrokhin, *Russkaia pravoslavnaia tserkov': sovremennoe sostoianie*, pp.. 174–234; Mitrokhin, "Infrastruktura podderzhki pravoslavnoi eskhatologii v sovremennoi RPTs. Istoriia i sovremennost'", *Russkii natsionalizm v politicheskom prostranstve (issledovaniia po natsionalizmu v Rossii)*, 1 (Moscow, 2007), pp. 196–250.

375. For more on the formation of the present episcopate of the R.O.C., see Nikolai Mitrokhin, "Sotsial'nyi lift dlia veruiushchikh parnei s rabochikh okrain: episkopat sovremennoi Russkoi pravoslavnoi tserkvi", in Kimmo Kääriäinen and Dmitrii Furman, eds, *Novye tserkvi – starye veruiushchie, starye tserkvi – novye veruiushchie. Sb. statei* (Moscow, 2007), pp. 260–324.

376. Mikhail Aksenov-Meerson, priest, *Pravoslavie i svoboda: Sb. statei* (Benson, VT, 1986); Liudmila Alekseeva, *Istoriia inakomysliia v SSSR: Noveishii period* (Benson, VT, 1984), pp. 217–36 (Chapter on "Pravoslavnye"); V. Zelinsky, *Prikhodiashchie v tserkov'* (Paris, 1982).

They were required also to accept uncritically the situation within the Church as it then was, and to conform to accepted standards in that community (for example, in dress). The dilemma between a readiness to "follow Christ in a spirit of self-sacrifice" and the practical requirement of accepting instruction from some semi-literate joiner who had become a monastic *starets*, or elder,[377] for some of the intelligentsia meant adapting to the practices of Orthodox life and "being received into the Church", but for others it led straight to disillusionment. As a liberal *samizdat* writer commented sardonically in 1987, "It's a joke to see someone who was yesterday (and still is today) an intellectual and book-lover pretending in church to be a primordial peasant of a kind which no longer exists. Archpriest Georgiy Florovsky warned long ago against confusing being received into the Church with 'going native'."[378]

Another *samizdat* author, who was a member of Father Dmitriy Dudko's community, had already noted the disillusionment back in the late 1970s:

> There are genuine ascetics in the monasteries, but they are in single figures. Few monasteries remain, and they are doomed to extinction. The monks are people with disabilities or whose spirit has been broken. They keep themselves to themselves and are terrified of the world outside their walls. They are frightened and incapable of living independently. Anything that deviates from their ascetic ideal is seen as the snares of the Devil. "The world has been damned, the end is nigh. We must pray and wait." Such is their motto. Any attempt at innovation scares them.
>
> Their longing for constancy often leads hermits [in the

---

377. Nikolai Mitrokhin, "Arkhimandrit Naum i 'naumovtsy' kak kvintessentsiia sovremennogo starchestva", in Kathy Rousselet (K. Russele) and Aleksandr Agadzhanian, eds, *Religioznye praktiki v sovremennoi Rossii* (Moscow, 2006), pp. 126–48; Anton Zhogolev, *Starets Ieronim* (Samara, 2004).

378. V. Iakubov (V. Frenkel), "Vtoroe obrashchenie (konets religioznogo renessansa)", *Materialy samizdata. Arkhiv samizdata radiostantsii "Svoboda"*, 8 January, 1988, vyp. 1/88, AS No. 6127, p. 13.

mountains of Abkhazia] to sectarianism, and they become opposed to the official Church. They have read the patristic literature, have a full understanding of asceticism, but you often encounter bigotry and ignorance among them. And yet, it would be wrong not to recognise their great merits. Living in the mountains, surrounded by marshes, often starving, hunted by K.G.B. agents, despised by the local population, they keep the faith, maintain a courageous, prayerful spirit and authentic Christian charity. If a neophyte is a graduate, he soon becomes aware that priests who were once country boys or come from an uneducated background, browbeaten by their teachers or the regime, have long ago become mired in what they learned at the seminary. They view young people with suspicion and wonder whether they have been sent to spy on them by the K.G.B. They aren't really capable of preaching, are servile when confronted by the authorities, avoid dangerous questions and are indifferent to the needs of their long-suffering neophytes, which they see as capriciousness. Enduring all these ordeals, the neophyte often comes to view the clergy with contempt. Undeniably, he is often much brighter than they are. He finds people and books, mostly through unofficial channels. He finds answers, accumulates a wealth of knowledge of the religious life, but cannot put it into practice on his own, and in any case sees no need to do so. The neophyte morphs into a smug "born-again" Christian who thinks he already has one foot in heaven.[379]

Not all those who became disaffected left the Church. Many rallied around more cultured and politically aware priests who were willing to welcome intellectuals. As outsiders within the Church, these parishioners came to an accommodation between their own religious needs and the

379. N. Shemetov, "Pravoslavie v SSSR segodnia. Piat' dialogov", Moscow, Autumn 1976–Winter 1978, typescript, pp. 20, 23, 26. Forschungsstelle Osteuropa an der Universität Bremen, Historisches Archiv, F.01, Vestnik RKhD.

compromised reality of the churchgoing community. On the other hand, priests who were prepared to speak to the intelligentsia on their own terms held a wide spectrum of views on life in the Church and the Church's role in society. As a result, the communities of their followers differed greatly. Even in the early 1980s there was an obvious gulf between churchgoing intellectuals.

Orthodox liberals aimed to replicate in the U.S.S.R. the ideological legacy and practices of Westernised Russian Orthodoxy, like that of the autocephalous Orthodox Church in America and the West-European Eparchy of the Constantinople Patriarchate. These were accepting of other faiths, in particular of the Roman Catholic Church. Their experience could be acquired through direct contact, as representatives of Western Orthodoxy regularly visited the U.S.S.R., particularly Moscow and Leningrad.[380] The corresponding literature was frequently available in these cities, especially the Paris-based *Herald of the Russian Student Christian Movement*, which was distributed in the U.S.S.R.'s major university cities.

The influence of Western liberal Orthodoxy was not a monopoly of the *Herald of the Russian Student Christian Movement*, however. Its spokesmen were virtually all the presenters of religious programmes on Western radio stations broadcasting in Russian, irrespective of their formal religious affiliation. Graduates of the St Sergius Institute in Paris, the ideological centre of European Russian Orthodox liberalism, regardless of which of the Russian Orthodox Churches they belonged to, coordinated their efforts closely, particularly in upholding the rights of believers in the U.S.S.R.

The process of formation within Russia of post-Soviet parishes of the

380. "Zaiavlenie v Preobrazhenskii federal'nyi sud Moskvy sviashchennika Gleba Iakunina po delu 'Bychkov protiv Chaplina'", "Portal-Credo.ru" website, 12 December, 2006; http://www.portal-credo.ru/site/print.php?act=news&id=49990. An important role in spreading liberal Russian Orthodox ideas in the U.S.S.R. was undoubtedly played by certain R.O.C. clergy with European citizenship: Vasiliy (Krivoshein), Metropolitan of Brussels, and Anthony (Bloom), Metropolitan of Sourozh. Metropolitan Anthony not only preached excellent radio sermons but regularly lectured to Orthodox audiences within the U.S.S.R., mainly at the Moscow theological colleges.

"Russian Orthodox Church Outside Russia" was an important event in 1990, and largely drew on fundamentalist groups within the Russian Orthodox Church. Fundamentalist Russian Orthodox intellectuals, as well as fundamentalist ideologists like Father Dmitriy Dudko, for the most part stayed within the R.O.C. and in the following years played an important part in steering the ship of the Church sharply to the right.

The last major group of Orthodox intellectuals were the traditionalists, who were perfectly happy with the way the Church had been run in Soviet times. They condemned any attempt to "politicise" the R.O.C. and involve it in secular matters. Intellectuals who were attracted to the traditionalists, often simple and self-effacing priests, were concerned about their personal salvation, were willingly drawn into the Church community, and accordingly integrated much more readily with the priesthood and monastic life.

The social and political changes taking place in the U.S.S.R. were of great interest to all Orthodox intellectuals. Firstly, they were restoring historical justice and gave hope of a "spiritual renaissance of the nation", a search for the "road back to church", which was understood as a national revival of the Orthodox religion and rituals. Secondly, the changes dramatically raised the social status of Orthodox intellectuals in their professional environment, or at least stopped them being viewed as outsiders. Thirdly, the large-scale influx of educated people into the Church increased the weight and influence of intellectuals in dealing with internal Church issues. The group of Orthodox intelligentsia that managed to attract the greatest number of newcomers would, it was supposed, be best placed to lobby for their view of which internal Church reforms were overdue. Some of the Orthodox intellectuals were undoubtedly hoping to use the changed situation and the influx of people into the Church to realise their own political aims.

The enthusiasm and demands of Orthodox or religiously inclined intellectuals were supported by many democrats. In November 1987, a remarkable document was published under the title of "An Appeal to the Soviet Government to Return to the Church All the Churches in the Soviet Union".

This early demand for the large-scale restitution of Church property (including St Basil's Cathedral, the Kremlin cathedrals, and the Kazan and St Isaac's cathedrals in Leningrad) was signed not only by Russian nationalists who had been political prisoners (Yevgeniy Pashnin, Ivan Cherdyntsev, Rostislav Yevdokimov) but also by leaders of the semi-mythical "free trade unions"[381] like Tatyana Pletnyova, Lev Volokhonsky and the future leader of the Democratic Union, Valeriya Novodvorskaya, who had instigated it; the underground Leningrad socialists Arkadiy and Irina Tsurkov and Aleksandr Skobov; and Yevgeniya Debryanskaya, co-founder of the Democratic Union and future spokeswoman of the Russian lesbian movement.[382]

The Emergence of Christian Associations

The legalisation of Orthodox intellectual associations occurred during 1990. These took three basic forms: Christian socio-political movements and parties, church fellowships and publishing projects.

The creation of Orthodox social and political movements and parties in Russia was not particularly fruitful, despite the widespread public interest in politics and the founding of political parties which mushroomed in the U.S.S.R. in 1989–90.[383] Of the five or six ambitious institutions whose names included the words *Christian* and *Russian*, none made a significant mark in Russian national politics. They paled into insignificance beside the likes of Democratic Russia or the Liberal Democratic Party of Russia, whose legacy continues to this day.

381. The Free Inter-professional Confederation of Workers (S.M.O.T.) was one of the dissident groups of the late 1970s–early 1980s which tried to revive itself in the perestroika period. See Liudmila Alekseeva, *Istoriia inakomysliia v SSSR*. On the revival of trade unions in the late 1980s, see the essay above by Sergey Khramov.
382. "Obrashchenie k sovetskomu pravitel'stvu s predlozheniem vernut' Tserkvi vse khramy na territorii SSSR, 18 November 1987", *Materialy samizdata, Arkhiv samizdata radiostantsii "Svoboda"*, 27 November, 1987, vyp. 44/87, AS No. 6110.
383. This is not true of every part of the former U.S.S.R. In the Baltic republics and Moldavia, the prospects for openly Christian political parties and movements were much better.

The main mistake of those seeking to establish Christian associations, most of whom were Moscow and Leningrad Orthodox intellectuals from the 1970s with experience of dissident politics, was to overestimate the level of support for religious revival among the Soviet intelligentsia generally. Another mistake was their attempt to transplant the Western experience uncritically. The prominence of Christian political parties in Europe gave optimists false hopes of replicating the situation in Russia.

Vitaliy (Utkin), head of Religious Education and Catechesis of the Ryazan diocese, in early 2006 posted on an Internet forum the details of how he had come to the Church. It had begun when, as a student at the Krupskaya State Pedagogical Institute in Moscow, he had attended a seminar conducted by Deacon Oleg Stenyayev, an active sympathiser and later member of the Russian Orthodox Church Outside Russia:

> One day, Father Oleg said, "Okay guys, let's go and preach on the Arbat!" At the time, the Arbat was a free speech zone for everyone. "Wow!" we responded. "How do you preach?" "It's easy," Father Oleg replied. "You just stand and listen to me. People will see you and they'll come over too." That's exactly what we did. Father Oleg was in a cassock (with an anorak on top), found a good pitch, and we gathered round. He took a Bible and started reading. Today it is difficult to believe how quickly people gathered. Father Oleg really worked the crowd. We "preached" like that for a couple of weeks, and then some Baptist alerted his lot that there were priests preaching on the Arbat. Baptists with guitars appeared. Father Oleg immediately went over to debate with them. We started attracting even larger crowds. One day in February 1990, Father Oleg said, "The Communists are allowing a large demonstration for the first time. Everybody will be there. We need to make posters and be there too." We got hold of a few bedsheets and made two banners: "After the Bolsheviks fall, only a tsar will save Russia from new Party slavery!" and "A public holiday to commemorate the New Martyrs of Russia!"

(It was New Martyrs' Day by the calendar of the Russian Orthodox Church Outside Russia.)

That Sunday morning we met at the Artists' Club. More and more people came. Father Oleg, as always, preached and we stood and listened. Suddenly we realised that, for quite some time, tens of thousands of people had been crossing the Crimean Bridge. We raised our banners and marched with them. If anyone is interested, I can bring a photo from the monastery of us marching with our banners and various onlookers reading them. Their expressions . . . Oh, dear! A year earlier, just a few months after leaving the Communist Party, I had been baptised in the Church of the Archangel Michael across from the new building of our university by South-west metro station. That's how I became an Orthodox Christian.[384]

The future Father Vitaliy combined involvement in his Christian society with active membership of the Confederation of Anarcho-Syndicalists, which at that time was one of the largest organisations of political noncon-formists. Its leading lights were graduates of the Krupskaya Pedagogical Institute.[385]

The numbers participating in the religious revival movement were small and tended to disagree among themselves. In 1990 they were, in any case, preoccupied with opening churches and all the other ecclesiastical activities they had been dreaming of for years. The "Christian politics" associations remained marginal, numbering several dozen or, at best, a couple of hundred active members. The leaders of these groups went on to consider-ably greater personal success. Several of the most active members of the Russian Christian Democrat Movement were elected to the R.S.F.S.R. Supreme Soviet and the Moscow City Council in 1990. As a member (and

384. monk_vitaliy. Byloe ;););) i dumy ;););) (iz ryazanskikh razgovorov), "Live Journal" website, 14 January, 2006; http://www.livejournal.com/users/monk_vitaliy [Website now purged – tr.]   385. Ibid.

now the historian) of the movement, Aleksandr Shchipkov recalls that they wisely kept all mention of "Christian Democracy" out of their campaigning. Another Christian Democrat, Aleksandr Ogorodnikov, did identify himself as a Christian Democrat and failed to be elected in that or any subsequent election.[386] Another leader of a 1990 dwarf party called the Russian Christian Democratic Party spent many years in the wilderness before resurfacing in an electoral bloc in 1999. Aleksandr Chuyev subsequently became Chairman of the subcommittee on relations with religious organisations of the State Duma (1999-2003).

Some Orthodox politicians in the provinces were more successful. Wilhelm Fast (1936–2005) became a people's deputy of the Tomsk Provincial Soviet. He was the elder brother of Father Gennadiy (Fast). A mathematician, professor at Tomsk University and one of the leaders of an amateur expedition to study the Tunguska meteorite, he was closely associated with a circle of dissidents in Moscow. In 1981–2 he was one of the main defendants in a major K.G.B. operation involving more than sixty raids in six cities, targeting the production and distribution of (largely religious) *samizdat* in Tomsk. Three of the defendants were convicted and another was sentenced to a term in a mental hospital. Fast and several other defendants avoided the labour camps, but he was sentenced to be dismissed from his teaching post and spent six years working as a yard-sweeper.[387] Under pressure from his family, who all converted to Orthodoxy, he was also baptised in 1989. As his name, Wilhelm, does not figure in the Russian Orthodox Church calendar, he required special permission from the Dean to retain it. By the time of the March 1990 elections, he was

---

386. Aleksandr Shchipkov, "Transformatsiia pochvennicheskikh idei ("Patrioty"). Glavy iz knigi 'Khristianskaia demokratiia v Rossii'", "Religiia i SMI" website, 28 February, 2006; http://www.religare.ru/article26577.htm. Aleksandr Ogorodnikov currently heads a small Orthodox charitable organisation.

387. "Sud nad Chernyshevym, Kovalevskim, Kendelem", *Khronika tekushchikh sobytii*, 65, 31 December, 1982; http://www.memo.ru/history/diss/chr/index.htm; Liudmila Alekseeva, *Istoriia inakomysliia v SSSR*; "V Tomske ego nazyvali pravednikom: O zhiznennom puti izvestnogo uchenogo i pravozashchitnika Vil'gelma Fasta vspominaet ego brat prot. Gennadii Fast", *Kifa*, 3 (30) (2003); http://gazetakifa.ru/content/view/363/

co-chairman of the provincial organisation of Memorial, because of which his manifesto, posted on the Internet by his admirers, reads as a touching and typical example of the spirit of the times with its inclusion of "all things nice". To quote the first four points:

Our manifesto is based on the programmes of the Tomsk People's Movement; of People's Deputy of the U.S.S.R. Stepan Sulakshin; Academician Andrey Sakharov; the Memorial history education society; the Universal Declaration of Human Rights; and other international documents of which the U.S.S.R. is a signatory.

My guide to action is the teaching of the Gospel of Jesus Christ. My authorities are Friedrich Haas ("Hasten to do good"), Albert Schweizer ("Reverence for life"), Archbishop Luka (in the world, surgeon Valentin Voyno-Yasenetsky), Mother Teresa (Charity) and Aleksandr Solzhenitsyn ("Live not by lies").

Spiritual Rebirth. Restore people's original human under-standing of conscience; restore morality; revive, along with charity, chastity, piety, asceticism; teach people to appreciate and protect holiness. The spiritual needs of believers of all faiths in Tomsk (Orthodox, Muslim, Catholic, Baptist etc.), as well as of atheists, should be provided for without equivocation. Mosques, churches and chapels must be returned to their rightful owners.

In the province's educational institutions, the role must be enhanced of ideology-free, humanitarian, environmental, economic, sociological and legal education. At the same time, teaching should be permitted by qualified experts on religion, atheism, Marxism and other doctrines which exclude violence, mutual hatred and hostility. Nobody should be forced to study them.[388]

After 1993, Wilhelm Fast served with distinction for more than ten years as

---

388. "Fast Vil'gel'm Genrikhovich. Kandidat v narodnye deputaty Tomskogo oblastnogo soveta. Okrug No. 66", "Tungusskii fenomen" website; http://tunguska.tsc.ru/ru/science/tv/16/22/

chairman of the province's Commission for the Rehabilitation of Victims of Political Repression. He met and became a friend of Solzhenitsyn, and had a decisive impact on the moral climate in the region. This was partly because he was the head of a family of priests who included not only his brother but also his son and two sons-in-law, who actively worked with the intelligentsia.

Brotherhoods

Brotherhoods, a traditional form of male association of lay members of the Church, ceased to operate openly in the U.S.S.R. in the late 1920s, although they reappeared clandestinely at least from the second half of the 1960s. Officially revived in 1990, they were seen as providing support to the clergy and bishops in missionary and catechetical work, as well as in the restoration of churches and monasteries. From the outset, they included provision in their charters for economic and publishing activity. Sisterhoods existed unofficially throughout the Soviet period, but have never played a significant public or political role beyond providing an "Orthodox funeral bureau", or an association for women unable to decide to become, or as yet undecided about becoming, nuns.[389]

In 1990, the future of brotherhoods was still unclear, although state agencies were registering the constitutions of communities emerging from the underground, and on 12–13 October a founding congress of the Union of Orthodox Brotherhoods was held at the Moscow Cinema Club. The person elected as chairman was Abbot Ioann (Ekonomtsev), a graduate in classical philology of Moscow State University, former staff member of the Soviet Embassy in Greece, former employee of the Institute of World History of the U.S.S.R. Academy of Sciences, writer and playwright. In 1986 he was ordained as a priest, and in 1989 tonsured as a

389. There are currently thirty or forty relatively large sisterhoods in the R.O.C., each with between twenty and forty active members. They carry out many duties, from helping in diocesan administration to working in secular welfare institutions.

monk.[390] This was only the first step for brotherhoods as they moved from being unofficial communities of penniless enthusiasts gathered round a popular priest to the status of officially registered institutions with their own bank accounts and chairmen.

Even at this early stage, however, the brotherhoods were becoming centres of intellectual opposition to the majority in the Church. Although many of them later collapsed or became commercial or quasi-political organisations, some remain active to this day and play an important role in the Church. The best known is the Radonezh Brotherhood, which throughout the 1990s was an advocate of fundamentalism. Yevgeniy Nikiforov, head of the society from its inception, describes it at that time:

> From the outset we were a grassroots society. For example, [in the early 1980s] we wanted to read religious books, and then started publishing them for other people. We established religious *samizdat*. Aleksey Rogozhin, now in charge of Radio Radonezh, somehow managed to publish thousand-page books in print runs of a thousand copies. Yevgeniy Avdeyenko, a Classics scholar and philosopher who taught Ancient Greek, the language of the Eastern Fathers of the Church, founded a study group on patristic literature. Out of that grew a publishing house and grammar schools. When we obtained registration as a cooperative [their first way of becoming "legal" – N.M.], we got the official stamp and were able to sign a contract with the Meridian House of Culture to hold meetings there; the whole of Moscow turned up. Now we have three officially registered schools with their own bank accounts, a radio station, a newspaper, a pilgrimage travel bureau. They, in turn, have offices and branches. Our pilgrimage service recently celebrated its fifteenth anniversary. We held a seminar in Jerusalem for our thirty-five regional offices.[391]

390. Evlogii (Smirnov), *arkhiepiskop, Eto bylo chudo Bozhie. Istoriia vozrozhdeniia Danilova monastyria* (Moscow, 2000), pp. 300–301, 312.
391. Valerii Konovalov, "Tri chasa tishiny v efire", *Trud*, 18 March, 2005.

Another major confederation is the Transfiguration Association of Brotherhoods, which unites the followers of Father Aleksandr Men and the liberal priest Georgiy Kochetkov. It runs its own St Filaret Orthodox Christian College and regularly organises conferences. In the 1990s, it was the main focus for liberal Orthodox clergy and laity.

The Murder of Father Aleksandr Men

On 9 September, 1990 at 6.30 in the morning, on the way from his house to the railway station, Archpriest Aleksandr Men was mortally wounded by an axe blow to the head.[392] His murder had more far-reaching consequences for the Russian Orthodox Church than his killer (or killers) can have anticipated. Not only did the Church lose a charismatic preacher, one of its few personalities familiar to the general public from talks, television appearances and articles, but the churchgoing intelligentsia split irrevocably into liberals and conservatives.[393] Many might demur, however, from the view that his murder put an end to all prospect of missionary activity by the Church among educated non-Christians.

Father Aleksandr Men left behind a great community of people whom he personally had brought to the Church, and a rich literary legacy explaining convincingly to many, although not all, non-believing but thoughtful people why they should believe, and how and what Russian Orthodox Christians believe. That is why his books have been reprinted many times in the past two decades. Over this period, which could hardly have been more favourable for the Church's work, there has been little evidence of similarly successful Christian advocacy.

Who killed Father Aleksandr and why has yet to be established. I

392 Yves Hamant, *Alexander Men: A Witness for Contemporary Russia (A Man of Our Times)*, trans. Steven Bigham (Torrance, CA, 1995); Sergei Bychkov, *Khronika neraskrytogo ubiistva* (Moscow, 1996); Andrei Eremin, *Otets Aleksandr Men'. Pastyr' na rubezhe vekov* (Moscow, 2011); Zoia Maslennikova, *Aleksandr Men'. Zhizn'* (Moscow, 2002); *Pamiati protoiereia Aleksandra Menia* (Moscow, 1991).

393. Some of the latter degenerated into fundamentalists.

personally incline towards the widespread belief that he was murdered by nationalists who probably had links to the fundamentalist wing of the Russian Orthodox Church. In 1990, a presentiment of civil war was deepening in the U.S.S.R. It never came to all-out war, fortunately, but there was no shortage even then of people who considered themselves "urban guerrillas". In May and August 1990, arson attacks destroyed the apartments of Aleksandr Verkhovsky and Vladimir Pribylovsky, two leading figures in the Moscow Information Exchange Bureau, which at that time was the largest research organisation of oppositionists.[394] They unearthed and published information about the Russian nationalists, and shortly before had received threatening anti-Semitic notes through the post. Neither in the years before 1990 nor in the two decades since were these people, who were doing exactly the same work, subjected to the same kind of intimidation. At just this time, in August 1990, the St Petersburg apartments of Nina Katerli and Poel Karp, writers and campaigners against anti-Semitism, were also destroyed by arson. Needless to say, the law enforcement agencies failed to find the culprits.

Aleksandr Men did not just have a lot of people who hated him; he was surrounded by them. Even Archpriest Vsevolod Shpiller, very liberal by the standards of the Russian Orthodox Church and much respected, including by Jews who had converted to Orthodoxy, writes:

> I told [Archpriest Leonid Kishkovsky of the Orthodox Church in America, who visited on 24 May, 1978] that I find him [Father Aleksandr Men] intelligent, interesting, and would long ago have made him an archpriest, but only of an autocephalous Jewish church in Tel Aviv. "Tell me which of your priests you think are interesting . . . " I mentioned Father Valerian Krechetov, the village priest in Akulovo near Moscow, the brother of my deacon. He is not ardent but blazing in his Orthodox faith, but at the same time not a fanatic, intelligent, modest and well educated. Metropolitan

394. *Panorama*, 6 and 10 (1990).

Yuvenaliy recently appointed him to one of the suburban deaneries, and, in my opinion, this will do a great deal for our Church in Moscow. "Men-Men-Men . . ." Father Valerian is his equal in every respect, only also a pure Russian, with all the best traits of the Russian mind and heart.[395]

Today the clergy and laity in the Church of St Nicholas in Kuznetsy, where Father Vsevolod Shpiller was the archpriest, form a dominant group in the Church in Moscow and de facto largely determine the ideological atmosphere within the whole Church. It is institutionalised in the teaching staff of the St Tikhon Humanitarian University, which moved from a conservative (in the 1980s) to a fundamentalist (in the 1990s), and then back to a conservative (in the 2000s) position. In the latter half of the 1990s–early 2000s it was this group which actively opposed the followers and ideological legacy of Aleksandr Men.

Many clergy and Russian Orthodox believers were even more radically opposed to Men and what he stood for. For a long time even in Father Aleksandr's own parish of Novaya Derevnya, the rector, some of the women working at the church, and elderly parishioners were at war with the priest and his noisy young parishioners. One of his close collaborators writes in her memoirs:

The [regent of the Right Choir] spent most of her time writing denunciations, first of Father Aleksandr, believing that he was secretly setting up a "Jewish Choir" [of young Muscovite parishioners whom he grouped together in the Left Choir] and accusing him of intending to create "some sort of Greek or Jewish Church", and then of the church elder who supported him. [At the Trinity-Sergius Monastery, a few kilometres away from the village of Semkhoz, where Father Aleksandr lived, the archpriest of the

395. Otets Vsevolod Shpiller, *Stranitsy zhizni v sokhranivshikhsia pis'makh* (Moscow, 2004), p. 517.

378

church was] supplied with literature of a particular kind. First it was the infamous "Protocols of the Elders of Zion", next a collection of articles by Feliks [Karelin whom, in the first half of the 1960s, Men had known well but who later became a Russian nationalist *samizdat* author] and his friends, who hinted transparently that traditional Orthodoxy was being deliberately undermined by Zionists and Freemason Jews who had wormed their way into the Russian Orthodox Church in the guise of priests and pseudo-theologians and were writing subversive books in order to sabotage it. Their subversion was being printed by anti-Christian Catholics and spread all over Russia in order to subjugate Moscow, the Third Rome, to the Pope.[396]

It is as well to remember that many Russian nationalist writers had dachas in the village of Semkhoz itself.[397]

Shortly after the killing of Father Aleksandr, two murders of prominent Moscow priests followed a similar pattern (and also remain unsolved). On 26 December, one of Father Aleksandr's immediate superiors, Abbot Lazar (Solnyshko), was killed in his own apartment. He was head of the registry of the Moscow diocese. On the night of 1 February, 1991, Abbot Serafim (Shlykov), a monk at the Danilov Monastery, was also killed in his apartment. He had been a member of staff at the Russian Ecclesiastical Mission in Jerusalem.[398] In the decades since then, the Russian Orthodox Church has known no comparable murders, let alone a series of this kind.

Publishing Projects

In 1990, the revival of social initiative occasioned by perestroika, the expansion of legal opportunities for self-realisation and entrepreneurship, and

396. Zoia Maslennikova, *Aleksandr Men'. Zhizn'*, p. 188.
397. Ivan Shvetsov, *Tlia. Sokoly* (Moscow, 2000), pp. 412–13, 425.
398. This position would have ensured early consecration as a bishop.

an acute shortage of religious literature provided the right conditions for a rapid growth of Orthodox publishing. Almost every brotherhood and many private entrepreneurs, often with their own religious and political agendas, tried to move into publishing and distributing the printed word. It was a quick and reliable way of accumulating primary capital but also a welcome opportunity for Christian intellectuals to apply themselves, after years of semi-underground writing, translating and publishing (in minute print runs) of books which mattered to them.

We have already mentioned the success of the Radonezh Brotherhood, which started as an underground publisher and grew into an organisation with a sizeable media company. This is much the way in which the R.O.C.'s largest media enterprise, the *Orthodox Encyclopedia*, came into existence. The project was directed by Sergey Kravets, a member of a semi-legal society centred around the Moscow philosopher Aleksey Losev. It existed in the 1960s–80s and attracted intellectuals who, in religious terms, were predominantly conservative. In 1988–90, Kravets edited *Literary Studies* (*Literaturnaya uchoba*). He recalls,

In 1990, I was offered a Humboldt Fellowship. At the time, my wife and I were really counting the kopecks for milk and bread. It was a fantastic offer: three years in Germany with a scholarship of DM 8,000 to study the archive of the Russian religious philosopher Semyon Frank. Brilliant! We got ready to leave and dropped in on our good friend, Father Andronik [Trubachov] at the Trinity-Sergius Monastery. He had just been appointed Abbot of the Valaam Monastery. He suddenly said, "You shouldn't be going off anywhere. You need to stay to work here. We have an opportunity to create something we could only dream of for years: an academic Orthodox publishing house. We will be able to publish Pavel Florensky, Vladimir Solovyov!" We decided to stay. Right there and then, in the office of *Literary Studies* in the spring of 1990, we set up the Valaam Monastery publishing house. Then we had the idea of bringing out a complete, eleven-volume history of the Russian Church, based on the work of Metropolitan Makariy (Bulgakov), with new commentary and brought up to date from the mid-seventeeth century to the present by our own team. We invited secular scholars from the Academy of Sciences, and these authors are with us to the present day, at the core of our endeavours.[399]

Another of Losev's students, but more inclined to liberalism, was Sergey Averintsev, a People's Deputy of the U.S.S.R. and member of the Academy of Sciences. He became President of the Bible Society of the U.S.S.R., registered in January 1990 under the auspices of the Soviet Charity and Health Foundation. This quiet society, barely noticed by the media, created in the image and likeness of the Bible societies that exist in most other countries, retains to this day a virtual monopoly on the printing and distribution of Bibles in Russian for the needs of all of the country's Christian communities. It also assists international Christian institutions to translate the Bible, in whole or in part, into the languages of the former U.S.S.R. In 1990–91, Bible Societies were formed in Latvia, Armenia, Moldavia, and Ukraine and began to be created in Georgia, Byelorussia, Estonia and Lithuania.[400] The creation of the society did, however, deprive some of the leaders of the Russian Orthodox Church of a source of substantial income, derived from reselling editions of the Bible freely donated by Western Christian organisations. Accordingly, when in February 1990 at a meeting with bishops, Lukianov, the Chairman of the U.S.S.R. Supreme Soviet and by now effectively the second most powerful figure in the Church, asked Metropolitan Filaret (Denisenko) of Kiev for his opinion of Averintsev, he was told, "Oh, he's a very dangerous man. He is getting involved in matters which are none of his business. He should be getting on with

399. Valeriy Konovalov, "Entsiklopedist", *Izvestiia*, 3 April, 2003; http://www.peoples.ru/state/citizen/kravets/. Kravets states there that the Orthodox Encyclopedia publishing company is registered as a division of the Synod.
400. *Moskovskii tserkovnyi vestnik*, 21 (1991).

his philosophy and researches into philology and art history instead of trying his luck with this Bible Society. We were in talks about organising, cooperating, and jointly publishing the Bible and suddenly we are faced with this society. The Church's representation there is now in the hands of dissidents. It is very odd that Kharchev is in there with them."[401]

The Situation in Ukraine

In 1990, the Russian Orthodox Church was not only opening new parishes but also losing some it already had. At the beginning of the year there were a total of 10,100. This rose by mid-September to almost twelve thousand. By 1 January, 1991, the number had fallen to ten thousand, a net loss on the year of a hundred.[402] This was a serious setback from which the Church has not fully recovered to this day. The loss resulted from a massive crisis.

Legalisation of the Ukrainian Greek-Catholic Church

The crisis that developed in the Orthodox dioceses of Western and, to some extent, Central Ukraine in 1990 did not come as a complete surprise to the Church hierarchy, although the Moscow Patriarchate could hardly have anticipated its scale.

The Ukrainian Greek Catholic Church, commonly known as the Uniate Church, had been swallowed by the Russian Orthodox Church in 1946–9. In 1989 it forcefully reminded the world of its continuing existence. In the post-war decades, the population of Galicia and Transcarpathia was considered nominally Orthodox, although bishops, priests and monastics of the Ukrainian Greek Catholic Church lived and actively ministered there in

401. "Tserkov', kotoraia vsegda privykla doveriat' vlasti ...", *Ukrainskaia greko-katolicheskaia tserkov': preodolenie mifa. Materialy seminara* (Moscow, 2002), pp. 147–8; http://religion.gif.ru. For a full transcript of the meeting, see Rossiiskii gosudarstvennyi arkhiv sotsial'no-politicheskoi istorii, F. 89, Per. 8, Dok. 41.
402. Nathaniel Davis, *A Long Walk to the Church*, pp. 75, 87.
403. For details, see Nikolai Mitrokhin, "Khudshee, konechno, vperedi ..."; Mitrokhin,

secret. Many "Orthodox" priests in the region were covert Greek Catholics, and their parishioners had no wish to repudiate the Uniate rites.[403]

Legalisation of some of the Uniate clergy occurred early in 1989. Huge rallies in support, numbered in tens of thousands, took place during the summer in cities across the region. In the autumn of 1989, the Uniate Church regained its first church, in the capital of Ukrainian nationalism, Lvov. They wrested it from the Russian Orthodox Church, which denied the Uniates any right to exist, whether at a local level or indeed as a Church.[404] From 1 December, 1989, the state authorities were officially registering Greek Catholic communities.

Two aspects of the problem need to be borne in mind. First, the Greek Catholics laid claim only to buildings they had owned prior to 1946. The problem for the Russian Orthodox Church was that it had not built (and had not been allowed to build) a single church in Galicia since 1946 at its own expense. Moreover, during 1988–9, the Ukrainian S.S.R. authorities had handed over to it some eight hundred formerly Greek Catholic churches in the region which were unoccupied or had been used during the Soviet era for other purposes.[405] Second, despite the hundreds of conflicts over restitution of church property in 1989–93, most communities in the region made their choice entirely voluntarily between the Uniate Church and the several varieties of Orthodoxy on offer in Ukraine.

The reluctance of the Russian Orthodox Church to negotiate with the Uniate Church in 1988–9 certainly exacerbated the conflict, and in late 1989 caused it to spill over into violence in the streets. In many cases, where a battle was taking place in a particular parish over a church, it was the Russ-

"Russkaia pravoslavnaia tserkov' i greko-katoliki na Zapadnoi Ukraine", *Otechestvennye zapiski*, 7 (2002), pp. 381–93; http://magazines.russ.ru/oz/2002/7/2002_07_46.html
404. In the summer of 1989, Metropolitan Filaret (Denisenko) of Kiev described the U.G.C.C. as "an insignificant group of Uniates" and declared that "the Greek-Catholic Eastern Rite Church has not existed in Ukraine for more than forty years". See "Dva mneniia o sobytii, kotoroe proizoshlo 43 goda nazad", *Moskovskie novosti*, 30 July, 1989.
405. Viktor Elenskii, "Ukraina: Tserkov' i politika v posttotalitarnom sotsiume", *Logos*, 50 (1995), p. 158.

ian Orthodox believers who lost. At the end of January 1990, a hastily convened Council of Russian Orthodox Bishops noted instances in which Russian Orthodox congregations had been expelled from churches, but acknowledged that "Eastern-rite Catholics, like all citizens of our country who profess a religion, should enjoy equal rights, including the right to open and legal profession of their faith."[406]

In fact, many churches in Galicia and Transcarpathia remained Orthodox. A movement to repudiate the union with the Vatican had become fairly widespread in the Western Ukraine between the wars. Additionally, after the Second World War a substantial number of Orthodox Ukrainians had been deported to the region from Poland and now regarded all Catholics as enemies. As the decades had passed, many Galicians and Transcarpathians had grown used to being Orthodox and saw no reason to repudiate their new religious identity.

As a result, Orthodoxy in Western Ukraine has to this day retained a substantial measure of support. The ratio of Greek Catholic to Orthodox congregations in Galicia on 1 January, 2004 was approximately 6:4, with 2,875 Uniate parishes to 1,807 Orthodox.[407] Admittedly, the vast majority of these Orthodox Christians decline to recognise the authority of the Moscow Patriarchate or to consider themselves members of "the Russian Church".

The Ukrainian Autocephalous Orthodox Church

Another crack in the Russian Orthodox Church, which became visible in 1989 but rapidly grew wider in 1990, saw the creation of a Ukrainian Autocephalous Orthodox Church (U.A.O.C). An institution of that name had existed in the 1920s and was restored under the German occupation in the

406. "Iz opredelenii Arkhiereiskogo sobora", *Zhurnal Moskovskoi Patriarkhii*, 5 (1990), p. 7.
407. Calculated from statistics of the State Committee for Religious Affairs of Ukraine, published in *Lyudina i svit*, 1 (2004), pp. 30–31. At that time, the number of Orthodox parishes in Galicia acknowledging allegiance to the Moscow Patriarchate was half as many again as in the Byelorussian Exarchate or the Moldovan Orthodox Church.

early 1940s, but thereafter existed in the form of marginal religious groups in the Ukrainian diaspora in the West.

The concept of an anti-Moscow, pro-Ukrainian Orthodoxy neverthe-less persisted also in the Ukrainian Soviet Socialist Republic. On 15 Febru-ary, 1989, a group of Kievan intellectuals organised a committee to revive the Autocephalous Church. On 19 August of that year, the major Lvov parish of Sts Peter and Paul, headed by the most influential priest in the diocese, Archpriest Vasiliy Yarema, declared itself autocephalous. That is considered the date of the refounding of the Ukrainian Autocephalous Orthodox Church. In the course of the following two months, dozens of parishes in Galicia, as well as in neighbouring Volhynia, joined the nascent Church. In early October 1989, the Church was joined by Bishop Ioann (Bodnarchuk), who had resigned shortly before from the Moscow Patriar-chate and immediately became head of the re-established Church.

In 1990, then, Western Ukraine entered the furnace of awakening national feelings, both political and religious. Every month, hundreds more parishes switched their religious allegiance, split and fought for control of church buildings. Local authorities, under the windows of whose offices meetings attended by tens or even hundreds of thousands of people were being held in the winter of 1989/90, recognised the way the wind was blow-ing and began actively supporting the Greek Catholic and Autocephalous Churches' registration of their new acquisitions.[408] Elections to local and republican institutions in March 1990, which were won by the democratic-nationalist People's Movement of Ukraine, helped to mollify political passions. The hold of the Soviet regime and Moscow's influence in Western Ukraine were effectively at an end. This, of course, greatly accelerated the breaking away from the Russian Orthodox Church of parishes and whole rural deaneries, as well as the institutional entrenchment of the "schismatics" and the spreading of their influence to almost every other part of Ukraine.

---

408. The January 1990 Council of R.O.C. Bishops expressed its surprise at the transfer by local authorities of the functioning Russian Orthodox cathedral in Ivano-Frankovsk to supporters of the U.G.C.C.

In March 1990, Ioann (Bodnarchuk), as Primate of the Autocephalous Church, performed his first consecration of a bishop. On 5–6 June, a National Council of the Ukrainian Autocephalous Orthodox Church took place in Kiev at which Metropolitan Mstislav (Skrypnik), who had lived in the U.S. and been consecrated in the Church back in the 1940s, was elected Patriarch. In August 1990, the U.A.O.C. appointed a bishop for Kiev, finally moving outside the area where it really did have massive support. In October, the Council for Religious Affairs of the Ukrainian S.S.R. registered the U.A.O.C.'s charter, thereby officially recognising it. Metropolitan Mstislav (Skrypnik) then returned to Ukraine for the first time. On 1 December, a council of bishops of the U.A.O.C. assembled in Kiev, set up its permanent administrative headquarters there and gained a material institutional presence.

Earlier agreements negotiated by the Russian Orthodox Church with the U.S.S.R. and republican authorities and, indeed, with the Vatican, had no force in Galicia and Volhynia. The new Ukrainian authorities, reflecting the interests of a majority of the population, saw the Moscow Patriarchate as the accomplice of an occupying power, not a "source of spiritual guidance". To tell the truth, senior figures in the Moscow Patriarchate conceded as much themselves, but only in secret interviews with the U.S.S.R.'s political leadership:

> Orthodox believers are dismayed by this attitude. We believe we have served loyally and for that seem now no longer to be wanted. It seems to be the Catholics of the Eastern Rite who are wanted now. At the Council, the question was raised of how we should view the Board of Religious Affairs. Can it control what is happening? Can we trust it? Is it capable of applying the existing laws of our country or not? And what approach is being taken by the local authorities, from the secretaries of provincial committees of the Communist Party to chairmen of district executive soviets in these three regions of Lvov, Ivano-Frankovsk and Ternopol?[409]

409. "Tserkov', kotoraia privykla vsegda doveriat' vlasti ...", pp. 144–5.

The leaders of the U.S.S.R. frankly did not know what to do. In any case, against a background of developing "hot" inter-ethnic conflicts and the overall crisis engulfing the Soviet system, the issue of Church unity was plainly not a top priority. The Vatican, which on principle opposed violence, was not going to assume responsibility for the actions of a Greek Catholic Church over which it had virtually no control. On the other hand, neither was it prepared to condemn its followers and effectively come down against them on the side of the Russian Orthodox Church.[410] One group of Russian Orthodox bishops in Western Ukraine, only too aware of the scale of popular discontent, was packing its bags with the intention of moving to a see in a more peaceful part of the country, while another was preoccupied with the chances of Metropolitan Filaret (Denisenko) of Kiev becoming the next Patriarch.

Creation of the Ukrainian Orthodox Church (Moscow Patriarchate)

The new Patriarch was obliged to address the Ukrainian problem as a matter of urgency. A plan devised in late 1989 to accord pseudo-autonomous status to Ukrainian Orthodoxy was put into action and the "Ukrainian Exarchate" was transformed in January 1990 into the "Ukrainian Orthodox Church". This was intended to pacify the nationalists in the Church and prevent a split. The leaders of the Russian Orthodox Church saw it as a fiction, a sop which could probably be retracted at a later date. The future head of the Ukrainian Orthodox Church, Metropolitan Vladimir (Sabodan), explained to Anatoliy Lukianov the Holy Synod's thinking behind the Council of Bishops' resolutions:

---

410. Negotiations were regularly conducted with the Vatican. In January 1990, a joint committee was even set up but was overtaken by events. It was, in any case, not taken seriously by the main parties to the conflict. Attempts by the committee to share out churches between the Orthodox and Greek Catholic sides in the spring of 1990 led to the U.G.C.C. representatives walking out in April 1990. They felt little obligation to assist the R.O.C.

At the Council, taking full account of the situation, we changed the structure of the Russian Church. We have created a so-called Ukrainian Orthodox Church within the Exarchate and granted it a charter. They will have their own synod, so we are showing that Moscow is granting them full autonomy within the framework of the Russian Church without their having to break away. The aim is to paralyse this new movement. The new provision for the Exarchate and our attempt to respond to their national aspirations without destroying the structure of the Russian Church will, we hope, enable us to win some of these people over to our side when we introduce the new charter.[411]

At the same meeting, Metropolitan Yuvenaliy (Poyarkov) of Krutitsy and Kolomna (now a permanent member of the Holy Synod), put it even more clearly:

We have created exarchates in the Church, calling them the Ukrainian Orthodox Church and the Byelorussian Orthodox Church. We have granted these exarchates certain rights which allow them independence in matters of no fundamental importance. As far as policy is concerned, everything comes back to the Patriarchate and the Synod. Not a single policy decision can be taken by the synod of the exarchate. They can do this and that, but the final decision rests with Moscow and they cannot say, "The Synod has passed a resolution but we are not going to apply it in our exarchate."[412]

The fictitious nature of this "independence" was, however, equally obvious to Ukrainian believers, who were not unduly impressed by the creation of the "Ukrainian Orthodox Church". Only in the summer of 1990, after the election of the new Patriarch and an appeal from the U.O.C. bishops to the Synod, was this part of the R.O.C. offered a new status. The Ukrainian

411. "Tserkov', kotoraia vsegda privykla doveriat' vlasti ...", p. 147.   412. Ibid., p. 148.

Orthodox Church gained full independence in terms of its internal governance and financial management while remaining part of the Russian
Orthodox Church. The Chairman of its synod (the Metropolitan of Kiev)
became an ex officio member of the Holy Synod of the Russian Orthodox
Church.

By the time a Council of Bishops of the R.O.C. was convened on 25–7
October, 1990 to discuss the Ukrainian situation and grant autonomy to the
U.O.C., of the twenty-five hundred or so parishes in Galicia, only some seven
hundred remained in the Russian Orthodox Church.[413] A very large number
of parishes in the Transcarpathian region transferred to the Ukrainian Greek
Catholic Church,[414] while a similar exodus to the Ukrainian Autocephalous
Orthodox Church occurred in the Volhynia and Kiev regions. Even the
proclamation by Patriarch Aleksiy II of the edict granting autonomy to
the Ukrainian Orthodox Church in St Sophia's Cathedral in Kiev was accompanied by mass protests by supporters of the Ukrainian Autocephalous
Orthodox Church and the Ukrainian Greek Catholic Church.

The autonomous status granted to the Ukrainian Orthodox Church
was a compromise between the wish of some Orthodox believers, mainly in
southern and eastern provinces of Ukraine and in Transcarpathia, to
remain within the "Russian Church" and the determination of many
priests and laity (particularly in Galicia and Volhynia) to make the Ukrainian Church "autocephalous", with full canonical independence. The
Moscow Patriarchate failed to satisfy the latter, and, two years later,
many of them supported the Metropolitan of Kiev, Filaret (Denisenko),
when he decided to establish yet another Ukrainian Orthodox Church fully

413. Nathaniel Davis, A Long Walk to the Church, pp. 87–8. Even these statistics were out of
date, because parishes which had in fact left the R.O.C. had not yet been re-registered as
affiliated to other churches.
414. Specifically, in the Mukachevo diocese of Transcarpathia which, although formally in
the U.G.C.C., was in fact directly subordinate to the See of Rome. The Transcarpathians
resented any suggestion of Galician primacy, including in religious matters. Most of the
support for the U.A.O.C., and subsequently the Ukrainian Orthodox Church (Kievan Patriarchate), came from Galician parishes, which ruled out the possibility of significant
support in Transcarpathia.

independent of Moscow. Its bedrock was the disgruntled parishes of Galicia, where the Russian Orthodox Church lost the last vestiges of its influence.[415] To a lesser extent this was also true of the Volhynia and Kiev regions.

In 1990, saving the parishes of Galicia for the Russian Orthodox Church was a hopeless task. This reality had to be recognised in the first days of the patriarchate of Aleksiy II, and was evidently something of a "birth trauma" for his entire administration. The blame was pinned squarely on the Vatican and on Metropolitan Filaret (Denisenko) personally. Any mention in the last two decades of contacts with the Vatican or of the Ukrainian Orthodox Church (Kievan Patriarchate), which Metropolitan Filaret currently heads, has been accompanied by reproaches against them for plundering the Western Ukrainian dioceses and perpetrating a schism.

The Ukrainian Autocephalous Orthodox Church has not flourished. After numerous splits, mergers and perpetual changes of leadership, at the time of writing it continues as two warring synods, which between them represent only a few hundred parishes. Most of the parishes that initially transferred to it are today under the jurisdiction of the Ukrainian Orthodox Church (Kievan Patriarchate).

For the Russian Orthodox Church, the main event of 1990 was unquestionably the election of a new Patriarch. This is not because it marked the beginning of a new era in the life of the Church. Its significance was more in the fact that Aleksiy II, elected in a reasonably democratic way, affirmed that the Church should adhere in its internal management to the policies and procedures of his predecessor, Aleksiy I, during the most authoritarian period of Soviet rule, and perhaps of Russian history. No less important is the fact that Aleksiy II's decision accorded with the mood of other leaders of the Church, as the election itself showed. Cliques and personalities

415. There are currently still some two hundred parishes in Galicia owing allegiance to the Moscow Patriarchate, mainly in the Pochayiv Lavra region. However, many priests there are nervous of informing their parishioners of their canonical subordination to Moscow and omit mention of the Patriarch of Moscow in the liturgy. See Nikolai Mitrokhin, "Khudshee, konechno, vperedi ..."

rather than programmes had been contending. If society at large was seeking to change and introduce open competition between differing views of what the future should hold, believing that was key to effective progress, the Church, or at least its senior clergy, chose to move in the opposite direction.

By and large, Russian Orthodox believers, the clergy and most of the laity, supported the bishops' position. Their authoritarian approach appealed to the *babushki* who filled the churches, many of whom had been members of the Young Communist League in the 1920s–40s. Where their interests were challenged, these redoubtable old women were well able to stand up for themselves. They were not much bothered about K.G.B. infiltration of the clergy. Their favourite priest could, to exaggerate only a little, swagger around with a holster on his belt without risk of falling out with them.

Anti-Communist intellectuals among the laity or the clergy were an insignificant if active minority within the Church, and barely noticeable outside large cities. They most certainly were opposed to the Church's authoritarian style of government and eager to see it purged of priests who had been overly willing to collaborate with the regime during the Soviet period. Their opinion counted for little. In 1990, the Church authorities at best allowed them a little scope, particularly in areas where it knew there was a shortage of talent: politics, public outreach, diaconal work (giving practical help to the orphaned and needy), journalism and publishing.

The reality of the next two decades has seen Orthodox intellectuals realising only a modest part of their aspirations. It has not so much been the Church leaders' authoritarian style to blame for this, although that undermines personal motivation to work for the Church, as the modest intellectual, organisational and financial resources of the intelligentsia, combined with their extreme politicisation and often unjustified sense of grievance. To this must be added the fact that the intelligentsia in the Russian Orthodox Church is split. The spilling of the blood of Father Aleksandr Men in 1990 permanently alienated his relatively few liberal followers from the nationalistically, monarchistically and often anti-Semitically-minded majority of Russian Orthodox intellectuals.

The majority in the Church were meanwhile preoccupied with material matters, many involved in building or rebuilding a cathedral not in their souls but in the real world. A pressing need to reopen or build new churches to meet the needs of believers, or to provide monasteries for the few thousand people who for years had longed but been unable to become monks, began to be satisfied only in 1990. This, however, increased the Church's urge to restore as many of the churches and monasteries which had existed in the Russian empire before the 1917 Revolution as possible. The desire to avenge all the years of oppression, and not infrequently to stake out territory, obsessed ordinary believers and priests alike. Loving a church building for itself, as something which took priority in the minds of priests over the parishioners occupying it, was something new in Russian Orthodoxy. Such issues as the existence and restoration of thousands of church buildings for which there was no congregation, or the need to seize churches from thousands of congregations which were breaking away from it, had never previously been faced by the Russian Orthodox Church. Riding the wave of the religious resurgence, farming out to churchgoing intellectuals the work of catechesis and missionary activity, the clergy quite simply forgot the need to attract and, even more importantly to retain, their flock.

Investing all the Church's resources, material, logistical and moral, in an expensive programme of construction and restoration which began in 1990 set the Church's priorities for the next two decades. Over-hasty investment in restoring churches in Galicia just a few months before their congregations broke away in schisms should have been a hard lesson, but it did not hit home. The schism in Ukraine, or at least its extent, was only one of the disasters the Church in 1990 could have minimised, even if it could not have prevented it. The staunchly pro-Kremlin line and disagreeable personality, not only to parishioners but also to the clergy, of the head of the Kievan Exarchate as well as of some of the region's bishops served to radicalise the Greek Catholic majority, as well as Orthodox parishes which had no time for the Moscow Patriarchate. If, at the very beginning of 1990, it should have been possible for the Ukrainian Greek Catholic Church and the Moscow Patriarchate to come to a relatively amicable agreement on dividing revenues and property between them, after the victory of the national democrats in regional elections everything began to go seriously wrong for the Russian Orthodox Church. As a result, it lost not only everything the Greek Catholics wanted but also its standing in the region, which led to the bizarre schism in 1992 when Metropolitan Filaret (Denisenko) broke away from the Moscow Patriarchate, taking with him precisely the parishes he had been fighting on behalf of that patriarchate to keep under its control.

The year 1990 was one of missed opportunities for the Russian Orthodox Church. It proceeded along lines laid down in the preceding decades of its history. Whereas society was conscious of an imperative to change and reform itself, the Church, seeing itself as a much wronged victim, became even more convinced of its own own righteousness and felt no inclination to learn lessons from history. It chose not to appeal over the heads of its leaders, not to reform itself even in the spirit of the General Council of 1988, and is now harvesting the fruits of that decision.

How those fruits taste is for each member of the Church to decide for themselves.

OCTOBER

1 October

The Russian S.F.S.R. plans to start implementing the 500 Days plan on 1 October, and in the morning Mikhail Bocharov, Chairman of the R.S.F.S.R. Supreme Economic Council, announces on television that the countdown of days has begun. That evening, however, R.S.F.S.R. Prime Minister Ivan Silayev says on *Time* (*Vremya*) that it will start on 1 November, claiming that the U.S.S.R. Supreme Soviet has been unable to decide which of the (by now, three) programmes to choose. Ruslan Khasbulatov, Chairman of the R.S.F.S.R. Supreme Soviet, declares, "Whatever happens, we shall implement the Shatalin–Yavlinsky programme from 1 November. That is the final deadline" (*Izvestiia*, 274. p. 1).

3 October

Germany is proclaimed a unified state (*Izvestiia*, 275, p. 1).

4 October

A parliamentary commission is set up by the R.S.F.S.R. Supreme Soviet to enquire into publication of materials in *Pravda* and *Soviet Russia* on 26 and 27 September which alleged that democratic forces were preparing a "counter-revolutionary *coup d'état*" and "power grab" (*Izvestiia*, 276, p. 3).

Mandarin oranges go on sale in Moscow, but the price is also exotic at 15 roubles per kilo (*Moskovskii komsomolets*, 228, p. 1).

5 October

A presidential decree on "Urgent measures for transition to a market economy" proposes, firstly, "Transition to widespread use in the economy of negotiated wholesale prices", but then adds, "In order to prevent unjustified rises in the price of industrial and technological products, a maximum profit level will be introduced. All profit in excess of this will be transferred in equal proportions to the U.S.S.R. and republican budgets."

7 October

Aleksandr Solzhenitsyn proposes renaming Leningrad Nevograd, after the River Neva which flows through the city. In May 1991, on the eve of the referendum about changing the name, Solzhenitsyn next proposes St Petrograd (*Svyato-Petrograd*). The author's abiding dislike of the name St Petersburg, Sankt-Peterburg in Russian, had to do with his belief that it had been coined during the reign of Peter the Great by officials of German descent.

9 October

A U.S.S.R. law, "Concerning freedom of conscience and religious organisations", is published. It is a revolutionary measure and provides legal guarantees, making possible the existence of wholly legitimate religious communities in the U.S.S.R. Religious organisations are henceforth free to publish and to engage in economic activity (Arkadii Stoliar, "Gosudarstvo i Tserkov': po zakonu i 'na samom dele'", *Otechestvennye zapiski*, 1 [2001]; http://magazines.russ.ru/oz/2001/1/stol.html).

The prospects for implementing the Shatalin–Yavlinsky plan are discussed at a session of the R.S.F.S.R. Supreme Soviet. From an interview given by Grigoriy Yavlinsky:

> A centralised price reform has evidently been started. As a result, on a U.S.S.R.-wide basis, before a choice has been made of a plan for transition to a market economy, the decision has been taken to introduce "negotiated" wholesale prices between suppliers and customers on the basis of price lists which the U.S.S.R. State Committee on Prices has just drawn up. Furthermore, there is a limit on the permissible level of profit. We foresee that prices will

not be mobile and flexible, just very high. The stabilisation plan built into the 500 Days project was designed to ensure a reasonable standard of living and stable prices on over 150 goods and services needed for everyday living. It has just been made unrealisable. It will now be impossible to keep these prices down. I would like to emphasise that the difficult times we now face will be a direct result of decisions taken in accordance with the U.S.S.R. government's plan (*Izvestiia*, 282, pp. 1–2).

9–11 October

Economic and national policy is discussed at a plenum of the Central Committee of the C.P.S.U. Political analysts see its outcome as evidence of the growing influence of revanchist, neo-Soviet forces in the Central Committee and U.S.S.R. leadership. Presidential decrees having the status of law are being prepared without public participation and made known only after they have come into effect.

Analysts believed that Gorbachev had been unable since the summer to continue his policy of "splendid isolation". Economic counter-reforms and an abrupt worsening of relations with the Russian republic had considerably undermined the President's relations with the Left, most of whom supported Russian republican policy. Some believed this apparent reconciliation with the right-wingers was an inevitable consequence of his confrontational policies of the preceding three weeks (Maksim Sokolov, "Oktiabr'skii plenum: Mikhail Gorbachev vystupil kak General'nyi sekretar' TsK KPSS", *Kommersant*, 40 [15 October]).

12 October

At the hearing in the trial of Konstantin Smirnov-Ostashvili, the police are unable to cope with "national patriots" who unfurl banners with anti-Semitic slogans in the courtroom and hold up placards insulting the judges. The culmination is a rally of Smirnov-Ostashvili's supporters at the entrance to the Moscow City Court, at which it is declared that "this kangaroo court will result in civil war!" (*Izvestiia*, 284, p. 3).

The first issue of a weekly magazine titled *Hobbies* appears. The editors state that the new publication is "a newspaper for the soul": "We have had enough of politics, the battling of parties, leaders and movements. There is another life: everyday human life with its joys and interests. *Hobbies* is a newspaper for anglers, mushroom pickers, pet lovers, collectors, flower arrangers and gardeners – in short, for anyone who has a hobby in their spare time. Price: 6 kopecks" (*Izvestiia*, 284, p. 7).

13 October

A presidential decree is published "Concerning measures to uphold the inviolability of property rights in the U.S.S.R." (*Izvestiia*, 285, p. 1). Its objective is to counter the leaders of the R.S.F.S.R. and other Soviet republics who are seeking to take control of U.S.S.R. property. Another objective is to safeguard property which the C.P.S.U. had acquired at various times (Rudol'f Pikhoia, "Spory khoziastvuiushchikh sub"ektov", *Moskovskie novosti*, 27 [2003]).

15 October

It is announced in Oslo that the Nobel Peace Prize has been awarded to Mikhail Gorbachev, President of the U.S.S.R. (*Izvestiia*, 288, p. 1). The Nobel committee praises his contribution to the reunification of Germany, perestroika and beginning the process of disarmament.

16 October

A U.S.S.R. law "Concerning public associations" (*Izvestiia*, 288, p. 1) prohibits funding by the state of political parties and mass movements pursuing political goals, except for the financing of election campaigns in accordance with electoral law (Sergei Posudin, "Normativno-pravovoe regulirovanie deiatel'nosti politicheskikh partii v postsovetskoi Rossii", http://zhurnal.lib.ru/p/posudin_sergej_wladimirowich).

A presidential decree "Concerning the status of higher education institutions" states, "On application, higher education institutions will be granted the status of self-governing (autonomous) organisations, operating under their own charters, drafted in accordance with the laws of the U.S.S.R. and union republics" (*Izvestiia*, 288, p. 2).

At a session of the R.S.F.S.R. Supreme Soviet, Boris Yeltsin says of national economic reform: "When it is absolutely clear that the latest plan proposed is going to fall flat, the Russian republic must be ready to implement its own plan of economic stabilisation and transition to a free market. Perhaps by then not in five hundred days, but within whichever time limit our people will allow" (*Izvestiia*, 289, p. 2).

17 October

Grigoriy Yavlinsky informs the R.S.F.S.R. Supreme Soviet of his intention to resign as Deputy Prime Minister. The economic plan supported by the R.S.F.S.R. Supreme Soviet, representatives of the workers' movement and Western experts as an integral package to stabilise the economy and rescue the country from crisis can no longer be implemented because of increasing disintegration of the economy. This resulted from collapse of the Soviet system of under-the-counter bargaining and the increasing autonomy of union republics, which were implementing their own economic plans (*Izvestiia*, 290, p. 2).

19 October

Twenty-two members of the Warsaw Pact and N.A.T.O. sign a Treaty on Conventional Armed Forces in Europe, roughly equalising the overall armed forces of the two blocs.

A meeting of the leaders of the U.S.S.R. State Security Committee discusses measures to be taken by the K.G.B. to intensify the fight against organised crime. Vladimir Kryuchkov, Chairman of the committee, notes that material wealth and financial resources amounting to many billions of dollars are concealed in the shadow economy (*Moskovskii komsomolets*, 241, p. 1). The U.S.S.R.'s shadow economy was experiencing rapid growth in

1990, but already in the 1960s and 1970s had been inextricably linked to Party and governmental bodies. It became one of the most important elements of the entire national economy (Simon Kordonskii, "Stsenarii igrek, ili gipoteza o rukovodiashchei roli partii v 90-e gody", *Vek XX i mir*, 3; http://old.russ.ru:8080/antolog/vek/1990/3/kordon.htm).

From 19 to 29 October, an art fair is held at the Central Artists' Club on the Crimean Embankment, Moscow. Twenty-one Soviet galleries display modern "saleable" Soviet art (*Moskovskie novosti*, 42, p. 14).

20 October

The founding congress of the Democratic Russia movement is held in Moscow's Rossiya cinema. More than two thousand delegates assemble. The Chairman of the founding committee, Arkadiy Murashev, emphasises that Democratic Russia should be the body focusing all of the republic's progressive forces. It should provide support for the President of the R.S.F.S.R. when, in due course, he is elected (*Izvestiia*, 292, p. 2).

21 October

The Toyota-ASTO Service Centre opens in Moscow, to service Toyota vehicles to the highest international standards (*Izvestiia*, 292, p. 2).

23 October

Mstislav, Patriarch of Kiev and All Ukraine, flies in to Kiev from abroad. He is to head the newly restored Ukrainian Autocephalous Orthodox Church, one of three Ukrainian Orthodox churches in Ukraine (*Izvestiia*, 295, p. 2).

24 October

An underground nuclear explosion of between 20 and 150 kilotons is carried out at the nuclear test site in the Novaya Zemlya islands. This is to confirm the weapon's reliability and "increase the safety of nuclear weapons". Radiation in the test area is normal (*Izvestiia*, 297, p. 6).

26 October

A presidential decree is published "Concerning the introduction of a commercial rate for the rouble against foreign currencies, and measures to create a U.S.S.R.-wide foreign exchange market". From 1 November, 1990, a commercial rate of the rouble against foreign currencies will be introduced, based on the ratio of 1.8 roubles to 1 U.S. dollar (*Izvestiia*, 298, p. 1). In the early 1980s, the rate for the rouble had been set artificially by the U.S.S.R. State Bank at approximately 0.6 rubles per U.S. dollar. At that time, the black market rate was nearer 6 roubles to the dollar.

The T.A.S.S. correspondent in New York reports that Aeroflot will be flying into Sheremetyevo-2 Airport seventeen billion cigarettes (more than eight hundred million packs) of a number of brands under a long-term trade agreement with a subsidiary company of Reynolds Tobacco (*Moskovskii komsomolets*, 247, p. 1).

27 October

Independence and autonomy in managing its affairs is granted to the Ukrainian Orthodox Church (*Izvestiia*, 300, p. 6). See the article above by Nikolai Mitrokhin.

23–7 October

Moscow hosts the 19th Congress of Trade Unions of the U.S.S.R. Some ten years previously, the Soviet trade unions had given major financial assistance to the British coal miners. Through the Communist Federation of Trade Unions they had donated about £1.5 million (Sergey Khramov).

29 October

After a "popular, direct and secret ballot", Saparmurat Niyazov is elected President of Turkmenistan with 98.3 per cent of the vote (*Izvestiia*, 301, p. 2).

30 October

A boulder brought from the Solovki archipelago, where the first Soviet concentration camp was located, is positioned on Dzerzhinsky Square in Moscow, opposite the main K.G.B. building (*Izvestiia*, 302, p. 1).

Zoya Marchenko recalls the unveiling of the Solovki Stone on Lubyanka: "For decades we lived, not daring to show a photo, a letter, even to mention our departed relatives. Now we can come to the Solovki Stone and, together with our grandchildren, revere the memory of our loved ones who perished in the camps" (quoted from the Memorial website; Sergei Krivenko, http://www.bulletin.memo.ru/b21/35.htm).

In the Central Writers' Club, a meeting is held in memory of Father Aleksandr Men. It is organised by parishioners of his church in Novaya Derevnya (*Moskovskii komsomolets*, 251, p. 1).

31 October

At a session of the R.S.F.S.R. Supreme Soviet, Prime Minister Ivan Silayev delivers a report on economic reform. He emphasises that, despite the obstacles which have prevented implementation of the 500 Days plan throughout the U.S.S.R., the Russian government intends to act in full accord with its logic during the transition period (*Izvestiia*, 304, p. 1).

On the same day, the R.S.F.S.R. Supreme Soviet adopts a declaration of Russia's economic sovereignty. It will be declared invalid by the U.S.S.R. government.

AN INTERVIEW WITH VLADIMIR POZNER

*Vladimir Pozner in 1990 was a senior political commentator
for U.S.S.R. National Television.*

Interviewer: "1990 was the peak of your popularity on Soviet television. How did your own feelings alter between 1988 and 1990? Did your expectations for the future of society and politics change? Did you revise your own career goals in the light of a rapidly changing situation, or did you feel you would carry on much as before?"

Pozner: "My popularity was actually quite unexpected and started with the international television link-ups of 1986. The first of these was recorded in December 1985 and aired in February 1986. It was a link between Leningrad and Seattle and was something completely new. There had been link-ups before. The first with the United States was in 1982, and others followed in 1983 and 1984, but they were phoney, by which I mean that there was a preliminary agreement on both sides that everything would stay friendly. There would be no mention of problems and no arguments. That made everything fairly unreal. The programmes had little impact and were soon forgotten. Very few people remember them at all. What they do remember is the first television link-up of the perestroika era. The talk was edgy and angry. The Americans told us exactly what they thought about the U.S.S.R., and our viewers were far from complimentary about the United States. You have to remember that there was really only one Soviet television channel, so the whole country watched it. The situation was quite different from the United States, where it was shown only on channels which subscribed to the *Phil Donahue Show*, and not even all of them took that particular programme. If in America we had around eight million viewers, in the

U.S.S.R. there were tens of millions, perhaps even a hundred million. That was the moment I became well known. Nobody knew who I was before 1986: I worked in the Foreign Broadcasting Service, addressing American audiences, and spoke fairly frequently on American television from Moscow, but I wasn't allowed to travel abroad. I was a familiar face in America from appearances on popular programmes, of which the biggest was *Ted Koppel's Nightline*, but in the U.S.S.R. I was completely unknown.

"I don't think my career has had a peak of popularity, because that suggests something starting from nothing and gradually rising, whereas this was instant, explosive fame. I immediately became a political commentator and T.V. personality, and all but abandoned the Foreign Broadcasting Service.

"In 1988, my popularity was no higher than after the Leningrad–Seattle link-up. Why would it have been? I don't remember making any particularly outstanding programmes at that time. As glasnost went into decline and Gorbachev seemed to become disillusioned with the liberals, he started taking back people he was far more comfortable with, Soviet old-timers like Yanayev and Pugo, and I felt my scope decreasing. That actually started some time in 1989, and in 1990 it narrowed even more when the bloodshed started in Tbilisi, Baku and Vilnius. I could no longer understand Gorbachev's actions, and I suppose moved towards supporting Yeltsin. Things came to the point where I gave up on television completely in the spring of 1991.

"I was asked in an interview for America to say, if a presidential election were to be held the next weekend, whom I would vote for, Gorbachev or Yeltsin. I said that, although I had been an ardent supporter of Gorbachev, who literally changed my life (it was thanks to him that I had made a career in television, and thanks to him that I started being able to travel abroad), I could no longer understand what he was trying to do and would, most likely, vote for Yeltsin. Word of this interview got around and produced a negative reaction. I was informed through Leonid Kravchenko, then Chairman of State Television and Radio, that there had been a review of the organisation's political observers, and, in light of my views, the Party leadership no longer saw a place for me in television. I thought for a short time and decided they were right; I really shouldn't be working for their kind of television. I wrote a letter of resignation, but not just with the usual clichés about standing down 'at my own request'. I made it clear why I didn't want to work with Kravchenko or in Soviet television as it was. I had already moved over to the local team, hosting a talk show for the Moscow channel. It was called *Sunday Night with Vladimir Pozner*. We made good programmes, but they were broadcast only in the Moscow region. Later, in 1991, I went to live in the United States."

Interviewer: "Let us go back a little. We know that people working in Foreign Broadcasting knew far more about the Western media than those who worked in other areas of Soviet television and radio. Were you able, in the 1970s or early 1980s, to see at least something of Western television or listen to radio from the West? Which Western media formats did you find most interesting?"

Pozner: "You have to appreciate that it was impossible to watch Western television if you lived in the U.S.S.R. People who travelled did, of course, but I was not allowed to travel abroad. In 1977, I was let out for a short time to Hungary, and later to Finland, but those were very brief trips. A bit later I was sent to Canada and appeared on television there, but that was only for a week and I hardly had time to see anything for myself. After that I was again barred from foreign travel because I evidently didn't say quite the right things about our invasion of Afghanistan, so for the next five years the privilege of foreign travel was again withdrawn. It was only when Gorbachev came to power that I was able to travel outside the U.S.S.R. once more."

Interviewer: "You're saying that in Foreign Broadcasting you had no access to T.V. channels in the West?"

Pozner: "None whatsoever. Newspapers were not a problem. I had extensive access to Western writing which was brought back by friends. There was also the Foreign Literature Library in Moscow, and of course I read *Time*, *Newsweek*, US News, the *New York Times*, the *International Herald Tribune*, and French and British newspapers as well. I was fully aware of what people there were writing and what the media consisted of. I listened to the radio, that was possible, but I only started getting to grips with television as an industry and in a professional sense after 1991, when I worked in America."

Interviewer: "In a 1998 article for *Friendship of the Peoples*, you wrote about a conversation with Yeltsin in 1990 and how the Yeltsin of 1990 differed from the Yeltsin of 1998."

Pozner: "Yeltsin gave a very important interview when he was running for election as a People's Deputy of the U.S.S.R. in March–May 1990. His opponent was Yevgeniy Brakov, Director of the Likhachov Automotive Factory. I was asked to interview Yeltsin. He was in political disgrace at the time, occupying the position of Deputy Chairman of the State Construction Committee. I was told that we would have half an hour for the broadcast, so I took two cameras along and said, 'Boris Nikolayevich, we have half an hour of airtime so let's work in the format of a live broadcast. If it lasts exactly half an hour, they won't be able to cut anything.' I thought the interview went extremely well. Yeltsin fielded the questions expertly. He was in great shape, but permission to broadcast was withheld. Evidently it was rather too good. The cassette was stolen and later broadcast in Yekaterinburg (Sverdlovsk at that time) and then in Leningrad. Yeltsin quite unexpectedly phoned me at home and asked, 'Are you going to be in trouble?' I replied, 'Why should I be in trouble? I'm not the person who stole the tapes, am I?' He said, 'Well, remember, if there is any aggravation I am prepared to protect you.' I was surprised. People in power usually have very short memories."

Interviewer: "What kind of impression did Gorbachev make in 1990?"

Pozner: "I was disappointed that he talked so much – too much, in fact.

There was a feeling that he was not managing the situation very well, and that he had allowed some of the reins of power to slip from his grasp. I remember the way he behaved during some T.V. debates, in particular with the Azerbaijanis and Armenians. He was downright rude, telling them curtly just to pipe down. I was a fervent supporter of the new times because they had brought freedom. Books were no longer being banned, plays could be performed, but then there was this disappointment with Gorbachev's leadership. His indecisiveness about certain things had unpleasant consequences. I encountered that myself. I made a film with Stalin's personal interpreter, Valentin Berezhkov. He phoned me himself and said he wanted to make a film. He felt it was time to speak out. The film was called *The Witness*. At one point we talked about the secret protocols to the Molotov–Ribbentrop Pact of 1939 [on the dividing up of Eastern Europe], and when the decision had to be taken on whether to broadcast the film or not, it was sent 'upstairs'. I was summoned to the Central Committee and told to go to the Department of Propaganda. They said, 'Vladimir Vladimirovich, this is a very good film, but you mention the secret protocols. Was Berezhkov present at the signing of the protocols?' In fact, he hadn't been present. There was a second interpreter, Vladimir Pavlov, and he wasn't talking. I had to say, 'No, Berezhkov was not present.' 'There, you see? Your film is called *The Witness*! Let Berezhkov testify about what he actually saw. How can he be a witness to things he didn't see?' It was cleverly done, but the order came directly from Gorbachev. We had to cut all mention of the secret protocols."

Interviewer: "In *Sunday Evening with Vladimir Pozner*, did you have guests for the audience to question, or was it just a conversation between you and the audience?"

Pozner: "It was a genuine talk show in which the audience played a key role. First the guest would answer a few questions from the presenter, but then it was mostly over to the audience. The presenter acted as a facilitator between the audience and the guest. For me, I suppose, the most memorable programme was about the ethnic question. The U.S.S.R. was already crumbling; there were hot spots where trouble was flaring. We decided to invite children and young people aged from ten to sixteen from all the republics. They arrived literally from every republic except Estonia, if I remember, and Georgia. In effect, the programme was a conversation with them, very unusual and thought-provoking. The children spoke far more openly and honestly than adults.

"There were a few surprises. One boy, I think he was ten, from Kirghizia, said that people get married but, after all, they can get divorced too. We also had teenagers from Armenia and Azerbaijan. A bitter conflict had broken out between those republics over Nagorno-Karabakh. One Armenian sixteen-year-old produced a gun. I pointed a gun at him myself and asked, 'What are you going to do? Are you going to shoot?' He thought for a moment, then put down the gun and said he wouldn't shoot. It was a dramatic moment."

Interviewer: "Did they show the scene with the guns on television?"

Pozner: "Yes."

Interviewer: "Was it live or recorded?"

Pozner: "Live. We only did live broadcasts. I have no time for recorded television programmes. Pre-recorded political or news programmes are not T.V., they're plays staged in front of a microphone. When nobody, including you the presenter, knows what is going to happen next, the programme is far more highly charged. If you know absolutely anything can be cut, or adjusted, or rearranged, that is not television, it's something else. Almost everybody has gone over to pre-recording now – not because they are scared but because if you record a talk show today, fillet out the most striking bits tomorrow to make a trailer for the programme, and broadcast it in three days' time, you can attract more viewers. I understand the argument, but then you have to live with the fact that nothing unexpected is going to happen, or rather, everyone will be expecting it to happen. It's like sport.

What kind of football is it if everything is pre-recorded and you know that goal is going to be scored? Television is more immediate than radio. You are witnessing what is happening and don't know what will come next. That's a special strength of television. Unfortunately, it has been sacrificed to other interests."

Interviewer: "Did you have more freedom on the Moscow Channel in 1990 than on the national Soviet channels?"

Pozner: "I think we did, firstly because the man in charge was a different kettle of fish from Leonid Kravchenko. Kravchenko was very career-minded – smart, skilful, a good manager – but he always knew exactly what he was doing and who he was doing it for. When I said I would have voted for Yeltsin, he didn't care one way or the other who I supported, but at that time Gorbachev was in power so he decided my face didn't fit. Also, of course, the smaller the audience, the greater your freedom. The less impact you can have, the more freedom you get."

Interviewer: "What was your impression of T.V. in 1990, not so much at the top level as at the level of the professional staff? Was it rather inert or a creature throwing off its shackles?"

Pozner: "There were highly professional people from the old days, very good directors and line producers (who were called 'editors' at that time). The situation was worst, oddly enough, with the on-screen personnel, because there were none. We had newsreaders, professional people with excellent spoken Russian. There were various newcomers, but they had no idea how to behave on screen, how to work with the camera."

Interviewer: "Who were these newcomers?"

Pozner: "People who had no professional experience but who were soon turning up in droves. Reporters, for instance. Every profession has its own unwritten rules. Reporting is telling the story of what is going on without revealing your personal attitude. If you're a reporter, do everyone a favour:

show exactly what's happening. It's of no interest what the reporter thinks. We want to know exactly what happened. With perestroika a whole phalanx of very able people appeared who thought they had to volunteer their opinion, even within a straightforward news programme. Somebody presenting a news programme ought not to express his views. That's not his job!"

Interviewer: "Would you like to name some names?"

Pozner: "Yes, I can think of plenty of people who believed that, even very popular presenters like Tatyana Mitkova or Mikhail Osokin. I've always said that was wrong. The B.B.C., for instance, would never allow that sort of behaviour."

Interviewer: "Have you told them that to their faces?"

Pozner: "I talked about it publicly, but people didn't agree. 'We are in a different situation now, times have changed' – you hear it constantly. They invite a guest who puts one viewpoint, but where is the second guest to express an opposing view? Give the audience at least some diversity of attitudes and opinions, let them listen to both sides and then make up their own minds. Back in the early 1990s, new people appeared on the scene who very soon saw themselves as knights in shining armour. They were going to change the country. They were going to transform the world with their words, their speeches, their vision of the truth, but that is really not the job of a journalist. It is quite wrong. A good journalist is like a watchdog, always yapping about problems. If everything is fine, the regime doesn't need journalists."

Interviewer: "In 1990 you called for the establishment of a public television service. You said it was vital. Did you really think it would happen?"

Pozner: "Yes, in 1990 it was much more feasible than it is now, because in 1990 all the signs were that sooner or later non-state television was going to appear. Where there is commercial television, there is a real need for public service television, television which doesn't depend on advertising or the regime. It was feasible then. Nowadays it seems far less feasible."

Interviewer: "Were you hoping to participate in setting up that kind of service, or did you not see that as an option?"

Pozner: "If anyone had invited me, of course I would have taken part in it."

Interviewer: "Did you have a team of like-minded television people around you in 1990?"

Pozner: "No, there was nothing like that because the country was still Soviet. There was an elite of so-called political commentators who faithfully served the regime, and in return enjoyed the privileges reserved for high-ranking Soviet officials, from medical care and country retreats to access to distribution centres of scarce goods and trips abroad. But another group was growing up, one which eventually created the Television News Service programmes in 1990–91 for the First National Channel, and then they went on to work for N.T.V., but I was not part of that group. I was a lot older. I was fifty-two before I got in front of a camera, while the kids in the new group were thirty or thereabouts. I never belonged to the elite, because they always regarded me as an outsider, while people who were twenty years younger than me were just different; they belonged to a different generation. I was largely on my own, a lone wolf, if you like. In fact I still am."

Interviewer: "In 1990 and 1991 you had two books published in English. What drew you at that moment to a writing career?"

Pozner: "I didn't write those two books at the same time; there was a considerable interval between them. At an international film festival, I met a man whose father, Albert E. Kahn, had been a great friend of my father's. Kahn was famous as one of the 'Hollywood Ten'.[416] His son Brian was an environmentalist who had links with with the Biology Faculty at Moscow State

416. Although "blacklisted from mainstream publishing in the late 1940s" (Wikipedia), Kahn was not one of the "Hollywood Ten" jailed for contempt of Congress for refusing to testify in 1947 before the House Un-American Activities Committee.

University. There was a project to protect the Siberian White Crane. Anyway, Brian met me by chance and said, 'Listen, you ought to write a book. You have a really interesting biography.' I said, 'I don't think so. I'm not a writer.' Anyway, after much persuasion, I said, 'Okay, I could talk about politics, only I don't want to write about myself or my personal life.' He would come to see me, ask questions, and we accumulated around fifty cassettes of my stories. He took it all back to the United States, knocked it into some kind of shape, arranged it in chapters and sent it back to me. I read it and thought, Well, okay, maybe. Brian showed it to a major U.S. literary agent, who said, 'That's all very interesting, but if Pozner isn't going to talk about himself and his personal life, nobody is going to take the book.' Brian relayed this back to me, and I took the manuscript and rewrote it, filtering it through my own personal perspective. The book is titled *Parting with Illusions*.[417] It is an attempt to understand how I, who believed in the system, rooted for it and tried to bring about 'socialism with a human face', was disappointed, recognised that it was all an illusion, and that nothing was going to come of it all. Writing the book was very painful. Breaking with illusions and something you believed in is not easy. I found the book such hard work that, when I finished it, the idea of sitting down to rewrite it in Russian just seemed too much. It was published in America and to everyone's surprise, or at least to mine, became a bestseller. For twelve weeks it was on the *New York Times* bestseller list, rising to No. 7 despite the fact that there was no sex in it, no murders, no spy stories, and it was written by a foreigner. It was a very important book for me. My second book came out in 1992. As the first had been a bestseller, the publishers asked me immediately after the failed coup attempt in 1991 to write another. The book was called *Eyewitness: A Personal Account of the Unravelling of the Soviet Union* and was published by Random House. It was purely journalistic. I wrote it quickly and in English. It needed to be published as soon as possible, while readers were still remembering that

417. Vladimir Pozner, *Parting With Illusions: The Extraordinary Life and Controversial Views of the Soviet Union's Leading Commentator* (New York, 1991).

there had been an attempted coup in the U.S.S.R. The book did well, but it wasn't a bestseller. I consider it a piece of topical journalism."

Interviewer: "Did writing books at that time mean you were looking to find work outside of television?"

Pozner: "Absolutely not. I'm working on a book right now, and regularly provide a column for Esquire. I have never been looking for anything else. I also direct a college of television arts and teach at it. When the school is in session I see very clearly that television is in my blood. I realise that that is where I really found myself, that I enjoy working in it very much, and that I would not like to part with it. I took a long time deciding what I wanted to do, because by my third year in the Biology Faculty I knew I was not going to make a biologist or an academic. For a while I thought I might translate English poetry, but soon saw that that was not my thing either. By trial and error I arrived at what I really enjoy."

Interviewer: "My last question is about the college of television arts you set up when you returned from America. Did you feel in the late 1980s and in 1990 that a different approach to training television reporters was needed?"

Pozner: "It is important to point out that the college was the idea of my wife, Yekaterina Orlova. Without her efforts there would have been no college. I have always held that you can't go straight from school to a faculty of journalism and become a journalist. I firmly believe that journalism is not only a profession but a way of life. You can be trained as a doctor, and indeed it's a very good thing if you are, but I really don't think you can learn to be a journalist purely through study. You can teach someone to recognise a 'lead', you can teach them how to use a camera, but they can only become a journalist after they have some experience and feel the need to share it, when they have their own take on the world. I believe that journalism is a second education for which you don't need to study formally. You can come into it from other professions and gradually become a journalist. That goes both for television and for newspaper journalism. The idea of founding a college came later, mainly because of the development of regional television. We didn't have that in the Soviet period. When hundreds and hundreds of local T.V. companies sprang up and television professionals were in very short supply, former teachers and engineers started going to work for them.

"One of Russia's greatest drawbacks and problems is that it is so centralised. It will only become a normal country, and you can take that how you like, when the provinces are on the same level as the centre, when people are no longer desperate to get to Moscow or St Petersburg, in the same way that the French are not desperate to get to Paris and the Americans are not desperate to get to New York, because everywhere the quality of life is much the same. The Milan opera is in Milan, not Rome; Harvard is not in Washington or New York but in Cambridge, Massachusetts; and so on. When that happens, and the professional level of television in the provinces is the same as in the capital (which is important, because people trust their local television much more than the national provision), everything will change. We need to make sure the provinces get the right professionals, and this school was established precisely to cater for people already working in regional television, not Muscovites."

FROZEN EXPERIENCES, OR LOCAL TELEVISION REPORTING IN 1990

Pavel Pavlov

We know from social surveys that already in the Soviet period television was the primary cultural medium, the national channels having the most viewers. It became even more prominent during perestroika.[418] Boris Dubin of the National Centre for the Study of Public Opinion (VTsIOM) described its place in perestroika society:

> An important aspect is the behaviour of people at home, with their families, their daily, personal life after work. That would seem to be free from the demands of society, social obligations and expectations. Yet for Russians the focus of their private life is invariably the television set. It has become a kind of of synonym for home and family, which is why, as soon as anyone gets home, they either turn it on as automatically as turning on the light, or find someone else has already done so. If that didn't happen, the house would seem lifeless, as if there were nobody living there.[419]

This attitude towards the television existed already in the Soviet 1970s and 1980s, as we can see from films and literature of the period which depict everyday life.

Local television in the 1970s and 1980s was a good deal less developed than it is today, when every territory of the Russian Federation has several

---

418. On turning politics into spectacle, see Mikhail Iampol'skii, "Vlast' kak zrelishche vlasti", *Kinostsenarii*, 5 (1989), pp. 176–87.
419. Boris Dubin, "V strane zritelei", *Druzhba narodov*, 8 (2001).

television companies of its own. It was less influential than the local press, which during perestroika virtually regulated private time, and national television served to synchronise "local time" with the rest of society. The proportion of viewers watching national, as opposed to local, television has been steadily falling: in the mid-2000s, according to Gallup Media, 40 per cent of viewers in the Chelyabinsk region preferred to watch local television, as against 12 per cent in the late 1990s. Dubin's 2001 thoughts on local television can, however, be applied retrospectively to 1990: "Clearly, the technical, financial, and human resources of local television bear no comparison with those of the national channels, if only because their advertising revenue is minimal or nonexistent, making the companies almost completely dependent on local government and local budgetary allocations."[420]

In 1990, there was just one local T.V. station in the Southern Urals. It was operated by Chelyabinsk Television Studios, one of nearly a hundred state-owned local broadcasting enterprises in the U.S.S.R. Its staff produced *Channel 8*, a news programme, as well as popular science, art and current-affairs features. Unfortunately, back then archives were not kept very conscientiously, or they have not survived intact, so there are only a few programmes that can be dated with certainty in the fairly extensive archive of the Southern Urals State Television and Radio Company, as Chelyabinsk Television Studios' successor is known. Indeed, just three programmes are definitely known to have been broadcast between 1 January and 31 December, 1990. They are *A Day of Mourning and Hope* (*Den' skorbi i nadezhdy*) about the unveiling of a memorial to victims of Stalin's purges, at which Academician Andrey Sakharov spoke; *In Conversation* (*Sobesednik*), a forty-minute interview with the previously *samizdat* Chelyabinsk writer Tatyana Taiganova; and a short feature, *Traces* (*Sled*), about the aftermath of an explosion at the Beacon (*Mayak*) chemical plant in 1957.

By 1990, the media were becoming acclimatised to the concept of free speech, although this was more evident in print than in electronic media.

420. Ibid.

Journalists were nevertheless aware that they were skating on thin ice, and this gave their work a particular urgency.[421] So-called "taboo" topics were no longer taboo, and the general public were deluged with new information, to which previously only a select few had had access.[422] By 1990, television programmes on new topics were fairly common and a distinctive style had evolved for communicating sensitive information of public importance. The presenter's tone of voice conveyed controlled pathos and the message was delivered in an intimate manner, as if he were talking to each viewer personally. Mediating content of this kind was plainly a source of pride, and local television reporters could overdo some tricks of the trade of their senior colleagues on national programmes like *Perestroika Searchlight*, *Viewpoint* (*Vzglyad*), and *Before and After Midnight* (*Do i posle polunochi*). The Chelyabinsk equivalent was *The Fifth Wheel* (*Piatoye koleso*), where we find the same controlled emotion and impassive denunciation of the "higher echelons", the deadpan revelation of shocking facts which "speak for themselves", and the constant interaction with the viewer. The broadcast was designed to hold the viewer's attention, to oblige them to think, to break down stereotypical reactions. In 1988–9, the presenters of *Viewpoint* had, in their individual ways, honed these techniques to perfection. Local television struggled to keep up, sometimes lapsing into moralising or offering importunate conclusions and reactions.

This difference in the level of national and local television presenters was obviously related to the fact that many topics being aired for the first time on local television in 1990 had been discussed on national television and in the local press as early as 1988–9.

---

421. Occasional attempts were still being made at this time to ban or restrict reporting, particularly on television. An edition of *Viewpoint* was blocked in December 1989, and the programme was finally shut down in early 1991. Unlike in the past, such actions invariably prompted public protests.

422. Aleksei Levinson, "Arkhiv i prostota. Replika neistorika", *Novoe Literaturnoe Obozrenie*, 74 (2005), p. 38.

A DAY OF MOURNING AND HOPE [423]

This programme showed the unveiling in September 1989 of the Golden Mountain memorial in the north-west district of Chelyabinsk. It was repeated several times and caused a considerable stir. The memorial was a rock placed at the spot where huge numbers of victims of Stalin's purges had been shot and buried in mass graves. The chronology shows the extent of the delay in informing the public about the discovery and gives a sense of how far behind other media local television was.

Known as Bald Mountain until 1843, Golden Mountain was renamed after prospectors from Vyatka discovered gold there. It continued to be mined until 1935, when the workings were closed. In 1946, Yuriy Gerasimov, a prospector, found large numbers of bodies in the abandoned mines. He remained silent about his gruesome discovery until October 1988, when he wrote a letter to the editor of *Chelyabinsk Worker*. An article, based on his letter, was published under the title "Something's Not Right with Our Memory". On 14 June, 1989, a group of archaeologists began excavating one of the mine entrances. Over the summer months, the remains of 350 bodies were recovered, and specialists dated the "burials" to 1936–9. It proved impossible to establish the victims' names. According to the K.G.B., more than thirty-seven thousand people were arrested in the 1930s in the Southern Urals on political charges. Of these, 11,592 were shot.[424]

In December 1990, various publications appeared in Chelyabinsk whose authors flatly denied that the graves were those of victims of Stalin's purges, claiming instead that the mine had been used to bury unknown persons who had died in the cold and famine of the winters of the Second World War. Thousands of people were said to have been

---

423. An archive note indicates that the programme was repeated on 23 March, 1990, but we have been unable to establish the dates of earlier broadcasts. Reporter, Vasiliy Pavlov; cameraman, Nikolai Makhinya; producer, Galina Filimonova.

424. E. B. Druzhinina, "Zolotaia gora, mesto zakhoroneniia zhertv repressii", *Internet-entsiklopediia "Cheliabinsk"*; http://book-chel.ru/ind.php?what=card&id=5913

evacuated to Chelyabinsk who were unfamiliar with the region.[425]

On 9 September, 1989, a rally was held when the human remains found in the Golden Mountain mines were interred. It was attended by more than six thousand people, and addressed by Andrey Sakharov, Yelena Bonner and Galina Starovoytova. A report of the meeting was circulated by the Soviet T.A.S.S. news agency. (Speaking shortly afterwards in Lyons, Sakharov began his talk, "A few weeks ago I stood before a gaping mass grave . . .")[426] The television reporter covering the ceremony described the mass burials on Golden Mountain as one of the most terrible discoveries of our time, continuing, "Only in our days has it become possible to talk about it. People have not overcome their fear. They are still trying to overcome a fear which the administrative-command system has instilled in you and me. It was a system which acted brutally and inexorably, as the Golden Mountain knows, as do those who still carry its secret within themselves."

Staff at the Chelyabinsk Television Studios involved in making the programme say the commentary for A Day of Mourning and Hope was revolutionary for that time. Just a year or two previously, reporters could not have imagined being able to speak so openly in the course of a television broadcast. Golden Mountain put Chelyabinsk at the centre of a major revelation of the perestroika period, raising its status and putting it on the map of history. The local museum staged an exhibition, A Memory Recovered from the Mines, which continued for most of 1990.[427] The report was in two parts.

---

425. A permanent monument has yet to be erected on Golden Mountain, although several designs have been proposed. In winter it is used as a ski slope. [A further eleven mines containing human remains have been discovered in an area of some 15 hectares in the vicinity of Golden Mountain. See E. B. Druzhinina, "Memorial'nyi kompleks 'Zolotaia Gora' (Cheliabinsk)"; http://wikimapia.org/6650107/ru/Мемориальный-комплекс-«Золотая-Гора»]

426. I. Smychagina, T. Krylova et al., "Vse tol'ko nachinaetsia", Aktsioner, 13 February, 1998 [No longer available on the Internet–tr].

427. A further exhibition, Mountain of Grief, in Chelyabinsk Central Library, was devoted to the burials. See E. Turchenik, Muzei i muzeinye ekspozitsii v MUK TsBS g. Cheliabinska; website of Tsentralizovannaia bibliotechnaia sistema Cheliabinska [No longer available on the Internet].

Andrey Sakharov, frame from *A Day of Mourning and Hope*

The first related the history of the atrocity. After reporter Vasiliy Pavlov's introduction came an interview at the site with Yuriy Gerasimov:

Gerasimov: "I was a prospector. We went down looking for gold."

Pavlov: "And what did you find?"

Gerasimov: "We cut into an old working. It was sealed off and piled high with corpses. It was like they spilled out from there into our shaft. When my mate came up, I told him and he said, 'That's those enemies of the people that were shot here.' He said it had all been cordoned off round there. They didn't let anyone through, starting in 1937. They were shooting people."

Pavlov: "Did you believe him that they were enemies of the people?"

Gerasimov: "They weren't enemies. You put enemies to death openly. This was all done like thieves in the night."

Although the corpses spilling out of the workings was a grisly detail, it was retained in the broadcast.

Pavlov: "Here is the excavation site where the remains were recovered of victims of Stalin's purges. But these were only a small proportion. How many are left? Hundreds, thousands, tens of thousands? Golden Mountain reminds us that the system that produced wanton lawlessness on an unprecedented scale has not yet been broken, although it should have collapsed under the sheer weight of the crimes it committed. That has not happened, and will not happen until we overcome the legacy of 1937 within ourselves."

Those words identify the main problem which Soviet and post-Soviet society faced, and still faces.

This mournful segment concluded with three interviews at the site with relatives of people who had been shot. For those watching them on television, what they had to say was truly a revelation. For so many years these people had silently raged against a regime which had caused them such suffering, and now was their opportunity to relate everything, down to the smallest detail. They did not hesitate to name names and specify dates, and to publicly blame the Stalin regime for their miseries:

"I came to honour the memory of my father. My mother was arrested. I, an eighteen-year-old girl, was sentenced to a year of hard labour. We were considered children of enemies of the people. Shame on Stalin's butchers!"

"It is purely by chance that I am alive today, standing at the graves of people with whom I was imprisoned in the Chelyabinsk central prison. Of my twenty-year sentence, I spent eighteen months in Chelyabinsk. I had another eight and a half years in a concentration camp. Not all the people who were shot are buried here. More died in prison, and there were more than fifteen thousand people held in there."

The link to the second part was a piece about the Memorial society, which has made itself responsible for commemorating all those who were purged. The second part of the broadcast was an interview with Academician

Sakharov. His speech was undoubtedly longer, but two excerpts were chosen, the first of which went as follows: "We are not going to wait for anyone's strong arm. We will ourselves create, with our own democratic hands, a country under the rule of law, a country of truth and humanity. That will be our tribute to those we are burying today." Although Sakharov was clearly continuing an earlier line of argument, in the broadcast there was no lead-in to his speech, the producer emphasis-ing that no further comment was necessary. The supposed need for a "strong arm", which Sakharov was arguing against, was a line familiar to everyone in 1989 and the 1990s. His reference to "us" demonstrated the revolutionary thrust of his appeal to unite for the victory of a "land of humane values".

Even more telling is the second excerpt:

> What is happening now is a logical extension of the Stalinist system. I believe that perestroika must restore historical justice in this country and create abundance, without which there can be no social justice. We need perestroika so that people feel they are the masters of our country and its future. Perestroika must also bring people material well-being: an apartment, clothing, food. We have long and difficult years ahead of us, but we will cope.

No doubt the excerpts were chosen to appeal to the main aspirations of ordinary people in the Southern Urals, with the "three pillars" of the pere-stroika years being listed as an apartment, clothing and food. Sakharov was probably making these points in the course of a more sophisticated argu-ment, and they evidently come over more baldly in the broadcast than in their original context. "What is happening now" was devastation, the spectre of famine, the painful transformation of the economy. In the broad-cast, perestroika appeared to be an amorphous, transcendent force which would replace the "strong arm", but seemingly "us" too. It was perestroika which had come to destroy the Stalinist system and restore the people's violated rights. It seems clear that the editing intentionally selected from the available footage words consonant with the local understanding of perestroika and its anticipated results. It is instructive to compare this with interviews given by Sakharov to *Knizhnoe obozrenie* (*Book Review*) in the spring of 1989:

> I agree that society can improve only on a basis of morality. Our people have been gravely damaged as a result of terror, from living for many years in a climate of deceit and dissimulation. But I believe that moral strength always survives in the people. In particular, I believe that young people, who in every generation start life anew, are capable of choosing a highly moral position. It is not so much a matter of rebirth as of allowing that moral strength to develop which exists in every generation and which springs up again and again.[428]

Here, Sakharov's emphasis is on the human ability to morally conquer the slave mentality inculcated by years of terror. From this interview, we can infer the main points of his speech which were not included in the televised cut. The Chelyabinsk editors left in the robustness of Sakharov's appeal to his fellow citizens, but cropped his speech so that it appeared to support a passive expectation of progress. Perestroika, which began as a revolution from above, was presented as a self-sufficient redemptive power. From Sakharov's other texts we can easily see that he had never supported passivity of that kind, and his words acquired that sense only by being taken out of context.

The sense of shock and the expectation of a miraculous solution were very strong in the provinces, particularly among those not involved in the wave of strikes of the time.

---

428. Quoted from a re-publication no longer available on the Internet; partially available on "Human Rights in Russia" website, http://hro.org/node/11118/

IN CONVERSATION [429]

In the programme In Conversation reporter Vasiliy Pavlov talked to Tatyana Taiganova, a local samizdat author being published for the first time.[430] She talked about the current state of the country, providing an insight into the thinking of a member of the provincial intelligentsia. Her provincialism comes through primarily in the directness and personal colouration of her judgements and the absence of "professionalism" in her thinking. Taiganova made no reference to other authors or to other people's opinions. This was her personal take on reality, and that makes its survival from 1990 so valuable:

Pavlov: "What questions should I be asking you? I have only my knowledge of your writing to rely on. Your novellas The Loving Forest and The Limit contain the theme of a home for humankind. Do you see that as an ideal for organising the world?"

Taiganova: "No, we are outcasts, driven away from our mothers and fathers. We lack the one thing we most need, a base. Today, all this evil of perestroika . . . and good, but for the moment mostly evil, it seems to me . . . Why does nothing ever come right for us? Because people have no firm base. If someone has a home, I mean, everything just naturally falls into place. A home is not only a place where you live. It is the place you were born, and where you will die; where, perhaps, your children will live after you. I have come to see that we don't know the meaning of solitude. Russian solitude and Western solitude are two quite different things. We are isolated because we can never be alone. We have no home."

429. The programme was broadcast on 14 November, 1990. Reporter, Vasiliy Pavlov; cameraman, Anatoliy Nikolayenko; programme editor, Nina Vakhrusheva.
430. Tatyana Taiganova is a poet, writer and graphic artist. She was admitted to the Writers' Union in 1989. In 1998 she moved from Chelyabinsk to Vologda, where she still lives. First published in the late 1980s, her best-known work at the time of the programme was The Loving Forest (Laskovyi les), published in Literaturnaia ucheba, 2 (1989). For further information, see http://www.netslova.ru /tayganova/

Tatyana Taiganova, frame from the programme *In Conversation*

The question Taiganova addressed to the world, before going on to answer it herself, was why nothing ever came right in Soviet society. That was not the interviewer's question, but it was clearly what was preoccupying her at that moment. It reflected a common reaction in 1990 to the changes taking place: "Why does nothing ever come right for us?" The whole forty-minute interview was directed towards answering that question.

Taiganova's aphorism that "We are isolated because we can never be alone" is intriguing. Does it mean, "We are incapable of being alone with ourselves", or "We are incapable of thinking independently"? Is our home not truly ours because we have not built it ourselves?

Taiganova went on to say, "I have this idea in my head of gathering creative people together, finding a place with some houses, and going to live there, establishing a colony." She wanted to establish a utopian commune of like-minded individuals, but she was not proposing to take the lead herself. She was still talking about "we". Her commune could be seen as an attempt to escape from a world that was breaking down into individual destinies. Taiganova's other main suggestion was that there was a need for passive resistance to what was going on in society:

There is a great wave of aggression all around us, and at some point we shall need to build a dyke against it. I think the best tactic is, for a while, just to accept it in order to gain the necessary insight into the kind of world we live in, to see what is close to us in order to be ready, if need be, to fight it. We have lost our bearings in life. We have lost track of what is good and what is evil. We have lost ourselves. We need a pause to get used to the rest of the world and for it to get used to us. We should rest and then move on. People need to be given an opportunity to stand back.

The idea of temporary acceptance, of taking a rest from change in order to get a good look at what is happening, ran contrary to Sakharov's message. Intellectuals wanted a quiet backwater where they would have time to understand what was going on, but there was no time to spare. The television viewer was faced with someone who wanted to escape to an ivory tower, to bow out of perestroika intellectually and retreat to an unchallenging place.

Pavlov: "You once called your writing 'spiritual literature based on socialist material'. What did you mean by that?"

Taiganova: "Our life has become mythologised. It has no contact with reality. We live in a world we have dreamed up ourselves. We built it with the aid of a great concept, and now we live in it. It is a reality, but a fantastic reality. I suppose it is the realism of socialism. It is difficult to understand. I remember when my manuscript was being read, people said it was total bullshit 'but well written'. They wanted to find something complimentary to say about it but couldn't. They couldn't accept the mythological symbolism, which was entirely realistic. They found it contrived."

The fantasy nature of socialist reality created the need for an aesthetic response, and the reaction of such writers as Andrey Sinyavsky, Yuliy Daniel and Venedikt Yerofeyev was the heroic creation of a new literary language. By the 1980s, this sense of a fantasy world was common even among writers and artists not usually inclined to radical experimentation.

Taiganova was giving voice to many writers who, in 1990, felt they were living in a vacuum. Her idea of establishing a writers' colony would have provided them with a self-contained readership:

> Our Russian people have a soul, despite all the efforts which have been made to expunge it. It has survived in such a pristine, child-like form that we can take hope from that. It obliges literature to look to the soul, to the human. There are many challenges, but one of the greatest is to give people back their dignity. It is very difficult because there is a torrent of information which demeans the human. It is demeaning to be a Soviet citizen, to be a citizen at all, to consent to live in a city with five hundred factories within the city limits. That is demeaning.

Taiganova's belief that the human soul had survived despite the cruelty of the times, despite the universal decay, was more optimistic than the gloomier judgement of the Native Soil (*Pochvennik*) group of the intelligentsia, who categorically announced that the new Russia was spiritually dead. At the same time, if Taiganova's complaint about a torrent of information which demeans human beings suggested that it was the information, rather than the grim reality being reported (by the media, including, of course, television), which was demeaning, she seems logically to have been arguing for the return of censorship.

Pavlov: "There has recently been a lot of talk to the effect that we will soon be spiritually dead. People who proclaim this in the press seem to exclude themselves from their own strictures. What gives them that right?"

Taiganova [ignoring the question]: "We are impoverished only in terms of action. We have forgotten how to do and make things. I am not talking about manufacturing, but about living life. We have forgotten how to make our own lives. We will find our natural way back to this. We are living creatures. We will biologically relearn how to live. As regards spiritual decline, I cannot agree with that. I do not know any spiritually impoverished people. We have been through so much."

Taiganova's idea of a writers' colony, of a pause, and, in this excerpt, of a natural way back to "biological life", all developed her theme of a new life separate from what was evolving in the country. Her leitmotif was separation. A biological ability to live suggests the breaking out of the "Numbers" (citizens) through the Green Wall in Yevgeniy Zamyatin's novel *We*. Beyond the wall, the Mephi live "biologically". The system within the wall, which provides the Numbers with heat and food, reduces them to the same "impoverishment of action" to which Taiganova was referring.

Taiganova: You see, we are in a strange situation from an international perspective. We have somehow been left on the sidelines of history. The village has been destroyed, our cities too are in ruins. We were neither an urban civilisation nor a rural civilisation, neither East nor West, just a place on the map of the world. If we imagine history developing in a spiral, at some stage the most advanced society will return to where we are now. We are behind, but we are already at this point where there is conflict and crisis but also transition to the next level. Our country is at a critical stage of transition to a different level or quality. Some other countries may be seriously damaged before they reach this point, but we are already there."

This optimistic point of view is a commonplace of Russian philosophy, the notion that Russia has a special historical destiny. At the same time it is reminiscent of Marmeladov's belief in *Crime and Punishment* that the Lord will receive the "halt and maimed" just because they did not dare to hope for such favour. Taiganova appears, however, to have been saying more than this. Perhaps we should pause. Perhaps there is no need to go further. She seemed unexpectedly to be combining this view with a suggestion that destruction might have a positive value in freeing us from being readily categorised. We remained "neither East nor West". Our release from all manner of predestination, demands and plans of Providence might have been the key to our "transition to a different level".

Taiganova also used a persistent expression of the perestroika years: "on the sidelines of history". This was not geographical but temporal provincialism. Historical progress was pictured as a country in whose provinces, in whose "backyard", we were vegetating. This provincialism was understood in the perestroika years in terms of our lagging behind on the road to progress. Somewhere human beings were living at the cutting edge, steadily building a happy and fulfilled life, and somewhere else, out on the sidelines, in the servants' quarters, well away from the eyes of fine ladies and gentlemen, pathetic, backwards "we" were cringing. Taiganova, however, gave a twist to all this. Yes, we may have been the servants, we may have been living on the sidelines, but what if suddenly the last became first? What if all humankind renounced its towns and villages and transitted to this stage – not just to a devastated civilisation but to a new way of living outside the old "civilised" bonds, not to the jungle but to the triumph of spiritual, "non-material substance"?

TRACES [431]

The television programme *Traces* reported the consequences of an explosion at the Beacon chemical plant in the closed town of Chelyabinsk-40. The makers of the programme eschewed commentary by experts and themselves spoke directly about an environmental disaster, compiling an account from interviews with the inhabitants of Muslyumovo, a village

431. The programme was broadcast on 16 September, 1990. Reporter, Tamara Nikolayeva; cameraman, Nikolai Makhinya; producer, Galina Filimonova.

Frame from the
programme *Traces*

situated in the floodplain of the River Techa. The stories of these people
certainly had political significance. For a long time they were kept in ignorance of what was concealed behind the concrete walls of Chelyabinsk-40,
a restricted area code-named Ozyorsk in the passports of its residents.
(Ozyorsk is now the town's official name.) Neither did they know that the
chemical plant there was discharging radioactive effluent into the waters of
the Techa. Local people bathed in it, drank its water and scythed hay on its
banks. So almost everyone in Muslyumovo was exposed to large doses of
radiation. The film crew brought a dosimeter with them and established
that radiation levels were dozens of times higher than acceptable limits.

The feature started with a brief introduction to where the events occurred,
and then showed the house, now a museum, where Igor Kurchatov, founder
of the U.S.S.R.'s atomic programme, lived. A voiceover had Kurchatov
saying, "People worked for many years to build an atomic and hydrogen
bomb, because they knew that a threat hung over the state and that, if we did
not have such weapons, there were forces in the world which would bring
our land to its knees." The implication of this insert was clear: nobody was
concerned about the consequences of contaminating the entire territory

surrounding Beacon: the end justified the means. An interview with the Director of the Chelyabinsk branch of the Ministry of Health's Institute of Biophysics, the medical centre where irradiated people were observed, supported this view: "I could not even tell the medical orderly who saw these people in his village that the population had been irradiated."

A number of interviews with residents of Muslyumovo made it clear that they blamed their troubles on the U.S.S.R. government. Citizens of the U.S.S.R. had been the main victims of ensuring the nuclear security of the U.S.S.R. They had not been informed of their diagnosis, although almost all the villagers were dying of cancer. They were not resettled in safe areas, as they clearly should have been, and their children, who suffered from leukaemia, were being treated with aspirin.

Shocking statistics were quoted. An explosion had occurred at the chemical plant in 1957, and, twenty years later, 105 children from the radioactive zone had leukaemia. Five years later, the number had risen to 126, and five years after that it was 140. One mother, holding her sick child in her arms, said, "I appeal to the government of the U.S.S.R. and to Mikhail Gorbachev personally. Our children are seriously ill, but there are no drugs in the hospital here. We see on television how children are treated in the West. Help us! Otherwise our children will die."

The reporter, Tamara Nikolayeva, kept narration to a minimum. What needed to be said was said by those affected. One sequence was filmed in Chelyabinsk-40. The daughter of the director of the nuclear plant was interviewed. She complained that those involved in the Chernobyl disaster were treated like heroes, but everyone had forgotten Ozyorsk.

In 1990, when there was a shortage of everything in the country, Chelyabinsk-40 had no shortages. A full range of products was brought in to the stores. Residents of the secret city could choose from a selection of imported clothes, and their salaries were paid promptly and in cash. People in the town said in the film that they were entitled to these benefits because they paid for them with their health and their lives. At the same time, the village teacher in Muslyumovo said that the children in her school were often ill. She complained of suffering constantly from headaches herself.

The material was filmed in May 1990 but shown only in September. The presenter concluded her report this way: "That teacher did not return to work. In July she underwent surgery. She had a malignant brain tumour."

Traces was a documentary exposé. Revealing dark new aspects of life in the U.S.S.R. was a genre which dominated television in 1990. The tone of the programme was profoundly pessimistic, however. Although it followed the traditional positive approach of Soviet investigative journalism, with a special commission being set up at the end to tackle the problems of the Muslyumovo villagers and the townspeople of Ozyorsk, the overall mood was sombre. The programme was simply demonstrating some of the sad consequences of "building Communism".

Analysing these three broadcasts from 1990, which selected themselves largely by chance, shows us provincial television journalism copying the capital in terms of subject matter, editing and presentation. Although it had assimilated the rhetorical devices of 1987–9, provincial T.V. was clearly lagging behind the kind of programming being shown nationally in 1990, in which there was already much discussion of plans to move towards a market economy and new kinds of economic activity. Economic and cultural contacts with foreign (primarily the "capitalist") countries were being widely reported, and a lot of attention was being paid to the preoccupations of young people and the latest trends in popular culture. From 7.00 a.m. until 6.00 p.m. every day, the local Moscow channel was given over to 2 x 2, a music and entertainment station. The first national late-night broadcasts featured music videos.

During the transformation taking place both in society and in the media, some regions lagged behind while others were ahead of the game. This was particularly true of the Baltic States and Leningrad. Chelyabinsk, of course, was a laggard. Local television did not contribute significantly to the democratisation of provincial audiences, despite the fact that its local roots could have been a trump card in its struggle with the national channels for audience share.

Local television had yet another weakness in 1990 which arguably has applied to all post-Soviet television, even, indeed particularly, to the national channels. Dubin identified it as a sense of "watching from the sidelines", with viewers feeling completely detached from what they are seeing:

> There is a combination of dissatisfaction on the part of Russians with many television broadcasts and a feeling of being dependent on their television set, an inability to turn it off. In the circumstances of Russia, this has a particular, broader significance. This fissile symbiosis of conflicting emotions in the viewer is the standard mode of existence of the mass of modern Russians. We can widen this and apply it to the way Russians view the world in general, their country and its state, the people around them and, ultimately, themselves. They look at everything with a mixture of unfocused curiosity and watchful alienation, interest and mistrust, as if it is not happening to them, not here, not now. In this condition, what is seen, or shown on television, may be experienced (and even quite strongly), but the experience, because people are distanced from it and unable to influence it, is altered, frozen, unexciting. I am inclined to see this kind of behaviour as a "spectator syndrome" associated with a purely passive view of society, the "television democracy" which Yuriy Levada identified in his last years.[432]

432. Boris Dubin, "V strane zritelei"; Iurii Levada, "Indikatory i paradigmy kul'tury v obshchestennom mnenii", in his *Ot mnenii k ponimaniiu: Sotsiologicheskie ocherki 1993–2000* (Moscow, 2000), pp. 305–22.

NOVEMBER

1 November

The Presidium of the U.S.S.R. Supreme Soviet resolves that the anniversary of the October Revolution should be celebrated throughout the U.S.S.R. (*Noveishaia istoriia otechestvennogo kino*). A resolution is needed because the leaders of several union republics and other territories have already enacted legislation abolishing Soviet holidays and replacing them with their own.

3 November

The first issue of *Rossiyskaya gazeta* goes on sale. In his greeting "God grant Russia may find its way to the light", Aleksiy II, Patriarch of Moscow and All Russia, calls for a revival of Russia's age-old morality and spirituality. The newspaper regularly publishes laws and statutes of the R.S.F.S.R. Supreme Soviet.

Moscow City Soviet's commission for culture, arts and preservation of historic heritage approves a first list of squares, streets, side streets and metro stations whose names are to be changed.

4 November

Ukraine observes a Day of Remembrance of Victims of the Famine (*Izvestiia*, 307, p. 2). In the autumn of 1990, Ukraine Politizdat publishes *The 1932–1933 Ukrainian Famine Through the Eyes of Historians and the Language of Documents*, compiled by the Ukrainian Communist Party's Institute of Party History. It notes, "Archival materials reveal that the direct cause of the Ukrainian famine in the early 1930s was a coercive grain requisition policy. This was carried out with extensive use of repression and had devastating consequences for the peasantry" (Stanislav Kul'chitskii, "Prichiny goloda

1933 goda v Ukraine po stranitsam odnoi podzabytoi knigi", *Zerkalo nedeli* [Kiev], 16–22 August, 2003).

Representatives of Sotheby's auctioneers, headed by its chairman, Lord Gowrie, and the Soviet Cultural Foundation hold a joint seminar. The Foundation announces that it wishes to participate in the next auction of works by Soviet artists which Sotheby's is planning to hold in London (*Moskovskie novosti*, 44, p. 22).

5 November

The Moldovan Parliament is reviewing its policy towards national minorities and has stated its intention to pursue constructive dialogue with its Gagauz and Transnistrian communities (*Izvestiia*, 308, p. 1).

6 November

Addressing the Russian-speaking population on national television, Zviad Gamsakhurdia declares that relations between the Soviet army and the people of Georgia would not be artificially aggravated and that the presence of the Soviet Army in Georgia must be addressed, following the example of Eastern Europe, on the basis of international law. He also notes that Georgia needs its own security agency and that the K.G.B. "has no role to play on Georgian territory" (*Izvestiia*, 309, p. 3).

7 November

A military parade is held in Moscow and, contrary to Gavriil Popov's recommendation, there are other demonstrations on the anniversary of the October Revolution. This is the last state-sponsored Red Square parade in honour of the 1917 Revolution. Mikhail Gorbachev and Boris Yeltsin head the procession, both ascending the stand on the Lenin Mausoleum.

In Red Square, Sergey Stankevich reports that, "As the first parade approached the Mausoleum, two shots were fired from a sawn-off shotgun." Police detain the offender, thirty-seven-year-old Aleksandr Shmonov from Leningrad (*Izvestiia*, 310, p. 6). Shmonov held Gorbachev responsible for

Official rally on Palace
Square, Leningrad,
7 November, 1990

Below: Official rally on
Palace Square, Leningrad,
7 November, 1990

Democrats' demonstration,
Leningrad, 7 November, 1990

Below: Democrats'
demonstration, Leningrad,
7 November, 1990

Food coupons, receipts and labels from 1990

the deaths of civilians in Tbilisi in 1989 and in Baku in 1990. Gorbachev is saved by a police sergeant who deflects the barrel of the shotgun, causing one shot to go off in the air and the other to hit the wall of the GUM department store (Vladimir Tikhomirov, "Chelovek s ruzh'em", *Ogonek*, 46 [2005]; http://www.ogoniok.com/4920/38).

8 November

Gavriil Popov, Chairman of the Moscow City Soviet, announces at a plenary meeting that from 1 December food rationing will be introduced. Each resident of the capital will be entitled to buy produce totalling 31 roubles per month, including 1.5 kilograms of meat, 200 grams of butter, 500 grams of flour etc. (*Moskovskii komsomolets*, 258, p. 1).

11 November

Gorbachev and Yeltsin meet in Moscow. Yeltsin reports to the R.S.F.S.R. Supreme Soviet that agreements have been reached on reforming and transforming the political system of the U.S.S.R., which he says were minuted after the meeting. This information is disputed by Gorbachev's entourage (*Moskovskie novosti*, 48, p. 1; *Rossiiskaia gazeta*, 15 November, p. 1).

12 November

Emperor Akihito (b. 1933) ascends the throne of Japan.

At an extraordinary session of the Crimean provincial soviet, deputies resolve to restore the Crimean state and to hold a referendum among the population of the peninsula and Crimean Tatars living outside it (*Izvestiia*, 316, p. 2).

12–13 November

The inaugural session of the Moscow Central Stock Exchange opens.

13 November

The Armenian Supreme Soviet resolves to "depoliticise", in effect, to ban the setting up of U.S.S.R. Communist Party committees in state-run enterprises and educational institutions. The republic is thus able finally to eliminate the one-party system (www.parliament.am).

The prestigious French firm Lancôme opens a salon on Nevsky Prospekt in Leningrad in order to sell French cosmetics and perfumes for Russian roubles (*Izvestiia*, 316, p. 2).

14 November

Mikhail Nenashev, the liberal director-general of State Television and Radio, is replaced by Leonid Kravchenko, an experienced functionary expected to finally "tighten the screws". Kravchenko sets about the task energetically, in December effectively closing down *Viewpoint* (*Vzglyad*) for refusing to cut comment on the resignation of Eduard Shevardnadze. In January 1991, the presenters of the Television News Service, Tatyana Mitkova, Aleksandr Gurnov and Yuriy Rostov are suspended after refusing to read on air the official commentary on the invasion by U.S.S.R. troops of Vilnius, Lithuania. Kravchenko was sacked in 1991 after the defeat of the

The Lancôme salon on Nevsky Prospekt, Leningrad, November 1990

attempted August hard-line coup.

Zviad Gamsakhurdia is elected Chairman of the Georgian Supreme Soviet. In his inaugural address he rules out any possibility of Georgia signing the U.S.S.R. Union Treaty (*Izvestiia*, 318, p. 2).

15 November

Large-scale rioting breaks out in the evening in Chişinău after the funeral of a Moldovan man, murdered on 12 November by a group of [Russian] hooligans when he intervened to defend the honour of the national flag (*Izvestiia*, 319, p. 1).

16 November

At a session of the U.S.S.R. Supreme Soviet, Gorbachev says that the executive branch should have the power to carry out the programme adopted by the Supreme Soviet. Pressure is being exerted by destructive forces which are hindering the consolidation of Soviet society. At the root of this is a power struggle. At the very moment when the government is offering people a way

439

out of the crisis, forces interested in fomenting confrontation for their own political purposes are campaigning against it. After the break, Yeltsin, Chairman of the R.S.F.S.R. Supreme Soviet, says that the crisis in the country has arisen not from personal relationships between politicians but from the continuing existence of a totalitarian regime. The U.S.S.R. government has been attempting to implement a dead-end programme, not even through the Council of Ministers but by presidential decree. Yeltsin advises Gorbachev to stop clinging to the old institutions and the current U.S.S.R. government. The country's top problem, he says, is the food crisis. He urges setting false pride aside and seeking emergency aid from the West. Otherwise, there will be famine (*Izvestiia*, 319, p. 1).

17 November

At the morning session of the U.S.S.R. Supreme Soviet, Gorbachev focuses on the need for early signing of the U.S.S.R. Union Treaty (*Izvestiia*, 320, pp. 1, 3).

18 November

Military uniform is becoming fashionable; young people in Moscow are trying on military greatcoats, boots, breeches, tunics and astrakhan caps. It is also much cheaper than other clothing (*Moskovskie novosti*, 46, p. 2). Because of cutbacks in the army and a general shortage of money, there is a lively market in army property, which is being sold off by both ordinary soldiers and workers at army supply depots (*Moskovskie novosti*, 46, p. 2; Iu. Peshkova, "60-e – 70-e", *Kommersant-Weekend*, 3 November, 2006).

19 November

Following a meeting in Budapest of defence and foreign ministers, members of the Warsaw Pact decide to commence dismantling all the bloc's military institutions from 1 April, 1991. The Council for Mutual Economic Assistance (Comecon) is also to be wound up, on 27 June, 1991.

20 November

At a session of the U.S.S.R. Supreme Soviet, People's Deputy Viktor Alksnis claims to have received intelligence reports that C.I.A. agents in an East European country met representatives of democratic movements from the Baltic States, Belarus and Ukraine to discuss ways of bringing down the Soviet Union. He alleges that they were planning to form a union stretching from the Baltic to the Black Sea (*Izvestiia*, 323, p. 2).

Andrey Chikatilo (1936–1994) is arrested in Rostov province. The most notorious of Soviet serial killers, he had, according to investigators, killed fifty-three people: twenty-one boys aged seven to sixteen; fourteen girls aged nine to seventeen; and eighteen women. Information about his arrest was published in the Soviet press only on 28 December (*Izvestiia*, 361, p. 12). Chikatilo was sentenced to death and shot on 14 February, 1994.

21 November

An address from the Council of Baltic States to the U.S.S.R. Supreme Soviet notes:

> On 17 November, 1990 the U.S.S.R. Supreme Soviet violated the sovereign rights of our states and peoples by, among other things, issuing blatant threats to forcibly remove democratically elected governments and to repeal the laws of Latvia, Lithuania and Estonia. In the face of these threats, we declare that the Baltic countries will avail themselves of their inalienable right to offer resistance to violence. We call upon the U.S.S.R. Supreme Soviet to desist from its policy of intensifying threats and military pressure against the Baltic States, which are pursuing a course of peaceful restoration of their rights. Latvia, Lithuania and Estonia do not intend to sign the U.S.S.R. Union Treaty, but remain willing to negotiate and conclude bilateral agreements with the U.S.S.R. and union republics in respect of political relations, economic, and other cooperation (*Echo of Lithuania*, 240, 22 November, p. 1).

In the R.S.F.S.R. Palace of Soviets, a treaty is signed by the R.S.F.S.R. and Kazakhstan declaring a policy of equal rights; non-interference by the two republics in each other's internal affairs; renunciation in their relations of pressure, violence and intimidation of any kind; and guarantees of the rights and freedoms of the Russian population in Kazakhstan and of the Kazakh population in Russia. An economic cooperation agreement is also signed (Izvestiia, 325, p. 1).

23 November

At a session of the U.S.S.R. Supreme Soviet, deputies propose that the President should within two weeks submit to parliament a proposal for restructuring and strengthening the U.S.S.R.'s executive institutions (Izvestiia, 326, p. 1). "I am today present at the funeral of the Council of Ministers," Prime Minister Nikolai Ryzhkov tells the meeting. Ryzhkov lays blame for the economic crisis on hasty and ill-considered actions by the Russian republican parliament and Yeltsin personally (Izvestiia, 327, pp. 1–2).

23–5 November

In Grozny, a Congress of the Chechen People is organised by leaders of national, social and environmental organisations; liberal deputies of the Supreme Soviet of the Chechen-Ingush Autonomous S.S.R.; and representatives of the Chechen diaspora. The congress elects an executive committee, with Major General Dzhokhar Dudayev as its Chairman. It further adopts a Declaration of the Formation of the Nokhchi-Cho Chechen Republic. On 26 November, a session of the Supreme Soviet of the Chechen-Ingush A.S.S.R. declares it a sovereign state.

While asserting the independence of the Chechen-Ingush Republic, the declaration carefully avoids almost all mention of the R.S.F.S.R. or U.S.S.R., other than in Article 10, which condemns the "genocide perpetrated against the Chechens and Ingush, and other peoples of the U.S.S.R.", and asserts their right to compensation for moral and material damage caused to their country and its peoples in the period between

1944 and 1957 (Dzhabrail Gakaev, "Put' k chechenskoi revoliutsii", *Chechnia i Rossiia: obshchestva i gosudarstva* [Moscow, 1999]; http://www.sakharov-center.ru/ chs/chruso8_1.htm).

24 November

The draft Union Treaty is published, under which the Soviet Union would be transformed into the "Union of Separate Sovereign Republics". Its main principles are as follows:

> 1) each republic party to the Treaty is a sovereign state with full state power over its territory; 2) the U.S.S.R. is a sovereign federal state, formed as the result of a voluntary association of its constituent republics and exercising state governance within the powers delegated to it by the parties to the Treaty; 3) the republics recognise as fundamental to their union the principles of human rights enshrined in the Universal Declaration of the United Nations and international covenants. Citizens of the U.S.S.R. are guaranteed the opportunity to study and use their native language, with unobstructed access to information, freedom of religion, and other political and personal freedoms; 4) the republics see as crucial to their freedom and prosperity the formation and development of civil society. They will strive to meet people's needs on the basis of a free choice of forms of ownership.

The draft treaty does, however, leave fairly extensive powers in the hands of the central leadership of the Union (*Izvestiia*, 327, p. 1).

25 November

Before being allowed to exchange roubles for hard currency in Moscow banks, people intending to travel abroad have first to "buy a place in the queue" from the mafia battening onto the banking system. The price is 1,500 roubles to ensure that foreign currency can be obtained within one

Banquet to celebrate Agricultural Workers' Day, Istra-Senezh Broiler Production Association, Moscow Province, November 1990

day. A "place in the queue" had, until recently, required payment of not more than 300 roubles (*Moskovskie novosti*, 47, p. 2).

In 1990, the money supply increases three times more rapidly than provided for in the budget. Boris Fyodorov, R.S.F.S.R. Finance Minister, warns, "The measures now required will be tougher than those foreseen under the 500 Days plan." Viktor Kucherenko, Chairman of the Planning and Budgetary Finance Committee of the Soviet of the Union of the Supreme Soviet of the U.S.S.R., states, "Increasing the money supply cannot cause a financial crisis. It is merely a consequence of it" (*Moskovskie novosti*, 47, p. 10).

26 November

The U.S.S.R. Supreme Soviet considers the state plan and budget for 1991. Yuriy Maslyukov, Valentin Pavlov and Leonid Abalkin present U.S.S.R.-wide forecasts for the functioning of the economy, also for the State Plan in

444

areas under central U.S.S.R. management, and the U.S.S.R. budget for the coming year (*Izvestiia*, 329, p. 1).

27 November

A directive of the U.S.S.R. Supreme Soviet proposes that in the event of violation of rights laid down in the U.S.S.R. Constitution of citizens of the U.S.S.R. and of threats to their lives, health and property, the President of the U.S.S.R. should take all measures, including emergency ones, provided for by U.S.S.R. legislation. Distribution of food arriving from abroad, whether purchased or in the form of humanitarian aid, should be placed under the control of the U.S.S.R. Security Council. The Soviet state security agencies should be required to take effective action to combat economic sabotage – that is, they should ensure imported products are used for their intended purpose. It is announced that the President of the U.S.S.R. will establish a special agency to combat the most serious crimes (*Moskovskii komsomolets*, 272, p. 1).

The Minister of Defence, Dmitriy Yazov, states on national television that, "[u]nder no circumstances will the pilfering of nuclear weapons be tolerated. The army will be deployed wherever necessary in order to perform its primary functions of defending the state and ensuring its security. In the event of violence and armed attacks on soldiers of the Soviet army, military installations, military arsenals and weaponry, troops have orders to open fire" (*Izvestiia*, 331, p. 1).

28 November

Margaret Thatcher resigns as Prime Minister of Great Britain. The new Prime Minister is John Major.

29 November

U.N. Security Council resolution No. 678 authorises the use of force to liberate Kuwait from Iraqi forces. Operation "Desert Storm" is initiated by the United States on 17 January, 1991.

Agricultural Workers' Day, Istra-Senezh Broiler Production Association, Moscow Province, November 1990

In the first nine months of 1990, 133,000 drug addicts were officially registered in the U.S.S.R. Officials of the U.S.S.R. Interior Ministry admit that there are almost no schools in Moscow which do not have drug addicts among pupils in their senior classes. Of particular concern to the Soviet law enforcement agencies and Interpol is the Chu Valley in Kirzhizia and Kazakhstan, which is putting the "golden triangle" of South America in the shade. The West is seriously concerned about the possible exporting of Central Asian opium and cannabis to Europe and the U.S. (*Moskovskii komsomolets*, 274, p. 1).

30 November

A plane carrying 30 tonnes of food from Germany lands at Sheremetyevo-2 Airport, Moscow. It has been sent by Olympia-Reisen, a company that is helping Soviet Germans to emigrate from the U.S.S.R. and find work and an apartment in Germany (*Izvestiia*, 333, p. 1).

THE MINERS IN 1989–90:
A VENTURE INTO NATIONAL POLITICS

Sergey Turkin

How are miners involved in politics? The expected answer is, they go on strike. True, but not quite the full story. In 1989–90, when the present-day political system was just beginning to take shape and the miners were just beginning to become politically active, for a short time they aspired to a good deal more than just trying to pressurise the government by going on strike. The miners were politicised by the course of events. In July 1989, they were still heckling off the platform anyone who mentioned politics.[433] By June and July 1990, those same miners were holding their own congress and conducting a political strike. Why?

A GALA IN THE SQUARE

July 1989 saw the start of the miners' protest movement. There had been strikes before; appeals had been signed and sent to provincial authorities; spokesmen for some of the mines had done the rounds of national publications and been featured on television in *Perestroika Spotlight*.[434] None of it had had much impact, which made the surprise all the greater in the summer of 1989 when all the mining regions went on strike simultaneously.

Mining came to a halt in all the major centres – the Donets Basin, Kemerovo, Vorkuta – and to a lesser extent in the Moscow region and northern

---

433. "I was several times nearly driven from the platform for daring to use the word politics" (A. Vasil'ev and M. Krans, "Shakhterskaia 'al'ternativa'", *Kommunist*, 13 [1990], p. 60).
434. For example, D. Mendel', "Zabastovka shakhterov: vpechatleniia, kommentarii, analiz", *Sotsis*, 6 (1990), pp. 55–8; *Kommunist*, 9 (1989).

Kazakhstan. Looking at the Donets Basin, from which the most detailed documentation is available, we find the strikers' organisations completely replacing the local authorities. No doubt this was partly because the authorities decided to steer clear of trouble and not intervene in the strike but also because local people saw the miners as "their" government. In Donetsk, for example, the widow of a miner killed in an accident asked the strike committee to have her house redecorated.[435] Observers particularly commented on the fact that no drunks were to be seen in the streets during the strike. Indeed, in both the Donets and Kuznetsk basins, shops selling alcohol were closed at the miners' request for the duration of the strike.[436] The motivation was to reduce the authorities' ability to influence the course of events. Indeed, the authorities were accused of trying to step up delivery of vodka and wine to the stores.

The miners' strikes were based from the outset on their sense of being in opposition to everybody else, not only to the local authorities and mining management but to "civilians" in general. They saw themselves as a professional guild, and that was the basis, not without a certain theatricality, on which they appealed to the central government. In every location, the strike was played out in public squares. In the Donets Basin, only miners who turned up in their working clothes or with their working badges were allowed into the square, and failure to appear without good reason was regarded as delinquency. The aim was to publicise dramatically the fact that the strike was taking place.

From the beginning, the miners' specific aim was to secure the signatures of General Secretary Mikhail Gorbachev and Prime Minister Nikolai Ryzhkov on a document the strikers had adopted. They believed the only way they could avoid being double-crossed was by not leaving their own territory. There were protests against the suggestion that a delegation

435. *Moskovskie novosti*, 31 (1989), p. 9.
436. Z. Ibragimova, "Ploshchad' Boli, ili Drugogo vykhoda u Kuzbassa ne bylo", *Ogonek*, 32 (1989), p. 2; I. Bestuzhev-Lada, "Kak pri zabastovke, no bez zabastovki", *Gorizont*, 11 (1989), p. 22; *Informatsionnyi biulleten' Informatsionnogo agentstva Svobodnogo mezhdunarodnogo ob"edineniia trudiashchikhsia* (IA SMOT), 24 (1989), p. 1.

should go to Moscow, and it was insisted that Gorbachev and Ryzhkov must personally come to them. The miners even offered to pay the politicians' fares. Alternatively, they suggested, a peripatetic session of the U.S.S.R. Supreme Soviet could be held in the Donets Basin. When this idea was rejected, they suggested a television bridge, broadcast live nationwide. An audience of millions as witnesses was thought likely to ensure fair play.[437] The miners' perception of a wholly dysfunctional outside world was so entrenched that when their delegation did eventually leave Donetsk for Moscow, it was assigned a bodyguard of four ex-soldiers hardened in the war in Afghanistan.

When, at 10.00 p.m. on 24 July, 1989, the Donetsk miners were informed by the head of the delegation in Moscow that agreement had been reached, they insisted on continuing the strike until the delegation had returned to base and they could see the signatures of Gorbachev and Ryzhkov for themselves. The miners suspected that as soon as they left the square a decree banning strikes would be passed to prevent them from holding on to their gains. Everything that was so near would be lost and nothing would change.[438] After the document was publicly read out, there was a great burst of applause, and only then was it time for general "fraternisation"; only then were they openly supported by "civilians" in the square. In his final speech, the leader of the strike committee said, "For the first time we have felt ourselves to be not a grey mass but human beings; not slaves but people capable of winning when we unite in a disciplined manner and in solidarity, to gain what rightfully, by our work, belongs to us all. Thank you, brothers, for your unity. Thank you for your trust."[439]

The miners were conscious of a gulf separating their own world from the world outside, and believed they should negotiate directly with the Party and government in Moscow as the only force capable of bringing change to their lives. Like the heroes in a myth, the representatives of their community, defying entropy, had voyaged out to alien realms, endured many ordeals there and returned home with a pearl of great price. Those

437. Ibid., p. 4.   438. Ibid., pp. 7–8.   439. Ibid., p. 7.

left at home meanwhile performed ritual actions to give power to the explorers, enabling them to see their mission through to a successful conclusion. The people were waiting for a miracle to happen, and doing everything in their power to bring it about. There was a great sense of occasion: "Food was brought in, 'snap' for the miners; the cafeteria was doing brisk business selling water, soft drinks, pies and biscuits. The Bistro mobile café arrived with pizza, roast meat, pies and ice cream, and kvas was poured free into miners' flasks."[440] And: "The miners came in shifts to the square in front of Government House. Wives brought dinner to their husbands. There was a real sense of celebration and unity."[441]

The strike was not generally viewed as political. The miners themselves had no time for talk of political struggle. They said that things were wrong, and they were taking the action they believed might put things right. Their ideas about the causes of the strike were extremely vague. Judging from our sources, the miners were delighted when witnesses to the strike commented that "the mines were stuck in the twelfth century,"[442] and vehemently insisted that every aspect of their life and work was just not fair.[443] A major result of the strike was that the miners came to see the central government as their natural negotiating partner.

Following the strike, several agreements were signed. Those signed with mining provinces differed from those signed with cities, and there was also U.S.S.R. Government Directive No. 608, which summarised the miners' main demands. The implementation of these agreements was to prove highly selective, with the result that the miners' subsequent contacts with Moscow were mainly attempts to get them honoured. There were no political demands initially; these only arose when it became clear that the U.S.S.R. government was sabotaging implementation of Directive No. 608. After the strike, the miners tried for a time to resolve their difficulties piece-

440. Ibid., p. 1.   441. V. Iankulin, "Stachka", Stolitsa, 14 (1991), p. 6.
442. Z. Ibragimova, "Ploshchad' Boli", pp. 2–3.
443. E.g., "When there's nothing to buy, it's fair to go on strike." See V. Yankulin, "Stachka", p. 6.

meal through contacts they had made in the capital. They had not yet developed an "interaction theory" or a political understanding of what was going on.

THE BEGINNINGS OF POLITICS

The major asset of the miners' leaders in their dealings with politicians in Moscow was the impression the miners' strike had made nationally. There was no immediate need to put additional pressure on the central government, and large-scale industrial action in the Kuznetsk Basin and Vorkuta in early August 1989 and strikes at various other mines were mostly in response to local conflicts, like the building of the Krapivinsk hydroelectric station in the Kuznetsk Basin.

Only in Vorkuta, where the miners had been more radical from the outset, was an August strike partly targeted also at the government in Moscow. Their greater radicalism may have been due to the [forced-labour-camp origins of the mines there] (which meant the miners' traditions had a shorter history) or to a situation popularly referred to as serfdom. Under Soviet labour law, a miner could not switch from one mine to another without losing his "northern weighting".[444] Be that as it may, in Vorkuta the miners moved from economic to overtly political action in a relatively short time. In late 1989 they tried to persuade their comrades in the struggle in other areas to put forward radical political demands. At the Fourth Conference of Kuznetsk Basin Workers' Committees in November 1989, the Vorkuta representative, S. Mosolovich, urged the Kuznetsk miners to call a strike demanding the U.S.S.R. government's resignation. On that occasion, the conference delegates confined themselves to sending a telegram to Prime Minister Ryzhkov, warning of the possibility of a sympathy strike, and demanding unfreezing of the Vorkuta strike committee's bank account, restoration of its legal status and lifting of the news blackout imposed on it. In response to a telegram from the Vorkuta miners asking

444. See L. Nikolaeva, "Protivostoianie", *Pozitsiia*, 5 (1989), p. 5

for a strike, the Kuznetsk Basin Soviet of Workers' Committees expressed support but also asked their comrades in Vorkuta and Inta to "show responsibility, caution, prudence, and not provide opportunities to those wishing to discredit the workers' movement". A report on the visit of a delegation of miners' leaders to Vorkuta at the end of 1989 reproached the Vorkuta miners for their reluctance to seek forms of struggle other than strikes, the untimeliness of their political demands, and their collaboration with the Russian Popular Front and Democratic Union parties.[445]

Mainstream miners' politics prior to 1990 mostly involved regular visits by regional delegations to Moscow. Until the end of September 1989, these were attempting to extract the food and equipment promised in the agreement reached during the July strikes, which had included "improving the supply of consumer goods and food to mining regions". This had been a particular demand of the Kuznetsk miners' leaders.

The bodies in contact with Moscow were workers' committees, which had been universally formed, or rather re-formed, from strike committees:

> At mines, and in some other enterprises, workers' committees were elected which then delegated representatives to a city committee, and these in turn to a provincial committee. Some members received sabbatical pay from voluntary contributions made by their fellow workers. This gave a degree of assurance that they would act in accordance with the wishes of their constituents rather than of the bureaucrats.[446]

The miners' was a grassroots movement. For example, a decision to strike had to be taken by each mine separately. Representatives of workers' committees at every level, from those representing a single mine to provincial representatives, travelled to Moscow individually. Attempts by the provincial workers' committee to coordinate the activities of the city and

445. *Rabochee dvizhenie Kuzbassa. Dokumenty i materialy* (Kemerovo, 1993), pp. 173, 188, 196.
446. Ibid., p. 92.

mine committees were met with understandable suspicion and ultimately failed. The miners never did manage to organise themselves as an integrated group for dialogue with the central government. Individual spokesmen from the mines and cities were, as the shortages worsened, more often effectively foraging for groceries and equipment which the workers' committees they represented were to distribute. Officials not infrequently found ways of buying them off. In the autumn of 1989 this approach was stopped – in the Kuznetsk Basin by a decision of the province's workers' committee – but not before it had discredited the very principle of "unorganised" representation, whose main feature seemed to be a simple lack of coordination between the different levels of workers' committees. It became evident that "unauthorised" contact with the regime could cost the miners' leaders their independent stance. Once this was recognised, the movement progressed towards greater centralisation and rapidly became politicised.

A turning point for the mainstream miners' movement, including Vorkuta, was the Fourth Conference of Workers' Committees of the Kuznetsk Basin. This was convened when it was becoming obvious to everyone that the government was reneging on key aspects of Directive No. 608. The first strike related to this backsliding took place on 23 October, 1989 in the Kuznetsk Basin. The conference was intended from the outset to be political, as was signalled by convening it under the aegis of the Union of Kuzbass Workers, a political organisation set up after the July 1989 strike, but which had not been very visible since. The conference was broadcast on radio to the entire Kuznetsk Basin, which gave it some similarity to the First Congress of People's Deputies of the U.S.S.R. in May 1989. It was the setting for the first political statements referring not to narrowly defined miners' issues but to the situation in the country as a whole. The realisation had dawned that the miners' problems resulted from a wider background of major political blunders and the inefficiency of the current regime itself.

One speaker protested that, instead of the socialist goal of maximum

453

satisfaction of the individual's material and spiritual needs, the people had been fobbed off with a penurious existence. Instead of the elimination of exploitation there was economic and non-economic coercion. Instead of public ownership of the means of production there was state property, which alienated the producer from the fruits of their toil. Instead of the power of the people there was the power of the Communist Party and government officials. Instead of developing culture and creating the right conditions for all-round development of the personality there was an ideology of deceit. The conference declared that the main objective of the Union of Kuzbass Workers should be to create a society which would fundamentally improve the development of productive forces, where power and property would belong to the people, and where the rights and interests of the individual would be respected.[447]

There were as yet no radical demands for the government to resign. However, reference was made in conference speeches to the need to reject the "Stalinist model of socialism", a phrase evidently borrowed from liberal historians and economists. In the language of the time this was an attack on the bureaucracy. Shortly after the conference, a token strike was held in the Kuznetsk Basin which included political as well as economic demands, for abolition of Article 6 of the U.S.S.R. Constitution, a new parliamentary electoral law and changes to the law governing resolution of labour disputes. At several meetings during the strike there were declarations that the workers' committees would not be disbanded until the bureaucracy had ceased to exist.

Politicisation of the miners was related also to the forthcoming election of people's deputies of the R.S.F.S.R. and provincial soviets, just as various unofficial proto-parties had appeared in 1988 and 1989 in connection with election campaigns for the 19th Communist Party Conference and the Congress of People's Deputies of the U.S.S.R. Miners' leaders, on behalf of the workers' unions which by early 1990 had sprung up in all mining regions, stood in elections and gained many seats in regional soviets.

447. Ibid., p. 113.

The workers' unions were to some degree carrying on the miners' claim during the first strikes that they were a closed, professional guild. The miners' organisations continued to distance themselves from unofficial political movements, claiming they were "too different" from them. Nevertheless, the political viewpoint emerging in their documents was moving rapidly in the direction of "Left" dissident ideas, which argued that past decisions had perverted the course of history and produced unsatisfactory results. Unlike the dissidents, the miners' leaders had no intention of embarking on academic studies of when exactly and why the fatal mistakes had been made. Nevertheless, the need for a "rearrangement" of life, including national politics, was becoming increasingly obvious to them.

By late 1989 to early 1990, the miners had at least partly centralised their movement, fashioned a political organisation to speak for it and formed a clear political view of what was taking place. Despite differences over appropriate methods of struggle, it can be said with little exaggeration that politically the miners were united. Leaders were also emerging from their ranks, some of whom would head up the workers' unions while others strengthened the workers' committees. Finally, the miners had every reason to want to continue to put pressure on the government. By early 1990, it was obvious that all their contacts with Moscow in connection with Directive No. 608 had produced nothing worthwhile. The government refused outright to ratify the documents, claiming they would undermine the entire concept behind its reforms.

THE SEARCH FOR POLITICAL LEGITIMACY: PUBLIC RITUALS AND THEIR IDEOLOGICAL UNDERPINNINGS

In 1990, the miners' movement was very different from what it had been in 1989, and from what it was to become in 1991. If 1989 had seen numerous strikes and two unsuccessful invasions of Moscow by workers' committees, and 1991 saw numerous strikes from the beginning of the year, 1990 in contrast had only one significant strike, on 11 July. Instead it had three congresses, two of miners and one of the Confederation of Labour.

What did a congress signify in the perestroika era? It was the model of an ideal community and that community's political expression. During perestroika, no more legitimate political entity could be imagined than a properly convened congress. It differed from a run-of-the-mill political meeting in that all congresses (or soviets, which were much the same thing) were idealised models, and thus theoretically independent and all of equal status. My own favourite example is the District Soviet of Avtozavodsky in the city of Gorky, which in the summer of 1990 proclaimed the independence of its part of the city.[448] By the end of year, even Moscow district soviets were thinking of doing the same. The national power structure, a multiplicity of congresses and soviets, was described at the time as a "layer cake".[449] This had the corollary that any community aspiring to a role in politics had little option but to hold a congress. The word *sovereignty* was on everybody's lips. Given the sense of growing crisis, everyone wanted their own lifeboat, so at least there was no shortage of congresses.

But to return to the miners. It can be argued that actually there were more than three miners' congresses in 1990, because they were politically active in the local soviets in areas where they had influence. Miners were the backbone of the democratic faction in the Kemerovo provincial soviet. They were, however, very much a minority in their local soviets. We estimate that between a quarter and a third of seats were typically held there by "democratic" deputies. This seemed all the more reason to convene their own congresses and strengthen their independent political voice.

During the first months of 1990, the miners' leaders were still preoccupied with fruitless negotiations with the government in Moscow over the fate of Directive No. 608, and were participating in the work of their local soviets. They were, however, simultaneously preparing a First Congress of Independent Workers' Movements and Organisations of the U.S.S.R., which set up the Confederation of Labour. The congress was held between 30 April and 2 May, 1990 in Novokuznetsk. A group of activists in Moscow had been

448. *Panorama*, 7 (1990), p. 1.   449. Nikolai Travkin's expression.

456

planning a congress of independent workers' movements back in June 1989 after rumours spread that plans for a "workers' congress" were being hatched in the bowels of the Central Committee of the Communist Party. In other words, there was a struggle for ownership of a political entity to be called a "workers' congress". There was subsequently to be a struggle between the mining management and leaders of the workers' committees over who should "own" the miners' congress.

The Confederation of Labour congress was different from the workers'/miners' congresses in that a large proportion of the papers for it were drawn up by Moscow intellectuals, in particular Viktor Sheynis, an economist, and Leonid Gordon, a sociologist. The confederation's congress reports differed significantly from the resolutions passed at the conferences of workers' committees in that they contained no mention of socialism. The confederation's congress put forward major political demands. It called for withdrawal of the official status of Communist Party committees in enterprises, the armed forces, the Interior Ministry, the K.G.B., the Public Prosecutor's Office and the courts. It called for nationalisation of the Communist Party's property, the resignation of Gorbachev's government and its replacement by a new, fully democratic regime.[450] At the same time, it emphasised that political and economic change should be brought about peacefully.

There never was a second Confederation of Labour Congress, but the first set up a fifty-eight-person Council of Representatives of the Confederation of Labour with a coordinating council consisting of one representative each from Donetsk, Kemerovo, Moscow and Sverdlovsk. In the future, it was this council which played the main role in the workers' movement, whose leaders were largely those of the miners. By the end of 1991, the workers' committees were under its jurisdiction.

The congress demonstrated that the miners and dissident intellectuals were not in perfect harmony. Documents proposed to it were adopted largely because 52 per cent of the delegates were from Kemerovo province and

450. *Rabochee dvizhenie Kuzbassa*, p. 165.

generally went along with the leaders. The resolution on the congress's attitude towards the Communist Party was of overriding interest to the dissidents, but so eager were they to discuss it that the miners' leaders proposed that it should be excluded from the agenda. The Confederation of Labour Congress was, in any case, too cumbersome to play an active role in politics. The logical alternative was the First Miners' Congress.

That congress is of great interest. The First Miners' Congress was held between 11 and 15 June, 1990 in Donetsk. It was wholly organised by the miners themselves, unlike the second. In our opinion, it was highly representative of the miners' movement. The participants saw it as a "real" congress, and spent considerable time verifying the representativeness and credentials of delegates to ensure that all the formalities were duly observed which make for a true congress. The threat that it might go the same way as the Congress of People's Deputies of the U.S.S.R., which by the summer of 1990 had lost its sacral status, was a matter of great concern. "We watch the congress debates on television and are outraged by the games played by the organisers, yet we ourselves are allowing the person presiding to put pressure on our delegates," one participant complained touchily.[451]

The fact that the congress played strictly by the rules increased its prestige in the eyes of the miners themselves. For Nikolai Travkin [founder in 1990 of the Democratic Party of Russia], a guest there, such procedural meticulousness seemed perfectly normal: "I would not be too concerned about losing a day due to the fact that we are unable to agree on the agenda. We have all watched on television the First Congress of the Soviets of the U.S.S.R., Ukraine, the Leningrad Soviet, the Moscow City Soviet, and there these issues took up not just a day but whole weeks."[452]

The members of the congress clearly saw it as the equal of other congresses and soviets representing territories. Despite some awkward moments, like when the greetings from the Moscow City Soviet concluded with the hope of "close collaboration between the renewed soviets of

451. I S"ezd shakhterov (Donetsk, 1990), pt 1, p. 14.   452. Ibid., p. 28.

Moscow and Donetsk",[453] the miners in attendance set great store by this idea. In the pecking order of congresses, they saw themselves as only slightly below republican level.

The miner's main priority at their first congress was to assert their independence. They made it clear that they were not affiliated to any political party by stating,

> The First Miners' Congress, expressing the will of its delegates, emphasises the complete independence of workers' organisations of the coal and mining industry from all political bodies. Independent workers' movements and workers' organisations are subject only to the will of their members, and believe they should be under the control of no political forces or parties. Our desire for independence also defines our relationship with the Communist Party.[454]

When the resolution about their attitude towards the Communist Party was debated, representatives of one delegation questioned whether it was "democratic" to adopt a resolution about another organisation. In response, one of the congress's leaders commented, "We have the right to adopt a resolution in respect of any political institutions of the U.S.S.R., including the Communist Party".[455] In the speeches of ordinary miners, this sense of independence was expressed particularly strongly:

> Dear Rulers of the U.S.S.R.,
> Dear President,
> You can probably stop worrying about us now. Nobody is going to take care of me better than I will myself. Give me freedom! Give me freedom to work and earn as much as I can so I can feed myself and my children, buy clothes for myself and my family, decide for myself how my children are to be taught, what medical care they

453. Ibid., p. 11.   454. Ibid., p. 2, p. 92.   455. Ibid., p. 87.

are to get, and, when the time comes, how to provide for my old age, live where I want to, love and believe in what I choose, and perhaps every year take my holidays in the Canary Islands and ride in a Cadillac.[456]

This congress's attitude towards the politics of Moscow was little different from that of the Congress of the Confederation of Labour:

We all live under the administrative-command system. Its state monopoly over property and the absence of market competition condemn the economy to stagnate and fall behind, and the people to live in poverty. The top leadership of the country promised to change that situation, but experience has shown that reforms are not being implemented in earnest. What is needed now is a government with the ability and determination to end the state's monopoly of property and the effective monopoly of the Communist Party in politics, and bring about a real transition to democracy and the market.[457]

The miners had a fairly abstract idea of what the market was. More than one speaker repeated that it would be a means of providing a decent life, like people had in the West.[458] The safeguard against the dangers of the market was a real trade union, also like in the West. Foreign guests attending the congress were bombarded with questions about the right way to organise trade unions. The congress documents enumerated many obligations the state should accept and honour. The miners were fully aware that a number of mines would need to be closed, but they also had no doubt that it was the government's duty to minimise the social impact of the closures.

456. Ibid., pt 1, p. 48.   457. Ibid., pt 2, p. 87.
458. According to opinion polls, 1990 was the year when the desire of citizens of the U.S.S.R. (and later Russia) to live "like they do in the West" reached a record high. See V. Sogrin, *Politicheskaia istoriia sovremennoi Rossii* (Moscow, 1994), p. 69.

The delegates did not agree on all issues. It was physically impossible to take account of the wishes of representatives of particular mines. There was a promise in one of the resolutions to process requests made at the congress after it closed and forward them to the authorities, but it was obviously not going to be possible to take account of all of them. More seriously, there was a confrontation from the outset between the Kuznetsk Basin miners and those from Ukrainian regions, particularly the Donets Basin. The Ukrainians were in a majority at the Congress with 58 per cent of the seats, and decided to take it over. The Kuznetsk delegation, with 24 per cent of the seats, tried at first to resist, requested an adjournment and even threatened to walk out, but then decided not to aggravate the situation. No Kuznetsk delegates were included on the organising committee for the second congress, and they also failed in their bid to have it held in the Kuznetsk Basin, the second-largest mining region. For all its outward unity, the First Miners' Congress revealed a serious rift between these blocs, which Moscow was able to exploit in the run-up to the second congress.

The ideology, and even the terminology, used by the miners at their congress were for the most part borrowed from democratic forces. Not surprisingly, both while preparing the congress and especially after it, the leaders' contacts with the authorities of the union republics were strengthened. On 23 June, 1990, Yeltsin had a meeting with the Kuznetsk Basin workers' committees to coordinate efforts for "united action in the event of any emergency".[459] In August, during his visit to Novokuznetsk, a statement of intent was signed in which both sides undertook to support the other in implementing reforms.

Immediately after the first congress it was decided to hold a twenty-four-hour political strike to mark the anniversary of the July 1989 strike. This had been agreed by workers' committees of the Donetsk and Kuznetsk basins, Vorkuta and Rostov province, and had the support of the Council of

459. *Nasha gazeta*, 26 June, 1990.

Representatives of the Confederation of Labour.[460] The need for an anniversary strike was discussed repeatedly at the congress, although there is no mention of it in the resolutions. Nevertheless, the date of the strike, 11 July, is mentioned as the day when the miners were to have made their demands known to the U.S.S.R. authorities. The only general strike of 1990 was thus a symbolic echo of a strike a year earlier, and it was a direct consequence of the miners' congress.

The strike and the holding of a second miners' congress, already scheduled for August, need to be seen as crisis measures. The congress provided the miners' community with a means of rapid political response to events in the country, and the strike renewed the positive energy of the miners' movement. It is no surprise that their leaders wanted to recapture the euphoria of July 1989. As in the previous year, the miners went to great lengths to ensure good order during the strike. A workers' militia was set up and relations established with the police; points where alcohol would be on sale were monitored. It was decided to hold the strike not, as in 1989, in city squares but at the mines. Clearly, if the strike became disorderly it would not have the hoped-for moral impact.

This time, the strike's demands were handed down by the leaders, but detailed organisation remained in the hands of workers' collectives. The demands included: resignation of the government of the U.S.S.R.; conclusion of a new Union Treaty; bringing the U.S.S.R. Constitution into line with the constitutions of the union republics and the Universal Declaration of Human Rights; nationalising the property of the Communist Party; introducing competition law; depriving members of social organisations of ex officio seats as people's deputies of the U.S.S.R.; and depoliticising the armed forces, the Interior Ministry, the K.G.B., court institutions, the Prosecutor's Office, the state and national press, and education.[461] Clearly, these were radical demands which the government would never accept. They were also more radical than anything which had been discussed at the miners' congress less than a month before.

460. *Glasnost'. Ezhednevnaia khronika*, 6 July, 1990.   461. *Rabochee dvizhenie Kuzbassa*, p. 190.

The radicalisation of the miners' demands was affected by events at the 28th Congress of the Communist Party of the Soviet Union, which took place between 2 and 11 July, 1990. Not only were representatives of democratic circles in Moscow barred from the miners' congress, specifically members of the Communist Party's Democracy Platform, but Party members from the miners' movements also were. The Russian republican authorities were preparing a showdown with the U.S.S.R. centre at the C.P.S.U. congress. They presented a programme for dealing with the economic crisis and, when it was, predictably, blocked, announced they were resigning from the Party. It is highly probable that the Russian republican authorities coordinated their actions with the miners' leaders (who specifically supported the R.S.F.S.R.'s demands for a Union Treaty), since a politically inspired general strike during the Party congress would have had significantly less political impact.

In the Kuznetsk Basin, following the strike, the conservative Kemerovo Provincial Soviet took a number of liberal decisions. In particular, it established a commission to inventory Party property in anticipation of its possible nationalisation. Other interesting events in the summer of 1990 were rallies held in the Kuznetsk Basin on 2 June to commemorate the anniversary of the 1962 shootings [by the Khrushchev government of protesting workers in Novocherkassk]. These rallies were an initiative of the Congress of the Confederation of Labour, but if participation in the July strike was almost total, only two or three hundred people in each city supported them. The rallies were much more radical than the strike. They were overtly anti-Communist with slogans like, "The ideology of Leninism is the ideology of Red fascism". They demanded a parliamentary commission of inquiry into the 1962 massacre, in order to bring its perpetrators to justice; complete rehabilitation of the victims; and payment of pensions to the families of those who died.[462] The modest turnout indicates that the miners were not that interested in seeing justice for the victims of political repression.[463]

462. *Nasha gazeta*, 5 June, 1990.   463. Possibly the fact that the events in Novocherkassk occurred outside the Kuznetsk Basin region meant that there were no local witnesses.

A much higher priority was the problems of the present day and measures to resolve them. They evidently did not share the view that analysing and correcting past wrongs were prerequisites for moving the country forward.[464] This was at a time when even top Party officials were being forced, through the efforts of Moscow intellectuals, to acknowledge the need to rehabilitate victims of state repression. Indeed, the 22nd Kemerovo Provincial Conference of the Communist Party, which was in session at this time, supported an appeal from the rallies for crimes in Novocherkassk to be investigated.

THE END OF POLITICS

The summer of 1990 was a turning point for the political future of the miners' movement. Their leaders opted for a robust confrontation with a regime that was in no hurry to listen to proposals from their congresses and conferences. The miners were making friends with Yeltsin and the Russian republican authorities, and the U.S.S.R. government began to view them as dangerous opponents. The hardening attitude showed in the aftermath of the July 1990 strike, when, for the first time, strikers were deprived of bonuses and began to find their summer holidays being rescheduled to the winter months. Mine directors and managers were fired for "unsatisfactory educational work" among the workforce.

The period of increasingly acute confrontation came just as the miners' movement began to experience a political crisis of its own. As conditions deteriorated, some became less willing to contribute towards paying their representatives on the workers' committees. Not infrequently, mine and even city committees collapsed. The miners' workers' unions were unable to compete with emerging political parties. In some cities, their membership had halved by the autumn of 1990. The Fifth Conference of Workers'

464. On the importance of remembering history, see Sergei Turkin, "'Vspominanie istorii' v period perestroiki: kak protsess, i ne tol'ko ...", Neprikosnovennyi zapas, 47 (2006), pp. 67–76.

Committees of the Kuznetsk Basin was attended by 321 delegates instead of the 577 expected. The delegates adopted all the reports they were supposed to, including radical political declarations, but the conference had little impact. The workers' committees decided, as recommended by the miners' congress, to concentrate on establishing an independent miners' trade union. As a result, the political arm of the workers' committees, which is what the workers' unions were, ceased to exist. The Council of Representatives of the Confederation of Labour, which included some of the miners' leaders, tried with variable success to coordinate the activities of affiliated political parties. It was to survive but, by its very nature, was unable to generate political initiatives.

The Second Miners' Congress was the last throw of the political dice for the miners. It was held, not in August 1990 as planned, but only at the end of October, and again in Donetsk. In the months preceding it, Mikhail Shchadov, U.S.S.R. Minister of the Coal Industry, outplayed the miners by obtaining agreement that his report would be the main item on the agenda. He also negotiated the right for several dozen of his ministry's civil servants and mine managers to be full members of the congress.[465] Next, it was found that a number of miners' leaders, mainly from the Kuznetsk Basin, had "accidentally" been listed as guests rather than voting delegates, and the predominantly "Ukrainian" congress chose not to correct the mistake.

The crucial decision the congress needed to take concerned setting up a miners' free trade union. This was blocked in a debate at the congress's main session, which led to 130 delegates meeting separately and announcing that a free trade union would nevertheless be formed. This split discredited the notion of the miners' congress as a model of representativeness and put an end to its aspiration to be a channel for the miners to participate independently in the political process, as equals, even, of the soviets in the republics. The miners' leaders went back to attempting to coerce the government by calling mass strikes, which they duly did in 1991.

465. *Rabochee dvizhenie Kuzbassa*, pp. 212–13.

GAME, SET AND MATCH

What motivated the miners to try to enter politics? They were following a familiar route in the footsteps of critically-minded citizens who start out intending to protect the environment or preserve historic monuments, only to find themselves obliged to sign up sooner or later to left- or right-wing oppositional politics. The miners were different only in terms of speed: the trajectory started in 1989 and brought them to politics in just six months.

Was their political project doomed from the outset? Most probably, yes. Their politicisation was as predictable as the outcome of their attempts to negotiate with a regime that had no interest in honouring its agreements. By entering the political fray, however, the miners lost twice over. First, they lost to political parties which could offer better quality. The vulnerability of their leaders and the weakness of their political "product" reflected the untimeliness of social-democratic values in 1990. Liberal ideology sounded more convincing when delivered directly by intellectuals. In addition, they had only one year in which to grow to political maturity and simply ran out of time. Second, they were outplayed by the U.S.S.R. government in Moscow. At the Third Congress of People's Deputies of the R.S.F.S.R. in March–April 1991, Yeltsin was to win a much more difficult battle, while the miners' leaders lost control at their second congress, largely because there was no single leader who could unite the different regions.

As a result, Yeltsin's victory over Gorbachev at the R.S.F.S.R. congress was, for a time at least, seen as "iconic". No more was heard of the miners' congress, and their own iconic image was to manifest itself only in 1998. It was miners forlornly beating their helmets in impotent rage on the hump-back bridge [in front of Moscow's White House in protest at the Russian Federal Government's deceitfulness and incompetence, and demanding Yeltsin's resignation].

DECEMBER

2 December

Boris Yeltsin is interviewed by Yegor Yakovlev, editor of *Moscow News*:

Yakovlev: "It is fashionable nowadays to criticise Gorbachev. Yeltsin by contrast is seen as a very radical leader. I think that, nevertheless, it will not be long before increasing criticism starts coming in your direction. Society always expects more than is actually achieved, and in addition, because of the exceptional situation, you will have to take unpopular decisions which will do nothing for your image. Are you prepared for that?"

Yeltsin: "No doubt it will happen, but, travelling through half of Russia, I have said at every meeting, 'Bear with the new Russian Supreme Soviet and its leaders for two years while we stabilise the economy. After that, in the third year, you will see living standards rise. If we don't deliver, you can kick us out, but in any case we will leave of our own accord.' We seem already, within limits, to be making inroads into the most pressing problems affecting food supplies, although the decline still has some way to go. If everything just stayed the way it is at present, a wave of discontent would sweep both Gorbachev and Yeltsin away. That could begin in the spring. Then more decisive action would be needed. If our hands weren't tied by the U.S.S.R. government, we could be doing a lot more. We have lost three months because of their wretched economic plan" (*Moskovskie novosti*, 48, p. 5).

U.S.S.R. Prime Minister Nikolai Ryzhkov's approval ratings over the past year: December 1989: 52 percent; January 1990: 44 per cent; July: 25 per cent; October: 15 per cent (*Moskovskie novosti*, 48, p. 7).

PIK publishers are preparing *In the Dock*, a three-volume study of the circumstances surrounding the trial of Konstantin Smirnov-Ostashvili [Chairman of the Pamyat' (Memory) Union for National Proportional Representation], recently sentenced to two years' imprisonment on charges of inciting anti-Semitism and ethnic hatred.

3 December

At the R.S.F.S.R. Congress of People's Deputies, opponents of introducing private land ownership continue to prolong the discussion (*Izvestiia*, 336, p. 1). An amendment proposed by Sergey Shakhrai, allowing peasants to sell allotted land only after they have held it for ten years, is passed by 602 votes to 369, with 40 abstentions. At a press conference afterwards, Yeltsin says the land has now been placed in the hands of the people (*Izvestiia*, 337, p. 1).

A presidential decree relieves Vadim Bakatin of his duties as Interior Minister. He is replaced by Boris Pugo (*Izvestiia*, 336, p. 3).

Eduard Shevardnadze: "I knew Bakatin, but not particularly well. He was generally considered a good interior minister. After my resignation, I didn't see Gorbachev for three or four months. Aleksandr Yakovlev resigned along with me. Gorbachev phoned one day and said, 'Drop by. Let's talk.' It wasn't an easy conversation. He was in a dire state. Anyway, at that most difficult time for him, while we sat talking for two hours, just Yakovlev, Gorbachev and me, the only person to phone him was Bakatin. I imagine he just offered him moral support. We are on your side, that sort of thing. No-one else at all phoned Gorbachev in the course of our meeting.

"I didn't know Pugo well, but I'd heard he was educated and well read. Then he turned out to be one of the coup plotters.

"Why did I resign? Because I had specific information that the counter-revolution was preparing an offensive on the R.S.F.S.R. government's White House in Moscow. People were already assembling 50 or 60 kilometres outside Moscow, including army people. I had completely reliable information that an attack was coming. Later, the August coup plot was hatched in much the same way.

"Incidentally, when the 1991 plot was under way, I arranged a meeting with Yeltsin. I wanted to warn him about the same thing: the counter-revolution being on its way to attack the White House. In his office some-one asked, 'You don't know where Gorbachev is, do you?' I said, 'Yes. He is on holiday in the Crimea.' 'Do you think this is a sensible time for the President to be on holiday?' I replied, 'If Gorbachev knew about the plot and went off to holiday in the Crimea, he is a traitor too.' But Gorbachev didn't return to Moscow with the plotters. He came back in a separate plane and got on with his work as President."

7 December

In November, the price of potatoes and fresh and pickled cabbage had increased by 170 per cent compared with 1989. The price of pickled gherkins had increased by 240 per cent; pickled tomatoes by 190 per cent; apples by 40 per cent; meat and poultry by 230 per cent; eggs by 410 per cent; honey by 190 per cent; and vegetable oil by 200 per cent (*Moskovskii komsomolets*, 281, p. 1).

9 December

According to the R.S.F.S.R. Interior Ministry, during the first ten months of the year eighty-eight crimes against individuals (murder, grievous bodily harm, etc.) were committed, an increase of 12 percent on the whole of 1989 (*Izvestiia*, 342, p. 2).

12 December

Lech Wałęsa, leader of the Solidarity trade union movement and Nobel Peace Prize winner, is elected President of Poland with a landslide majority. In Leningrad, Aleksandr Nevzorov, presenter of the popular *600 Seconds* television programme, is shot during the night but recovers (*Izvestiia*, 346, p. 8; *Moskovskii komsomolets*, 286, p. 1).

14 *December*

For the first time in many years, there are queues of depositors wishing to pay money into the U.S.S.R. Savings Bank. The attempt to "tether" the population's cash by raising interest rates on fixed-term deposits is one of the measures to stabilise the financial system (*Izvestiia*, 347, p. 1). Unfortunately, it was not a sign of incipient economic recovery.

15 *December*

A presidential decree insists that enterprises must without delay sign contracts for the supply of centrally distributed products in 1991, in compliance with the state's requirements and through existing economic channels (*Izvestiia*, 348, p. 1).

16 *December*

Aleksandr Kabakov: "After a rally at the unveiling of the memorial stone to the victims of the terror, on the eve of International Human Rights Day, mortification and an ossified persistence in evil, the striving for good and persistence in intolerance again confronted each other on Lubyanka. People with icons and banners circled Dzerzhinsky Square, whose very name has come to symbolise our shared, inescapable guilt. People walked in a religious procession, but still an ominous shadow fell on them, and perhaps that too had symbolic significance. We circle again and again the horror of the past, which seems not to allow us to break the damnable ring of hatred" (*Moskovske novosti*, 50, p. 1).

Inflation in 1989 was 7.5 per cent against 9 per cent in 1990, according to the State Statistics Committee. Independent experts put the figures at 12 and 18 per cent respectively, and forecast that it will break through the 20 per cent barrier before the end of the year (*Moskovskie novosti*, 50, p. 10).

17 *December*

The Fourth Congress of People's Deputies of the U.S.S.R. opens. Gorbachev acknowledges that "in the course of perestroika the country's leaders have made serious mistakes and miscalculations," but, he adds, ". . . we have never known such freedom of thought. A totalitarian, command-administrative system has been razed to its foundations." He calls on the Party to show discipline: "What is most necessary at this moment to over-come the crisis is to restore order in the country. It all comes down to the issue of power. If we have strong government, discipline, and keep a close watch to ensure that decisions are properly implemented, we will be able to provide satisfactory food supplies, rein in the criminals and put an end to inter-ethnic strife" (*Argumenty i Fakty*, 51, p. 1). A lively debate follows. Pres-ident Nursultan Nazarbayev of Kazakhstan strongly criticises the U.S.S.R. government, as well as the weakness of the U.S.S.R.'s top leadership. According to the Interregional Deputies Group, the underlying cause of the misfortunes is that the country had so far failed to introduce serious change. Viktor Alksnis complains that there has been no sign of a programme for dealing with the crisis in the President's report (*Izvestiia*, 351, pp. 1–2).

18 December

T.A.S.S. reports that Iraq is to send food aid to the U.S.S.R. Baghdad announces that 500 tons of dates will be sent as "a gift from the people of Iraq" (*Moskovskii komsomolets*, 289, p. 1). This "act of charity" is primarily a propaganda move. In the 1970s and 1980s the U.S.S.R. had been a close ally of Iraq. After supporting military action against Saddam, Gorbachev vacillated. In October–November 1990, supporters of a more lenient policy towards Saddam and of more criticism of the U.S. line on Iraq had become influential in the Soviet leadership (Iuliia Khitrukhina, "SSSR i Kuveitskii krizis 1990 goda", *Obozrevatel'*, 9 [2003]; http://www.rau.su/observer/N9_2003/9_11.htm).

From Shevardnadze's memoirs:

> In spite of the clearly stated position of the U.S.S.R. government, there were people who believed we could find a common language

471

with Saddam, who was considered a friend. With this in mind, Yevgeniy Primakov, a personal friend of Saddam, visited first Baghdad and then Washington in an attempt to mediate. I opposed the visit and told Gorbachev, "The country cannot have two international positions."

Primakov's travels proved fruitless. He was unable to persuade Saddam to moderate his stance, and George W. Bush interrupted Primakov abruptly by saying, "Hussein has committed the same kind of crime as Hitler. There can be no talking with him and no concessions!" (Eduard Shevardnadze, "O proshedshem i budushchem", trans. Viktoriia Zinina, Druzhba narodov, 11 [2006]; http://magazines.russ.ru/druzhba/2006/11/zi10.html).

19 December

At the U.S.S.R. Congress of People's Deputies, Yeltsin says the situation in the country has deteriorated seriously since the last congress. It is now out of control and it sometimes seems that disaster is inevitable (Izvestiia, 353, p. 1).

During the night of 18 December, explosions were heard in Riga, Latvia. Windows were broken in the buildings of the Council of Ministers, the military commandant's office and the District Party Committee (Izvestiia, 352, p. 1). The Deputy Chairman of the National Front of Latvia, Ivars Redisons, said, "We have established that no democratic organisation in Latvia or the N.F.L. had any part in these recent bombings" (Diena, 20 December, p. 7).

20 December

At the U.S.S.R. Congress of People's Deputies, Shevardnadze reports on the situation in the Persian Gulf. Regarding the political situation, he says, "All the reformers have now run for cover. A dictatorship is in the making. I am resigning. Let this be my contribution, my protest against the impending dictatorship. I have supported Gorbachev. I am his friend and share his views, but I cannot go along with what is happening." The reason for his resignation was said to be "blatant harassment" by, among others, Pamyat' nationalists. At a press conference, Vladimir Ignatenko says that Shevardnadze's resignation came as a complete surprise to Gorbachev (*Izvestiia*, 353, p. 1).

Commentary by Shevardnadze:

> A summary of my report was circulated to the deputies, I went to the podium and said this would be the shortest speech in my life. Everybody was watching: what was going on? I said counter-revolution was imminent. We had all run for cover. The counter-revolution could undo all that democracy had achieved, and so, in protest at the onset of dictatorship, I was resigning. It was a call to all the people. We needed to unite and put a stop to the threat of dictatorship, whose supporters were standing right beside us.
>
> I had told my colleagues that soldiers were preparing to attack Moscow and, specifically, the White House, but no-one believed me. When I announced my resignation, Gorbachev said, "I know nothing about this. I should know if something is afoot, but I have heard nothing. Where is the K.G.B., where is the Interior Ministry?" I knew about this myself because, of five thousand staff at the Ministry of Foreign Affairs, half were K.G.B. I knew them all personally, who was a real diplomat and who was a K.G.B. officer. I was on good terms with them. They had very extensive connections and I got all the information, more than the K.G.B. chiefs. When no-one believed me that counter-revolution was imminent, that was when I resigned. Was it the right thing to do? I think my action was justified. It turned out later that even people sitting in that hall knew something was being readied, but what it was, no-one was saying.
>
> By then, I had established good relations with the leaders of

various countries. They were alarmed and wanted to know what was happening. I could not tell all of them.

A day and a half later, I went to see Yeltsin. I went in and said, "Do you know where these rebels are right now? Just 50 miles from the White House, and they can be here within two days. What will you do then?" Yeltsin took a slip of paper out of his folder and showed me his decree: Troops deployed on Russian territory are subordinate to the head of the Russian government. In other words, Yeltsin would become commander-in-chief. That decree could save the day. He asked me, "What do you think? Should I sign this or not?" I said, "Sign it straight away. It will be too late tomorrow." From that day, he was commander-in-chief. Thanks to the army, he went on not only to disperse but to destroy many of the conspirators and preserve democratic government. Later, after the defeat of the plotters of the August 1991 coup, a rally was held on 22 August at City Hall. I spoke. Luzhkov was there too, and Popov, the former Mayor. Ten thousand people came, a huge crowd. That was the end of that story, but not of the battle between Gorbachev and Yeltsin.

22 December

At the U.S.S.R. Congress of People's Deputies, Vladimir Kryuchkov denies that there is a threat to democracy from the K.G.B. Among domestic threats, he singles out the nationalist organisations with armed detachments, and also agitation by a number of other movements (*Izvestiia*, 355, p. 1).

24 December

The R.S.F.S.R. Supreme Soviet passes a law "Concerning ownership of property in the R.S.F.S.R." The act makes it legal for state and municipal property to pass into private ownership (*Izvestiia*, 358, p. 1).

25 December

The R.S.F.S.R. Supreme Soviet passes a law "Concerning enterprises and entrepreneurial activity" (*Izvestiia*, 359, p. 8).

26 December

Gorbachev informs the U.S.S.R. Congress of People's Deputies that the previous night Nikolai Ryzhkov suffered a heart attack. His life is not currently in danger. The President nominates [hard-liner] Gennadiy Yanayev for the post of Vice-president of the U.S.S.R. A request from deputies for the President to consider alternative candidates is refused (*Izvestiia*, 360, p. 1).

The R.S.F.S.R. Supreme Soviet approves the republican budget for 1991. The contribution to the U.S.S.R. budget is set at 23.4 billion roubles, a reduction of 119 billion roubles on the current year (*Izvestiia*, 359, p. 8).

Rossiyskaya gazeta publishes an appeal from Yeltsin for "compatriots abroad" to contribute to the revival of Russia (*Rossiiskaia gazeta*, 43, p. 1).

Produce [donated as humanitarian aid] has already appeared on the stalls of traders at the Car Market in front of the secondhand store on Komsomolsky Prospect, and more has turned up in commercial shops and kiosks. A small packet of chocolate wafers will cost you 2–3 roubles; Maoam chews, described as chewing gum, are 10 roubles; and biscuits sell at 25–40 roubles a packet. A box of chocolates normally sold only in Czech hard currency shops is retailing at a cool 70 roubles (*Moskovskii komsomolets*, 296, p. 1).

"Now I can get into the Writers' Union restaurant," Vasiliy Aksyonov jokes at a presentation of his novels *The Burn* and *The Island of Crimea* at the Cinema Club. His Writers' Union membership card had just been returned to him with the inscription, "For Aksyonov, who was always with us and who has returned, not been admitted, to the Writers' Union". Aksyonov gives his impressions of Moscow roughly as follows, "The city is like someone with typhoid who is showing signs of recovery" (*Moskovskii komsomolets*, 297, p. 1).

27 December

The four-month session of the R.S.F.S.R. Supreme Soviet concludes. It has issued some one hundred directives and twenty-four laws on, among other things, land reform, peasant farming, an R.S.F.S.R. referendum, freedom of religion, state pensions and property (*Izvestiia*, 360, p. 1).

28 December

The Director of television's *Viewpoint*, People's Deputy of the R.S.F.S.R. Aleksandr Lyubimov, says bluntly, "We are extremely concerned by a succession of resignations among the country's top leaders. Gorbachev's new team so far consists of old players and it is difficult to be even cautiously optimistic about the future. We will fight for *Viewpoint* in the new year and expect to win" (*Moskovskii komsomolets*, 299, p. 1). After the conflict over reporting Shevardnadze's resignation, *Viewpoint* was taken off air until August 1991 (apart from one programme broadcast on Latvian television).

Commentary by Shervardnadze:

> I knew the lads from *Viewpoint*. They were very critical of the country's leaders but treated me quite gently. I think we understood each other. I thought their programme was a first sign of spring, a television show in which people spoke honestly and openly about the shortcomings and failures of the state. I greatly respected them and thought they told the truth.

30 December

The last 1990 issue of *Ogonyok* publishes Aleksandr Genis's "The View from a Dead End": "At the point where the disparate genres of crime fiction, science fiction and belles-lettres proper intersect, we find they have one thing in common: they reject the reflection of reality in favour of modelling it" (*Ogonek*, 52, pp. 17–19).

HISTORY AS ECONOMICS, OR A JOURNEY
FROM 1921 TO 1906 VIA 1990

Olesya Kirchik

1990s Russia saw a precipitate discrediting of the concepts of democracy and freedom, which became associated in the public mind entirely with savage market capitalism. Back in the time of the 1905 Revolution, Max Weber had warned of the less than straightforward relationship between these concepts, and his words ring true today. "It is utterly ridiculous," he wrote, "to attribute elective affinity with democracy or even freedom (in any sense of the word) to today's advanced capitalism – that 'inevitability' of our economic development – as it is now imported into Russia and as it exists in the United States. Rather, the question can be phrased only in this way: How can democracy and freedom be maintained in the long run under the dominance of advanced capitalism?"[466] Nevertheless, in Russia in the 1990s we believed that the market and democracy were as inseparable as Siamese twins. To understand this "ridiculous attribution", we need to travel back to 1990 and recall how it was intended to approach building an independent Russia.

The year 1990 was above all a time of enthusiasm for transition to a free market economy, and economic issues were predominant on public platforms, in parliamentary debates and in the pages of the periodical press. The economic guru became the intellectual most sought after by politicians as there was a belief that economists would find a solution to all the crises and save us from imminent disaster. Girded with the prestige of science,

466. Weber's answer to the question is: "They can be maintained only if a nation is always determined not to be ruled like a herd of sheep" (Max Weber, "On the Situation of Bourgeois Democracy in Russia", quoted in Guenther Roth and Wolfgang Schluchter, *Max Weber's Vision of History: Ethics and Methods* [Berkeley, 1984], p. 202).

they would show the way to a better future, because it was time to choose how Russia should go forward, with a new form of government and a new economy. If up until now the rhetoric had been about improving the existing economic mechanism, the admission in 1989–90 that the situation was critical[467] was tantamount to admitting that the problems could not be solved within the existing framework. The rhetoric of crisis opened up the possibility of publicly discussing innovative ways of transition to a fundamentally different social system.

In 1990–91, various crisis-management programmes were proposed and widely debated, and every one of them was predicated on a move to market economics. They differed only in terms of the pace of change, the state's role, and how relations between the republics and the U.S.S.R. centre should be altered. This was a time also noteworthy for the admission of economists actually into government,[468] to elected office and as advisers to the U.S.S.R. and Russian republican governments. The alliance between government and academe was symbolised by economists with differing outlooks and from different generations: Leonid Abalkin, Grigoriy Yavlinsky and Yegor Gaidar. With the discourse of power all but coinciding with the discourse of economics, the ambiguous status of economics as an exact science and as a moral discourse became very obvious, as did that of an economist who was both technical adviser and politician. Nikolai Kondratiev, shot in 1938, had offered the observation that, "very often, if not always, scholarly analysis becomes advocacy of a particular social ideal".[469]

The ambiguity derives from the fact that economics, like history, is the name both of a scholarly discipline and of the area it studies.[470] Differenti-

467. See, for example, Egor Gaidar, *Gibel' imperii. Uroki dlia sovremennoi Rossii* (Moscow, 2006), pp. 303–18.
468. Like late 1991, the period from February to October 1917 was "a golden age for economists", with several at the pinnacle of government power. See Alessandro Stanziani, *L'Économie en révolution: Le cas russe, 1870–1930* (Paris, 1998), p. 182.
469. Quoted in N. A. Makashev, *Eticheskie osnovy ekonomicheskoi teorii: Ocherki istorii* (Moscow, 1993), p. 7.   470. Michel de Certeau, *L'Écriture de l'histoire* (1975) (Paris, 2002), p. 37.

ating between the discourse and its object enables us to avoid presenting a market economy as normative, as in: "The free market was chosen as the most rational and efficient, even the only possible, way of coordinating the economy and society." It enables us to avoid bundling the market with democracy, and also to deal with simplistic conspiracy theories that market ideology was imposed by foreigners intent on weakening Russia. We shall see below that some element of ideology is never far from the discourse of Soviet economists.

This is not to question the scholarly credentials of economics or the validity of particular economic theories. We are interested primarily in the meanings and images that were associated with the concept of market reforms, and ultimately determined how they were perceived. How was "radical economic reform" discussed in public, rather than in a strictly political or academic context? How did the market come to be seen as the only possible solution? Why was it judged essential to take immediate action if otherwise inevitable disaster was to be forestalled?

NEW ECONOMIC THINKING

"The omniscient physicists seem to have been squeezed out of our national consciousness by practical economists. In a circle of friends, a business-like economist trumps not only a physicist but even, on a good day, a top-flight ice hockey player," claimed Vasiliy Selyunin in *Novy mir* in 1985.[471] This was a major change.[472] His article was one of the first examples of perestroika economic journalism, which was destined to become the dominant genre of writing in magazines and journals in the latter half of the 1980s. He discussed and criticised the economic experiments conducted in the U.S.S.R. from 1983 onwards, the first since Aleksey

471. Vasilii Seliunin, "Eksperiment", *Novyi mir*, 6 (1985), p. 173.
472. Economics had not always been a prestigious profession in the U.S.S.R. In the mid-1950s, Timofey Lysenko even questioned its legitimacy: "Why do we need economics? Is there such a science?" Quoted in Aleksandr Nikonov, *Spiral' mnogovekovoi dramy: agrarnaia nauka i politika Rossii (XVIII–XX vv.)* (Moscow, 1995), p. 215.

Kosygin's attempts to "improve the economic mechanism" were halted.

Perestroika started with the intention of accelerating Russia's socio-economic development. It looked back to the economic reform of 1965, with its aim of ensuring financial viability by granting a degree of financial autonomy to enterprises, decentralising planning, democratising the workplace by drawing workers into the management of enterprises and improving the population's living standards.

In seeking an answer to the question of how to put everything right, Selyunin looked back to the economic discussions leading up to the 1965 reform, which crystallised the views of Soviet economists of the so-called "market" or "commercial" tendency. They proposed introducing bilateral contracts between enterprises in place of planning, and even wholesale trade in the means of production. In 1965, as in 1985, their proposals proceeded from an assumption that the Soviet planned economy was economically irrational and wasteful of resources and labour. They effectively proposed replacing cumbersome bureaucratic procedures with the economic logic of incentives and competition.

The first articles of perestroika economic journalism were crucial in turning public opinion in favour of reform.[473] What they had in common was a strong dislike of bureaucracy. They revived oppositions from the time of Khrushchev's Thaw: inefficient administrative levers versus regulation by the economy; the political arbitrariness of "home-grown Marats"[474] versus the objective laws of economics (whose determinist powers seemed oddly reminiscent of Stalin's iron "laws of the political economy of socialism"). The 1960s generation of economists, now finally able to discuss their views in public, gave high priority to social welfare and had great faith in the invisible hand of the economy, which was seen as the antithesis of

---

473. For example, Tat'iana Zaslavskaia, "Chelovecheskii faktor razvitiia ekonomiki", *Kommunist*, 13 (1986); Vasilii Seliunin and Grigorii Khanin, "Lukavaia tsifra", *Novyi mir*, 2 (1987); "Tri dnia v Poltave, ili Monologi o sel'skokhoziaistvennom trude i mirovozzrenii zemledel'tsa", *Znamia*, 3 (1987); Nikolai Shmelev, "Avansy i dolgi", *Novyi mir*, 6 (1987).
474. Seliunin, "Eksperiment", p. 173.

administrative compulsion. The concept gradually took shape of an ineffi-cient "administrative-command system"[475] which destroyed incentives to work, alienated the working class and peasantry from their ownership of the means of production, and which had installed itself in place of a truly socialist organisation of society.

The fist signs of this controversy in the press coincided with the official announcement of the policy of perestroika ("restructuring") at the January 1987 Plenum of the Central Committee of the Communist Party. Earlier, Gorbachev had called for the development of "new economic thinking". This was a direct political order to economists: "Our policy of accelerating socio-economic development needs to see economics rise to the theoretical level required to combat conservatism and inertia in economic thinking, the risk of a tendency towards crises in the economy, dogmatism and scholastic theorising in science."[476] The encouragement of "creative approaches" and "liberation from dogma" was evident also in the govern-mental directive "On the journal *Kommunist*", which emphasised the need for discussion, innovation and "enrichment of Marxism-Leninism". The directive effectively sanctioned an unusually frank discussion of Soviet history, and widened the historical perspective for debating the "economic problems of developed socialism". It resulted in the publication in *Kommunist* of a number of articles on the seventieth anniversary of the October Revolution, which were written in the new spirit of the times.

The years 1987–90 were a time when the old certainties of Soviet history were critically revisited. A craze for history developed which, although initiated by the Party, rapidly broke free of its ideological control. The Party's policy of glasnost and encouragement to challenge dogma led less to discussion of the current situation than to reassessment of the past. The new interest in history was stimulated primarily for reasons of political expediency rather than stemming from developments within the discipline itself. The intention had been to use the past as a weapon in an ideological

475. Gavriil Popov, "S tochki zreniia ekonomista", *Nauka i zhizn'*, 4 (1987).
476. *Materialy Plenuma TsK KPSS, 27–28 ianvaria* (Moscow, 1987), pp. 7–8.

battle for the present and future, and this was evident from the speed with which, in 1987–8, views on the pre-Soviet and Soviet past became radicalised and polarised. However, the historians' contribution to changing ideas about the past was soon put in the shade by the sheer energy of academic economists and economic journalists. The slackening of censorship and the policy of glasnost made it possible for a democratic press to emerge, periodicals at the liberal end of the political spectrum like the journals *New World* (*Novy mir*), *The Banner* (*Znamya*), *Friendship of the Peoples* (*Druzhba narodov*), *October* (*Oktyabr*) and *Youth* (*Yunost*), and the weeklies *The Spark* (*Ogonyok*), *Moscow News* (*Moskovskie novosti*) and *Literary Gazette* (*Literaturnaya gazeta*), which soon provided a platform for challenging the senescent regime and championing radical economic reform. Their most prominent authors included economists, journalists and well-respected academics, as well as those of a new generation.

Genuine economic analysis was virtually impossible, given that statistics and reliable data about the economic situation were still guarded as closely as state secrets and available only to an elite few close to the realpolitik of running the economy. This resulted in the discussion focusing on pre- and post-revolutionary economic history.

THE THEORY OF DEFORMED SOCIALISM

A preoccupation of 1987–9 was exposing the truth about the Soviet past, primarily during the period of Stalin's rule. Lifting the taboo on topics like the Great Terror and collectivisation of agriculture made possible the publication of Solzhenitsyn, Shalamov, Vladimov and other previously banned writers, as well as translations of the work of Western historians and Sovietologists from the 1960s. These were the main sources for gaining an understanding of the Stalin era. Articles were published in periodicals about collectivisation and the policy of "de-kulakisation", the dispossession of supposedly rich and exploitative peasants, although the term was largely displaced by the arguably more accurate "de-peasantisation". Investigations into the deliberately induced famine which took millions of lives gave a further sense of the repressive and destructive nature of Stalin's policies after 1929. As Viktor Danilov recalled, "In effect, we resumed our work, which had been halted in the second half of the 1960s and early 1970s, work which we, entirely justifiably, considered essential for an understanding of our country's past and present and for perestroika, the rebuilding of our society on genuinely socialist principles."[477]

In the ensuing debate about a past in which the essential key to understanding the present had to be found, three approaches to Soviet history collided. The apologists of Stalinism gave unconditional approval to his methods of industrialisation, most of them downplaying the scale of the violence perpetrated against the peasantry and the widespread repression of the urban population. They saw the success of Stalin's policies as deriving from discipline and argued that "reimposing order" was the best way to resolve the economy's current problems. The second view was that, despite the excessive cruelty of Stalin's methods, there had been no alternative so they were justified by the historical situation. Economists and historians who took that approach did not question the principles underlying the system as it had evolved. The third, and most widely held, view considered that a real opportunity to implement a humane transition to socialism had been missed at the end of the 1920s. Soviet government policy had taken a wrong turning in 1929, and the economy's subsequent failures resulted from distortion of the true principles of socialism. It was argued that a return to basics was needed, a purification of socialism to reverse its replacement by a powerful bureaucracy which only claimed to be socialism. Thus, the theory of Deformed Socialism became the rationale for perestroika, based on opposing the true "financially viable socialism" of Lenin to the "barracks socialism" of Stalin, the years of the relatively liberal New Economic Policy to those which followed the "Great Turning Point" of 1929.

477. Viktor Danilov, "Iz istorii perestroiki: perezhivaniia shestidesiatnika-krest'ianoveda", *Novyi mir istorii Rossii: forum iaponskikh i rossiiskikh issledovatelei* (Moscow, 2001).

The economists of the 1960s generation were instrumental in having the New Economic Policy accepted as the reference model of true socialism and enabling Lenin (as opposed to Stalin) to become firmly identified in the public mind not with the Dictatorship of the Proletariat and the Red Terror, but with the N.E.P. The myth of the New Economic Policy as Lenin's real economic policy reflected their view of what the economic model of socialism should be. The famous political slogan of 1921, "From requisitioning to taxation in kind", was now interpreted as a call to abandon intervention by the state in the activities of economic agents in favour of regulating the relationship between them with such economic levers and incentives as taxes, credits etc. At the same time, there was an insistence on the need for radical reform, as opposed to the tinkering of the mid-1950s and 1965, which had been inspired by similar ideas.

In order to refute the view, firmly established in Soviet historiography, that the New Economic Policy had been only a temporary manoeuvre before the rush forward to socialism, there was much quotation of Lenin's statement of the need to "review our entire outlook on socialism", and that the N.E.P. was a serious, long-term policy. In an article titled "Loans and Debts", published in Novy mir in 1987, Nikolai Shmelyov argued that it was at this time that "the underlying principles of a scientifically-based, pragmatic approach to the task of constructing a socialist economy were formulated. From the passionate, emotional push of war Communism, which was partly due to the extraordinary circumstances of the civil war, there was a changeover to routine, considered, constructive work."[478]

The successful affirmation of the N.E.P. as the reference model of socialism stimulated interest in the work of Soviet economists of the 1920s, whom Stalin had stigmatised as the "bourgeois" and "neo-populist" school and who were purged after the Great Turning Point of 1929. This ultimately led to the complete rehabilitation of Nikolai Kondratiev, Nikolai Makarov, Aleksandr Chayanov and their economist colleagues, and the

---

478. Nikolai Shmelev, "Avansy i dolgi", Novyi mir, 6 (1987).

reprinting of their works.[479] The political equivalent of their economic ideas was to be Nikolai Bukharin's alternative approach to building socialism with the aid of the market.[480]

The theory of Deformed Socialism was incorporated into official discourse, not least because it explained the otherwise inexplicable paradox of the alienation of Soviet workers from the means of production, which were under Soviet public ownership. The only options were to disavow socialist principles or admit they had been distorted in the process of building socialism. In a report to the Central Committee plenum of March 1989, Gorbachev acknowledged that the Party's entire agricultural policy as practised since Stalin's collectivisation had resulted in serious errors which caused a human tragedy, and whose most serious consequence was alienation of the peasants from the means of production, leading to the loss of their sense of ownership. Close control of producers' economic activity, the centralisation of decision-making and strict planning control had led not to the supposed socialisation of property but to its nationalisation.

The debate on economic reform constrained within a socialist framework was thus a consideration of ways of "re-socialising" nationalised property through, for example, self-management or leasing arrangements. The strategic decision needing to be made was, according to Gorbachev, to return to the "genuine socialism of Lenin" and the principles of the N.E.P. by introducing leasing,[481] and by gradually introducing elements

479. Kondratiev, Makarov, Chayanov, Leonid Yurovsky and their colleagues were arrested in 1930 and sentenced on trumped-up charges to various periods of imprisonment. Many were subsequently shot. They had been partly rehabilitated in 1956, and were fully rehabilitated in July 1987.

480. In 1988, there was a great celebration of Bukharin in connection with his rehabilitation and centenary. The first articles about him and a selection of his works were published. See Nikolai Bukharin, *Izbrannye proizvedeniia* (Moscow, 1988), etc.

481. The concept of leasing became the cornerstone of perestroika agrarian policy. It was to allow legal separation of ownership of the means of production from their possession as the object of management, taking the managerial function away from the state. Vladimir Tikhonov, "Chtoby narod prokormil sebia sam", *Literaturnaia gazeta*, 10 (1988).

of commercial relations through an increase in enterprises' economic independence.[482]

ANTI-SOCIALIST DISCOURSE: FREEDOM – DEMOCRACY – PRIVATE PROPERTY

In parallel with the official discourse of perestroika, a radical anti-socialist discourse of the democratic opposition emerged. This did not appeal to socialist ideals but instead argued in favour of the liberal theory of natural rights. If the basic proposal of official discourse was "More socialism!", the democrats claimed that the inefficient system which had developed in the U.S.S.R. was already socialism, whose principles were accordingly demonstrably flawed.[483] The most striking, if not the first, example of this trend was Vasiliy Selyunin's article "The Origins", published in early 1988.[484] While giving the enthusiasm for going back to the 1920s its due, Selyunin made an important ideological advance in representing the N.E.P. not as a reference model of socialism but as a successful implementation of the "standard commercial model" based on private enterprise. Aware of the controversial nature of this interpretation, he pointed to a "moot point" in Bukharin's plan for building socialism. How was the private sector to mesh with nationalised industry? Was it even logically possible to insert the owner of private property into the socialist scheme (p. 173)?

A detailed excursion into history, encompassing the French Revolution, Ivan the Terrible, Peter the Great and the reforms of Alexander II, provided support for Selyunin's main thesis that "forced labour at all times and for all peoples has proved unproductive" (p. 178). As Russia's socialist enterprise was based on forced labour, it followed that the Soviet economic

---

482. Mikhail Gorbachev, "Ob agrarnoi politike KPSS v sovremennykh usloviiakh", in *Izbrannye stat'i i rechi*, vol. 7 (Moscow, 1990), pp. 350–52.

483. See L. Popkova (Larisa Piasheva), "Gde pyshnee pirogi?", *Novyi mir*, 5 (1987).

484. Vasilii Seliunin, "Istoki", *Novyi mir*, 1 (1988), pp. 162–89. It is estimated that between fifteen and seventeen million copies of this article were published in the U.S.S.R. See S. Larin, "Pamiati V.A. Seliunina", *Novyi mir*, 12 (1994).

system was by definition inefficient. Selyunin saw the Soviet experience of a mobilised economy as striking evidence of a direct connection between good husbandry and human rights. For him, the rights of the individual were a necessary restraint on "ruthless economic freedom", whereas state ownership of property was tantamount to expropriation of the individual (p. 170). Selyunin was essentially repeating Adam Smith's defence of the individuals' innate human right to dispose of their property as they choose to, even if all they possess are their own two hands. From this there follows a requirement for freedom of labour, which is crucial in terms of both human rights and economic efficiency. According to the classical liberal formula, possession of property equals possession of civil liberties equals an efficient economy. Hence the key to economic efficiency is emancipation of the producer from the tutelage of the state, collective or any other supra-personal authority. Historically, Selyunin argued, only private property had been able to deliver this.

This consideration of a liberal model of modernisation for Russia gave rise to a discussion of the Russian peasant commune, or *obshchina*, which had played a crucial role in the economy in the early twentieth century. Russian patriots, represented in the the media by the Village Writers, who included Solzhenitsyn, saw the commune as a pledge of the spiritual revival of the nation by returning to ancient Russian values.[485] Democrats saw it as a symbol of stagnation and "equal misery". Extraordinarily, the democratic discourse of the late 1980s revived the myth of the proprietor, the land-owning peasant, as it had been created in the discourse of the tsarist government. The proprietor, the smallholder who was supposed to appear as a result of Pyotr Stolypin's reforms (which aimed to promote peasant land ownership), would be endowed, in the view of liberals and economically aware government officials of the early twentieth century, with such virtues as enterprise, diligence and "culture". He was the antithesis of the "ignorant, impoverished masses" in

485. A platform for the "Slavophiles" or "Native Soil" writers was provided by the journals *Moscow (Moskva)* and *Our Contemporary (Nash sovremennik).*

the communes who were "drunkards and layabouts".[486] This opposition was precisely replicated in the radical discourse of perestroika, where collective and state farms took the place of the demoralising commune, and the first leaseholders and farmers replaced the pre-revolutionary smallholder. According to this logic, the Stolypin reform (which gave the peasant private ownership of land) and the New Economic Policy helped agriculture to progress. Collectivisation, on the contrary, was a step backwards because it reintroduced feudal dependency, servitude, and hence unproductive labour. Selyunin emphasised the continuity between the peasant commune and the Soviet collective farm (p. 186). In 1989, Yuriy Chernichenko, a prominent journalist and founder of the neo-liberal Peasant Party, introduced the term *Agrogulag* into public discourse, representing the collective and state farms as forced-labour institutions.[487] He turned the official Soviet interpretation of history upside down, likening the lot of collective farm workers to that of serfs before the Great Reforms of Alexander II.

This view saw a war against the peasants in the 1930s destroying not just a few "exploitative kulaks", as Soviet propaganda would have it, but an important social group of peasant landowners, and with them a particular peasant way of life, work ethic and reservoir of farming skill. The process of "de-peasantisation", which had continued through the entire Soviet period, was responsible for the permanent crisis in agriculture, and the only way to recover the situation was to revive the peasant smallholder: "In social terms, this means we need to reverse the policy which destroyed peasant land ownership. That is what we need to restore."[488] Journalists set about rehabilitating the image of the prosperous kulak peasant farmer,[489]

---

486. Petr Stolypin, "Rech' ob ustroistve byta krest'ian i prave sobstvennosti, proiznesennaia v Gosudarstvennoi Dume 10 maia 1907 goda", quoted from P. A. Stolypin, "Nam nuzhna velikaia Rossiia ...". *Polnoe sobranie rechei v Gosudarstvennoi Dume i Gosudarstvennom Sovete. 1906–1911* (Moscow, 1991), pp. 86–96.

487. Iurii Chernichenko, "Podniavshiisia pervym", *Novyi mir*, 9 (1989). *Novy mir* also serialised George Orwell's *1984* and Solzhenitsyn's *The Gulag Archipelago* in 1989.

488. V. Tikhonov, "K istokam", *Pogruzhenie v triasinu* (Moscow, 1990), p. 64.

489. E.g., Mikhail Zaraev, "Kak vozrodit' kulaka?", *Ogonek*, 3 (3313) (1991), pp. 12–19.

a product of Stolypin's reforms and the N.E.P., a model of sturdy independence, the "salt of the earth of Russia". Stories appeared in newspapers and magazines of the extraordinary productivity of the small individual plots workers on Soviet and collective farms were allowed to cultivate.[490] The famous Arkhangelsk peasant Nikolai Sivkov, who left a Soviet farm to set up his own animal-rearing farm, became a talisman of the democratic movement and has gone down in history as the "first Russian farmer".[491]

The Russian republican government appropriated the anti-socialist and anti-Soviet discourse of "de-peasantisation", which fitted in well with the notion of the sovereignty of the R.S.F.S.R. and the "rebirth of the Russian people". At the Second (Extraordinary) Congress of People's Deputies of the R.S.F.S.R., Ivan Silayev, head of the Russian republican government of the time, drew a direct parallel with events at the beginning of the twentieth century, inviting the deputies to remember the years 1906–11. "Dear Comrades," he told them, "almost exactly eighty-five years ago, on 9 November, 1906, a law was passed in Russia which gave peasants the right to withdraw from the commune and demand the transfer to them, as their personal property, of part of the land of the village Mir. What purpose has been served by our having anathematised the name of Stolypin and his land reform?"[492]

The "Stolypin phenomenon" in the autumn of 1990 facilitated publication in Zvezda of the book devoted to him in Solzhenitsyn's cycle The Red Wheel. Simultaneously, three articles were published in Issues in Economics (Voprosy ekonomiki) analysing Stolypin's reforms. The anti-socialist discourse of perestroika combined criticism of the Soviet agricultural system and, more generally, of the Soviet economic system with outright rejection of

490. A. Pushkar', "Zhivye dushi", Izvestiia, 24–6 July, 1989.
491. Featured in the 1986 award-winning eponymous documentary film by Marina Goldovskaya.
492. "Doklad predsedatelia Soveta ministrov RSFSR po Zakonu "O krest'ianskom (fermerskom) khoziaistve", Vtoroi (vneocherednoi) s"ezd narodnykh deputatov RSFSR, 17 noiabria–16 dekabria 1990 goda: stenograficheskii otchet, 6 vols (Moscow, 1992), vol. 1, p. 58.

socialism as such.[493] Rejecting Soviet economics and politics, the discourse logically saw individual freedom, a market economy based on private property, and a democratic system as inextricably linked. The agrarian question, and especially the notion of "re-peasantisation", fuelled a more extensive ideological move away from "mending socialism" to full-blown free market economics. This shift, from the N.E.P. to pre-revolutionary reforms, from social-democratic to neo-liberal ideology, chimed with a perception that the entire Soviet experiment could and should be written off as an aberration, a temporary deviation from "normal" development.

THE MARKET AS THE BASIS OF AN INDEPENDENT RUSSIA: A STATE WITHOUT IDEOLOGY?

From late 1989, there was much talk of the inevitability of transition to a market economy as the only way out of the then current economic difficulties and in order to forestall a major crisis. In 1990 a variety of suggestions were made as to how to avoid this, based on different understandings of the nature of the market and of the way to effect transition to it. The main bone of contention was the nature of the economic and political system that should result from radical economic reform: a "socialist" or a "free" market.

The first option was based on the convergence theory that the world's two major social systems were coming closer together. The idea of a Third Way, which would combine a market economy with the "achievements of socialism", was advocated by such Western intellectuals as Ralf Dahrendorf and J. K. Galbraith, and also by Andrey Sakharov, an undisputed shaper of public opinion within the U.S.S.R., as well as by such Soviet economists as Leonid Abalkin, Stanislav Shatalin and Nikolai Shemlyov. Convergence theory accepted the equal validity of both social alternatives, which were viewed as representing two complementary aspects of human nature. The socialist market was thus, in the words of Shemlyov, a system

493. Vitalii Naishul', "Vysshaia i posledniaia stadiia sotsializma", in T. Notkin, ed., *Postizhenie* (Moscow, 1991), pp. 31–62.

which made it possible "to live your life on two legs rather than one".[494] The doctrine of market socialism, officially adopted by the U.S.S.R. government, associated democratisation – that is, political pluralism and a guarantee of basic civic freedoms – with mixed forms of ownership and development, a public sector in parallel with private enterprise.[495]

Opposed to the concept of market socialism was the neo-liberal philosophy that affirmed the primacy of the market and of economic rationality. If in 1988 Vasiliy Selyunin concluded that the state sector would remain the principal sector of the economy, only a year later he was arguing, quoting another economic journalist, Boris Pinsker, that "the public sector will always tend to inefficiency" and that true democracy could only be based on private property.[496] Pinsker was repeating the arguments of Western neo-liberal conservatives who criticised social-democratic governments for bureaucratic interference and subsidies which created a culture of dependency.[497] Decrying bureaucratic intervention in the working of the economy, Pinsker quoted the darling of neo-liberalism, Friedrich Hayek, to the effect that the state must be subordinated to neo-liberal principles, not the will of peoples, parliaments or governments (p. 202), thus anticipating the argument that it was impossible to carry out radical reforms in a democratic manner.

Market socialism was seen as an oxymoron, an "eclectic utopia" which should be repudiated in favour of a normal, natural market without any -isms.[498] Rejection of Soviet ideology in this period led to rejection of any form of ideology. Aleksandr Tsipko's publications gave the economic argument against socialism even as a system of ideas, which was one of the most damaging.[499]

---

494. Nikolai Shmelev, "Libo sila, libo rubl'", Znamia, 1 (1989), p. 147.
495. See, for example, Stanislav Shatalin, "Ekonomicheskaia programma politicheskoi partii", Kommunist, 7 (1990), pp. 32–3.
496. Vasilii Seliunin, "Planovaia anarkhiia ili balans interesov?", Znamia, 11 (1989), p. 195.
497. Boris Pinsker, "Biurokraticheskaia khimera", Znamia, 11 (1989), p. 195.
498. See Evgenii Iasin, "Sotsialisticheskii rynok ili iarmarka illiuzii", Radikal'naia ekonomicheskaia reforma. Istoki, problemy, resheniia (Moscow, 1990).
499. See Aleksandr Tsipko, "Khoroshi li nashi printsipy?" Novyi mir, 4 (1990), pp. 173–204).

While Marxism-Leninism was losing the scientific status it had claimed for many years, the early 1990s saw an attempt to purge economics, and society generally, of all ideology.[500] The dominant rhetoric was of emerging onto the great highway of human progress, integration into the community of nations, a return to universal human values and, first and foremost, to freedom. The affirmation of economic freedom is found in many publications of this time: "Property and Freedom", "Transition to Freedom", "Freedom as a Productive Force", "Free Enterprise and Free Labour," "Ordeal by Freedom" etc.[501]

The year 1990 was thus a moment when a belief that the free market was the normal form for any economy coincided with the collapse of the old economic system, both for economic reasons like excessive money supply, and because of political events like the "parade of sovereignties". With a backward glance to the New Economic Policy and the Stolypin reforms, this ideology saw the figure of the land-owning peasant as all-important. However, economic journalism remained blind to industrial policy and the actual mechanism of most sectors of the U.S.S.R. economy, whose problems could not be conveniently solved by calling for more freedom. These affected not the grand historical prospects of economic development but the reality today and tomorrow of the lives of readers of all that "thick journal" disputation.

TWO PROGRAMMES

The policy of market socialism was embodied in the U.S.S.R. government's reform programme, developed by a group of economists under Academician Leonid Abalkin and presented for discussion in May 1990. The

500. The opposition of "scientism" to "common sense" can be traced back to Hayek, who denounced the notion of scientific management of society as an inherent characteristic of socialist ideology. See Friedrich A. Hayek, *The Counter-revolution of Science: Studies on the Abuse of Reason* (Glencoe, IL, 1952).

501. Market romanticism, which linked political liberty with freedom of private enterprise and private property, usually resulted from uncritical acceptance of the principles of neo-classical economic theory.

programme favoured gradualist reform, recommending phased integration of market elements into the Soviet economy over a ten-year period. The first phase involved stabilising the financial situation and monetary circulation by administrative measures. The programme was criticised by the younger generation of neo-liberal economists, who included Larisa Piyasheva, Boris Pinsker, Vitaliy Naishul, Aleksey Ulyukayev, Boris Lvin and supporters of the democratic movement; they damned it as half-hearted, indecisive and overly ideological. Piyasheva saw the government's strategy of a planned transition to the market as liable to exacerbate the economic crisis: "The policy of 'renewing socialism' results in palliative legislation, proposal of ineffective measures and ambiguity in its positions."[502] A "phased, 'planned' transition to market-based price formation," she mocked, would "result in a very rapid transition of consumer prices in an upward direction, even further deterioration of the deficit, and expansion of the black economy". The only possible way out of the situation was immediate, radical market reform, giving priority to price liberalisation and privatisation.

A tactic of accelerated reform was the basis of an alternative transition programme developed by Grigoriy Yavlinsky and his colleagues in 1990 in parallel with their work on the government's reform proposal. The "500 Days" programme was adopted by the R.S.F.S.R. Supreme Soviet on 11 September, 1990, but its real significance was symbolic rather than practical. It became the banner for a coalition of democratic forces which renewed their attack on the U.S.S.R. government and Gorbachev's "centre-right bloc". In September 1990, Gavriil Popov, Chairman of the Moscow City Council and a leader of the democratic movement, criticised Gorbachev's programme in his opening speech at the "Transition to Freedom" international conference: "This bloc can only make changes in a manner and timeframe acceptable to the bureaucracy. As the bureaucracy is

502. Larisa Piiasheva, "Esli pravitel'stvo vse ponimaet ... Postup' ofitsial'nogo ekonomicheskogo myshleniia", *Vek XX i mir*, 3 (1990); http://old.russ.ru/antolog/vek/1990/3/piash. htm

the progeny of bureaucratic socialism and is incompatible with the new model of society, of all possible versions of perestroika, the one chosen is the most realistic and the least effective."[503] The new power centres thus derived legitimacy precisely from their alternative economic reforms, which were designed to ensure, first and foremost, greater economic efficiency. In the autumn of 1990, as again in the autumn of 1991, the plan for an independent Russia centred on the idea of escape from the authority of a U.S.S.R. government whose ideology of "equalisation and passive consumerism" (p. 6) was to be counteracted by economists acting as agents of purely economic logic.

The opposition of the politically acceptable to the economically effective was refined and logically honed in the debates of economists of the Moscow–Petersburg circle, some of whom went on to form the nucleus of Yeltsin's reform government in the autumn of 1991. Just two days after the formal adoption by the Russian republican leaders of the 500 Days programme, a future Russian republican prime minister, Yegor Gaidar, published an article criticising both the U.S.S.R. government's programme and the alternative programme for their lack of clarity about the division of power between the U.S.S.R. and republican governments, given the looming disintegration of the U.S.S.R. He also criticised populist promises on social welfare which were not properly costed against budgetary revenues.[504] If the success of a politician was measured in terms of his ability to be popular, the task of a specialist adviser was to "tell the truth to politicians and the public", and the truth was that it would not be possible to put the economy to rights without a lot of pain. We recognise the ideal, traceable back to John Maynard Keynes, of the neutral, politically unbiased economic expert who, for the common good, should guide the actions of politicians.

503. Gavriil Popov, "Vystuplenie na mezhdunarodnoi konferentsii 'Perekhod k svobode'", *Voprosy ekonomiki*, 12 (1990), p. 4.
504. Egor Gaidar, "Dve programmy", *Pravda*, 13 September, 1990. The inconsistency of the U.S.S.R. government's economic reform policies were criticised in the pages of the main Communist Party newspaper!

Underlying the plan for an independent Russia, largely drafted and substantiated not by politicians or representatives of the new social interest groups but by economists, was the economist's dream of abolishing politics.[505] As problems with the economy and the political crisis worsened, the market began to be seen as an ideal and self-sufficient engine of change. This was at the expense of politics, which was seen as an overly complex configuration of social and political forces. Ultimately, priority was given to the mechanism of reform rather than to those who were supposed to benefit from it. This was partly due to the unpopularity of the proposed reforms with the population at large and the relative narrowness of the reformers' support base, of which they were fully aware. Gaidar had explicitly written about this in his article in *Pravda* in mid-September 1990.[506] Even earlier, Anatoliy Chubais had expressed the following concern: "In the course of its implementation, this reform risks arousing the discontent and even resistance of most of the social groups and political forces in society."[507] The representative democratic institutions which had significantly contributed to undermining the old system came to be seen as more of an obstacle than a prerequisite for the imminent changes.[508] In particular, parliamentarians' social-welfare expectations inherited from the Soviet system were seen as a hindrance to development, their shift from "socialism" to "social welfare"

505. An expression coined by Pierre Rosanvallon, who warned of the need to distinguish between the neo-liberal utopia of a self-regulating market, which belongs to the realm of economists' ideology, and actual capitalism, which results much more from the interaction of various social and political forces and sundry lobbyists. See Pierre Rosanvallon, *Le Capitalisme utopique: Histoire de l'idée de marché* (Paris, 1977).

506. More information about Gaidar's views on the economic programme in 1990 is given in Egor Gaidar, *Gosudarstvo i evoliutsiia* (Moscow, 2003), pp. 234–41.

507. [Anatolii Chubais], "Zhestkim kursom ... Analiticheskaia zapiska Leningradskoi assotsiatsii sotsial'no-ekonomicheskikh nauk", *Vek XX i mir*, 6 (1990), p. 17.

508. In October 1991, Gennadiy Burbulis, while Secretary of State of the R.S.F.S.R., said in a television interview that "The representative bodies have become more of a hindrance than a help to our reforms. They were needed to destroy the totalitarian system but have now performed that task. Now the territories of Russia are crying out for a pyramid of power" (Burbulis in the R.T.V. programme *Bez retushi* on 9 October, 1991). Quoted from Tat'iana Vorozheikina, "Shestvie triumfatorov", *Vek XX i mir*, 1 (1992); http://old.russ.ru/antolog/vek/1992/01/voroj.htm

being largely terminological. Under this logic, which seemed to see the rational economic expert pitted against populist politicians and the ignorant masses, an authoritarian imposition of reform appeared unavoidable.

All the "foremen on the perestroika building site", whether the "commercial" economists of the 1960s or the democrats (who mainly inclined to neo-liberalism), as well as the younger economists included in the "reform government", shared a kind of economic determinism. They believed that the market, as the most effective economic system, would by its very nature bring about a strengthening of political freedoms and the resolution of social problems.[509] Disappointment with the early results of reform, which did not meet these optimistic expectations, led to widespread public disillusionment with the market and its associated concepts of freedom and democracy. Another important consequence of economic determinism was that, seeing social justice as no more than a function of economic efficiency and the freeing of labour (as opposed to the Soviet "equality of misery"), stopped people thinking about the role in the state of civil society. Belief in the primacy of the market overshadowed the issue of developing democratic institutions, establishing an independent judiciary and other fundamental questions regarding the new social order. Although in the past fifteen years the effectiveness of this deterministic economic credo has been periodically called into question,[510] the issue of the appropriate relative priority of economics and politics remains unresolved.

509. On how economic determinism blinkered the Gaidar team (which came together in 1990), see a later interview by Petr Aven at http://www.polit.ru/analytics/2006/12/20/ aven. html
510. See, however, Egor Gaidar and Vladimir Mau, "Marksizm: mezhdu nauchnoi teoriei i 'svetskoi religiei' (liberal'naia apologiia)", Voprosy ekonomiki, 5 (2004), pp. 4–27.

AFTERWORD:
THE CHALLENGE OF RECENT HISTORY

Irina Prokhorova

"Tell me, sir, shall we live under socialism for long?"
"No, mate, the food's already running out."[511]

Robert Darnton, an American cultural anthropologist and book historian, in 1999 said that he was intending to make "the leap into cyberspace" by creating an electronic book in which the material would be organised like a pyramid, with layers which would enable the reader to create their own reading, staying on the surface of something like a monograph or delving down into deeper, more detailed, layers by following hyperlinks.[512] Organising material in this way opens up new ways of thinking about the history of ideas, economics, politics and society, and will move us nearer to making a reality of the ideal which the French call "*histoire totale*".

This book springs from a special two-volume issue of *New Literary Observer* which set out to study recent history on the basis of a single year – 1990 – in just that way, by creating a hypertext-rich digital research project. In our case, the top layer was a chronology of 1990, capable of being added to and germinating commentaries, supplements, clarifications, notes, personal memories, analytical articles and audiovisual materials ad infinitum. The issue was intended from the outset to be an open-source project that would allow other researchers to make corrections and additions,

---

511. T.V. film, shot 6–7 November, 1990: "How They Did Things in Odessa, or Odessans of All Countries, Unite!"
512. Robert Darnton, "Lost and Found in Cyberspace", *Chronicle of Higher Education*, 12 March, 1999, pp. 134–5.

continually deepening and enriching knowledge of recent Russian history. The intention was to put this e-book online, providing an opportunity for many researchers in the humanities to refine our data.

The original two large printed volumes of *New Literary Observer* were accompanied by a DVD, but in fact it was this electronic version which was regarded as the original, with the two printed volumes, necessarily restructured and containing only about half the material, reduced in status to a cumbersome attachment.

The potential of a hypertextual approach to presenting historical facts has long been recognised in Russian literary studies, the most notable example being Roman Timenchik's 784-page *Anna Akhmatova in the 1960s*,[513] which attempted to provide an exhaustive apparatus for Akhmatova's notebook entries and the drafts of her poems and prose. The consternation with which some colleagues met this mammoth work would have been dispelled if the seemingly superfluous wealth of information could have been provided on digital media, with Akhmatova's fragments forming a top layer beneath which the drama of the lives and destinies of people in the twentieth century were revealed.[514]

We shall not discuss the relationship between the development of ideas about the world we live in and technical progress, beyond remarking that new technological tools available to students of the humanities have updated both the lens assembly through which their research subject is viewed and the professional tools available to the cultural historian. A symptom of this is the growing interest in writing history on the basis of detailed analysis, or close reading, of localised fragments of time, and particularly of a single year.

Back in 1975, Hans Robert Jauss, the founder of reception theory, explored the collision of art's new ways of seeing with the reader's horizon of traditional expectations. He did this on the basis of a large number of artistic events occurring in the single year of 1857 (of which the principal

513. Roman D. Timenchik, *Anna Akhmatova v 1960-e gody* (Toronto, 2005).
514. See "Kniga kak sobytie", *Novoe Literaturnoe Obozrenie*, 79 (5/2011), pp. 120–87.

498

ones were the appearance of Baudelaire's *Fleurs du mal* and the scandal around Flaubert's novel *Madame Bovary*). Jauss showed how significant these events were to prove, representing, indeed, a turning point for French culture.[515]

Two more recent studies were published almost simultaneously. Hans Ulrich Gumbrecht modestly described his groundbreaking *In 1926* as "an essay in historical simultaneity".[516] In it he aimed to reconstruct a 'web' or 'field' of (not only discursive) reality which strongly shaped people's behaviour in 1926. Gumbrecht explained that he chose 1926 because it was the year in which Martin Heidegger's *On Being and Time* was published, which incorporated a wide range of cultural codes connecting the different "worlds" of the year and which provided Gumbrecht with the foundation for his project. Gumbrecht's attempt at a total representation of 1926 is in full accordance with the logic of e-books – a collection of separate thematic codes ("Authenticity vs Artificiality", "Individuality vs Collectivity", "Uncertainty vs Reality") with an immense number of internal hyperlinks.

The Italian Slavist, Gian Piero Piretto, in his *1961 in Moscow* took that year as a key moment of "thaw" in the history of Soviet Russia, a year which formed the ideas and discourses of the liberal '60s generation.[517] He saw 1968 in Europe, famous for its youth movements, enthusiasm, romantic idealism and alternative culture, as having been anticipated seven years earlier in the U.S.S.R.

Research of this kind raises questions about the adequacy of traditional historical periodisation and chronology with their reliance on the dramatising of iconic events. Our own choice of 1990 for a study of Russia's recent past was entirely deliberate. The initial hypothesis was that this year, which has been ousted from cultural memory by the more spectacular years of 1989 and 1991, was a turning point in modern Russian history, and that

515. Hans Robert Jauss, "*La Douceur du foyer*: Lyric Poetry of the year 1857 as a Model for the Communication of Social Norms", *Aesthetic Experience and Literary Hermeneutics*, trans. Michael Shaw (Minneapolis, 1982).
516. Hans-Ulrich Gumbrecht, *In 1926: Living at the Edge of Time* (Cambridge, MA, 1997).
517. G. Piero Piretto, *1961: Il Sessantotto a Mosca* (Bergamo, 1998).

events of 1990 crucially affected Russia's subsequent development. Our "rich" description of this year has confirmed that premise, a year of revolutionary change which manifests extreme heterogeneity of socio-cultural phenomena, intensive work on the part of society in rethinking the past and finding new philosophical frameworks, immense political activism and social innovation, and the start of an abrupt modernisation of the Russian language (the "discourse revolution"). A sudden wealth of possibilities and institutional changes which had attained critical mass made irreversible the decaying of the Soviet empire. It was in 1990 that Article 6 of the Constitution of the U.S.S.R., which granted the Communist Party a monopoly on political initiatives in Russia, was abolished. New parties burgeoned, an epidemic of ethnic conflicts swept over the country, and the so-called "parade of sovereignties" in the republics began. New media appeared: independent television and radio stations, newspapers and magazines. A market in books began to form, and the brief era of cooperatives ended as big business emerged in the form of joint ventures, the first private banks, and commodity and stock exchanges. The first private art galleries opened, and the artistic underground came close to becoming the mainstream. To all intents and purposes, the Warsaw Pact disbanded, and reunification of Germany became a reality.[518] An era of mass foreign travel was ushered in. It was also the peak year for emigration out of the U.S.S.R. The Soviet economy finally collapsed, bringing shortages of all consumer goods.

For obvious reasons, Russian academics and the Russian public take a strong interest in "key moments" and "turning points" of history. The events of the late 1980s, culminating in the defeat of the attempted coup against reform in August 1991, clearly had a major impact on how Russian thinking in the humanities developed in the subsequent decades. The late Juri Lotman's final book, *Culture and Explosion*, profoundly reflects his own experience of the disruptive succession of epochs.[519] When working on the

518. The protocol formally dissolving the Warsaw Pact was signed by its member states on 1 July, 1991.
519. Juri Lotman, *Culture and Explosion (Semiotics, Communication and Cognition)* (Berlin, 2009).

present book, we were particularly influenced by Lotman's view of culture as a complex unity of layers which develops at different speeds and which combines explosive and gradual processes in its various spheres. Andrey Zorin, in his innovative *Feeding the Double-headed Eagle*, proceeds from Clifford Geertz's concept of the metaphorical nature of ideology. He traces the history of the crystallisation and sequence of the basic ideologemes of the Russian state at watersheds in Russia's past. Zorin acknowledges that his study's perspective on the exchange of metaphors between ideology and literature at moments when a new regime is establishing its identity and seeking legitimation is informed by his personal experience as an eyewitness of the historic tectonic shifts of the late 1980s and early 1990s.[520]

Without embarking on a detailed description of the very diverse intellectual activity in the humanities in modern Russia, one important trend should be noted. If we survey the work over the last fifteen or twenty years of such diverse (in terms both of age and of research methodology) scholars as Juri Lotman, Aron Gurevich, Mikhail Gasparov, Mikhail Yampolsky, Roman Timenchik, Andrey Zorin, Boris Gasparov, Valeriy Podoroga, Aleksandr Etkind, Igor Smirnov, Konstantin Bogdanov, Boris Dubin, Lev Gudkov, Aleksey Levinson and others, it is possible to identify an overall direction in which research in the humanities is moving in Russia. At the risk of oversimplification, there is a move away from a generalised approach, no matter how encyclopaedic in scope, towards a more flexible, detailed, individualised study of humanity and culture, away from "textocentrism" towards cultural and philosophical anthropology. There is no doubt that this anthropological trend is directly related to the collapse of the Soviet system and its whole superstructure of socio-cultural mythologems, which has obliged humanities researchers in Russia (and Slavists generally) to critically re-evaluate the perspectives and tools of their profession, to develop new categories and aesthetic guidelines, and to review the field of culture and its institutions.

520. Andrei Zorin, *Kormia dvuglavogo orla ... Russkaia literatura i gosudarstvennaia ideologiia v poslednei treti XVIII–pervoi treti XIX veka*, 2nd edn (Moscow, 2004).

The unique experience of living through history, being directly caught up in events, and the parallel process of reflecting on the symbolic construction of a new reality and evolution of new ways of living explain the intense interest in the present and recent past, the issue of temporality and proliferating identities which has been evident in the work of Russian scholars over the last two decades. It is not surprising, then, that since the early 1990s, among the most popular reading of Russian intellectuals have been the works of Roland Barthes, Michel Foucault, Gilles Deleuze, Paul Virilio, Walter Benjamin, Alain Badiou, and other philosophers and historians of culture who have focused on the development and formulation of new concepts of time and of the boundaries between past, present and future, as well as of the very concept of "the present" and new categories of subjectivity.[521] The present study of 1990 thus accords with major intellectual trends of Western and Russian humanities research, taking into account and developing many postulates and discoveries of our colleagues.

---

521. Hans-Ulrich Gumbrecht's *Production of Presence: What Meaning Cannot Convey* (Stanford, 2004), published in Russian by Novoe Literaturnoe Obozrenie in 2006, addresses the problem of neglect of "presence" (aesthetic impact) in the context of literary criticism and the humanities over the last thirty years.

ILLUSTRATION SOURCE NOTES

Photographs on pp. 39, 41, 42, 164, 167, 173, 288, 289, 291, 292, 444, 446 by Oleg Olegovich Smirnov, photographer and regular contributor to *New Literary Observer* projects; on pp. 44, 166, 255, 294, 435, 436, 439 from the archive of Kirill Vladimirovich Ovchinnikov (1932–2006), lecturer at the Chemistry Faculty of St Petersburg State University, secretary of the Commission for the History, Protection and Conservation of Architecture of the Architects Club, author of books and albums on the history of St Petersburg architecture; on pp. 66, 72, 104, 437 by Gennadii Nikolaevich Kalashnikov, poet, member of the Writers' Union of the Russian Federation, and Nikolai Gennadievich Kalashnikov, historian and local history specialist; on p. 143 reproduced from Tel'man Gdlyan and Nikolai Ivanov, *Kremlevskoe delo* (Moscow, 1994); on p. 272 by V. Leontiev and on p. 293 by Andrei Raizer. The poster on p.19 was designed by V. Chumakov, and the cartoon on p.323 has been taken from a 1990 issue of the satirical magazine *Crocodile*.

Every effort has been made to credit the source of images used in this book and to discover any existing copyright holders. The editor and publishers apologize if any have been missed and invite anyone claiming ownership not identified above to contact MacLehose Press.

INDEX

Figures in **bold** denote an illustration

religious public holidays 349
resigns from Communist Party 32, 190,
    251
Russian presidency 260, 298
Russian sovereignty 188
Supreme Soviet bilateral treaties 257
television celebrity 265
traffic accident 332
victory over Gorbachev 466
see also coup (1991); presidency of the
    R.S.F.S.R.; Supreme Soviet of the
    R.S.F.S.R.
Yerofeyev, Venedikt 171
Yevgeniy Popov's Gala 57
Yezhelev, Anatoliy 38
Young Communist League (*Komsomol*) 75,
    76, 78, 79, 101, 153, 156, 293, 304, 391

Youth radio station 34
Yugoslavia 150, 157, 158, 184, 199
Yurganov, Andrey 94
Yuriy Levada Centre 155
Yuvenaliy (Poyarkov), Metropolitan 388
Yuvenaliy, Metropolitan 89

Z
Zadornov, Mikhail 66
Zetkin, Clara 15–16
Zhitomirskaya, Sarra 208
Zorin, Andrey 501
Zoshchenko, Mikhail 210
Zubovskaya Square, Moscow 71

IRINA PROKHOROVA is a literary critic and cultural historian, and editor-in-chief of the magazine and publishing house New Literary Observer. She has been the recipient of numerous awards for her work, including the Liberty Prize for her contribution to the development of Russo-American cultural relations, the Andrei Bely Prize for literature, and in December 2012 she was made a Chevalier de la Légion d'Honneur. She came to international prominence in 2012 when, with her brother Mikhail Prokhorov standing for the presidency, she took part in a live debate against the filmmaker and Putin supporter Nikita Mikhalkov.

ARCH TAIT has translated many leading Russian writers of today. For his translation of Anna Politkovskaya's *Putin's Russia* he was the winner of the inaugural P.E.N. Literature in Translation Prize in 2010.

BRIDGET KENDALL is the B.B.C.'s Diplomatic Correspondent and presenter of the weekly Radio 4 discussion programme "The Forum". From 1989 to 1994 she was B.B.C. Moscow Correspondent.